AF818219

Kristen Ringdal | Sabrina P. Ramet |
Danica Fink-Hafner [eds.]

Small States, Big Challenges

Norway and Slovenia in Comparative Perspective

Nomos

edition sigma

The Deutsche Nationalbibliothek lists this publication in the Deutsche Nationalbibliografie; detailed bibliographic data are available on the Internet at http://dnb.d-nb.de

ISBN 978-3-8487-2420-8 (Print)
978-3-8452-6579-7 (ePDF)

British Library Cataloguing-in-Publication Data
A catalogue record for this book is available from the British Library.

ISBN 978-3-8487-2420-8 (Print)
978-3-8452-6579-7 (ePDF)

Library of Congress Cataloging-in-Publication Data
Ringdal, Kristen / Ramet, Sabrina P. / Fink-Hafner, Danica
Small States, Big Challenges
Norway and Slovenia in Comparative Perspective
Kristen Ringdal / Sabrina P. Ramet / Danica Fink-Hafner (eds.)
346 p.
Includes bibliographic references.

ISBN 978-3-8487-2420-8 (Print)
978-3-8452-6579-7 (ePDF)

1. Edition 2016
© Nomos Verlagsgesellschaft / edition sigma, Baden-Baden, Germany 2016. Printed and bound in Germany.

This work is subject to copyright. All rights reserved. No part of this publication may be reproduced or transmitted in any form or by any means, electronic or mechanical, including photocopying, recording, or any information storage or retrieval system, without prior permission in writing from the publishers. Under § 54 of the German Copyright Law where copies are made for other than private use a fee is payable to "Verwertungsgesellschaft Wort", Munich.

No responsibility for loss caused to any individual or organization acting on or refraining from action as a result of the material in this publication can be accepted by Nomos or the editors.

Print: Rosch-Buch, Scheßlitz

Preface

This book is the latest result of the cooperation between the Department of Sociology and Political Science at the Norwegian University of Science and Technology (NTNU) in Trondheim Norway and the Centre for Political Science Research at Faculty of Social Sciences, University of Ljubljana, Slovenia, dating back to 2002. The cooperation was initiated by Danica Fink-Hafner and Sabrina P. Ramet and has been supported by the Norwegian Research Council, the Faculty of the Social Sciences and Technology Management, and the Department of Sociology and Political Science, NTNU on the Norwegian side, and by the Slovenian Research Agency and by the Centre for Political Science Research at the Faculty of Social Sciences, University of Ljubljana on the Slovenian Side.

The idea for this book was developed in 2011 and led to a conference in Ljubljana in late 2012 where some of the chapters were presented and discussed. The main idea was to form the book by comparing the challenges of two small states in Europe, Norway and Slovenia, two countries with quite different histories and geopolitical locations but that share similarities attached to their roles as small states.

Kristen Ringdal, Trondheim,
Sabrina P. Ramet, Trondheim,
Danica Fink-Hafner, Ljubljana

Contents

Kristen Ringdal, Sabrina P. Ramet, Danica Fink-Hafner

1 Comparing Two Small States, Norway and Slovenia An Introduction

The number of small states in Europe has increased in stages from the breakup of the Habsburg Empire in 1919 to the collapse of the Soviet Union and socialist Yugoslavia in 1991.[1] Norway with a population of about 5 million and Slovenia with 2 million are both small European states, although Norway in terms of territory is slightly larger than Germany. It is commonly understood that small states have different security challenges and different foreign policy imperatives from larger states, let alone great powers. The constraints of size and limited resources also shape the domestic context in small states, resulting in policy challenges, opportunities, and dilemmas unique to them.

In this volume, we shall be focusing on parallels, similarities, and differences between Norway and Slovenia in challenges and policies in a number of sectors. This includes the political sphere, the economic sphere, the religious sphere, the environment, and history education. We hope to make a contribution to understanding the reasons for certain policy choices in these two states, the advantages as well as the costs associated with those choices.

Why study small states?

Making a definition of small states is not as easy as it may sound. One way is a residual definition: small states are those that are not considered great or medium powers.[2] Neuman and Gstöl also mention other popular traits that may be used to define small states: population size, territory, Gross Domestic Product, military capability. Based on the first criterion, the World Bank use 1.5 million as a criterion,[3] whereas others consider countries with a population size

---

1 Iver B., Neumann, and Sieglinde Gstöl. "Introduction. Lilliputians in Gulliver's World?", in Christine Ingebritsen, Iver B. Neumann, Sieglinde Gstöl and Jessica Beyer (eds.), *Small States in International Relations* (Seattle & Reykjavik: University of Washington Press & University of Iceland Press, 2006), p. 1.

2 *Ibid.*, pp. 8–9.

3 World Bank. Retrieved from http://www.worldbank.org/en/country/smallstates/overview.

as the Netherlands or less (16 million) to be small states wheras micro-states have a population below 100,000.[4] Another problem is power, based on specific strengths such as the power of Switzerland in the financial sector and Saudi Arabia based on the petrolium resources. In the latter sense, Norway challenges the definition of a small state. We follow Neuman and Gstöl's definition and this clearly identifies both Norway and Slovenia as small states.

The simple answer to the headline question is that most of the roughly 195 states in the world are small, and Europe is no exception to this pattern. In international relation studies of small states have a tendency to be ignored because they are not the main actors on the international scene. From a methodological point of view, since most states are small, a representative picture of world politics must also include knowledge about small states. Small states may also be used with profit in case studies for general research questions. Veenendaal and Corbett[5] argue that comparative politics is much poorer for not seriously utilizing small states as cases in studies of democratization and decentralization.

We see two perspectives on the study of small states: how small states may influence the international system, and how the politics of small states are affected by the international system and the great powers?

Examples of the first perspective are small states playing an important role in global agenda-setting. Ingebritsen mentions the Nordic countries as examples of states that have become norm entrepeneurs, pursuers of social power.[6] Ingebritsen mentions several areas where the Nordic countries have been important norm setters. The Nordic model emphasizing social equality and universal social provision of security have been extended to development assistance. The Nordic countries as promoters of green values and sustainable development. Nordic countries have also played important roles as bridges between East and West during the Cold War and as conflict mediators in several settings with the Oslo Agreement between Israel and the Palistinians as a prominent example.

Our book is inspired mainly by the second perspective: How small states are affected by their surroundings as regards both their foreign and their domestic policies. In terms of foreign policy, because of their limited capabilities, we would expect small states in general to rely on international law and

4 Iver B. Neumann, and Sieglinde Gstöl. "Introduction. Lilliputians in Gulliver's World?", in Ingebritsen et al. (eds.), *Small States in International Relations*, p. 6.

5 Wouter P. Veenendaal, and Jack Corbett. "Why Small States Offer Important Answers to Large Questions". *Comparative Political Studies* Vol. 48, No. 4 (March 1, 2015), p. 1.

6 Christine Ingebritsen, "Norm entrepreneurs. Scandinavia's role in worlde politics" in Ingebritsen et al. (eds.), *Small states in international relations*, pp. 273–285.

work through international organizations such as the UN and the EU. In international organizations all states are formally equal and small states may work to promote policies and attititudes that are favourable to them. An example of this is the Norwegian efforts to establish an Law of the Sea[7] that established economic zones extending 200 nautical miles from the coastline. This secured both the Norwegian petrolium resources and national rights to fish resources.

Small states are dependent on international trade and thus have open economies exposed to the forces of the gobal economy. This has important consequences for domestic policy. Peter Katzenstein's book, *Small States in World Markets*, is a classic study that opened the way for research on small states combining international relations perspective with domestic politics of small nations.[8] Small states need strategies to maintain the possibility of national choices in a world of great constraints. He saw political corporativism as a an institutional response to recurrent economic crises as well as to the threat of war. Katzenstein[9] maintains that democratic corporatism is an effective way of coping with a rapidly changing world. Open economies demands flexibility in adapting to changed conditions. This encourages cooperation between the state, the trade unions and employers organizations and agreement on the need for a genereous welfare state.

Norway: political history, economic and social development

Political history

During the Viking age, Norway was gradually consolidated as a kingdom. Harald Hårfagre is recognised as the first king of Norway from 872, although he controlled only the main parts of Norwegian territory. During the high period of the Old Norwegian Kingdom from around 1200 until 1380, it included Iceland, Greenland, and the Orkney and Faroe Islands, as well as parts of Sweden. Due to a combination of intermarriage and dwindling of the male heirs, Denmark, Norway and Sweden were united in the Kalmar Union under Queen Margrete in 1397. In Sweden, discontent with the increasing Danish domination in the union made Sweden leave the union in 1523 and appointed its own king. Norway and Denmark continued in the union, but from 1536

7 See http://www.un.org/Depts/los/.

8 Peter J. Katzenstein, *Small States in World Markets Industrial Policy in Europe* (Ithaca, N.Y: Cornell University Press, 1985).

9 Peter J. Katzenstein, "Small States and Small States Revisited", in *New Political Economy*, Vol 8, No. 1 (March 2003), p. 25.

Norway was defined as a province of Denmark. The same year, the Danish king decided that Denmark should adopt the Lutheran Reformation – which was accomplished by 1539.

In the Napoleonic Wars Denmark-Norway sided with France. In 1814, as a consequence, Norway was seceded to Sweden as a part of the Treaty of Kiel. Norway did not take part in the negotiations and a rebellion started in Norway. A broadly representative body (*Riksforsamlingen*) met at Eidsvoll and made a new democratic constitution that was signed on 17 May 1814. The *Riksforsamlingen* elected Christian Fredrik as king of Norway. This was unacceptable to Sweden and after a short war an agreement was reached in August 1814. According to the agreement the Swedish king became the monarch of both countries, but Norway was allowed to keep the new constitution, and could form its own parliament, the Storting. Except for military and foreign affairs, Norway enjoyed self-rule in the period of union with Sweden. Another important milestone in the development of democracy in Norway was reached in 1837-38 with the passing of two laws (*Formannskapslovene*) which established local self-rule for the administrative districts that were the forerunners of the municipalities. This was important for local democracy and for building political competence throughout Norway.

Political parties were established in the 1880s, first the Liberal Party (*Venstre*) in 1884 followed by the Conservative Party (*Høyre*), and the Norwegian Labour Party in 1887. An important event that marked the last phase of the union with Sweden was the conflict in 1884 about establishing parliamentary rule in Norway. This implied that government had to be based on the majority in the parliament and not on the preferences of the Swedish king. The Norwegian Liberal government continued the policy of expanding Norwegian self-rule to include foreign policy. The political conflict culminated with the passage of a new law establishing an independent Norwegian consulate system. As the Swedish king refused to sign the law, the parliament held that the King had stopped functioning as the King of Norway since he now was unable to form a new government, and the union was, thus dissolved. After a period of tension, close to war, an agreement was reached on dissolving the union and Norway became independent in 1905.

Since 1814, the suffrage in Norway had been limited and reserved for men. After several amendments, general suffrage for men was passed in 1900 and in 1913 this was extended to women. After 1905, Norway followed Sweden in adopting a policy of neutrality and nonalignment. Norway's neutrality policy succeeded in keeping the country out of World War One. After the war, Norway saw the need for collective security and joined the League of Nations in 1921. The neutrality policy failed to prevent the German occupation of Norway during 1940-45. When the occupation ended in 1945, Norway joined the UN.

However, World War Two showed the shortcomings of the neutrality policy and the weakness of collective security. Thus, Norway joined NATO in 1949.

The period from 1945 to 1965 has been described as the golden period of the Norwegian Labour Party. In most of this period the party formed majority governments. This period of stable Labour rule ended in 1965 when the Conservatives formed a centre-right coalition government. It was short-lived, but it marked the start of a period until 2005 with alternating labour and centre-right coalition governments. The political climate changed with more emphasis individual freedom and opposition to state regulations. This has been described as a "wave towards the right" in Norwegian politics. It culminated in the Willoch government (1981 – 1986) with the deregulation in many areas from banks and opening hours for shops and restaurants, to the ending of the state monopoly in broadcasting by allowing, first local radio and television, and later commercial television.

Norway's relationship with the EU is thoroughly described in chapter 12. Here it suffices to mention the main political events. The Labour government headed by Trygve Bratteli started negotiations with the European Community (EEC). The results of the negotiations were put to a referendum in 1972 where the voters turned down membership with a narrow margin. In 1992 the Labour government felt that the situation for Norway had changed and wanted to apply for membership in the European Union. The government wanted an advisory referendum before going to negotiations. The outcome of second referendum was, however, another "No" to Norwegian membership. Since 1994, Norway's relation to the EU is regulated through the Norwegian membership in the European Economic Area.

In the period 2005 – 2013, the Labour Party headed a coalition government together with the Socialist Left Party and the Centre Party. After 8 years in power, the "green-red" government lost the parliamentary election and the Conservatives formed a coalition government with the Progress Party for the period 2013-2017.

Economic history

Historical statistics indicate an average growth in the Gross National Product per capita of 2.2% for the period 1865 to 2011 and from 1900 to 2007 the average annual growth rate was 2.6%.[10] This made Norway one of the richest countries in the world. A closer examination reveals both times of boom and

10 T. Eika and Ø. Olsen, "Norsk økonomi og olje gjennom 100 år", in *Samfunnsøkonomen,* Vol. 43 No. 8, (2008). Retrieved from http://www.ssb.no/a/filearchive/norsk-okonomi_og_olje_gjennom_100_aar.pdf.

times of stagnation and decline. From the Middle Ages until about 1900, the Norwegian economy was dominated by the primary sector, farming, forestry and fishing. The export products were mostly dried fish and timber, often transported on an increasing Norwegian merchant fleet. The first period of strong economic growth after 1814 was the great boom 1843 to 1975 driven by improved productivity in the primary sector and growth of exports and an expansion of the merchant fleet.[11] The next period 1875-1914 is a period of relative stagnation, but it marks the start of industrialization in Norway. The industrial take-off period in Norway was 1905-1920. Norsk Hydro was founded in 1905, the first firm to utilise hydroelectric power in manufacturing. Another factor that influenced industrialization was the rapid increase in the work force due to the slowing down of emigration to the USA.

Grytten describes the period from 1914 to 1945 as a period of deep crises mixed with periods of growth. The years of economic hardship saw a series of serious labour conflicts. In 1935, the national labour organization (*LO*) and the employers' association (*NHO*) made the Basic Agreement (*Hovedavtalen*) to regulate industrial disputes. This agreement represents an important change in climate from a conflict mode to cooperation between labour and capital in Norway. In the decades to follow the cooperation was extended into tri-lateral cooperation where the state contributed by providing social security as well as contributing to the successful end of the annual centralised wage negotiations.

After the war, the Labour government introduced centralized economic planning and strict regulations of the economy during the first period of reconstruction. The period from 1950 to 1975 is described as the golden period of the Norwegian economy with an annual growth rate in the GDP/cap of 3.3%. Grytten comments that this achievement has often been explained with the large public sector combined with economic planning. However, the growth was actually lower than in countries with more liberal economic policies.

The period from 1973 to the present is characterized by the importance of the oil industry and by neoliberal economic policies. The increasing dominance of the oil sector had several consequences. Norway was able to run a counter-cyclical financial policy in the 1970s securing full employment, but this hemmed industrial development outside the oil sector. High labour costs also contributed to loss in competitive power. The combined effect was a rapid de-industrialization and the growth of the service sector.

The economic policy based on a mixed economy with extensive regulations did not stand up to the challenges in the 1970s. The result was a spiral of infla-

11 Ola Honningdal Grytten, "The Economic History of Norway", in *Encyclopedia*, edited by Robert Whaples: Economic History Association. Retrieved from https://eh.net/encyclopedia/the-economic-history-of-norway/.

tion and increasing wages. The conservative government that came into power in 1981 deregulated the credit market including the strict control of the lending policy of the banks. The rapid increase in loans overheated the economy and led to a sudden collapse in the housing market. This resulted in a major finance crisis (1987-1992) when the government had to intervene to keep the major banks solvent. The crisis was followed by a period of strong growth until 1998, mainly due to the high oil prices. Since 1998, the economy has remained strong through periods of international financial crises until the recent dramatic drop in the oil prices which has increased the efforts to make the economy less dependent upon the contracting oil sector.

The Norwegian welfare state

The present extensive Norwegian welfare state is the result of a long period of development since the start in the second half of the 19th century. One of the fore-runners was the poverty law of 1845 which put the responsibility for the poor on the municipalities. Towards the end of the century, industrialization, urbanization and population growth undermined the traditional form of welfare provided by the family, charity organizations, and the municipalities. The rise in productivity resulting from industrialization did, however, create resources that could be used to address the increasing social problems.[12] This period also saw the rise of mass democracy as well as trade unions and political parties which articulated the needs for new forms of social insurance.

We may distinguish between four periods in the development of the Norwegian welfare state.[13] The first period 1870-1920 is described as the entrepreneurial period. The increasing social problems in the factories were the background for the National Accident Insurance Scheme for factory workers in 1894. This is often seen as the start of the Norwegian welfare state. This was followed by various insurance and pension schemes for fishermen and seamen. Child labour was a serious problem in the new factories and a child labour law was passed in 1915.

The second period, 1920-1934, was characterized by many years of economic depression which overwhelmed the social assistance system and indicated the need for a more comprehensive insurance system. The third period

12 Francis G. Castles, Stephan Leibfried, Jane Lewis, Herbert Obinger, and Christopher Pierson, "Introduction", in Francis G. Castles, Stephan Leibfried, Jane Lewis, Herbert Obinger and Christopher Pierson (eds.),*The Oxford Handbook of the Welfare State* (Oxford: Oxford University Press, 2010), pp. 3–5 .

13 Gyldendal, "Velferdsstatens Utvikling - Fra Fattigvesen Til Trygd." Retrieved from http://web2.gyldendal.no/sosialkunnskap/html/velferdsstaten/8.htm.

from 1935 to 1980 starts with the first Labour government in 1935 and in this period the welfare state, much as the present one, came into existence. The labour government succeeded in passing the Worker Protection Act for all employees in 1936 and Old Pension Act was passed the same year. After 1945, the labour government worked to prepare a more comprehensive and universal insurance scheme. It was not realised until 1967 with the passing of The National Insurance Scheme Act which include health and sickness cash benefits, unemployment insurance, old age pensions, and infirmity pensions. Another milestone is the passing of The Working Environment Act in 1977. Universal social security was advocated to prevent crises, and increasing the flexibility of the economy. The Acts were also advocated from moral points of view and seen as parts of human rights. Universal, state financed social security is the core features of the Nordic model.

The last period from the 1980s and to the present saw a consolidation of the welfare state in Norway. The period is also characterized by increasing concerns in all European welfare states because the rapidly increasing costs in periods with low economic growth and increasing state debts. This has been followed by changes in welfare provision to save costs. In Norway, however, the oil revenue has made it easier to hinder re-entrenchment of the welfare state.

Slovenia: political history, economic and social development

Political history

The self-perception of Slovenians as primarily cultural ethnic group has deep roots in history of conflicts with other peoples and nations struggling over the same territory positioned between the Central Western part of current Europe and its Southern-Balkan region. In the period between the early history when Southern Slav ancestors of Slovenes migrated to this territory and World War Two many conflicts over territory emerged. Among them, most notable had been those involving Germans, Austrians, Italians, Hungarians, Ottoman Turks and even Napoleon's France. As pagan Slav ancestors were forced in the past to accept Christianity they were again pressured to abandon Protestantism under the Habsburg rule.

With an exception of the Slav state of Karantanija in the area of the present-day Austrian province of Carinthia (established in the 7th century and remained an independent entity until the middle of the 8th century) Slovenia was under foreign rule until the 20th century, mostly by the Habsburg monarchy. It was Protestantism in 16th century that constituted the ethnic linguistic basis of Slovenian ethnicity, which could not be fully expressed in political terms. Indeed, it is the March revolution of 1848 in frame of the Austrian-Hungarian Empire, which is considered to be a milestone in a political struggle for a united Slovenia / *Zedinjena Slovenija.*

Political modernization in terms of the development of party life started in Slovenia (as part of the Austrian-Hungarian Empire) in the second half of the 19th century. First a catholic conservative party (in 1890) and a liberal party (in 1891) were established. In 1886 a weak social-democratic party joined them. By 1920 also the Communist party was established due to the split of social-democracy.[14] Parties from other ideological political families appeared sporadically and achieved weak influence (e.g. a branch of pro-fascist ORJUNA). The process of democratization in Slovenia (as part of the first Yugoslavia created after World War One) was interrupted by a dictatorship and after World War Two it experienced a one-party authoritarian regime in frame of the second (socialist) Yugoslavia, which insisted on communist party rule also after Tito's split with Stalin in 1948. Both, with experiences under Austria and in frame of both Yugoslavias, Slovenians mostly lived in multinational countries, which were laggards in democratization processes compared to Western Europe.

Slovenia (as part of Austria at the time) gained a general, equal, direct and secret voting right for men older than 24 years as late as in 1907.[15] Women only got the right to vote at the local level for a limited period of time when conservatives realized that they could get more electoral support by including at that time mostly conservative oriented female voters. It was only the new government in the territory governed by partisans (politically controlled by the Communist party), which in 1942 introduced the active and passive voting rights to Slovenian women. As the period between the two World Wars had been mostly under the undemocratic regime and World War Two prevented the normal party functioning, followed by a period of socialist system under the Communist Party rule, it was not until the end of the 1980s that pluralist party life started to re-emerge.

The newly established party system did reflect some traditional cleavages among the conservative, liberal and social-democratic (reformed Communist) parties. However, the key political issues of the time had been transition to democracy, transition to capitalism and the establishment of an independent state. Nevertheless, joining European integration processes had been seen as an

14 See more in Danica Fink-Hafner, *Politične stranke* (Ljubljana: Fakulteta za družbene vede, 2001).

15 Flora, Peter, Kraus, Franz, Rothenbacher, Franz, eds, *The Societies of Europe. Elections in Western Europe since 1815. Electoral Results by Constituencies* (London, Basingstoke and Oxford: Macmillan, 2000).

economic necessity as well as a socially and politically desirable goal as well. Although joining the NATO was not as consensual as joining the EU, in the end the majority of votes at both referenda created a legitimate basis for Slovenia's voluntary shifting the exercise of some Slovenia's sovereignty to the EU and for making Slovenia's defence part of a supra-national organization.

The high hopes of Slovenians for higher standards of politics, economy and social life in general after joining the EU soon turned to disappointment, with voters increasingly blaming the political elite for not being able to envision further Slovenia's development after achieving the major consensual goal since the brake-up of Yugoslavia. Increasingly also noticing of EU's democratic deficit and the critical lack of leadership have found a way into public opinion. With low levels of turnout Slovenian voters have been adding to the second-order rating of European elections[16]. At the local and national level citizens turned to protest politics. At the national elections voters radically shifted from older parties to newly established parties. The crisis of the leadership of the older parties, as well as their inability to manage the impacts of international financial and economic crisis, have led to a complete disintegration of the party system.

Starting with the 2004 parliamentary elections, the 1992 party system came to an end. The previous three-polar party competition (with the Liberal Democracy in the party system metric centre) dominating by the time of joining the EU turned into a two-polar competition between centre-left and centre-right clusters of parties and alternative government coalitions (both always including the Democratic Party of Pensioners). At two recent early elections (in 2011 and 2014) voters have turned not only to new political faces, but also entirely changed the political landscape. Currently Slovenia is led by a majority of completely new MPs and by the government with a Prime Minister, who established his party just before the elections and immediately took over the coalition government. The recent refugee crisis[17] may add to further destabilization of the party system by possible open articulation of extreme right voices either within the existing parties, which had shown sympathies to them in the past, or through potential newly established parties.

---

16 See more in Danica Fink-Hafner and Tomaž Deželan, Slovenia, in Viola, Donatella M., ed., *The Routledge Handbook of European Elections* (Abingdon, Oxon and New York: Routledge, 2016), pp. 471-490.

17 Jamie Merrill, "Refugee Crisis: Slovenia Struggling to Cope in Chaotic Scenes At Border as Violence In Syria Forces More to Flee*t", The Independent* (30 October 2015), at http://www.independent.co.uk/news/world/europe/refugee-crisis-slovenia-struggling-to-cope-in-chaotic-scenes-at-border-as-violence-in-syria-forces-a6715176.html [accessed on 1 November 2015].

Economic history

By 15th century craft, trade, monetary economy, urbanization and land reform created a basis for capitalist developments in the territory of today's Slovenia. Nevertheless, Slovenia economically truly modernized in the 19th century as part of the Habsburg Empire. However, the key source of the capitalist accumulation was Slovenian agriculture while the main promotors of industrialization had been non-Slovenian capitalists.[18]

Slovenia's early and more substantial industrialization compared to other parts of the first and the second (socialist) Yugoslavia, had allowed Slovenia an advantage in internationalization of its economy after World War Two. As the former Yugoslav republic with very open borders to the West Slovenia contributed the largest share of Yugoslav exports to the West. Compared with the other federal units it also had good economic pre-conditions for economic survival after the break-up with socialist Yugoslavia[19]. It was only marginally hit by the war in the former Yugoslav territory in the 1990s. With a help of economic ties with West European countries (particularly Germany), the economic growth and increasing real GDP growth rate[20] it not only economically prospered, but was also able to keep social inequality at a rather low level.

Already in the 1980s, the economic elite from Slovenia, had pressed in favour of introducing market economy. When this did not appear to be politically feasible within the former Yugoslavia, it pushed the Slovenian political elite toward the full legalization of market economy as part of gradual legal transformation of Slovenia's economy and politics – eventually creating a basis for the creation of an independent state.[21] Joining the EU was not only the employers' goal, also employees' organizations believed it would not hurt the employees in Slovenia.

In economic terms, joining the EU has brought about some un-anticipated disappointments. Indeed, Slovenia (previously used to the leading position in

---

18 See more in Janko Prunk, "Politično življenje v samostojni Sloveniji", in Janko Prunk, and Tomaž Deželan, (eds.), *Dvajset let slovenske* države (Maribor: Založba Aristej, 2012), pp. 17-56.

19 Jože Mencinger, "Costs and Benefits of Secession", in Danica Fink-Hafner and John R. Robbins, eds, *Making a New Nation. The Formation of Slovenia* (Aldershot, Brookfield USA, Singapore, Sydney: Dartmouth, 1997), pp. 204-215.

20 Maša Filipovič Hrast and Miroljub Ignjatović, *GINI Country Report Slovenia: Growing Inequalities and Their Impacts in Slovenia*, at http://gini-research.org/system/uploads/506/original/Slovenia.pdf?1372768022, p. 7. [last accessed on 12 November 2015]

21 Franci Grad, 'Establishing State Authority', in Danica Fink-Hafner and John R. Robbins, eds, *Making a New Nation: The Formation of Slovenia* (Aldershot, Brookfield USA, Singapore, Sydney: Dartmouth, 1997), pp. 83-93.

economic terms in former Yugoslavia) found itself in the economic periphery of the EU together with many post-2014 EU-newcomers. Hugh amounts of money available to national banks after Slovenia's joining the Eurozone had not been spent wisely for economic development, but rather for a new wave of non-transparent privatization. Parts of the economic elite with political connections had been able to use the situation for their private gains. They used the externally available money for privatizing public enterprises. The international financial and economic crisis revealed this aspect of the privatization process and the illegitimate participation of a part of the political elite in these processes. Furthermore, the political elite postponed the solving of the impacts of international financial and economic crisis by a quick increase in borrowing money abroad to maintain the public sector and welfare policies. Such a response has made Slovenia financially dependent on international loans and subordinated the national executive to the supranational centers of power.[22] Former Slovenia's exceptionalism in successful resistance to the pressures of international liberalization ended. The newly established country's dependence on the international financial organizations opened the door to the international dictate of neoliberal policies including pressures in a direction of austerity measures and privatization. Indeed, by becoming dependent on international loans, Slovenia has become increasingly similar to other post-communist countries, which have become *de facto* economically and politically peripheral countries within the EU. The fact is that Slovenia joined the 'problematic' countries pressured to adopt austerity measures as a mechanism for solving the crisis at a time when these measures were already severely questioned.[23] Although the IMF has openly admitted it may have been wrong when recommending such policy, the EU still insists on the austerity paradigm. Unlike the economic crisis in 1980s and early 1990s currently unemployment in Slovenia is increasingly being 'solved' by emigration, particularly brain-drain.

---

22 Danica Fink-Hafner, 'Toward the Dominance of the Executive', *Anali Hrvatskog politološkog društva*, vol. 10 (2013), pp. 71-90.

23 See e.g. Howard Schneider, An Amazing Mea Culpa from the IMF's Chief Economist on Austerity, The Washington Post on-line, 3.1.2013, http://www.washingtonpost.com/blogs/wonkblog/wp/2013/01/03/an-amazing-mea-culpa-from-the-imfs-chief-economist-on-austerity/ (30.8.2013); Larry Elliott, Phillip Inman and Helena Smith in Athens, IMF Admits: We Failed to Realize the Damage Austerity would do to Greece, *The Guardian*, Wednesday, 5.6.2013, http://www.theguardian.com/business/2013/jun/05/imfunderestimated-damage-austerity-wouldo-to-greece (30.8.2013).

Welfare state

In Slovenia traditions of social solidarity are rather strong. They are rooted both in Christian Socialist traditions from the 19th century and workers' movement since the end of 19th century. In addition to that the experience with the socialist period of full employment and welfare broadly and rather generously provided by the state had brought about the widely spread expectation among people that it is the state, which needs to take care of citizens' welfare. These values have persisted also after the transition to capitalism. Indeed, Slovenia's 1991 constitution established Slovenia as a welfare state (*socialna država*). Subsequently adopted policies effectively maintained the welfare state.

Unlike many other post-socialist countries, during the transition Slovenia had been able to rely on its solid financial and economic basis.[24] This is why various governments were able to opt for gradualism in capitalist economic transformation. Comparatively looking, also trade unions at the beginning of the building of a new state in Slovenia had been rather strong and were able to achieve the establishment of social partnership within the new political system, including the establishment of the tri-partite Socio-Economic Council. Indeed, neo-corporatism is believed to have enabled the compromises in balancing economic and socially inclusive development in Slovenia since the transition to democracy and capitalism.[25]

Nevertheless, in practice the welfare state has been increasingly amended by private funding (health-care being the particular case in point). This was possible because collectivist values have been increasingly challenged by individualist values and due to a gradualist approach to changing the economic and the welfare state system. The state-socialist welfare system with a predominant role of the state had changed during the 1990s by inclusion of some policy solutions from capitalist countries. Among the changes had been a shift from passive to active employment policy, adding the private insurance market (the third pillar) to the obligatory insurance (first pillar) and to the collective insurance by enterprises and individual schemes (second pillar) as well as privatiza-

---

24 Mencinger, J. (1997) Costs and Benefits of Secession, in: D., Fink-Hafner, J.R. Robbins, eds., *Making a New Nation:The Formation of Slovenia*. Aldershot and Brookfield: Dartmouth.

25 Bohle, D., Greskovits, B. (2007) The State, Internationalization, and Capitalist Diversity in Eastern Europe. *Competition & Change* 11 (2): 89-115; Stanojević, M., Krašovec, A. (2011) Slovenia: Social Pacts and Political Exchange, in: S. Avdagic, M. Rhodes, J. Visser, eds., *Social Pacts in Europe: Emergence, Evolution, and Institutionalization*. New York: Oxford UniversityPress.

tion of the housing sector - previously entirely state sector.[26] During the last ten years Slovenian welfare system has been gradually loosing similarity with social-democratic system. This shift started with a policy change under the centre-right government adding to the decrease in the systemic solidarity and to the increase in social inequalities.[27] Such a paradigmatic shift became even more obvious in the context of recent financial and economic crisis and the prevalence of austerity measures in its managing. The paradigm shift from rather rigid employment model toward the imported model of 'flexicurity' became feasible exactly in the window of opportunity provided by the financial and economic crisis. While Slovenia was the most equal among the OECD countries at the international level in the late 2000s with a Gini coefficient measuring the level of social inequality of 0.24 even after the recent crisis (when Slovenia lost more than 9% of GDP between 2008 and 2013 and experienced one of the largest economic contractions among euro area countries[28]), it has remained in a group of countries with rather low Gini coefficient.[29] However, despite the fairly egalitarian nature of the current Slovenian society, there are social groups with greater risk for falling into material depravity, poverty or social exclusion – the unemployed and inactive persons, a growing segment of flexibly employed, mainly young individuals with precarious and insecure positions and older (mostly retired) persons.[30]

---

26 Zinka Kolarič, Dvajset let postopnega spreminjanja slovenske socialne države, in Janko Prunk, and Tomaž Deželan, eds., *Dvajset let slovenske* države (Maribor: Založba Aristej, 2012) 283-298.

27 Zinka Kolarič, Tatjana Rakar, Anja Kopač-Mrak, Slovenski sistem blaginje v procesu postopnega spreminjanja, in Valentina Hlebec, ed, *Starejši ljudje v družbi sprememb* (Maribor: Založba Aristej, 2009), pp. 45-75; Zinka Kolarič ,From Socialist to Post-socialist Social Policy, in Ivan Svetlik, ed., Social Policy in Slovenia . Between Tradition and Innovation (Avebury, Aldershot, Brookfield USA, Hong Kong, Singapore, Sydney, 1992), pp. 15-32; Zinka Kolarič, Dvajset let postopnega spreminjanja slovenske socialne države, in Janko Prunk, and Tomaž Deželan, eds., *Dvajset let slovenske* države (Maribor: Založba Aristej, 2012) 283-298

28 *Commission Staff Working Document: Country Report Slovenia 2015*, European Commission, Brussels March 2015, {COM(2015) 85 final} at http://ec.europa.eu/europe2020/pdf/csr2015/cr 2015_slovenia_en.pdf [last accessed on 12 November 2015]. p.3.

29 Klemen Košak, Povečevanje neenakosti. Slovenija je na zanesljivi poti v večjo razslojenost, *Mladina* 2nd November 2012, at http://www.mladina.si/117364/povecevanje-neenakosti/ [last accessed on 12 November 2015].

30 See Filipovič Hrast and Ignjatović, *GINI Country Report Slovenia*, pp.27-32.

Similarities and differences between Norway and Slovenia

The two countries are rather similar small states in terms of population size. In terms of area, however, Norway is more than 15 times as larger than Slovenia. The two countries have a quite different geopolitical location. Norway is situated in stable Scandinavia with a few similar neighbours and with a common border with Russia. Slovenia lacks a common border with Russia, but both countries share security concerns about Russia's role in their respective neighbourhoods.

Both countries are bordering the sea, Norway with a 15,148 km coastline compared to Slovenia's 47 km. This is reflected in the importance of the sea. The maritime environment is far more important for Norway than for Slovenia both in terms of the economy and security. The merchant fleet and export of fish products have been important for the economic development of Norway for centuries and more recently even more important with the off-shore petroleum resources.

Both countries gained full independence relatively recently, Norway in 1905 and Slovenia in 1991. Both countries are presently democracies with several institutional commonalities. The two countries are however, quite different as regards experiences with democracy. Whereas Slovenia is an emerging democracy with only 25 years of continuous experience, Norway has a 200 year long stable democratic tradition.

The main research question that motivates this book is to what degree the comparison of Slovenian and Norway on a range of dimensions will reveal similarities that can be traced back to their status as small countries and to what degree their different regional and historical context are visible in different approaches to domestic and international politics? How the long democratic tradition in Norway versus the emerging democracy in Slovenia with its background of 45 years of communist rule is reflected in the aspects of domestic and foreign policy covered in this book?

A preview of the book

The book is divided into four parts. The first one is about the political system and democratic culture. The second part includes three chapters on gender equality and religion. The third part covers the economy and the environment, and the final part includes two chapters on aspects of the foreign relations of Norway and Slovenia. We will now give pre-views of each chapter and end with some general conclusions.

The first part includes four chapters. Chapter two, written by Kristen Ringdal and Mitja Hafner-Fink, compares the democratic cultures of Norway and Slovenia for the period 1990 – 2008 with data from the European Value Study. The point of departure for this chapter is the concept of "Civic Culture" first presented by Almond and Verba in 1963 and further developed by Ronald Inglehart and colleagues in books and articles since the late 1980s to the present. The civic (democratic) culture is based on values, attitudes and practices that work to sustain participatory democratic institutions. The empirical analysis is based on social tolerance, participation in civil activities and in untraditional political activities (political action). The results for social tolerance (homosexuality, abortion, divorce) were rather surprising. In 1992, the level of social tolerance in Slovenia was higher than in Norway and surpassed by only a few Western countries. In 2008, however, the level of social tolerance in Slovenia showed only a marginal increase, whereas in Norway it increased substantially from 1992 to 2008.

For activities in voluntary organizations, Slovenia did approach Norway both in terms of membership and doing unpaid work. Norway showed a stable and very high score for both 1992 and 2008, whereas Slovenia started out with low scores in 1992, but had halved the gap in membership in organizations in 2008, and almost closed the gap in doing unpaid organizational work. For unconventional political activities or political action (signing a petition, joining in boycotts, attending lawful demonstrations, joining unofficial strikes, occupying buildings and factories) both countries showed an equal increase from 1990-92 to 2008 with a level of participation of more than 30% higher in Norway than in Slovenia for both time points. The final country-level cluster analysis of social tolerance, social participation and unconventional political participation indicated that during the period of consolidation of democracy from 1990-92 to 2008, Slovenia approached the average of West European old democracies and the differences between Norway and Slovenia were also reduced. We may argue that this process of strengthening the civic culture in Slovenia has being supported by the democratic changes in the political system. However, the authors emphasize that some social processes, especially new social movements and civic activity actually started in the early 1980s. This is in line with thesis of relationship between cultural changes, modernization process, and democratization: cultural change can lead to political change.

The third chapter, written by Alenka Krašovec and Ola Listhaug, is titled "Political parties in Norway and Slovenia". The chapter describes the origins of the party system with a special emphasis on the developments since 1990. In addition, the authors also describe changes in political trust. The Norwegian party system emerged as responses to social and geographical cleavages with roots back to second half of the 19th century. The Liberal Party and The Conservative Party was the first to be formed in 1984 followed by the Labour Party in 1894. The differentiation in the party system continued with the establishment of the Centre Party and the Christian People's Party. The resulting party system was remarkably stable in the golden period of Labour Party rule period from 1945 to 1960. The period was followed by alternating Conservative-Centre coalition governments as well as Labour-dominated coalition governments. In recent years the voters' attachments to political parties have weakened. However, the levels of political trust have been relatively high, especially the general trust in democracy. There is also an increase in political action on the part of citizens.

The Slovenian party system likewise has roots in the 19th century. The three first parties the Catholic People's Party, the National Progressive Party, Yugoslav Social-democratic Party were all established in the 1890s. However, in the period between 1945 and 1989, only the Communist party was allowed in Slovenia. In 1989, pluralism was again formally adopted in Slovenia with the first democratic national election held in 1992. The new parties evolved from socio-political organizations that had been part of the socialist regime, the most important being the Liberal Democracy of Slovenia and the United List of Social Democrats (now the Social Democrats). In the period from 1990 to 2010 the Slovenian party system has been described as a relatively consolidated and stable system compared to other countries in Central and Southeastern Europe. In the 2011, the stability of the party system seems to break down with the emergence of two new parties that received more than a third of the votes. In 2014, another new party also received a third of the votes. Although general political trust may be described as relatively high compared to other Balkan countries, the trust in political parties collapsed with the global financial crisis in 2008.

Norway and Slovenia have similar institutional arrangements in the form of a parliamentary system with proportional representation and a similar number of political parties. Instability in the party systems was found in both countries, although since 2011, the instability is far higher in Slovenia than in Norway. The main explanation of the difference in stability may be sought in the different democratic traditions and historical circumstances. Whereas modern democracy in Slovenia only dates back to 1990, Norway has had a stable democracy since 1814.

In chapter four, Toril Aalberg and Marko Milosavljević compares the media systems in Norway and Slovenia. The Norwegian media system may be classified as "democratic corporatist", characterized by a historical coexistence of commercial media with ties to organized social and political groups and by an active but legally limited role of the state. Slovenia belongs to the "polarized pluralist model" with a weaker tradition of commercial media and a clear integration of media into party politics and a strong role of the state. From 1945 and until 1991, public media in Slovenia were, with a few minor exceptions, owned and controlled by the state.

The Norwegian media landscape was quite different. The multiparty representative democracy rooted in the 19th century gave rise to a strong expansion of the press with close ties to the political parties. The depolitization of the press from the 1970s coincided with a professionalization of journalism in Norway. Although broadcasting in Norway started as private services in the 1920s, a state owned monopoly was established in 1933. In 1981, the Conservative minority government abolished the state monopoly. This opened the way for the commercialization of the radio and television while retaining the state owned Norwegian Broadcasting Corporation (NRK) as the major public service provider.

During the last few decades, the media environment in both Norway and Slovenia has experienced dramatic changes due to the common trends of commercialization and globalization. Comparing the media systems on the four dimensions of Hallin and Mancini brings to light some differences between the Norwegian and the Slovenian media system. The *structure* of the media market in Norway may be characterized as being newspaper-centred with a long tradition of mass circulation, whereas the Slovenia press has a narrower coverage and the media system may be described as being television-centred. There are also differences in *political parallelism* between the two countries. In Slovenia pluralism is achieved by external diversity, i.e., between the newspapers, television stations. Media pluralism in Norway is increasingly achieved through internal diversity within each media channel. The Norwegian media system is characterized by a strong *journalistic professionalization* with institutionalized systems for self-regulation. Journalistic autonomy is weaker in Slovenia where various techniques are used by politicians to control the media. Both countries share strong *state intervention* into the media system including ownership and subsidies. In Slovenia, the state ownership of the media industry continued until the mid-1990s, when the state sold most of its shares in key media companies. However, political actors still retain their influence over the media through indirect deals and agreements. In Norway, there is also strong state intervention but this is balanced with an equally strong protection of press freedom.

"Narratives of the Nation" by Ola Svein Stugu and Peter Vodopivec looks at the national identities in Norway and Slovenia as seen through history textbooks. As an important vehicle of socialization, education is one of the main integrative mechanisms in modern societies and important in building collective identities, especially through the presentation of narratives and explanations of the past. During the last couple of centuries, Norway and Slovenia experienced very different political histories. Since 1814, Norway had its own constitution and independent government institutions, although until 1905 within the union with Sweden. Norway's recent political history is characterized by gradual change within stable boundaries. This contrasts with Slovene history, which is marked by three fundamental raptures during the last century: the break-up of the dual monarchy of Austria-Hungary in 1918, World War Two and the coming of the Communist regime, and the break-up of Yugoslavia in 1990-91. These differences in the recent history of the two countries are also reflected in the way history is recounted in schools. Norwegian textbooks are characterized by gradual change influenced by changes in scholarly accounts as well as reflecting changes in the political culture in the direction of a more widened democracy and more active public participation.

During the two centuries since 1814 two successive grand, national narratives of Norwegian history may be discerned. The first one was retrospective looking back to the Viking age and the times of the medieval Norwegian kingdom as a golden age in the nation's history. The second one was progressive, highlighting the national achievements as a narrative of fundamental changes in the conditions of life, closely tied to Norway's transition from a mainly agrarian society through industrial society to present Norway; from a society marked by hardships and toil to a modern society of prosperity and welfare.

A striking feature of Slovenian history textbooks is a two-layered structure, with an inner core of relatively stable Slovene identity, surrounded by dramatically changing contexts not only of statehood, but also of hegemonic political ideologies. Fundamentally, however, there seems to be a clear convergence in Slovene and Norwegian approaches to history teaching and its textbooks. The identity making potentials of historical narratives have been gradually substituted by more scholarly approaches and a higher degree of willingness to confront more contested themes and topics, something which is a prerequisite for good history teaching in a functioning democracy.

The second part of the book is comprised of one chapter on gender equality and two chapters on the Church-state relationships in Norway and Slovenia. Anders Todal Jenssen and Aleksandra Kanjuo-Mrčela compare Norway and Slovenia with respect to gender equality. They cover a broad range of indicators of gender equality, from the representation of women in politics and the elites, through gender differences in work, to attitudes on gender equality. In both countries a combination of a women's movement and a strong state support contributed to the present relatively high levels of gender equality. This is indicated in that Slovenia is ranked number one in 2013 (with the lowest score) on the UNDPs Gender Inequality index covering 149 countries, with Norway ranked number nine. Both countries have a strong welfare states encouraging, both practically and ideologically, high participation of women in paid employment providing for opportunities for women to combine work and family obligations.

Although the history of the development of the economic and political systems in the two countries has been different in many respects, contributing to the economic equality of women and men, many problems regarding gender equality are similar. This includes vertical and horizontal segregation in many spheres of society. The representation of women in politics is supported by quotas of 40% on the party lists. Women are more equally represented in government in Norway (50%) than in Slovenia (21%). In both countries the representation of women decreases as with the level of position both the private and the public sector. As an example, women in both countries are poorly represented in the business elite. The labour market in both countries is gender segregated. In Norway, gender segregation has been found to be the main source of the gender gap in wages. In addition, the high rate of part-time employment among women further contributes to gender gap in incomes from work. In Slovenia, the gender gap seems to be smaller, but recent studies show it to be increasing. Furthermore, women earn less for the same work in the same firm/organization. In terms of gender role attitudes, there are both similarities and differences. In both countries women and men are seen to have equal responsibility for household income, as well as having equal responsibilities for children. However, some results from the European Value Study indicate more traditional attitudes in Slovenia than in Norway.

The two chapters on Church-state relations – in Norway (Christine Hassenstab) and in Slovenia (Marjan Smrke) – reveal both similarities and differences between the two countries. Both countries were initially equally affected by the Protestant Reformation. In 1537 [King Christian III] established the Evangelical-Lutheran faith as the official religion of Norway and Denmark. In Slovenia, the Protestant Reformation was contested and came to an end with the Counter-Reformation towards the end of the 1590s when the Catholic Church became the state religion. However, Protestantism maintains its influence with both a historically recognized role in the establishment of the Slovenian nation (expressed also in a special state holiday – the Reformation Day – 31st October) and in much more liberal views on some important policy issues compared to other Catholic countries.

The predominance of two different religions/Churches took the two countries on different paths. In Slovenia, the marked predominance of Catholicism included a religious ideology that promotes a model of obedience to the clerical hierarchy as a necessary and indeed the sole intermediary between man and God. This is in direct opposition to the ideals and values promoted by Protestantism, such as religious exploration, the development of a personal and direct relationship between an individual and God, and the rejection of unquestioning respect of hierarchies. In practice, the schism between literal or fundamentalist interpretation of the faith and a more liberal interpretation is found in both countries. In Norway, an expression of this is the establishment of Menighets-fakultetet in 1907, which from 1913 were given rights to educate priests (cand.theol.) based on a conservative interpretation of the bible. In Slovenia, this is expressed in the tensions between those who advocated the Church's notion of a perfect Catholic society (so-called integrism), and the anticlerical forces who strived for a reduction of the role of the Church in society as well as for secularization at the societal level. This tension or cultural battle culminated in the 1930s. Whereas such tensions gradually weakened in Norway up to the present, they reappeared in Slovenia after the independence in 1991.

The Churches came out of World War Two quite differently. In occupied Norway, after a period of neutrality, the Church committed itself to a full scale opposition to the infamous Quisling government and thus emerged from the war strengthened. In Yugoslavia, the Communist Party won the war and separated state and Church, partly due to Marxist ideology, and tried to persuade the Catholic Church to break with Rome and to establish itself as a "national" Church in collaboration with the Communist party.[31] In the period between 1945 and the breakup of socialist Yugoslavia, the Roman Catholic Church was demoted from a central role to the margins of society (although its situation improved measurably after the signing of a protocol between the Yugoslav government and the Holy See on 25 June 1966[32]). After Slovenia became independent in 1991, the local branch of the Roman Catholic Church tried to revive its ideological hegemony from the pre-1941 period. In 1991 it regained all its former estates, but in the context of the recent financial crisis suffered heavily from a financial scandal that resulted in the resignation of three archbishops. Even before that its influence on social and political life had been much smaller than in the neighbouring catholic Croatia.

In Norway, after decades of debate, the Norwegian Parliament amended the Constitution to allow a separation of the national Church from the Norwegian state. This change allowed the Church to name bishops and deans without governmental approval, but the state would continue to finance the Church very much as before. The Constitution was also changed to reflect the fact that the foundation of the state rests on both Christian and humanist traditions.

---

31 Pedro Ramet (Sabrina P. Ramet), "The Catholic Church in Yugoslavia, 1945-1989", in Pedro Ramet (ed.), *Catholicism and Politics in Communist Societies* (Durham, N.C.: Duke University Press, 1990), p. 186. See also Jakov Blažević's interview with *Polet* (8 and 15 February 1985), as quoted in *Glas koncila* (Zagreb), 24 February 1985, p. 3.

32 See Sabrina P. Ramet, *Nihil Obstat: Religion, Politics, and Social Change in East-Central Europe and Russia* (Durham, N.C.: Duke University Press, 1998), p. 168.

In terms of structure, both countries have seen changes from religious homogeneity to more diversity. In Norway, this was influenced by the gradual changes towards a multicultural society due to increasing immigration since the 1970s. Even now, however, the traditional Churches – the Lutheran Church in Norway, the Catholic Church in Slovenia – remain dominant in their respective countries. Both countries have experienced secularization in terms of laws on abortion, marriage laws and on decline in religiosity. Again, according to the European Social survey 2012 39% in Norway and 33% in Slovenia reported to never attend religious services apart from social occasions, and one out of four in Norway and only one out of three in Slovenia attended only on special holy days.

Part 3 covers the economy and the environment. The chapter on the economic developments in Slovenia and Norway is written by Jože Mencinger and Jonathon Moses. In terms of population size, Norway is about 2.5 as large as Slovenia, but the Norwegian economy as measured by the GDP is about 11 times larger than the Slovenian economy. While Slovenia has been, similarly to other countries in the EU, constantly facing budget deficits, Norway has, mainly due to the oil exports, experienced increasing budget surpluses. Both countries do, however, share a similarity: they are among the OECD countries with the lowest income inequality. The Norwegian economy appears as stable and developed, while Slovenia is a new country undergoing many systemic changes, first as part of Yugoslavia and since 1991 as an independent nation.

In the period from 1919 to 1991, Slovenia was a part of Yugoslavia, with a socialist market economy. Mencinger describes the ups and downs of Yugoslav economic policy until the severe economic crisis at from the middle of the 1980s and the failure of the economic reforms and stabilization program ended in the break-up of Yugoslavia. In 1991, Slovenia became independent. The early economic performance of the new country was satisfactory and the social costs of transition were rather low. Mencinger explains this by favourable initial conditions and the choice of economic policies. Slovenia had already many elements of a market economy and was the richest of the Yugoslav republics. Mencinger distinguishes between four period of economic history since 1991: a short period of transitional depression, followed by a more than 10-year period with balanced economic and social development, a financial "gambling" period in a years leading up to the global financial crisis in 2008, which was a hard blow to country's small and open economy with a negative annual growth rate until 2013. The latest statistics indicate that the Slovenian economy is improving with a positive growth rate. Mencinger's main explanation for the lack of recovery in Slovenia is the political stalemate and mistrust rather than the Communist legacy.

Moses starts by stating that Norwegians since the beginning of the 1990s have continued to manage the economy to secure full employment and broad-based economic security. As a result, Norway is one of the richest, but also one of the most egalitarian, countries in the world. Moses finds the explanation of Norway's economic bounty only with reference to the oil resources to be misleading. It is the market-based, regulated, capitalist economy mixed with an active state in institutionalized cooperation with the trade unions and the employers that best explain how the country has secured its enviable economic record. Moses describes in more detail three important elements of Norwegian economic policy: securing full employment, low levels of poverty, and maintaining a high level of state ownership. In the last paragraph Moses observes that although Norway, through its EEA obligations, has also lost some of its policy independence, it has retained an autonomous monetary policy and a model of economic management that allows it to pursue a more social democratic and autonomous line of policy.

The two chapters on environmental issues are written separately by Matej Knep (Slovenia) and Espen Moe (Norway). Knep uses the concept of "policy paradigms" as his analytical tool. The three paradigms introduced, the *conservationist*, the *modern environmental*, and the *sustainable environmental paradigm*, represent historical stages in in development of environmental policies common in general and is relevant for both Norway and Slovenia. The underlying assumption of the conservationist paradigm is that nature has an intrinsic value. Establishing natural parks or protecting desired life-species are examples of environmental policies based on the conservationist environmental paradigm. In Slovenia, pressure from civil society led to the establishment of the Triglav National Park in 1924. In Norway, the first national park in Jotunheimen was proposed in 1921, but it was not realised until the 1960s together with the establishment of 16 additional national parks. Both countries are unquestionably among the most successful in Europe in terms of nature preservation and they share the image of being clean, progressive, and environmentally conscious.

At present, about a third of the hydropower in Europe is produced in Norway. Since the start of production of hydroelectric power in the 1920s, a recurrent theme in Norwegian politics is the conflict between the conservation of waterfalls and the expansion of hydropower. Two examples of this conflict are the 1970 Mardøla action, and the action in the late 1970s against the regulation of the Alta River. In recent years the conflict between conservationists and those who want to exploit nature resources, has found expression in protests against the building of new power-lines and over the establishment of wind-power parks.

The rapid increasing pollution from industrial production, made the ground for the *modern environmental paradigm.* In Slovenia, civil society played a crucial role in introducing this paradigm in Slovenia, already during the socialist period. After the establishment of the Green political party in 1989, environmentalists were able to establish normatively the modern environmental paradigm for Slovenia at an earlier stage than were other post-communist countries.

In Norway, the relationship between conservation and growth is a recurring theme. Until the 1960s most of the Norwegian political actors saw nature as a resource to be harvested for economic gain, rather than as something that should be preserved. This gradually changed into "growth with conservation" in the 1960s and the 1970s and the "polluter pays" principle was adopted in 1970. When sustainable development was launched by the World Commission in 1987, the concept was already well-established in Norway. In Slovenia, the *sustainable environmental paradigm* is still in the phase of policy experimentation and is not yet consolidated.

Norway is also different from Slovenia in being one of the largest exporters of oil and gas in the world. This key role in the Norwegian economy has established a sort of petro-industrial complex that exerts considerable influence on policies of energy and conservation. Moe concludes that a lot of work has gone into creating a thorough and well-developed framework for nature conservation. If we expand our discussion to include climate and energy, however, environmental standards are under threat because of both strong industrial interests and strong institutional biases pointing Norwegian energy interests in the direction of more petroleum. Even if Slovenia may be considered to be among environmental leaders, Knep's analysis shows that Slovenia lags behind when dealing with contemporary environmental challenges. This is evident especially when it comes to the slow implementation of anti-pollution measures and the reluctance in switching to environmentally sustainable development.

The next chapter, written by Damjan Lajh and Jonathon Moses, describes Norway's reluctance and Slovenia's enthusiastic relations with the European Union. Since the European Community opened for British membership in the beginning of the 1970s, the economic and political elites in Norway have sought to join the European Community/European Union. In two referendums, first in 1972, then in 1994, a majority of the voters rejected Norwegian membership. The main argument against membership was that membership would harm Norwegian agriculture, weaken national control of natural resources, and weaken democracy by ceding some decision-making authority to Brussels. Since the second referendum, Norway's relations to the EU have been regulated through an Agreement on the European Economic Area (EEA). After 1994, opinions polls showed a stable, narrow, majority against EU-membership. In recent years, with the economic crisis, the sentiment towards EU-membership for Norway has been increasingly negative and no political parties will at present seriously propose another debate and a third referendum.

In Slovenia, the sentiment vis-à-vis the EU has been quite different. In 1993, as a result of the democratization of post-socialist countries in Central and Eastern Europe, the EU opened for post-socialist countries to become members. The road to membership was to be accepted as a candidate and next to be able to fulfil a set of criteria posed by the EU. This included institutional stability, protection of human rights and the establishment of a market economy. All Slovenian political parties except one agreed to support Slovenian membership in the EU. A referendum on membership resulted in an overwhelming majority of 96% in favour of membership.

In 2007, Slovenia became a member of the Eurozone as the first of the post-socialist member states to adopt the Euro. The strong public support for the EU has continued, although enthusiasm has been weakened by the economic crises in Europe since 2007.

EU-membership has offered Slovenia an opportunity for rapid political and economic transition to development. However, the lack of national leadership in the formation and implementing a post-EU accession developmental strategy and the international economic and financial crisis pushed Slovenia to EU's periphery.

The final chapter in the book compares Norwegian and Slovenian foreign policy. The authors, Torbjørn Knutsen and Zlatko Šabič structure their analysis by four general concerns for any country: security, welfare, autonomy, and the prestige of the state. Norway and Slovenia have different geopolitical locations and differ in political history and foreign policy orientations. The authors observe that over the last 15-20 years Norway and Slovenia have become more similar in outlook and political orientation. A part of this is that both countries now are members of NATO and the EU is important for both countries although Norway is only member of the EEA. However, for Slovenia NATO and EU were instrumental in introducing liberal values and liberal-democratic institutions and guaranteeing the autonomy of the state, whereas for Norway EU has rather been perceived as a threat to national autonomy and a challenge to a smoothly working democracy.

One of the most striking differences between the two countries is the degree to which they have been affected by the maritime environment. The merchant fleet has been central to the Norwegian economy for many centuries and fish products are a significant part in Norway's foreign trade. Knutsen and Šabič conclude that some of the similarities between the foreign policies of the two countries can be traced back to the fact that both countries are small, democratic states that benefit from the present international system and which support the status quo and the work of the UN and international law. But there are also profound differences between the two countries that may be traced back to their different historical experience and geographical location.

Conclusions

Two decades ago, Bojko Bučar and Stein Kuhnle brought out a collection of papers comparing Norway and Slovenia.[33] Focusing exclusively on the political systems in these two states, the editors noted that, alongside their various similarities, there were also differences – among other things, that Norway's path to parliamentarism was gradual, unfolding over the decades following 1814, while Slovenia's emerged rapidly in the course of 1990-91.[34] In this volume, we have cast a wider net, bringing in analyses of environmental policy, history textbooks, Church-state relations, gender (in)equality, and foreign policy, among other topics.

Interest in small states is by no means a purely recent phenomenon. On the contrary, one can mention, for example, T. Hytten's article on the difficulties which small states face, published in 1930,[35] Annette Baker Fox's 1959 book, *The Power of Small States,*[36] Amry Vandenbosch's article devoted to small states in international politics, published in 1964,[37] and a 1965 article focusing on Western Europe's small states and their activity in the United Nations, again by Annette Baker Fox.[38] Few, if any, scholars would contest Vandenbosch's contention that one of the crucial earmarks of small states is their inability to compete with great powers in wartime "on anything like equal terms."[39] There can be external threats to security also in peacetime but, as Jonathan Alford has pointed out, the most vulnerable states are precisely the poorest states, which are likely to be the least attractive to hungry neighbors.[40] Legitimate regimes –

33 Bojko Bučar and Stein Kuhnle, *Small States Compared: Politics of Norway and Slovenia* (Bergen: Alma Mater, 1994).

34 Bučar and Kuhnle, «Foreword», in *Ibid.,* p. v.

35 T. Hytten, «The Difficulties of the Small States», in *The Australian Quarterly,* Vol. 2, No. 7 (September 1930), pp. 50-60.

36 Annette Baker Fox, *The Power of Small States* (Chicago: University of Chicago Press, 1959).

37 Amry Vandenbosch, «The Small States in International Politics and Organizations», in *Journal of Politics,* Vol. 26, No. 2 (May 1964), pp. 293-312.

38 Annette Baker Fox, «The Small States of Western Europe in the United Nations», in *International Organization,* Vol. 19, No. 3 (Summer 1965), pp. 774-786.

39 Vandenbosch, «Small States in International Politics», p. 294.

40 Jonathan Alford, «Security Dilemmas of Small States», in *The World Today,* Vol. 40, No. 8/9 (August-September 1984), pp. 363-369 at p. 363.

which increasingly means representative democracies with free and fair elections, a free press, separation of powers, and governmentally imposed limits to economic inequality – tend to be more resistant to external challenges, precisely because their domestic legitimacy means that a foreign power wishing, for example, to annex territory from the small state in question, will find little support among that state's population.

Since 1989, the breakup of the Soviet Union, Czechoslovakia, and Yugoslavia has added 18 new states to the European community of states – all but Ukraine and Belarus counting as small states. Only in the case of Czechoslovakia's "velvet divorce" was breakup completely peaceful. Where Slovenia is concerned, separation from the defunct Yugoslav federation involved a 10-day war, with relatively few casualties.

What emerges from the chapters collected herein is the broad similarity of challenges faced by Norway and Slovenia, in spite of their differences, as well as some general comparability in terms of the strategies adopted locally to meet these challenges.

The different experiences with democracy, Norway with a democratic tradition dating back to 1814, and Slovenia, an emerging democracy with only 25 years of continuous experience, is reflected in the democratic cultures of the two countries. Results from The European Value Studies indicate a higher level of civic culture in Norway than in Slovenia, evident both in democratic attitudes and in participation in civil society. However, we also observed a narrowing in the gap in democratic culture since 1990.

The party structure of Slovenia was relatively stable for a 20-year period from independence. However, the advent of the economic crises in 2008 severely weakened the trust in the established political parties, and revealed the shallow foundation of the party system. This became evident in the 2011 and 2014 election where three newly formed parties were successful at the expense of the established parties. Currently Slovenia is led by a majority of completely new MPs and by the government with a Prime Minister, who established his party just before the elections and immediately took over the coalition government.

The media structure in Norway has been more newspaper centred than Slovenia, where the press lacks the long Norwegian tradition of mass circulation. The Norwegian media at present are characterized by loose ties to political parties and internal diversity, whereas Slovenian media show closer ties to political actors and is characterized by external diversity, such as between various newspapers. Both countries share a high level of state intervention in the form of subsidies, however, with a stronger commitment in Norway than in Slovenia to the freedom of the media.

The study of history textbooks showed that the focus earlier on was on constructing national identity. This had two components: differentiation (Norwegians are not Danes or, for that matter, Swedes; Slovenes are not "alpine Croats", as they were once called); and the promotion of national mythologies (e.g., the cult of St. Olav in Norway). In both countries, however, the focus on identity-building has now given way to more scholarly narratives.

Again, where gender equality is concerned, both countries have had strong women's movements and, in both countries, the state has adopted legislation to promote relatively high levels of gender equality, when compared with the rest of the world. In Slovenia, the promotion of gender equality was linked, for nearly half a century after the end of World War Two, to the socialist project. In Norway, thanks to the quota imposed in Norwegian elections, the proportion of women in the Norwegian Storting is 40 percent. In Slovenia recent imposed quotas have increased the proportion of women in the Slovenian Državni zbor (the National Assembly) to 32%. The representation of women in the government is, however, still much higher in Norway than in Slovenia.

On the other hand, Norway and Slovenia have had different approaches to environmental challenges, with Norway embracing the concept of sustainable development even before it was adopted by the World Commission on Environment and Development, while Slovenia still lags behind in terms of environmental policy. And again, there is the contrast between the two states in terms of their respective orientations vis-à-vis the European Union. For Slovenes, entry into the EU was a clear goal (achieved in 2004), while Norwegian rejected an offer of membership twice over, preferring to regulate relations with the EU via the Agreement on the European Economic Area.

Comparisons between Norway and Slovenia bring about several interesting questions for further research into small states. States may nurture *values of social equality* over time in spite of changing political and economic systems – as particularly shown in the Slovenian case. Such a persistence of values and policies cannot be fully explained by the available economic basis only – as it is clear from rather big differences in wealth and sources of wealth in the two compared countries.

The two countries are small, democratic states that benefit from the present international system and which support the status quo and the work of the UN and international law. But there are also profound differences between the two countries that may be traced back to their different historical experience and geographical location.

Over the last 15-20 years Norway and Slovenia have become more similar in outlook and political orientation in their foreign policies. They are both members of NATO and both have close ties with the EU, Slovenia as a member and Norway through the EEA. However, for Slovenia NATO and EU were instrumental in introducing liberal values and liberal-democratic institutions and guaranteeing the autonomy of the state, whereas for Norway EU has rather been perceived as a threat to national autonomy and a challenge to a smoothly-working democracy.

Comparisons between Norway and Slovenia also bring about questioning the existing notions of centre and *periphery*. In the context of the last wave of globalization Slovenia opted for joining the regional integration including the shift of the execution of a part of its sovereignty to the EU level. In fact, it shifted from its long-term economically superior position within former Yugoslavia to the peripheral economic (and political) position within a much broader entity primarily led by several powerful West European countries. Contrary, Norway opted for many particular social, economic and cultural linkages with the EU searching for an optimum of its interests without fully joining the integration. Nevertheless, it consciously positioned itself on a kind of periphery as it is not included into EU policy-making as EU member states are, but still is affected by these policies.

Last but not least, the status and role of small states cannot only be measured by their economic power. Also the characteristics of their *agency* seem to matter – perhaps even more increasingly in the context of the last globalization wave. Norway has had a tradition of national leaders capable of grasping the changing world and formulating the conscious active positioning of Norway in the world. Contrary, Slovenia – as part of multinational states – has a rather poor history of national leadership-making and current agency capacity in many fields, which used to be managed by centres of multinational states (including monetary, foreign and defence policy). As a rule, Slovenia would rather wait and follow bigger countries in taking particular policy decisions. With the recent financial subordination to international financial organizations and key Eurozone decision-makers, recent Slovenian governments in fact also agreed to follow externally dictated domestic policies.

One surprising finding in this volume is how little difference the nearly half a century of socialism has made for Slovenia in the long run. Far more important in determining the trajectories of both Norway and Slovenia have been the relative stability of their respective parliamentary systems, their relative economic prosperity, the relatively high level of education of their respective populations, and their commitment – more clearly visible in Norway – to a concept of social justice.

Part One –
The System &
Democratic Cultures

Kristen Ringdal and Mitja Hafner-Fink

2 Changes and Stability in Democratic Cultures Norway and Slovenia 1990 – 2008

In this chapter we compare some aspects of the democratic cultures in Norway and Slovenia since 1990. The analysis will proceed at two levels. First, we will describe the democratic cultures of the two countries in a European perspective by means of data from the European Value Study (EVS) 1990 and 2008. Next, we will compare the two countries to answer the following research questions: What are the main similarities and differences in democratic attitudes and activities between Norway and Slovenia? Do we find evidence of convergence between the two countries after 20 years of experience with democracy in Slovenia? Do the within-country differences in democratic attitudes and practices by age, gender, education, and populations density show similarities between the two countries and stability over time?

The introduction will proceed with a discussion of the choice of democratic attitudes and practices to be used in the empirical analysis. Thereafter, a short version of the political history of the two countries will be presented. The introduction ends with stating some expectations about similarities and differences in democratic values between the two countries and about changes over the time period studied.

What are the main aspects of a democratic culture?

We will start with attitudes to democracy and present two approaches. The first one is based on basic values inherent in the concept of democracy. The second and wider approach is based on the concept of civil culture.

Møller and Skaaning[1] distinguish three basic attributes of liberal democracy: electoral rights, civil liberties, and the rule of law. The first attributes imply regular, free, general elections. Political liberties include freedom of speech, opinion, association, demonstration, and petition. The rule of law implies civil rights, that is equal access to and treatment by the law. Democratization may be seen as a sequence of steps that through gradations from liberal

1 Jørgen Møller and Svend Erik Skaaning (2010), "Beyond the radical delusion: conceptualizing and measuring democracy", *International Political Science Review* 31(3), pp. 261-283.

democracy to minimalist democracy. In this sense, both Norway and Slovenia satisfy the requirements of a liberal democracy at present.

Almond and Verba published *The Civic Culture* in 1963[2] based on political attitudes and democracy in five nations. In their landmark study, the civic culture was seen as the link between the micro and macro levels of the political system. The civic (political) culture is a mixture of modern participatory as well, traditional and parochial values that ensures stability. It is based on values and attitudes that work to sustain participatory democratic institutions. This includes political interest, feelings of political efficacy and active participation in civil society and politics. Also relevant are trust in people, and confidence in the political institutions of society as well as being proud of being a citizen of one's country. The civic culture also includes political tolerance. Some of these aspects of the political culture, especially trust in people and participation in civil society have also been conceptualized as indicators of social capital deemed important for the development and sustainability of democratic political systems.

Ronald Inglehart[3] used data from the World Value Survey to study the relationship between political culture and economic development. His main finding is that the civic culture is a crucial link between economic development and a stable democratic society. Inglehart's concept of civic culture consists of three elements: interpersonal or social trust, life satisfaction, and attitudes to societal change. Inglehart and Baker[4] link modernization and democracy in a more comprehensive way. They see modernization as driven primarily by economic growth and leading societies away from absolute standards of moral values and towards values that are increasingly rational, tolerant, trusting, and participatory. This indicates that the dimension of traditional versus modern, secular and rational values could be seen as an extension of the set of values that are important for developing a democratic society. Part of this is in opposition to Almond and Verba's view of the civic culture, since they saw traditional values, such as religion, as parts of the structure of society that fosters stability.

The two approaches open for a wide range of indicators of political values that may be important for maintaining a vibrant democracy. The first narrow approach points at indicators on attitudes to the various aspects of liberal democracy, whereas the wider approach based on the concept of civic culture

2 Gabriel Almond and Sidney Verba, *The Civic Culture: Political Attitudes and Democracy in Five Nations*. (Princeton, N.J.: Princeton University Press, 1963).

3 Ronald Inglehart, "The Renaissance of Political Culture", *American Political Science Review*, Vol. 82, No. 4 (December 1988), pp. 1203-1230.

4 Ronald Inglehart and Wayne Baker, "Modernization and Cultural Change, and the Persistence of Traditional Values" *American Sociological Review*, Vol. 65, No. 1 (February 2000), pp. 19-51

opens for indicators such as social and political trust, life satisfaction, political and cultural tolerance, as well as indicators of modern versus traditional values. The choice of democratic values or indicators of a democratic political culture will also depend on available indicators that are common to the EVS 1990-92 and the EVS 2008. We will examine indicators of social tolerance, participation in civil activities, and untraditional political activities or political action.

About Norway

There are two important years in modern Norwegian political history: 1814 and 1905. In 1814 Norway sought its independence from Denmark and formed a new modern democratic constitution. The independence lasted only a few months as Norway was forced to enter a union with Sweden as a result of the agreements after the Napoleonic wars. Based on the 1814 constitution, Norway was still able to establish a national parliament (Storting). The first parliamentary election was held 1815. From 1900 voting rights were extended to all men and universal suffrage was extended to women in 1913. The parliamentary system was adopted after a constitutional crisis in 1884. In 1905, Norway finally gained its independence from Sweden. The independent Norway followed Sweden in adopting a policy of neutrality in relation to the conflict between the major powers in Europe and remained neutral until the German invasion in May 1940.

During the German occupation, 1940-45, democratic rule in Norway was suspended. Norway joined the western coalition in the war against Germany and joined NATO in 1949. After the unions with Denmark and Sweden, "union" was not a popular word in Norway and in two referendums in 1972 and 1994 Norway said no to join the European Economic Community/European Union. In 1973 Norway made a free trade agreement with the EU. In 1994 Norway's relation with the EU was expanded with the European Economic Area (EEA) agreement which still regulates the country's relations with the EU.

About Slovenia

Slovenia is a new state with a long history of being divided and ruled by other states. By the end of the First World War (1918), the territory of present-day Slovenia was part of the Austro-Hungarian Empire. Then, the greater part of the Slovenian territory was included in the Kingdom of Yugoslavia, while the second part of the territory was connected to Italy. After the end of World War

II and until 1991, Slovenia was, in today's territorial extent, one of the federal units (republics) of communist Yugoslavia. Slovenia was the most developed federal unit of communist Yugoslavia having also important economic and cultural connection with the West. Indeed, the fact is that "the Iron Curtain" between Yugoslavia and the West was not completely veiled. After the breakdown of communism in Yugoslavia in 1990, Slovenia held free elections, and on plebiscite in December voted for independence. On June 25, 1991 Slovenia (simultaneously with Croatia) declared its independence of Yugoslavia.

Expectations on similarities and differences

Norway has experienced a 200 years of democratic tradition whereas Slovenia is a more recent democracy with a little more than 20 years of experience with democracy. Norway joined NATO in 1949 whereas Slovenia became a NATO-member in 2004. The same year, Slovenia became an EU-member whereas Norway rejected membership in two referendums in 1972 and 1994 and became member of the European Economic Area (EEA). Both countries are small, Norway with a population of about 5 million and Slovenia with about 2 million. Both countries are also homogeneous as to ethnicity as well as religion in that about 90% belong to the major ethnic groups, Slovenes and Norwegians, and most Slovenes are Roman Catholics whereas most Norwegians belong to the (Lutheran) Church of Norway.

Let us look at expectation on the themes covered in this chapter: social tolerance and political participation. In Slovenia, the new institutions showed high popularity in 1990, but recent economic problem may have created more critical attitudes towards democracy. However, we only have the EVS data from 1990/92 and 2008. Thus, we are not able to detect the effect of economic crisis, which has become the subject of (public) discussions only towards the end of 2008. This means, however, that we can observe "pure" effect of democratisation process since the first free multiparty elections in 1990, appended with the fact of becoming independent state in 1991. In Norway almost 200 years' experience of stable democratic rule may be expected to be associated with high levels of support for democracy and stability over the period studied.

In general, social tolerance is rather low in Eastern Europe compared to countries in the West. Again, with increasing levels of education, modernization, and experience of democracy one would expect social tolerance to improve. In Norway, we expect social tolerance to be high for the period studied, although we expect a shift in liberal direction from 1990 to 2008.

The experience of communism may have inhibited civil and political participation in Slovenia, although this may be expected to show change in the period studied. In Norway, participation at local levels in voluntary organisations and political activities has generally been high. Therefore, we expect high levels of participation both in civic and unconventional political activities.

We also have some common general expectations about within-country differences. On gender we expect men to participate more in civil and political activities than women, and women to be more social tolerant than men. However, in line with findings of various authors about closing the gender gap for at least the new types of political activities (e.g. unconventional, protest, individualized),[5] we expect that the role of gender (in favour of males) would be reduced from the first measurement (1990/92) to the second measurement (2008). We further expect a negative relationship between age on the one hand and participation and social tolerance on the other hand. We also expect a positive relationship between education and all aspects of democratic culture. We further expect that people living in cities to be more social tolerant than people in rural areas.

About the European Value Study

The European Values Study (EVS) has administered surveys of beliefs, values and attitudes of Europeans every nine years since the start in 1981.[6] The EVS is a large-scale, cross-national, and longitudinal survey research program on basic human values initiated by the European Value Systems Study Group in the late 1970s, at that time an informal grouping of academics. We will use data from the second and the fifth wave. The second wave was fielded 1990-92 and the fourth wave in 2008. The EVS includes surveys with identical questions in 26 countries in 1990-92 and 47 European countries and regions in 2008. In the latter round, more than 70,000 persons were interviewed. The surveys cover a

5 For example, Dietlind Stolle, Marc Hooghe, and Michele Micheletti (2005): Politics in the Supermarket: Political Consumerism as a Form of Political Participation. *International Political Science Review* 2005, Vol. 26, No. 3, pp. 245-269. DOI: 10.1177/0192512105053784; , Aina Gallego, "Unequal Political Participation in Europe", in *International Journal of Sociology,* vol. 37, no. 4 (2005), pp. 10–25. DOI 10.2753/IJS0020-7659370401; and Li, Yaojun and David Marsh, "New Forms of Political Participation: Searching for Expert Citizens and Everyday Makers", in *British Journal of Political Science,* Vol. 38, no. 2 (2008), pp. 247–272. doi: 10.1017/S0007123408000136

6 See http://www.europeanvaluesstudy.eu/evs/about-evs/.

range of topics including life satisfaction, attitudes, and values relating to family, work, religion, politics, and society.

Results

The analysis is divided in two parts. First, indicators of the democratic cultures of Norway and Slovenia will be compared with other European countries at around 1990 and 2008. This will show how the two countries compare with each their geographical neighbours in terms of democratic values and practices. In the second analysis, we will compare similarities and differences in democratic culture between groups formed by individual characteristics at both points in time.

Norwegian and Slovenian democratic values in a European comparison

The chosen indicators of a democratic culture are found with identical questions in 1990-92 and 2008. We start with social tolerance. The questions available in the EVS are far from ideal indicators of social tolerance. We base our measurement on a set of identical questions with the following introduction: "Please tell me for each of the following statements whether you think it can always be justified (10), never be justified (1), or something in between, using this card." From the list of 20 statements, we chose the ones on homosexuality, abortion and divorce as the bases for our social tolerance scale. The scale was computed as the means score of the answers on each question ranging from 1 to 10. High scores on the scale mean high social tolerance. The scale has satisfactory psychometric properties; it is one-dimensional and the reliability as measured by Cronbach's alpha is 0.80.

Figure 2.1 shows the country means on the social tolerance scale for 1990-92 and for 2008 for the countries included in both waves. As expected, social tolerance at the two time points is rather strongly correlated (r=0.80) at the country level, but the figure also shows some changes. At the first time point Slovenia scored somewhat higher on social tolerance than Norway. Compared to other European countries the tolerance in both countries was relatively high. The highest level of social tolerance was observed for the Netherlands, Finland, Iceland and Sweden. In the other end of the scale we find Malta followed by Lithuania and Poland.

Figure 2.1. Social tolerance

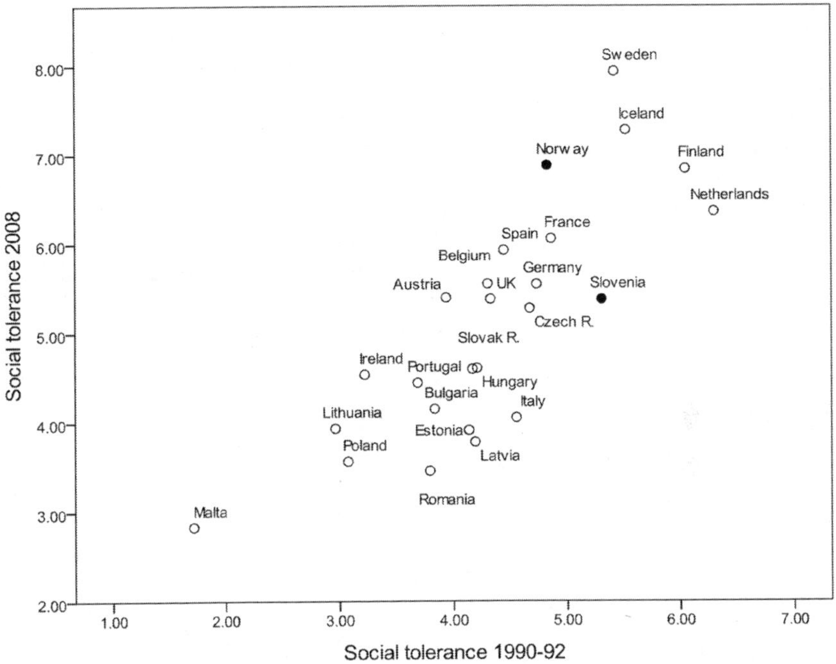

From the early 1990s to 2008, the average level of social tolerance increased from 4.3 to 5.3. The mean social tolerance score in Norway changed from 4.8 to 6.8, keeping Norway among the top ranked countries in 2008. The mean social tolerance score of Slovenia did, however, stay at the same level as in 1992. From being among the countries with the highest level of social tolerance in 1992, Slovenia is found close to the average for all nations in 2008.

The next theme is participation in voluntary organisations. The question on membership and doing work for voluntary organisations was introduced in this way: "Please look carefully at the following list of voluntary organisations and activities and say ... a) which, if any, do you belong to? b) which, if any, are you currently doing unpaid voluntary work for?" The list includes 14 types of organisations from "Social welfare services for elderly, handicapped or deprived people", through "Political parties or groups" to "Peace movement". Since the distributions were heavily skewed, we decided to distinguish between the ones who were members/did unpaid work for one or more voluntary organisations and those who were not engaged in voluntary organisations. The results are reported in the two following figures.

In Figure 2.2, the percentage in each country who were members of one or more organisations at the two time points are reported. As expected, the cluster in the upper right corner with the highest levels of membership in organisations, are Denmark, Iceland, the Netherlands, Norway and Finland. At the opposite corner we find countries from South and Eastern Europe with the lowest level of membership in organisations. This placement may at least partially be explained by the experience of communism and authoritarian rule which did discourage civil activities. The level of organisational membership in Norway is stable at around 80% both in 1990 and in 2008. In Slovenia, 39% reported to be member of one or more voluntary organisations in 1992. This has risen to 53% in 2008, moving Slovenia from a rather low to a medium rank among the European countries.

Figure 2.2. Member of one or more voluntary organisation

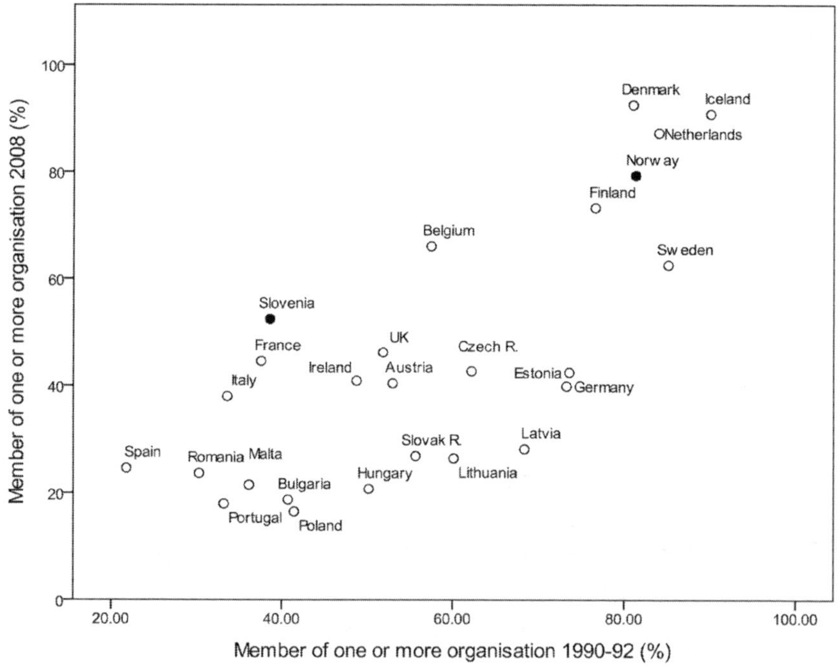

In Figure 2.3, the results for "currently doing unpaid work for voluntary organisations" are reported. The percentage are lower than for organisational membership, as unpaid voluntary work is more demanding than being a member only. At the upper right corner, we find the countries with the highest participation at both time points; the Netherlands, Finland and Norway. At the opposite corner with lowest activity, we find Spain, Hungary, Portugal, Bulgaria, Romania and Malta.

As for our two countries of interest, Norway remains rather stable with 35-40 % of the respondents being involved in unpaid voluntary work. Slovenia scored second lowest in 1992 with only around 15% involved in voluntary work. However, by 2008 the percentage had risen to 32 quite a bit above the mean of 24% for all countries.

Figure 2.3. Unpaid work in voluntary organisations 1990-92 – 2008

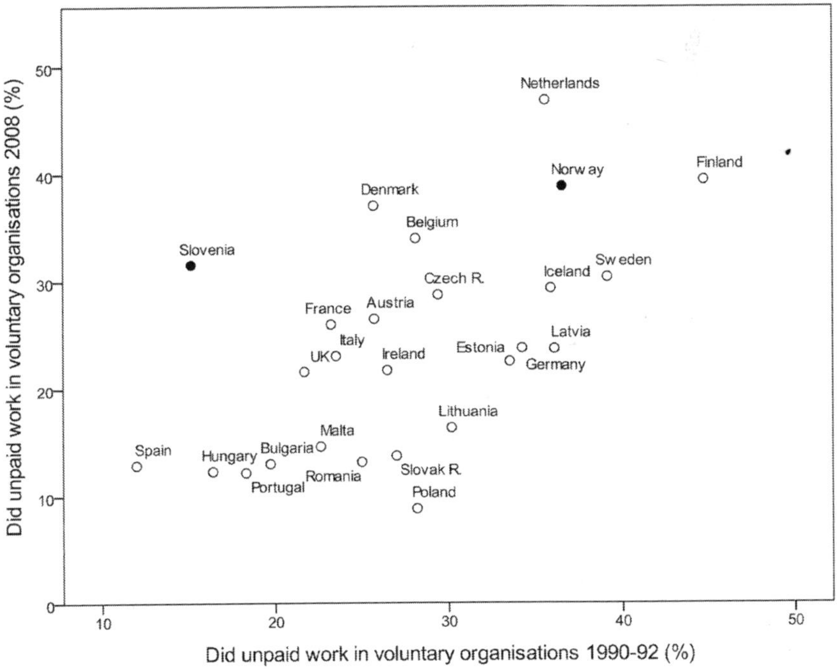

Next, we turn to political activities. In both waves a question about participation in five unconventional political activities were asked: "Now I'd like you to look at this card. I'm going to read out some different forms of political action that people can take, and I'd like you to tell me, for each one, whether you have actually done any of these things, whether you might do it or would never, under any circumstances, do it." The five types of political action on the card were: "Signing a petition", "Joining in boycotts", "Attending lawful demonstrations", "Joining unofficial strikes", "Occupying buildings and factories". Again, the distributions were skewed. Therefore, we will only distinguish between people who reported to have participated in at least one of the activities and those who had not participated in any of them. The results are reported in Figure 2.4, which shows the percentage in each country who have participated in political action in 1990-92 and in 2008.

Figure 2.4. Participated in one or more unconventional political activity (%)

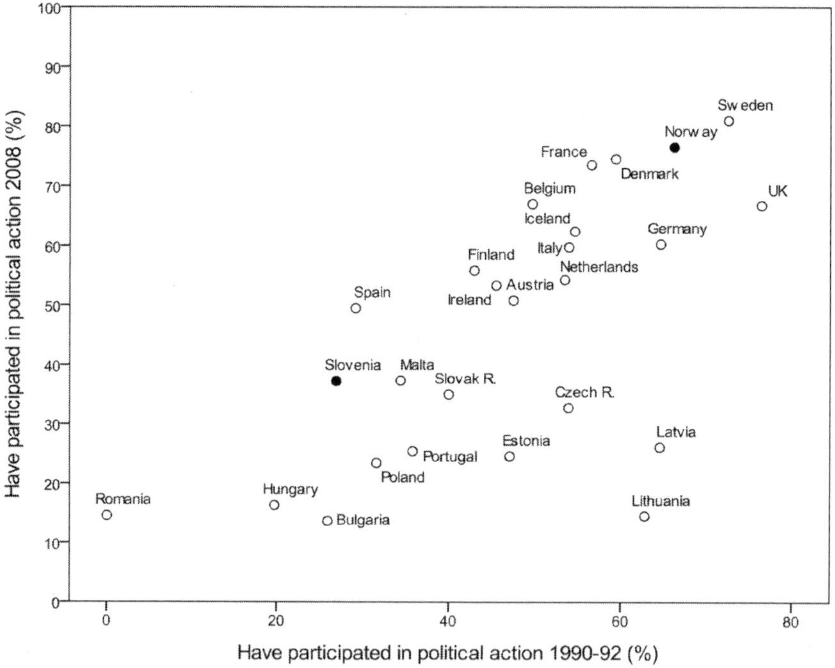

In 1990-92, the United Kingdom showed the highest level of political action in Europe with a participation of close to 80%. Next, with high level of political action followed Sweden, Norway, Latvia, Germany, and Lithuania. At the other end of the scale, with the lowest level of political action we find Hungary, Bulgaria and Slovenia. Most countries in the upper right hand of the figure, show stability in political action from the 1990s to 2008, but there are some notable exceptions. Latvia and Lithuania both show a strong decline in political action along with the Czech Republic and Estonia. Others show marked increase in political action, especially Spain and Slovenia. In Spain there was an increase in participation in political action from less than 30% to more than 50%. The increase for Slovenia is also substantial from 27 to 38%.

Democratic cultures in Norway and Slovenia

In this section, we analyse data for Norway and Slovenia. We perform pooled regression analyses of social tolerance (Table 2.1) and of participation in civil and political activities (Table 2.2). In all models, age, gender, education and town size are included as independent variables along with dummy variables for survey years and country. All models for the complete data sets with two time points also include the survey year by country interaction. This enables us to estimate adjusted differences between the two countries in attitudes to democracy and in civil and political activities as well as adjusted estimates of change in attitudes and activities. Finally, the inclusion of socio-demographic characteristics of the respondents also enables us to study within-country differences in the dependent variables.

In Table 2.1, we report the results from the OLS regression analyses of social tolerance based on the EVS 1990-92 and 2008 waves. Since we have data for both time points, the full model is applied, with the country by survey year interaction. The latter is statistically significant and consistent with the impression from the unadjusted differences (Figure 2.1). The interaction effect displayed in Figure 2.5 builds on the coefficients at the bottom of the table. The crossing lines show that the average level of social tolerance in Slovenia was about 0.6 higher than in Norway in 1990-92. Since that time social tolerance has increased weakly in Slovenia but more strongly in Norway so that their relative position is 2008 has become reversed. In 2008 the Norwegian respondents are substantially more tolerant than their Slovenian counterparts.

Table 2.1. Social tolerance; multiple regression analyses of data from Norway and Slovenia, EVS 1990-92 and 2008

	Coef.	
Gender		
Male (ref. cat.)	0.000	
Female	0.392	***
Age categories		
17 - 30 (ref. cat.)	0.000	
31 - 45	-0.166	
46 - 60	-0.543	***
61 - 89	-1.279	***
Level of education		
Prim.- low sec. (ref. cat.)	0.000	
Upper secondary	0.898	***
Tertiary	1.281	***
Town size		
-5000 (ref. cat.)	0.000	
5000 - 100 000	0.450	***
100 000 -	0.816	***
Country		
Slovenia (ref. cat.)	0.000	
Norway	-0.640	
Survey year		
1990-92 (ref. cat.)	0.000	
2008	0.394	***
Country by survey year		
Norway*2008	1.662	***
Constant	4.515	***
R^2	0.210	
Sample size	4288	

Note: Coef.: Unstandardized (OLS) regression coefficients, coefficients for reference categories are set to 0.000 for comparison. Statistical significance is marked in this way: * $p < .05$, ** $p < .01$, *** $p < .001$.

Figure 2.5. Adjusted predicted margins of social tolerance by country and survey year

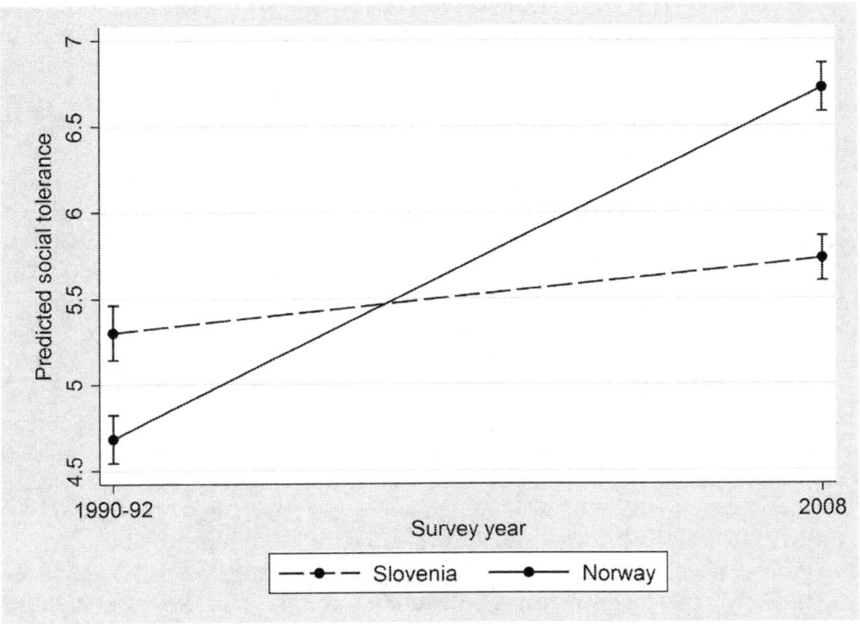

On the average, the differences between the socio-demographic groups are larger for social tolerance than for the attitudes towards democracy. Women are clearly more social tolerant than men. The difference is about 0.4 on a scale from 1 to 10. The differences between the age groups are more substantial. The oldest respondents (61-89 years of age) score about 1.3 points lower in social tolerance the youngest age group. Social tolerance is also significantly related to levels of education. Persons with tertiary education score about 1.3 higher on the social tolerance scale than respondents with primary or lower secondary education. There is a significant country by education interaction: the difference between the groups by education is larger in Slovenia than in Norway. Finally, town size is positively related to social tolerance. People living in large towns score around 0.8 point higher on the social tolerance scale than people in sparsely populated areas.

In Table 2.2 the focus is on participation in civil and political activities. All three dependent variables in the table are dichotomous and accordingly analysed by logistic regression. The first two distinguish between those who are currently (at the survey year) member of (and doing unpaid work for) one or more voluntary organisation and those who are not member of any such organisation. Let as start with the country differences and the evidence of change at the bottom of the table. All the relevant coefficients are significant for both indicators of participation in voluntary organisations. To make the results easier to interpret, the predicted probabilities of being member of one or more voluntary organisation by country and years, are displayed in Figure 2.6 and similarly for doing unpaid work in Figure 2.7. It is evident from Figure 2.6 that in Norway the probability has been high for the whole period, but slightly lower in 2008 than in 1990.Slovenia was far behind Norway in 1992 with a predicted probability of 0.4 in 1992. In 2008, the differences between the two countries are smaller as the membership rate has increased markedly in Slovenia. The impression that Slovenia is catching up is even stronger for the probability of doing unpaid work for a voluntary organisation in Figure 2.7. The large difference in 1990-92 has almost disappeared by 2008 when Slovenia is just slightly below the Norwegian level of participation.

Let us move to within-country differences. For gender and age, the average differences for membership as reported in Table 2.2 are small, but they conceal country differences. The regression coefficient for gender implies that women are less likely to be members of voluntary organisations. This finding is, however, only valid for Slovenia. This also applies to differences between the age groups, which are small in Norway and markedly larger in Slovenia, where we can see a pattern of decreasing probability from the youngest category to the oldest category. The age differences also vary by country for doing unpaid voluntary work, but here the pattern is the opposite. There are smaller age differences for Slovenia than for Norway. The gender difference is larger for doing unpaid work than for membership. Women are clearly less likely to engage in unpaid voluntary work than men. The differences between the groups by education are quite similar for membership and for doing unpaid work. Furthermore, there are stronger differences by town size for doing unpaid work than for membership. In both instances people in large towns show less participation than people living in small towns.

Table 2.2. Participation in civil and political activities. Logistic regression analyses of data from Norway and Slovenia, EVS 1990-92 and 2008

	Member of one or more voluntary organisation			*Do unpaid work in voluntary organisations*			*Have participated in unconventional political activities*		
	Coef.		OR	Coef.		OR	Coef.		OR
Female									
Male (ref. cat.)									
Female	-0.181	**	0.834	-0.417	***	0.659	0.033		1.033
Age categories									
17 - 30 (ref. cat.)	0.000			0.000			0.000		
31 - 45	0.186		1.204	0.387	***	1.472	0.199	*	1.220
46 - 60	0.001		1.001	0.356	***	1.428	0.004		1.004
61 - 89	-0.258	*	0.773	0.079		1.082	-0.550	***	0.577
Level of education									
Prim.- low sec. (ref. cat.)	0.000			0.000			0.000		
Upper secondary	0.351	***	1.421	0.521	***	1.683	0.666	***	1.946
Tertiary	1.101	***	3.008	1.030	***	2.802	1.033	***	2.811
Town size									
-5000 (ref. cat.)	0.000			0.000			0.000		
5000 - 100 000	-0.039		0.962	-0.246	**	0.782	0.064		1.067
100 000 -	-0.186		0.830	-0.409	***	0.665	0.178		1.194
Country									
Slovenia (ref. cat.)	0.000			0.000			0.000		
Norway	1.865	***	6.456	1.118	***	3.057	1.692	***	5.430
Survey year									
1990-92	0.000			0.000			0.000		
2008	0.716	***	2.047	1.117	***	3.057	0.722	***	2.058
Country by survey year									
Norway*2008	-0.801	***	0.449	-0.948	***	0.388	-0.132		0.877
Constant	-0.769	***		-2.161	***		-1.670	***	
Pseudo R2	0.139			0.072			0.167		
-2 Log Likelihood	5169.3			5270.2			5272.9		
Sample size	4570			4570			4570		

Note: Coef.: Logistic regression coefficients, coefficients for reference categories are set to 0.000 for comparison. OR: odds ratios, computed as exp(coef.). Statistical significance is marked in this way: * $p < .05$, ** $p < .01$, *** $p < .001$.

Figure 2.6. Adjusted predicted probability of being member of one or more voluntary organisation by country and year

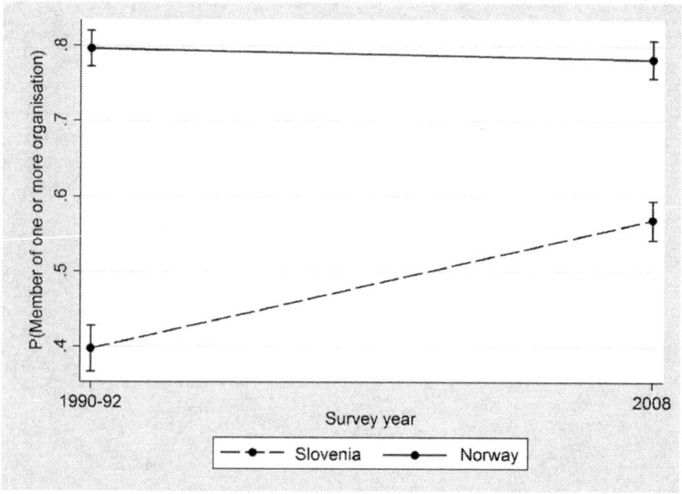

Figure 2.7. Adjusted predicted probability of doing unpaid work in voluntary organisations by country and year

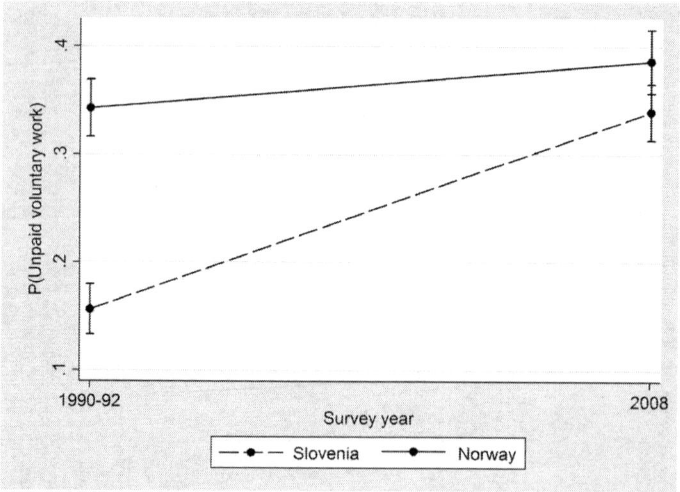

Let us move to participation in unconventional political activities or political action. Here we observe a markedly increase in participation from the early 1990s to 2008, slight lower for Norway than for Slovenia, but the latter difference is not statistical significant. Moving to within-country differences, there are obviously no gender differences in political action. We find differences between age groups; the largest one implies that people from the oldest age group are much less likely to engage in political action than people below 60 years of age. As to be expected, education is positively related to political action. The table shows the average relationship for the two countries combined, but this relationship is actually stronger in Slovenia than in Norway.

Signs of decreasing differences in democratic culture

An overview of changes on individual dimensions during the period from 1990 to 2008 indicates a possible (hypothetical) conclusion that differences between Slovenia and Norway have decreased. To support this conclusion, we conducted additional analyses combining three key dimensions: social tolerance, social participation (unpaid voluntary work), and unconventional (protest) political participation. More precisely, we classified countries in both time points (1990-92 and 2008) on the basis of these three dimensions, which were "measured" with aggregated individual data. We used a hierarchical cluster analysis of 25 countries (countries with missing data on any individual dimension were excluded). Ward's method was used for the clustering, while the squared Euclidian distance for standardised data (Z-scores) was used to measure the (dis)similarities amongst the countries.[7]

In both time points we can see clear division into two groups. However, this division is not the same in both time points. In 1990-92 the classification is as follows (Figure 2.8): The group with the highest means on all three dimensions consists of Nordic countries (Norway, Sweden, Finland, Iceland), Germany, Netherlands and Latvia. The second group is more differentiated and includes all other countries. Slovenia fits in this group. More precisely, together with Bulgaria, Hungary, and Spain, Slovenia forms a subgroup with the lowest group means on both participatory dimensions, and (especially in Slovenia) with higher values on social tolerance dimension.

In 2008 the classification is different (Figure 2.9): The group with the lowest mean values on all three dimensions includes new democracies (but not Slovenia and Czech Republic) and three more countries: Portugal, Spain, and Malta. The second group is more diversified and could be divided into two

7 See Joe H. Ward, Jr., 'Hierarchical Grouping to Optimize an Objective Function', in *Journal of the American Statistical Association*, Vol. 58 (1963), p. 301

subgroups: The group of Nordic countries (+ the Netherlands) with the highest group means values on all three dimensions, and West and Central European countries including Slovenia with intermediate values on all three dimensions.

This indicates that during the period of consolidation of democracy from 1990-92 to 2008, Slovenia approached the average of west European old democracies. The differences between Norway and Slovenia were also reduced since the countries were in different groups in 1990-92, but fitted within the same broad group with Western democracies in 2008. Another indication of the decreasing differences between the two countries is changes in the distance measures that used as input in the cluster analysis. The average standardized squared Euclidian distances between Slovenia and Norway on the three dimensions (social tolerance, social participation, political action) in 1990-92 was 14.3, while in 2008 this distance decreased to 4.8.

Figure 2.8. Classification of countries in 1990/92 according to level of social tolerance, social participation and protest participation

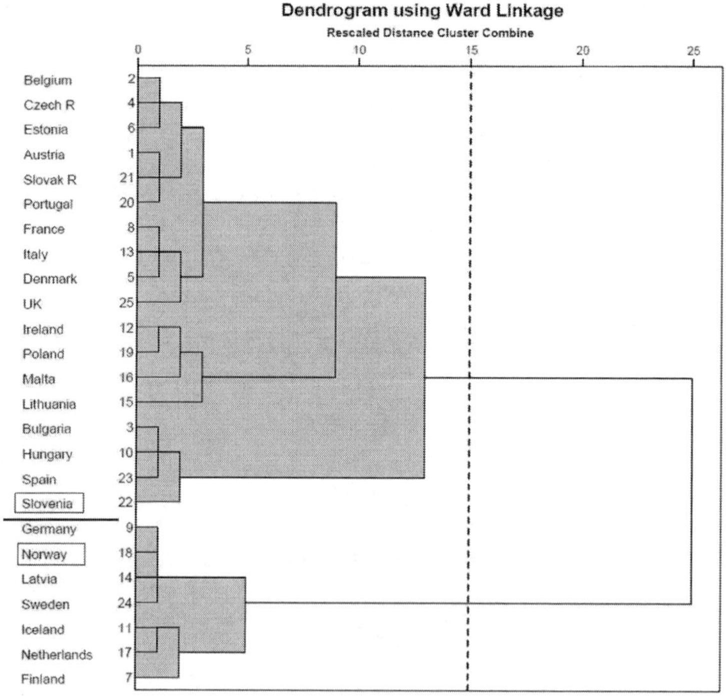

Figure 2.9. Classification of countries in 2008 according to level of social tolerance, social participation and protest participation

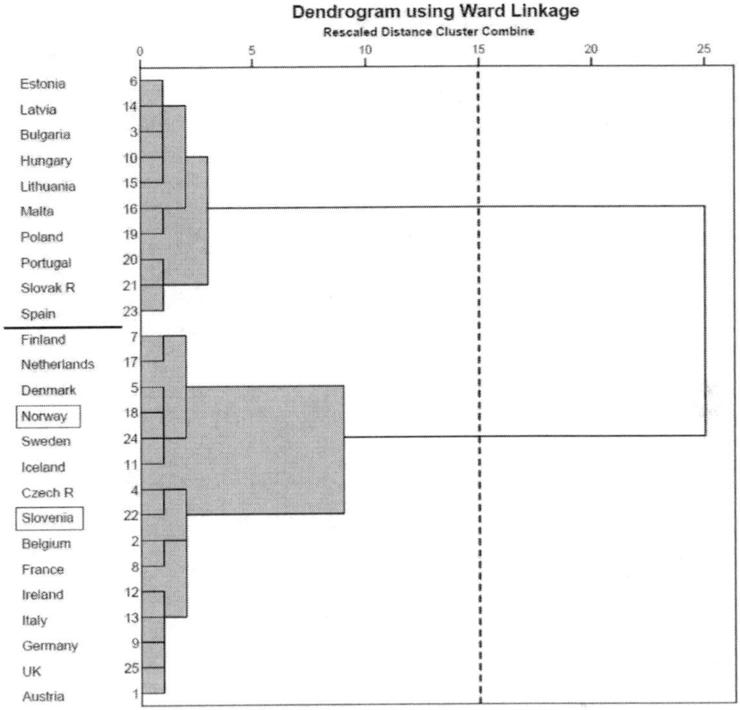

Conclusions

Our empirical analysis of the democratic (civic) cultures in Norway and Slovenia used data on social tolerance and participation in civil activities and in unconventional political activities (political action) from the European Value Study (EVS) from 1990-92 and 2008. The general expectations were that Norway with a democratic culture matured for 200 years would in most respect rate better on our indicators than Slovenia with 20 years of experience with democracy. We did however, expect Slovenia to catch up, especially on social tolerance and civic and political activities in the period studied.

First, we presented Norwegian and Slovenian democratic values in a European comparison followed by a more thorough analysis of Slovenian-Norwegian differences adjusted for socio-demographic control variables gender, age, education and town size. A cluster analysis of the countries based on basic indicators of a democratic culture concluded the empirical part of the chapter.

The results for social tolerance (homosexuality, abortion, divorce) were rather surprising. In 1992, the level of social tolerance in Slovenia was higher than in Norway and surpassed only by a few Western countries. In 2008, the picture had changed. Whereas, the level of social tolerance in Slovenia showed only a marginal increase, it increased markedly in Norway from 1992 to 2008.

For activities in voluntary organizations, a tendency for "catching up" is observed for both membership and doing unpaid work. Norway showed stable and very high score for both 1992 and 2008, whereas Slovenia started out with low scores scored in 1992, but had halved the gap in membership in organizations in 2008 and almost closed the gap in doing unpaid work. For unconventional political activities or political action (signing a petition, joining in boycotts, attending lawful demonstrations, joining unofficial strikes, occupying buildings and factories) the pattern is different. The level of activity increased about equally from 1992 to 2008 in both countries with a rate of participation of more than 30 percentage points higher in Norway than in Slovenia for the period studied.

The final country-level cluster analysis of social tolerance, social participation and unconventional political participation indicated that during the period of consolidation of democracy from 1990-92 to 2008, Slovenia approached the average of west European old democracies and the differences between Norway and Slovenia were also reduced.

Comparing Slovenia and Norway, we were able to show differences between an old democracy (Norway) and a young democracy still in the period of consolidation (Slovenia). We can clearly see differences which persist during the observed period (from 1990-92 to 2008) indicating a higher level of (democratic) civic culture in Norway. Simultaneously we can see a trend towards reduction of these differences. We can argue that this process of strengthening the civic culture in Slovenia has being supported by the democratic changes in the political system. At the same time it should be noted that certain processes (emergence of new social movement, secularization process) already started in the beginning of the 1980s, which means well before the first free multi-party elections in 1990.[8] This is in line with thesis of relationship between cultural changes, modernization process, and democratization: cultural change can lead

8 For example, Danica Fink-Hafner and Sabrina P. Ramet, "Slovenia since 1988: Building Democracy and Liberalism", in Sabrina P. Ramet and Danica Fink Hafner (eds.), *Democratic transition in Slovenia: Value Transformation, Education, and Media* (College Station, Tex.: Texas A&M University Press, 2006), pp. 30-51; and Veljko Rus and Niko Toš, *Vrednote*

to political change.[9] This means that changes (reducing differences between Slovenia and Norway) could be understood as continuation of (post) modernization process already present in 1980s and additionally supported with various aspects of democratic changes.

Slovencev in Evropejcev (Ljubljana: Fakulteta za družbene vede, IDV, CJMMK (Dokumenti SJM, 2005), p. 13)

9 For example, Ronald Inglehart and Christian Welzel , *Modernization, Cultural Change, and Democracy: The Human Development Sequence* (Cambridge and New York: Cambridge University Press. 2005).

Alenka Krašovec and Ola Listhaug

3 Political Parties in Norway and Slovenia

Norway and Slovenia are in many ways different countries. One of the important differences is the tradition of democracy and democratic life. While Norway is commonly treated as an old, established democracy, Slovenia only recently experienced a transition to democracy and is commonly treated as a young democracy. Given such discrepancy democratic concerns facing these two countries should be different, whether we talk about trust in institutions, involvement of citizens in politics, instability of the party system or development and characteristics of political parties. On the other hand, some similar institutional arrangements both countries opted for should lead to similar solutions but also to similar challenges both countries are facing. In the following sections development and characteristics of parties and governments will be analysed.

Norway

Norway is an old nation and by most standards also a well-established democracy. Although it is possible to go further back in time when discussing Norwegian political development, our interest of studying elections, parties, and government is primarily related to the last 200 years – from 1814 when the Norwegian Constitution was established – and until today. The political change in this period has been gradual rather than disruptive, although it is possible to observe key points of conflicts in the Norway's political development during the period. One distinct pattern is the continuous expansion of democratic rights to an increasing proportion of the population. A significant breakthrough of political parties came in the 1880s, and the main parties that were founded – the Liberal Party, the Conservatives, and the Labour Party – still exist, although they are necessarily highly transformed from the original parties.

In 1898 all men had achieved the right to vote and in 1913 all women were allowed to vote. In parallel with the expansion of voting rights the power of the parliament was extended. The key period for this was also in the 1880s, when the struggle to increase the power of parliament was linked to the national question – how Norway should increase the independence from Sweden (which Norway was in a political union with since 1814). Independence was achieved in 1905 and confirmed in a referendum where almost all voters said yes to leave the union with Sweden. This double democratization – political independence and the expansion of voting rights to all citizens and the broadening of political participation – laid the foundation for the working of electoral democracy which included a new set of political parties that developed in the first third of the new century.

The party system that evolved in this period was conditioned by an electoral system implemented in the 1920s which was more proportional than the old system, and thus increased the number of competitive political parties. The support for the Liberal party and the Conservative party, which had been dominant at the end of the nineteenth century and the early period of the twentieth century, was partly replaced by parties that appealed to more well-defined sets of voters than the old parties which were more like coalitions of voter groups. Important examples of parties that evolved under the new system are The Farmer's Party, and somewhat later, the Christian People's Party.

The new proportional system contributed to the formation of the cleavage model of voting as described by Rokkan and Valen.[1] In their research they emphasized that a set of cleavages based on geography, culture, and economic conflicts were the most important for the formation of parties and also for the voting choices of citizens. The geographic dimension included both important regions with distinct voting patterns, especially Southern and Western Norway on one side and Eastern Norway on the other. There were also important divides within these regions, for example between coastal and inland areas in Western Norway. A second geographic dimension was formed by the conflict between centre and periphery, where the political centre of the capital and surrounding areas stood in some conflict to the interests of the periphery.

Norway is a country with huge geographic distances and scattered population, which of course were even stronger in the period when communications were much less efficient than today. The centre-periphery factor created conflicts over many aspects of public policy and the distribution of economic transfers from government to counties and municipalities. In the two referendums on EU membership in 1972 and 1994 opponents of membership saw the European Union as an extension of the centre-periphery system of the Norwegian nation state, increasing the distance from the Norwegian peripheries to the power centres of the European Union.[2]

The cultural dimension included religious conflicts – especially between the state church and Lutheran groups. In the 1930s, the Christian People's Party

1 Henry Valen and Stein Rokkan, "Norway: Conflict Structure and Mass Politics in a European Periphery", in Richard Rose (ed.), *Electoral Behavior* (New York: Free Press, 1974).

2 Anders Todal Jenssen et al., (eds.), *To Join or Not to Join* (Oslo: Scandinavian University Press, 1998).

was formed to champion political issues from a religious point of view. Other moral and cultural issues, like anti-alcohol views and support for a more nationalist form of Norwegian language (nynorsk) were also part of the cultural divide where several parties took positions in favour of teetotalism and nynorsk. It is important to note that the Christian People's party did not become a party for the whole country until after World War Two as before the war the party had elected representatives to the parliament only in Western Norway.[3] Any student of Norwegian electoral politics will find that religion and other cultural cleavages are correlated with geography, and should be analysed together with the geographic dimension.

An important economic cleavage that increased in saliency in the first half of the twentieth century was the divide in the labour market between workers and capitalists. Several parties placed themselves on either the left or the right. The Labour Party soon became the most important party in advocating a socialist ideological positon, with the Communists and a smaller social democratic party losing support. In contrast to the Labour party's radical past from the 1910s and 1920s the party in the 1930s advocated pragmatic and reform-oriented policies. As a result of this policy shift Labour achieved the status as a governing party in 1935, which was the first step toward a long term period as the dominant party of government in Norway. In addition to the working class, the party also defended the economic interests of small farmers, those who were employed in the fisheries, and other groups in rural areas. At the time the government was formed in 1935 with a new election in 1936, it was of course impossible to know that the next democratic election would not occur until 1945 – nearly ten years after the previous election.

The election of 1945 is important because it was the first election which fully demonstrated the impact of the political cleavage structure. It may be quite common to say that the party structure was developed in the 1920s (after the proportional reform), but an important party alternative like the Christian People's Party was formed as a national party only after World War Two. The interwar years were a period with low stability in party alternatives. The primary cause of this was the economic depression, which also had a political impact, the conflicts in the labour movement which led to splits of the parties, and, as we have noted above, that the electoral reform made it easier for small parties to elect representatives to the Storting.

From 1945 the party structure achieved an unprecedented level of stability that with minor exceptions was to last through the 1960s. On the far left there was for the first part of the period the Communist Party which in 1945 received

3 See «Kristelig folkeparti», article in *Store norske leksikon* https://snl.no/Kristelig_Folkeparti [last accessed on 7 September 2015].

a record of more than 10 per cent of the vote – largely explained by the voters' impression that the party had been active in the resistance to the Nazi occupation of Norway. However, in the years that followed the support for the Communists dwindled and in 1961 the new Socialist People's Party took over the position to the left of the Labour. Labour stayed in power with a majority government until 1961. In 1961 Labour lost its absolute majority in the parliament, a signal that the period with strong Labour dominance was over and that other parties than Labour might be able to form a government. In 1965 (and with a short-lived government in 1963) this was also what happened. The nonsocialist parties ("bourgeois" parties as they are named in Norway) formed a government with a prime minister from the Centre Party (which had changed the name from the Farmer's Party). This government remained united for a period, until the question of Norway's membership in the European Union came on the agenda and the nonsocialist parties took different positions on the issue. To simplify, we may group the nonsocialist parties in two groups, the centre parties – the Liberal Party, the Centre Party, and the Christian People's Party as one group, and the Conservative Party in a group for itself. The bourgeois parties were strongly divided on the EU-question and the issue made it difficult for the parties to govern in a coalition for some time.

Several factors contributed to the political stability of the first post-war period. Some of the stability was based on the social cleavages that formed the foundation of the party structure. Cleavages are stable from one election to the next, but suddenly the stability was threatened by new issues. The question of Norwegian membership in EU emerged as a dividing issue both between parties and within parties, peaking in the first EU referendum in 1972. A second referendum on the issue came in 1994. The consequences were much the same as in 1972 – Norway stayed out, and many of the parties suffered from internal conflicts although not as quite as strongly as in the first round.

Although a single issue like the EU question can be powerful in creating political upheavals, change can also be initiated from processes of broader socioeconomic transformations. The prevailing view is that the voting behaviour was built on cleavages that were "frozen" when the party system was founded and all groups of citizens had access to the political system, primarily through voting rights. The famous "freezing hypothesis"[4] suggested that what happened a couple of generations back in time would be relevant for the voting behaviour of citizens in the 1950s and 1960s. And there was much in the voting studies based on survey data to support this view. However, at the same time many scholars of Norwegian elections (and in other countries) started to

---

4 Seymour Martin Lipset and Stein Rokkan (eds.), *Party Systems and Voter Alignments* (New York and Toronto: Free Press, 1967).

observe that the traditional cleavages were melting away. The weakening of social class in deciding the choice of party is maybe the most discussed example of the decline of the traditional cleavages.[5]

In addition to the weakening of traditional cleavages, new cleavages emerged. Much focus has been placed on new politics questions – including post-materialism, environmental issues, and gender conflicts, just to mention some of the new cleavages. It is maybe fair to say that new politics is related to the left-right dimension. But new cleavages have not been limited to various aspects of new politics, and in Norway like many other countries populist parties on the right have emerged. For many of these parties, questions related to immigration have been salient, but other questions are also on their agenda. For example, the Norwegian Progress Party has focused on tax questions and has wanted to reduce taxes. Similarly, the party wants to reduce government bureaucracy. Such questions were on the top of the agenda when the party was founded in 1973 (the name of the party then was Anders Lange's Party – after the founder), and they are still highly important for the party in the current government. The Socialist People's Party was replaced by the Socialist Election League in 1973, also including other groups on the left, and in 1975 they formed the Socialist Left party.

Recent years have seen some interesting variations in the formation of coalition governments. The more recent Labour government has included both a party to the left of Labour, the Socialist Left Party, and the Centre Party. The current government consists of two parties from the right, the Conservatives and the Progress party, and has normally support in the parliament by the Liberals and the Christian Peoples Party. It is important to see that both new parties on either side of the ideological divide, the Socialist Left Party and the Progress Party, joined the government for the first time. This confirms that the two parties are now brought into the mainstream of Norwegian politics. It is also a striking development that the Centre Party has joined a left-centre government while before the party was normally in governments on the centre-right side.

While the decline of traditional cleavages and the emergence of new cleavages are important developments in Norwegian electoral politics, we have also observed a general weakening of attachment to political parties. This is a long term trend and includes a decline both in membership in political parties and in identification with parties. This trend is quite strong and have important consequences for the working of the democratic system. Parties are voluntary organizations and the strength of parties was traditionally dependent on the activities of the members. The decline in membership rates as well as the weakening of

5 Oddbjørn Knutsen, *Class Voting in Western Europe* (Lanham, Md.: Lexington, 2006).

strength of identification with the parties are important signals that the bond between members and their political organization are looser than they used to be. Replacing the traditional forms of activities is a very strong professionalization of party organizations, with a strong growth of paid professionals.[6] Obviously, financial support from government will contribute to a more egalitarian political influence across rich and poor parties. Many will see this as a strengthening of democratic ideals. At the same time is the funding of the activities of parties by government sources in practice a replacement of voluntary activity and engagement of citizens by a professional political elite.

The transformation of the party system, with a decline of membership and unstable party identification, and a professionalization of party organizations dependent on funding from government raises the question of how political trust has developed. We can only answer this question for the recent decades as data are not comparable for the longer period. There are several interesting findings. For the first period, we observe that trust in politicians declined from the 1960s to the early 1970s, and then increased considerably in the 1977 election.[7] The standard interpretation of this is that the EU issue increased the political conflict level and created openings for new political parties on the far left and right, primarily the Socialist Left Party and the Progress Party. Actually the name of the latter party was Anders Lange's Party named after the founder of the party. It was only after his death that the party took its present name. For the Socialist Left, the opposition to membership in the European Union was the issue that generated support from socialist voters. For the Progress Party it was not the EU question directly as both anti-taxation and anti-regulations questions generated support from voters on the right. The EU referendum was just a triggering event that opened the room for political forces that were latent in the political system. Relevant discussions can be found in the studies of Henry Valen.[8]

The EU-referendum in 1972 was won – narrowly - by the no-side, and both Labour and the Liberals suffered party splits. The strong showing by the Socialist Election League and the Progressive Party in the 1973 election did not last long. In the 1977 elections the two winners from 1973 were losers and the Labour Party continued to govern with a much larger support than in 1973 when they lost heavily to the Socialist Election League (which became the

---

6 Knut Heidar and Jo Saglie, *Hva skjer med partiene?* (Oslo: Gyldendal, 2002).

7 Ola Listhaug and Bernt Aardal, «Politisk tillit – et mål på demokratiets helsetilstand?», in Bernt Aardal (ed.), *Det politiske landskap* (Oslo: Cappelen Damm, 2011).

8 Henry Valen, "The Storting Election of September 1977: Realignment or Return to Normalcy?", in *Scandinavian Political Studies,* Vol. 1, Issue 23 (September 1978), pp. 83-107.

Socialist Left Party in 1975). This can be seen as "normalizing" election,[9] and it is also possible to see the following elections with the competition between Labour and the Conservative Party taking centre stage as a return to "normal" politics. This corresponds to the pattern we find for political trust. Trust in politicians declined from 1969 to 1973 and increased from 1973 to 1981 and peaked in 1985. But normal times stopped there as in 1989 both the Socialist Left and the Progressive Party came back with good elections. For the Progressive Party immigration played a role, and for the Socialist Left pro-environment issues explained some of the increased support.

At the 1989 election there was a marked decline on trust in politicians, and for the remaining set of elections that we have studied (ending in 2009), there was only a weak recovery so that political trust only rose slightly above the all-time low from 1973.

We know from previous studies of political trust[10] that trust in politicians tend to have lower scores than many other trust measures. This is not necessary a weakness of measurement– what is important for our study is to rely on the same measure over time – assuming of course that change over time is what we want to study. It is common to make a distinction between specific aspects of trust, for example trust in politicians, and general aspects such as satisfaction for how democracy works. The time series for democracy from 1977 to 2009 shows two things – a very high score in Norway – and an impressive stability.[11] This means the variations in trust in politicians that we have observed is not translated into support – up or down - for democracy.

Since this book is about Slovenia and Norway a comparison between the two countries is of interest. A similar question for how democracy works measured on a scale from 0 to 10 where 0 is not satisfied at all and 10 very satisfied shows that for 2008 the score for Norway is 6.7 and for Slovenia the score for the same year is 4. 8. Norway is number 3 on the list (Denmark is on top of the 29 countries) while Slovenia is number 16.

The high trust level for Norway is confirmed by a study of confidence in European parliaments.[12] Dividing the countries into two groups – Western Europe and Eastern Europe, we find that level of confidence is quite stable in Western Europe while there is some decline in Eastern Europe in the period

9 *Ibid.*

10 For example, Listhaug and Aardal: «Politisk tillit», pp. 291-292.

11 *Ibid.*

12 Karin Dyrstad and Ola Listhaug, "Citizens' Confidence in European Parliaments: Institutions and Issues", in Wolfgang C. Müller and Hanne Marthe Narud (eds.), *Party Governance and Party Democracy* (New York: Springer, 2013). Denmark is again on top, followed by Switzerland and Norway (data are from 2008-2009).

leading up to 2008-2009 (the length of the period varies). Norway shows a decline in confidence in parliament while Slovenia has an increase. Among the five post-Yugoslav countries that we have data for, confidence in parliament is highest in Slovenia.

In sum, there is some good news and some bad news as well. Norway is one of the countries with highest trust- levels when compared with other European countries. Even with the decline in confidence in parliament at the most recent time point, Norway remains near the top among democracies in Western Europe. The picture for the time series for trust in politicians shows a long term decline although the level at the end of the period is marginally higher than at the low point from 1973.

There are some parallel patterns in the cases of Norway and Slovenia, different as they otherwise might be. Norway is a rich country with a working welfare state and a stable democracy. If would be unlikely if trust should not be high in this country due to the positive effects of a successful economic and political performance of the country.

The situation in Slovenia is, of course, different from that in Norway, but with some similarities as Slovenia is seen as a relatively successful case of the post-Yugoslav countries, which should lead us to expect high levels of trust compared to the other post-Yugoslav countries. We have data for five countries for 2008-2009, and we find some support for the expectation as Slovenia is the top-end in the distribution for confidence in parliament among post-Yugoslav countries.[13]

For Norway, Listhaug and Grønflaten have extended the research to cover other aspects of the hypothesis of a civic decline.[14] Based on the observation that electoral turnout at local elections has showed a long term decline, and that turnout in parliamentary elections has weakened somewhat, although not nearly as much as elections in counties and municipalities, they analyse a larger set of indicators of political participation and political involvement. The decline of turnout at official elections is not matched by a decline in political participation like activities in party organizations and contact with the political system. Similarly, there is an increase in political action among citizens. Also for political interest and engagement in political discussions the trend is upwards rather than downwards. We should be aware that for many of these indicators only small numbers of citizens are very active. But there is no general support for the hypothesis of civic decline.

---

13 *Ibid.*

14 Ola Listhaug and Lars Grønflaten (eds.), "Civic Decline? Trends in Political Involvement and Participation in Norway, 1965-2001", in *Scandinavian Political Studies*, Vol. 30, Issue 2 (June 2007), pp. 272-299, 2007.

Slovenia

Political life in Slovenia was for a long time dependent on developments in the Habsburg Empire, since Slovenia was an integral part of that empire until its dissolution in 1918. One of the most notable breaks in Slovenian political life during that era came with the March 1848 Revolution, when several national and political programs were presented; among them the most prominent was the United Slovenia Program, although Slovenes did not have any effective instruments of power to realize it.[15]

The development of modern parties started in the 1890s with the establishment of parties representing three rival ideological families: namely, the Catholic People's Party (in 1892), followed by the National Progressive Party in 1894, and finally, in 1896, the Yugoslav Social-democratic Party. The development of parties was closely connected with the introduction of universal suffrage (in national elections) of men, while women in Slovenia were granted suffrage only in 1946. In the first two decades of the twentieth century several other parties were formed. Slovene political life in the Kingdom of Yugoslavia was defined by two characteristics. There were strong ideological and political battles between the conservative party and the liberal party on almost every political issue and the struggle of these parties against Yugoslav national unitarism and state centralism.[16]

During World War Two, several parties joined the Communist Party to form the Liberation Front to fight against the occupation forces. But the Dolomitska Statement, signed by these parties in 1943, formally diminished political pluralism within the Front and had important consequences for political life after the war, when the communists had a leading role in all sectors of the state and society. Until 1989, other political parties were not allowed, although there were some socio-political organizations (the Socialist League of Working People, the League of Trade Unions, the League of the Socialist Youth, and the League of Veterans' Associations) which acted as 'transmission belts' of the leading communist party, and had representatives on all levels of the political system.[17]

In 1989, for the first time after World War Two, political pluralism was formally allowed in Slovenia and several parties were formed. These parties are frequently distinguished according to whether they are newly established or

---

15 Janko Prunk, *A Brief History of Slovenia* (Ljubljana: Založba Grad, 2000), p. 75.

16 Prunk, "A Brief History", p. 103.

17 Danica Fink-Hafner, "The Left in Slovenia", in Charles Bukowski and Barnabas Racz (eds.), *The Return of the Left in Post-Communist State* (Cheltenham, Northampton: Edward Elgar, 1999), pp. 107-129.

transformed; the transformed parties evolved from socio-political organizations that were part of the former socialist regime, the most important being the Liberal Democracy of Slovenia and the United List of Social Democrats (now the Social Democrats). New parties were heterogeneous in origin, with some developing from new social movements, some being the result of the mobilisation of new social groups, some arising from regional interests, and some being established as the classical social opposition to the old regime.[18] In December, 1989, several of these parties formed the Democratic Opposition of Slovenia (DEMOS) as a very loose coalition of political parties with poor organisation and a political programme chiefly based on the "sovereign state of the Slovenian people, parliamentary democracy, human rights and liberties, and a social and political system which is able to provide its citizens all their human rights" (Article 4 of DEMOS' founding agreement). It soon became clear that there were important ideological differences between these parties. Therefore, DEMOS can be described as many other such coalitions in Central and Southeastern European (CSEE) countries; i.e., as an umbrella organization or so-called movement party comprised of a loose coalition of organisations[19] which disintegrated soon after the first goal of transforming the old regime was achieved.

The first multi-party and democratic elections in Slovenia after World War Two were held in 1990; however, there were still three representative bodies that were designed during the socialist era. After a new constitution was adopted in December 1991, the first elections to fill the seats in the new representative bodies were held in 1992. The Slovenian Parliament is formally bicameral; the National Assembly is the lower house, which has 90 members, including two seats reserved for representatives of the country's Italian and Hungarian national minorities; and the National Council is the upper house, which consists of representatives of local and functional interests (trade unions, employers, farmers, universities, etc.) and has relatively limited powers. Perhaps the most important of the National Council's powers is the ability to issue a veto to laws passed in the National Assembly; in the 1996-2014 period, the Council issued 99 vetoes. In almost all cases, when vetoes were cast, they were overridden by the National Assembly.

Since the 1990 elections, Slovenia has had a PR electoral system, with a rather low threshold for the National Assembly; e.g., 2.5% in 1990, which slowly increased to 4% in 2000 and has continue to be the same also in 2015. Due to such an institutional arrangement, the fact that there was a relatively

18 Danica Fink-Hafner, *Politične stranke* (Ljubljana: Fakulteta za družbene vede, 2001).

19 Attila Agh, "The Hungarian Party System and Party Theory in the Transition of Central Europe" in *Journal of Theoretical Politics*, Vol. 6, No. 2 (April 1994), pp. 217-238.

large number of parties in the National Assembly, many of them small, should come as no surprise (in 1990, there were nine parties in parliament; later there were between seven and eight). The formal process for establishing a new party is relatively simple in Slovenia: despite the introduction of some stricter rules in 1994, just 200 signatures along with a party programme and internal party rules are needed to set up a new party.

Although Slovenia's institutional context has been fairly stable and open to new parties[20] and some new, mainly small parties (either genuinely new or offshoots from other parties) have joined the National Assembly at every election since 1990 (excluding the 2004 elections),[21] Slovenia's party system has, until recently, been described as a relatively consolidated and stable system in CSEE terms.[22]

In the 2011 early elections, Slovenia recorded the first important signs of instability, not only in the usual Pedersen's index volatility measurement of party system change, but also in terms of some new volatility measurements, which take into account the appearance of important new parties and the disappearance of old parties[23]. Specifically, just before the elections, two new parties emerged: the List of Zoran Janković – Positive Slovenia (PS) and the Citizen List of Gregor Virant (DL). Together they received 37% of the votes; the former party received 28.5% of the votes and was also the winner of the elections. This story was repeated in the early elections of 2014, when the Party of Miro Cerar (SMC), which formed a month and a half prior to the elections, won the elections with 34.5% of the votes and later formed the current governmental

20 Danica Fink-Hafner and Alenka Krašovec, "Factors affecting the long-term success of new parliamentary parties: findings in a post-communist context" in *Romanian Journal of Political Science*, Vol. 13, Issue 2 (Winter 2013), pp. 40-68.

21 So far, only two new parties (the Slovene National Party and the Democratic Party of Retired Persons of Slovenia) have remained in the National Assembly for more than two consecutive mandates following their first entry into parliament (as a new party, New Slovenia entered the National Assembly for the first time in 2000 and again in 2004, but failed to surpass the threshold in 2008; however, it returned to parliament in the 2011 and 2014 elections).

22 Danica Fink-Hafner and Alenka Krašovec, "Konsolidacija slovenske strankarske arene v primerjalni perspektivi", in Danica Fink-Hafner and Miro Haček (eds.), *Demokratični prehodi I* (Ljubljana: Fakulteta za družbene vede, 2000), pp. 155-176; Paul Lewis (ed.), *Party Development and Democratic Change in Post-Communist Europe. The First Decade* (London and Portland: Frank Cass, 2001); Danica Fink-Hafner, "Značilnosti razvoja strankarskega sistema v Sloveniji", in Janko Prunk and Tomaž Deželan (eds.), *Dvajset let slovenske države* (Maribor: Aristej, 2012), pp. 193-213.

23 Tim Haughton and Kevin Deegan-Krause, "Hurricane Season: Systems of Instability in Central and East European Party Politics" in *East European Politics and Societies and Cultures*, Vol. 29, No. 1 (February 2015), pp. 61-80.

coalition. There was another successful newcomer in the 2014 elections: The United Left (ZL) Coalition, which received 6.0% of the votes. The Alliance of Alenka Bratušek (ZaAB), a party formed by the former PM after the split in Positive Slovenia, also managed to cross the threshold. While Janković, the winner of the first elections (2011) during the financial and economic crisis, in the electoral campaign primarily relied on his success as a manager in biggest Slovenian company,[24] Cerar, the winner of the 2014 elections, called for the re-establishment of the rule of law in Slovenia and a change in the country's political culture. He has also made great strides in the fight against corruption. This is why Slovenia has experienced a more common pattern of competition, recently observed in many CSEE countries,[25] in which the "uncorrupted but inexperienced" challenge the "tainted but experienced.[26]

Slovenia's party system has not been immune to radical/extreme parties, in fact, radical stances of parties have been seen in particular periods. For example, Rizman[27] and Mudde[28] both mention the radical Slovene National Party (SNS) which, before the 1992 parliamentary elections, faced an attempt by the court to ban it[29] due to the suspicion that the party had its own military forces. The party entered the National Assembly for the first time in 1992, when it played on nationalistic and xenophobic sentiments[30] and continued to be a parliamentary party until the elections of 2011. Since the mid-1990s,[31] the

---

24 Tim Haughton and Alenka Krašovec, "The 2011 Parliamentary Elections in Slovenia" in *Electoral Studies,* Vol. 32, Issue 1 (March 2013), pp. 201-204.

25 But not only in these countries, as found by Andreas Bågenholm and Nicholas Charron, "Do Politics in Europe Benefit from Politicising Corruption?" in *West European Politics,* Vol. 37, Issue 5 (2014), pp. 903-931.

26 Haughton and Deegan-Krause, "Hurricane Season", p. 70.

27 Rudolf M. Rizman, "Radical Right Politics in Slovenia", in Sabrina P. Ramet (ed.), *The Radical Right in Central and Eastern Europe since 1989* (Pennsylvania: The Pennsylvania State University Press, 1999), pp. 147-170.

28 Cas Mudde, *Populist Radical Right Parties in Europe* (Cambridge: Cambridge University Press, 2007).

29 Tadej Bratok, "Slovenska nacionalna stranka", in Igor Lukšič (ed.), *Stranke in strankarstvo,* (Ljubljana: Slovensko politološko društvo, 1994), p. 209.

30 Rudi Rizman, "Radikalna desnica na Slovenskem", in *Teorija in praksa*, Vol. 35, No. 2 (1998), p. 254.

31 According to a longitudinal Slovene Public Opinion Poll, voters perceived SNS as a radical right wing party in the first half of the 1990s, whereas afterwards, the party was seen as a more radical left wing party than a radical right wing party (see Niko Toš et al., *SJM 2013/1. Pregled in primerjava rezultatov* (Ljubljana: Fakulteta za družbene vede, 2013).

SNS has represented an eclectic combination of (radical) left and (radical) right political values.[32]

Three radical right wing parties emerged alongside the SNS in the early and mid-1990s; however, individually, they received between 0.3 and 0.5% of the vote at the elections in 1992 and 1996 and therefore stayed out of the National Assembly. The Slovenian National Right, established by a former SNS MP, even formed a recreation/sports society called Slovenski sokoli (SS) (*Slovene Falcons*) as protective forces, de facto a paramilitary organisation. The National Social Union of Slovenia established special unarmed forces, called triplet. There were also Republicans.[33] It seems that the formation of such radical right wing parties coincided with a relatively high number of refugees in Slovenia (a result of the war in the territory of former Yugoslavia) and bad economic conditions in Slovenia (very high inflation, between 300% and 100%; high unemployment, between 11.5% and 14%; and a huge drop in GDP *per capita*).[34] In addition, the subjective perceptions of citizens, revealed in longitudinal public opinion polls, indicated poor living conditions for a large part of the population in the first half of the 1990s.[35] Despite "favourable" socio-economic conditions for the development of radical right wing parties during the first half of the 1990s, most of the electorate identified with moderate positions on the ideological spectrum. During that period, the electoral body was mainly centre-left-oriented (between 45.0% and 55.0% of voters found themselves in a left or centre ideological position), while later, a shift towards the centre became more predominant.[36] On the current left ideological pole, it seems that the United Left coalition can be classified as an organization with a more radical left agenda, since it is seeking to change fundamental thinking in politics and the economy, and in the election campaign of 2014, it clearly directed its wrath at austerity (neo-liberal economic) policies.

It is important to note the absence of an anti-system party in Slovenia, although during the 1990s, parties occasionally challenged the legitimacy of the elected elite or expressed doubts about the fairness of elections. However, the

32 Alenka Krašovec and Tim Haughton, "Money, Organization and the State: The Partial cartelization of Party Politics in Slovenia", in *Communist and Post-Communist Studies,* Vol. 44, Issue 3 (September 2011), pp. 199-209.

33 In 1998, Rizman claimed that in the 1990s, the Slovenian Democratic Party (SDS) and the Slovenian People's Party (SLS) frequently flirted with radical/extreme or some other populist politics. See Rizman, "Radikalna desnica na Slovenskem", p. 256.

34 Alenka Krašovec and Damjan Lajh, "Have Democratization Processes been a Catalyst for the Europeanization of Party Politics in Slovenia?", in *Journal of Southern Europe and the Balkans*, Vol. 10, Issue 2 (2008), pp. 183-203.

35 *Ibid.*, p. 188.

36 Toš et al., *SJM 2013/1.*

most important of such claims was made after the 2014 elections. Poor electoral results (20.7%), combined with the fact that the party leader Janša was sent to prison just a month prior to elections due to corruption in the Patria affair,[37] provoked the Slovenian Democratic Party (SDS) to claim that the elections were not free and fair and, therefore, not legitimate.

Although in Slovenia there is political pluralism one cannot ignore the fact that since the 1930s, several prominent ideas regarding the corporate state in Slovenia have been exposed.[38] Lukšič argued[39] that there have only been two periods in Slovenian history during which partisanship flourished (the early 1920s and the early 1990s), while Fink-Hafner said it is possible to talk about important anti-party sentiments in Slovenian society. All these observations have found ground today. To low electoral turnout (51 % in 2014), data on party membership can be added. While significant decreasing trends in party membership have been recorded in all European countries,[40] in Slovenia, this has not been a huge problem. It is also true, however, that in democratic Slovenia, very few voters are party members (the percentage has remained relatively stable since the mid-1990s at around 5%).[41]

As far as political trends go, the bigger problem has been very low trust in parties. In Slovenia, the people's trust in political parties collapsed with the global financial crisis 2008. In 1991, 12% of the people had a high level of trust in Slovenia's political parties; at the turn of the century, this share was similar; but in 2013, it was only 1%. Nevertheless, in 2015, 85 parties were registered (indicating a clear increase in the number of parties in relation to the early 2000s, when a little over 50 parties were registered). At the same time, disap-

37 See Damjan Lajh, "Slovenia", in Lisa Mootz (ed.), *Nations in Transit 2009: Democratization from Central Europe to Eurasia* (New York, Washington: Freedom House, Lanham Rowman and Littlefield, 2009), pp. 475-489; and Damjan Lajh, "Slovenia", in Sylvana Habdank-Kolaczkowska (ed.), *Nations in Transit 2013: Democratization from Central Europe to Eurasia* (New York and Washington D.C.: Freedom House and Lanham Rowman & Littlefield, 2013), pp. 532-548.

38 See Igor Lukšič, "Preoblečeni korporativizem na Slovenskem", in *Časopis za kritiko znanosti,* Vol. 20, No. 148-149 (1992), pp. 47-56; and Milan Zver, "Korporativizem v slovenski politični misli v 20. in 30. letih", in *Časopis za kritiko znanosti, domišljijo in novo antropologijo* Vol. 20, No. 148/149 (1992), pp. 37-45.

39 Igor Lukšič, "(Ne)strankarstvo na Slovenskem", in Igor Lukšič (ed.), *Stranke in strankarstvo* (Ljubljana: Slovensko politološko društvo, 1994), pp. 23-32.

40 See Ingrid van Biezen et al., "Going, going... gone? The Decline of Party Membership in Contemporary Europe" in *European Journal of Political Research,* Vol. 51, Issue 1 (August 2012), pp. 24-56.

41 Niko Toš et. al., *SJM 2000/1. Pregled in primerjava rezultatov* (Ljubljana: Fakulteta za družbene vede, 2000); and Toš et al., *SJM 2013/1.*

pointment and distrust in Slovenia's political parties helped to make room for new and electorally very successful parties, which took advantage of anti-corruption sentiment and the people's desire for new faces, as discussed by Haughton and Deegan Krause. The disintegration of the Liberal Democracy of Slovenia (formerly the most important party in the system) after 2004 and the disastrous performance of the Social Democrats as the main governmental party from 2008 to 2011 also help to explain the success of new centre(-left) parties after 2011. Last but not least, a kind of a strategic voting happened on the 2011 and 2014 elections. To prevent a victory of a centre-right SDS under Janša's leadership many centre-left oriented voters decided to support new parties with good pre-electoral prospects of the victory.

Slovenia has not avoided the more recent European-wide pattern of the personalization of politics.[42] This pattern has been in full effect since 2011, when new and electorally successful parties in the elections competed under the name of their "founding fathers" (e.g., the List of Zoran Janković – Positive Slovenia, the Civic List of Gregor Virant, the Party of Miro Cerar, and the Alliance of Alenka Bratušek). Although this trend was not yet in full swing, several indicators of the personalization of politics were already in effect in the 1990s and the early 2000s; for example, Janez Drnovšek in the Liberal Democracy of Slovenia (LDS), Borut Pahor in the Social Democrats (SD), and Janez Janša, whose importance to the Slovenian Democratic Party (SDS) can still be seen today.

When speaking about the party system and parties in Slovenia, it is impossible to ignore the LDS's decade-long dominance, which ended with the 2004 elections.[43] In the Slovenian context, the long-term dominance of the LDS (1992-2004) was assured by several developments. As discussed by Kropivnik,[44] only the LDS had, from the mid-1990s to the early 2000s, been up-to-date with modest changes in the position of the electoral body on the ideological spectrum, i.e., the party was the only one to explicitly follow the movement of the electoral body to an even more centre position on the ideo-

42 Lauri Karvonen, *The Perosnalisation of Politics: A Study of Parliamentary Democracies* (Colchester: ECPR, 2010).

43 The LDS's dominance ended for several reasons, among them were clientelism, which spread in the party (at a party congress after the electoral defeat, the LDS leader acknowledged that some party members were involved in clientelistic practices), and the withdrawal of Drnovšek from the party leadership position due to his election as the President of the Republic of Slovenia, both of which gave rise to internal disputes that led to the disintegration and later marginalization of the party.

44 Samo Kropivnik, "Družbeni in ideološki profili slovenskih političnih strank v preteklem desetletju", in Danica Fink-Hafner and Tomaž Boh (eds.), *Parlamentarne volitve 2000* (Ljubljana: Fakulteta za družbene vede, 2002), pp. 27-48.

logical spectrum. In addition, Fink-Hafner[45] observed that since 2002, no important politician in Slovenia has been positioned in the so-called metric centre to act as a link between different party poles, as Drnovšek did in the 1990s.

The LDS had also been trying to introduce a liberal-market economy while simultaneously preserving the welfare state and social cohesion.[46] Prior to the 2004 elections, there was a kind of informal consensus between parties regarding economic issues, which can be described as Bobbio's "liberal socialism".[47] Therefore, for a decade, the cleavage around economic issues in the party system was less profound. Slovenia opted for a specific economic transition in the context of other CSEE countries, (i.e., gradualism), and the population's clear expectations that the welfare state would be preserved led all parliamentary parties to advocate similar, social-democratic socio-economic policies.[48] With the 2004 elections, the SDS (a relative winner of the 2004 elections) made a final turn towards the conservative party camp[49] and significantly contributed to the saliency of an economic cleavage in inter-party competition. Since a financial crisis began in Slovenia in 2009, the economic split has

45 Fink-Hafner, "Značilnosti razvoja", p. 203.

46 Janko Prunk, "Politično življenje v samostojni Sloveniji", in Janko Prunk and Tomaž Deželan (eds.), *Dvajset let slovenske države (*Maribor: Aristej, 2012), pp. 17-56.

47 Danica Fink-Hafner and Alenka Krašovec, "Ideološko-politički rascjepi u slovenskoj stranačkoj arena poslije 1989. godine" in Danica Fink-Hafner and Mirko Pejanović (eds.), *Razvoj politikog pluralizma u Sloveniji i Bosni i Hercegovini* (Ljubljana, Sarajevo: Fakulteta za družbene vede, Promocult, 2006), pp. 71-104.

48 Miroslav Stanojević and Alenka Krašovec, "Slovenia: Social Pacts and Political Exchange", in Sabina Avdagić et al. (eds), *Social Pacts in Europe: Emergence, Evolution, and Institutionalization (*Oxford: Oxford University Press, 2011), pp. 232-256; Fink-Hafner, "Značilnosti razvoja", p. 202.

49 In 1989, the party was established as a social democratic party. Some authors claimed that in the early 1990s, the Social Democratic Party of Slovenia could without a doubt be regarded as a social democratic party, especially in terms of socio-economic issues (Prunk, "Politično življenje"), while others, for example, Pikalo (Jernej Pikalo "Vrnitev (ali samo vztrajanje) levice na Slovenskem", in Danica Fink- Hafner and Miro Haček (eds.), *Demokratični prehodi I.* (Ljubljana, Fakulteta za družbene vede, 2000), p. 205) believed that the party has always been strongly connected with the Catholic Church and thus has never been a centre-left party. With the selection of Janša as its leader in 1993 (still currently the party's leader), the party *de facto* started to turn towards the (centre-)right of the ideological continuum Zver (Milan Zver, "Value systems and the cleavage of the party space – EU and Slovenia", in Ladislav Cabada and Alenka Krašovec (eds.), *Europeanisaton of National Political Parties (*Plzen: Fakulta humanitnich Studii ZĆU v Plzni, Katedra Politologie a Mezinnarodnich Vztahu, 2004), pp. 239-246) even though it formally retained the Social Democratic name until 2003, when it became the Slovenian Democratic Party.

become even more prominent, although now, generally speaking, Slovene parties appear to have moved to the economic right.

On the other hand, the libertarian-authoritarian split has been continuously more prominent, and, even more importantly, it frequently overlaps with other cleavages (centre–periphery, state–church, urban–rural, modernism–traditionalism, liberalism–conservatism (clericalism), and communism–anticommunism). In this way, the libertarian-authoritarian cleavage has led to strong polarisation in the political arena as well as in society.[50] In Slovenia, this cleavage is usually referred to as an "ideological cleavage." It is mostly associated with questions over the role of the Roman Catholic Church in Slovenian society and politics, the rights of ethnic and sexual minorities, and events during World War Two (e.g., Partisans versus Home Guard or opponents of the occupation forces versus their collaborators). According to a Slovenian Public Opinion Poll, conflicts between leftists and rightists are the sharpest conflicts among social groups in Slovenia and have greatly intensified recently: in 2005, 15% of the respondents evaluated these conflicts as very extreme, while in 2013, 40% of respondents felt the same.[51]

Based on these divisions, some established/mainstream parties have usually been perceived as centre-left (for example, the Social Democrats, the Liberal Democracy of Slovenia, and the Democratic Party of Pensioners of Slovenia) and some have been perceived as centre-right (for example, the Slovene People's Party, the Slovene Democratic Party, and the New Slovenia).

There are two additional points worth mentioning when speaking about the Slovenian party system and its political parties. First, despite many divisions, examples of large-scale unity between parties can also be observed. However, this unity has, in large part, been connected with parties' attitudes toward the European Union and its policies.[52] Unlike in some other CSEE countries,[53] it seems that the impact of the EU environment on the Slovenian party system has been almost invisible. Slovenian EU membership was defined as a national project and, as such, was marked by a broad consensus within the political elite

---

50 Fink-Hafner, "Politične stranke", pp. 178-179.

51 Toš et al., *SJM 2013/1.*

52 Alenka Krašovec and Damjan Lajh, "The European Union: A Joker of Just an Ordinary Playing Card for Slovenian Political Parties?" in *Journal of Communist Studies and Transition Politics,* Vol. 25, No. 4 (2009), pp. 491-512.

53 Paul Lewis and Zdenka Mansfeldova, eds. *The European Union and Party Politics in Central and Eastern Europe* (Basingstoke: Palgrave. 2006); Aleks Szczerbiak and Paul Taggart, eds. *Opposing Europe: The Comparative Party Politics of Euroscepticism* (Oxford: Oxford University Press, 2008); and Tim Haughton, "Driver, Conductor or Fellow Passenger? EU Membership and Party Politics in Central and Eastern Europe," in *The Journal of Communist Studies and Transition Politics*, Vol. 25, Issue 4 (2009), 413-426.

on the process of joining the EU.[54] This led to a situation in which all major EU-related topics (the EU membership, the introduction of the euro in 2007, and the Slovenian Presidency of the Council of the EU in 2008) were defined as national projects. Taking into account the generally favourable public opinion regarding the EU, only a few small and/or non-parliamentary parties and occasionally the parliamentary SNS tried to play the Eurosceptic card, which, however, proved not to be a trump card in the electoral competition. Krašovec and Lajh[55] conclude that EU issues did not directly influence inter-party competition and therefore EU issues held particular significance for national politics but little salience for party politics. This situation has changed somewhat since a newcomer in the 2014 elections, the United Left coalition, directed its criticism of the EU towards a systemic set of ideological positions and arguments. Still, its disapproval has been directed more at the policies of austerity than at the EU as such.

Second, the long-term success of the single-issue Democratic Party of Retired Persons of Slovenia (DeSUS) is in comparison to other European countries, an exception. The party has been continually taking part in government coalitions (the only exception was the short-lived 6-month-long Bajuk's government) since its entrance into the National Assembly in 1996 as an individual party. Moreover, the party's position has changed over time from a supplementary role to a more decisive one in forming both centre-left and centre-right governmental coalitions. A strange situation emerged with the 2000 elections, when two "generational" parties entered the National Assembly: alongside the DeSUS, the Youth Party of Slovenia (SMS) was also electorally successful; however, it soon faced internal disputes, and the 2004 elections proved that it was, unlike the DeSUS, a fleeting organization.

Finally, we must devote some attention to governmental coalitions in Slovenia. Given the PR electoral system and low threshold, all Slovenia's governments have been coalitions of several parties, and all were, in the beginning of their terms, majority coalitions. Regarding the ideological distance between coalition parties, both ideologically mixed and homogenous coalitions were formed. The first type of coalition occurred under PM Janez Drnovšek and the LDS leadership from 1992 to 2004 (with a short interruption of six months in 2000). One reason for forming ideological coalitions was Drnovšek's wish to overcome ideological bi-polarisation in Slovenia, while also the opposition simultaneously stayed ideologically heterogeneous. However, this did not help Drnovšek ensure that his governments would stay as they were originally

54 Danica Fink-Hafner and Damjan Lajh, *Managing Europe from Home: The Europeanisation of the Slovenian Core Executive* (Ljubljana: Fakulteta za družbene vede, 2003).

55 Krašovec and Lajh, "The European Union", p. 508.

formed, since one of the most outstanding characteristics of governmental coalitions under Drnovšek was a pattern of slow "departures" of parties from coalitions as the legislative terms approached their end. Indeed, only Janša's first government (2004-2008) has survived the entire four-year legislative term in its initial composition. Nonetheless, it wasn't until 2011 that real instability of governments occurred, since two governments' disintegration led to two early elections (2011 and 2014). With the 2004 elections, the second type of coalition emerged: more ideologically homogenous governmental coalitions (centre-left or centre-right), which started to alternate in power, with only one party being a constant (the DeSUS). In addition, in the period between 1992 and 2014, all parliamentary parties (except the Slovenian National Party) experienced cooperation in governments.

Conclusion

Norway and Slovenia have some similar institutional arrangements, for example a parliamentary system with the prime minister as the head of government, a largely ceremonial head of state – the King of Norway, the President of Slovenia, and a PR electoral system with rather low threshold. In Slovenia the threshold is 4 %. In Norway the threshold is not determined by an exact figure, but for small parties 4 % is a key figure as parties that achieve this level of support is guaranteed to receive a number of representatives that roughly reflect the strength of the parties in the whole country. There are some important differences between the two countries; the structure of the parliament is one of them – one finds a unicameral parliament in Norway and a bicameral parliament in Slovenia with rather uncommon structure of the upper house – with representatives of local, but also functional interests (representatives of trade unions, employers, farmers, universities etc.). While the almost identical number of parties in Norway (8) and in the Slovenian parliament (7 or 8) is not surprising given the rather similar PR electoral systems used in the countries. We should note, however, that the Norwegian Green Party has only one member in parliament.

Larger differences can be found in the instability of the party systems. Overall, instability is higher in Slovenia than in in Norway. But instability is important in Norway as well. Of the parties that have emerged in the 1970s the most important to achieve representation in the Storting is the Progress Party, a right-wing populist party founded in 1973. But also on the left we have a new party from about the same period – The Socialist Left Party (which is the name for the most of the period). Recently, in Slovenia the last two elections (in 2011 and 2014) were won by political parties established just month(s) before elections, in 2011 List of Zoran Janković - Positive Slovenia, and in 2014 the Party of Miro Cerar, the current prime minister.

Another difference is that the reformed communist party in Slovenia still manages to get deputies elected to the parliament, while neither the Norwegian Communist Party nor the Red Party (with links to the Maoists groups from the late 1960s/early 1970s) have had any representatives in the Storting in recent election periods, but the latter party had one member of parliament elected in 1993. Slovenia is an exception regarding a permanent (since mid-1990s) electoral success of a Pensioners' Party; even more, it participates in the ruling coalition almost continuously since. In Norway, the Pensioners' Party has not succeeded in electing representatives to the Storting.

The differences between Norway and Slovenia can be contributed to very different democratic traditions and history (Norway has been independent since 1905 (but occupied by Germany 1940-45), while Slovenia gained its independence only in 1991), but another plausible explanation can be hidden also in four decades of self-managing socialism in Slovenia. This system definitely has had impact not on political culture, but also on values more generally.[56] Yet another difference has to do with the role of the dominant religious association. In Slovenia, the Roman Catholic Church has repeatedly intervened in politics in the years since the country gained its independence and formed a de facto alliance with Janez Janša, the head of the Slovenian Democratic Party. Nonetheless, the Catholic Church proved unable to obtain a ban on abortion or to see religious instruction introduced into state schools – two priorities for that association. In Norway, the Norwegian Church – a Lutheran denomination – has been less visible in party debates. As a state Church, its bishops were, until recently, appointed subject to the approval of the government, and this play a role in producing a more compliant Church, whereas in Slovenia, this is not the case. In spite of all these differences, both countries are facing similar democratic challenges, for example, trust in parties and other political institutions, decreasing or low party membership, and some dissatisfaction with democracy. We should note, however, that trust in politics is high in Norway and there is not a general negative trend. Based on the comparative material we find that trust is higher in Norway than in Slovenia. When we compare Slovenia with other post-Yugoslav countries, Slovenia rates favourably. This means that the shorter democratic history of the country has not precluded support of a democratic system.

56 For more on Slovenian values, see Sabrina P. Ramet and Danica Fink-Hafner (eds.), *Democratic transition in Slovenia: Value Transformation, Education and Media* (College Station, Tex.: Texas A&M University Press, 2006).

Toril Aalberg and Marko Milosavljević

4 The Norwegian and Slovenian Media System Compared

During the last few decades, the media environment in both Norway and Slovenia has experienced dramatic changes. Although they are both small states – and share certain trends and characteristics – there are also major and significant differences between the two countries, not only when it comes to their pre-1990 media systems, but also in terms of the current state of affairs. In this introduction we will review and explain the most important differences and similarities.

In *Comparing Media Systems* Hallin and Mancini classify Norway as representing what they called the prototypical Democratic Corporatist Model.[1] While they never classified Slovenia in their media and politics typology, other scholars have argued that Slovenia clearly belongs to the Polarized Pluralist Model of media and politics.[2] While the Democratic Corporatist Model, to which Norway belongs, is characterized by a historical coexistence of commercial media and media tied to organized social and political groups, and by a relatively active but legally limited role of the state, the Polarized Pluralist Model (as in the Slovenian case) has a weaker historical development of commercial media and a clear integration of the media into party politics and a strong role of the state.

Pre-1990s

The Slovenian media system, as a polarized pluralist model, is clearly linked to its socialist self-managing system as a founding member of the Socialist Federated Republic of Yugoslavia, but also to the political systems before the establishment of Yugoslavia and later socialism. Slovenia in the 19th century was

1 Dan C. Hallin and Paolo Mancini, *Comparing Media Systems. Three Models of Media and Politics (*Cambridge: Cambridge University Press, 2004), pp 67–68)

2 Sandra Bašić-Hrvatin and Brankica Petković, *You Call this a Media Market? The Role of the State in the Media Sector in Slovenia***.** (Ljubliana: Peace Insitute, 2008), p. 196; Barbara Pfetsch, Peter Maurer, Eva Mayerhöffer, Tom Moring, and Stephanie Schwab Cammarano, "Context of the Media-Politics Relationship: Country Selection and Grouping", in Barbara Pfetsch (ed.), *Political Communication Cultures in Western Europe: Attitudes of Political Actors and Journalists in Nine Countries* (London: Palgrave Macmillan, 2014), pp. 48-49.

marked by a strongly polarized political environment, particularly by the division between liberals (often referred to as Young Slovenes) and conservatives (Old Slovenes, mostly Christian Democrats). This was reflected also in a strongly polarized and partisan media environment. Later, after World War Two, and before Slovenia became independent in 1991, the media landscape was one where "public media were performing an activity of special social significance generously co-founded by society from the State budget". [3] The founders of the public media, that is the state, approved programming concepts and appointed editors-in-chief, while the media employees performed socio-political work, in fact all important conditions and mechanisms involved in the operation of the public media were practically determined and controlled by socio-political bodies (in particular the Socialist Association of Working People SZDL). According to Bašić-Hrvatin and Milosavljević Slovenia did not have a media market in the traditional sense before the political change took place in the early 1990s. Although media products had their consumers, the consumers were also media "owners", by way of their representatives in the founders' bodies. The media companies determined the production price, for instance, of newspapers, which was usually much higher than their sales price. Certain more market-oriented projects were, however, launched already during that period, clearly distinguishing the Slovenian (and Yugoslav) media environment from other socialist countries in Eastern Europe: a licensed version of French women magazine *Elle* was established already in 1968, the first more consumer-oriented domestic women magazine *Jana* was founded in 1972, and the first daily tabloid *Kaj* was launched in 1984. Cable systems were developed after 1985 and immediately started with distribution of Western European television channels such as Music Box, Sky, and MTV. However the ownership of Slovenian media was still "public", with SZDL defined as official founder. Prior to the privatization Slovenia's newspapers and broadcasters were "socially owned" and received generous subsidies out of the State budget. [4]

The Norwegian pre-1990s media landscape was clearly different from that found in socialist Slovenia. The multi-party representative democracy gave birth to a strong expansion of the press, as it was cheap to establish new newspapers and they could survive even with a small circulation. Until the 1970s most, but not all, newspapers were oriented toward one or another political party. The party press was, however, not *owned* by the parties, but formed

---

3 Sandra Bašić-Hrvatin and Marko Milosavljević. *Media Policy in Slovenia in the 1990s: Regulation, privatization, concentration and commercialization of the media* (Ljubljana: Mirovni inštitut, 2001); and Bašić-Hrvatin and Petković, *You Call this a Media Market?* [note 2]), pp. 18-19.

4 *ibid.*, pp. 20-24.

lasting alliances with their respective parties for mutual benefit. In certain periods, the parties gave financial support to loyal newspapers with a poor economy.

After the 1970s local market competition in Norway became more intense, and the largest newspaper in each market acquired a very large share of the local advertising, which made the stronger newspaper survive and increase its circulation, while the smaller papers in each local market tended to lose out and in many cases eventually close down. While broadcasting in Norway started up as private local or decentralised services, the parliament agreed to establish a state owned broadcasting monopoly in 1933. This company were given public service obligations and it was generally agreed that *broadcasting* should not become 'politicised' like newspapers had become.

At the beginning of the 1990s, the Slovenian system was still clearly dominated by the state and strong presence of political instrumentalization and utilization of the media, while the Norwegian system included some state ownership and regulation, it was more commercialised and the party-press ties were weakening.

The four major dimensions

According to Hallin and Mancini there are four major dimensions according to which media systems in advanced democracies can be compared. Briefly, these four dimensions are *(i) Structure of media markets, (ii) Degree of political parallelism (iii) Degree of journalistic professionalism,* and *(iv) The role of the state.*

The *structure of media market* refers to the fact that some societies are more newspaper-centred whereas other societies are more radio- or television-centred, both historically and today. Moreover, in some societies the newspapers are mainly addressed to an elite, whereas in other societies they are mass circulated. One of the main characteristics of this media market structure is therefore to look at the development of a mass circulation press. As is characteristic for the Democratic Corporatist Model, Norway has always had a very high newspaper circulation and an early development of mass-circulation press. At the start of the new millennium the newspaper circulation in Norway was 86%, while it only was 45% in Slovenia, indicating that newspapers in Slovenia to a larger extent mainly addressed the elite. [5] While Norway had 81 daily titles in 2002, the same number in Slovenia was six, indicating that Norway is a more newspaper-centred media system while Slovenia is more centred on broad-

5 Word Association of Newspapers, World Press Trends 2003. (Paris: WAN/ZenithOptimedia, 2003), pp. 210 – 244.

casting (however, in international perspective, Slovenian viewers are still among the lighter television users, according to AGB Nielsen international figures).[6]

The second dimension is the media system's *degree of political parallelism*, which refers the extent that the media is rooted in and reflects political or other social divisions in society. One component, and perhaps the most important one, is the degree to which the media content reflects political orientations in their news reporting. Other components include, but are not restricted to, organizational connections between media and political organizations, the tendency for media personnel to be politically active, and the partisanship of media audiences. Systems with a high degree of political parallelism are also characterized by external diversity, that is pluralism achieved through different media offering different viewpoints. Systems with a low degree of political parallelism are characterized by internal diversity, that is pluralism in viewpoints achieved within each individual media outlet.

While Norway used to have external pluralism, as expressed through the strong party press, this parallelism has diminished during the last decades with a shift toward neutral and commercial press and a system of internal diversity. In Slovenia, however, the rather strong link between political (and religious) groups and the media system has remained. Media Ownership Project investigated 37 media outlets in Slovenia and found that 62% don't have transparent ownership and 48% have connections to politics.[7]

As Bašić-Hrvatin and Petković argue, the (former) political elites became the economic elites, and were able to acquire the majority stake in media companies through an almost free of charge privatization. They saw the media not as an economic investment but as a political one, and the media stage as the centre of a power struggle.[8] The political clientelism through various post-socialist periods have also given the Roman Catholic Church a strong position within the Slovenian media sphere, with a particularly strong role in radio broadcasting and weekly print, but also with attempts with daily newspapers and television[9].

The third dimension, in which the two countries differ is the d*egree of journalistic professionalism.* The professionalism primarily refers to the degree of journalistic autonomy, or the existence and strength of distinct professional norms, often combined with a clear public service orientation among media

6 AGB Nielsen Media Research, Telemetric Summary commissioned by APEK, 2011.

7 https://www.reportingproject.net/media/author/Slovenia/

8 Bašić-Hrvatin and Petković, *You Call this a Media Market?* [note 2], pp. 24-31.

9 Marko Milosavljević. "Vseh šest dnevnikov najbrž ne bo preživelo. In stari so žilavi" ("All he six dailies will not survive. And the old ones are tough."). *Delo, Sobotna priloga*, 4 May 1996

workers. In Norway, journalists have over the years received a strong professionalization, with institutionalized systems for self-regulation. The professionalism, or rather, the journalistic autonomy is much weaker in the Slovenian system, where techniques used by politics to control the media include "moving of intractable journalists to other positions, the censorship of journalistic texts and the abuse of the right of reply and the right of correction on the part of politically and economically strong groups."[10]

Finally, the *role of the state and the degree of state intervention* in the media systems is considered the fourth major dimension. Such state interventions might include subsidies to newspapers in order to stimulate a plurality of newspapers, the existence and governance of public service media, and laws enabling or restricting journalistic gathering and presentation of news. Still, both Norway and Slovenia have media systems where the state plays an active role. In Slovenia, the state played a large role as an owner, main shareholder, or important shareholder of a number of companies, for more than 15 years after the independence and democratic transition in 1991. It was not until the mid-1990s that the state mostly sold its shares and ownership in the key Slovenian media companies; however the (party) politics retained its influence through indirect deals and agreements with specific media owners with other business interests (particularly controversial was the case of political and government influence at the daily newspaper *Delo* as an alleged part of an agreement between its official owner, brewery Laško, and the then-government, led by the right-wing SDS party and prime minister Janez Janša).[11] Today the key state owned media outlet remains the Slovenian Press Agency (STA) which is 100% owned by the government and which is an important source of news and agenda-setter for many, particularly smaller media. In Norway, there is also strong state intervention but with equally strong protection for press freedom. The role of the state is most evident in the generally high support for a strong public service broadcaster, as well continued policy aid and regulations introduced to secure market diversity and public service obligations.

10 *ibid.*, p. 199.

11 Jure Ugovšek. "Šrot: Delo je Janšev cilj, Mercator pa sredstvo za izsiljevanje" ("Šrot: Delo is Janša's aim, and Mercator is the means for the blackmail." Finance, 22 December 2007. See http://www.finance.si/200209/%C5%A0rot-Delo-je-Jan%C5%A1ev-cilj-Mercator-pa-sredstvo-za-izsiljevanje (accessed on 15 June 2015). See also Sabrina P. Ramet and Roman Kuhar, "Ownership and Political Influence in the Post-socialist Mediascape: the Case of Slovenia", in *Südosteuropa,* Vol. 60 (2012), no. 1, pp. 2-30-

Similar trends, but differences remain

According to Hallin and Mancini countries belonging to the Democratic Corporatist Model, like Norway, and those with a Polarized Pluralist Model, like Slovenia, are currently experiencing a "transition" towards a third model called the Liberal Model (typical of the Media System in countries like the United States and Australia). In the Liberal model, the media are deeply involved in the economic sphere and therefore subject primarily to market laws. Indeed, some of the recent trends experienced in Norway and Slovenia are related to commercialisation, market mechanisms and waves of privatization of their media industry.[12] This transition has been most apparent in Slovenia, who did not have a private market during the Yugoslav era, but the end of the public broadcasting monopoly in Norway has also clearly influenced the number of media channels available to the Norwegian public, but also given publicly owned media some healthy competition.

Related to the trend of privatization is the trend of globalization. The globalization of a media environment is partly illustrated by big international companies entering the media system through buyouts or by introducing new media channels and products to the consumers. As both Norway and Slovenia are small states, the introduction of foreign media owners have raised similar concerns about the preservation of national identity, language and culture. Related to this is the typical concern that foreign media-owners will be more concerned with profit, and less concerned with producing high quality content or media workers professional rights.

Finally, globalization is also linked to a third trend that has influenced the Norwegian and Slovenian media environment in similar ways for the last couple of decades. The introduction of new media has given traditional media channels competition, and both countries have experienced a decline in exposure to traditional non-digital media outlets. The next two sections will provide more details on these and other trends in the Norwegian and Slovenian media landscapes respectively.

---

12 For Slovenia, see for example Bašić-Hrvatin and Milosavljević, *Media Policy in Slovenia in the 1990s* [note 3].

The Media in Norway*

The basic legal principles for the Norwegian media system were established in the 1814 constitution: a general freedom of the press, which included a right for anybody to establish a newspaper, and a ban on advance censorship. Since then Norway has been known for its very high newspaper circulation as well as its strong state intervention in the country's media system through the use of press subsidies and a dominant public service broadcaster. This state intervention in the media system has however always been combined with an equally strong protection for press freedom. In this part of the chapter, I will present the main characteristics and structures related to the Norweigan media system. First we will take a closer look at the traditional media outlets, like newspapers and broadcasters, before we turn our attention to the internet and new media forms. The second half will provide a discussion of the relationship between media and politics in Norway and how this has changed over the years.

Newspapers

The first Norwegian *newspapers*[13] had already been established in major cities in the 1760s, but growth was very slow and it took more than 60 years before ten papers were published throughout the entire country. It took another 40 years before newspapers' readership started to spread into all segments of the society.

A development leading to a constitutional conflict in the 1880s polarised the political debate and politicised the newspapers. Almost all the newspapers took a stand in the conflict and when political parties were established, the newspapers formed alliances with these.[14] The period between 1860 and 1920 was characterised by a strong expansion of the press. It was cheap to establish new newspapers and they could survive even with a small circulation. Most newspapers were oriented toward one or another political party and spread within their party's group of supporters.[15] The newspapers were not *owned* by the parties, but formed a lasting alliance with their respective parties for mutual benefit. In certain periods, the parties gave financial support to loyal newspa-

* Toril Aalberg

13 The description of the Norwegian newspaper history is to a large extent based on Rune Ottosen, Lars Arve Røssland and Helge Østbye, *Norsk pressehistorie* (Oslo: Samlaget, 2002).

14 Svennik Høyer, "The Political Economy of the Norwegian Press", in Per Torsvik (ed.), *Scandinavian Political Studies,* Vol. 3 (1969), pp. 85-143).

15 Jörgen Westerståhl and, Carl-Gunnar Janson, *Politisk press* (Göteborg: Statsvetenskapliga institutionen, Göteborgs universitet, 1958).

pers with a poor economy. The parties also ran news agencies, supplying 'their' newspapers with everything from party propaganda to chess and bridge columns.

The newspaper structure which developed from 1880 to 1925 meant that all the major parties had their own newspapers in urban areas all over the country. This is the period when Norwegians in general became newspaper readers. Almost all newspapers had a geographically concentrated readership, and from 1900 and well into the 1950s almost all towns and cities had more than one newspaper, often three, four or more, each representing a different party. This system continued into the 1960s, with an interruption from 1940 to 1945. The Conservatives (Høyre), the Liberals (Venstre), and the Labour Party were represented with newspapers all over the country, while parties established after World War One were disadvantaged because they had to introduce their papers at a time when the newspaper market was already saturated. Only the Centre Party had a limited success.

The reconstruction of the Norwegian press after World War Two restored the ties between the newspapers and the parties, but local competition became more intense. The determining factor was the distribution of advertisements between local competitors. The largest newspaper in each market acquired a very large share of the local advertising. This newspaper tended to survive and increase its circulation, while the smaller papers in each local market tended to lose out in the competition. Newspapers with an ambition to reach beyond their political supporters, tended to tone down their political profile. In this way, the two processes – monopolisation of the local market and depoliticisation – were closely linked: Most newspapers ended their formal ties with the parties during the 1970s. But the previous party coloration is still visible, for instance in the coverage of election campaigns.[16]

During the party press era, politicians were often recruited as journalists and editors and vice versa, and the same people were active simultaneously in both arenas. The depoliticisation of the newspapers coincided with a professionalization of journalism. Formal education at college or university level became the starting point for many journalists. The journalists' and editors' organizations had already established professional codes of ethics.

The increased competition between local newspapers led to a reduction in the number of newspapers. In order to reverse or halt this development, state subsidies to the press were introduced in 1969. The subsidies slowed down, but were not sufficient to halt the local monopolisation process. Since the introduc-

---

16 Sigurd Allern, "From Party Press to Independent Observer? An analysis of Election Campaigns Prior to the General Elections of 1981 and 2005 in Two Norwegian Newspapers", in *Nordicom Review*, Vol. 28 (2007), pp. 63-79.

tion of the subsidies, many small newspapers have been established outside major towns and cities.

Some of the Oslo-based newspapers were read all over the country, but most of the papers have been local or regional. Really national newspapers appeared for the first time in the 1960s, when two newspapers started to be disseminated by air all over the country. This way, the two popular newspapers from Oslo – *Verdens Gang* and *Dagbladet* – developed as genuinely national newspapers.

Today the national level of the newspaper market consists of two tabloid newspapers and few more specialised papers, most of them with a small circulation. The national papers account for about 20% of the total national newspaper circulation. Four large regional or large city newspapers account for approximately one sixth of the total circulation. This means that local newspapers dominate the market with more than 60% of the circulation, and with approximately 200 out of a total of almost 230 existing newspapers.[17] The local press represents a complex and varied group of newspapers, but altogether they cover local life and politics in minute detail. The national papers, the regional papers and some of the local papers also cover the national and international level. Especially compared to the British tabloid press, the two popular Norwegian newspapers have much higher proportion of serious content about culture and politics.

Table 4.1. Some key figures of the Norwegian newspaper market 1995-2013

	1995	*2000*	*2005*	*2010*	*2013*
Titles	218	218	226	226	229
- of which: daily (5+ editions per week)	85	81	74	73	71
Total circulation in thousands	3,173	3,103	2,939	2,572	2,230
Daily reading (%/min)	84%/ 40 min	77%/ 34 min	74%/ 29 min	64%/ 23 min	51% 21 min

Note: Entries do not include newspapers

Source: SSB and Avisregisteret via MedieNorge, at http://medienorge.uib.no/statistikk/avis

The total circulation continued to increase for the Norwegian newspapers until the mid-1990s, but during the last twenty years there has been a decline of approximately 30%. Nevertheless, the total circulation per 1,000 inhabitants still gives Norway the top position among European countries.

17 Sigurd Høst, *Avisåret 2006* (Fredrikstad: Institutt for Journalistikk, 2007), pp. 42 - 47.

Broadcasting

While the newspapers were embraced in party politics for more than a hundred years, the norm has always been that *broadcasting* should not become 'politicised'. However, both radio and television play an important role in the political system. Broadcasting in Norway[18] started as local or decentralised services. Private companies in four cities (Oslo, Bergen, Tromsø, and Ålesund) were given a five-year licence to broadcast – they were granted a monopoly in an area surrounding the city. The first of these companies, *Kringkastingselskapet* in Oslo, started in 1925. *Kringkastingselskapet* expanded outside its original territory, and established the framework for a national service (with the exception of the western parts of the country). The companies were financed by a licence fee, a stamp duty on radio receivers sold in their district, and commercials. The programme content was serious – close to what would be expected of a public service broadcasting company, *Kringkastingselskapet,* did broadcast some talks on controversial issues of that time, but avoided party politics.

In 1933, the state was ready to take over responsibility for broadcasting in Norway. A minority government headed by the Liberal Party was supported in parliament by the Labour Party in a vote in favour of state ownership. The Conservatives supported the government in a vote on an integrated organisation for the new broadcasting company. This was in opposition to a system with two companies, one with responsibility for technical production and distribution, and one company with responsibility for content. The Broadcasting Act of 1933 established *Norsk Rikskringkasting* (NRK) – The Norwegian Broadcasting Corporation – as a national broadcasting monopoly. High priority was given to the creation of a genuinely national network of transmitters (it took almost until 1960 before radio reached 100% national coverage). NRK created a genuinely *national* radio: there were no regional variations, but the radio programme was to reflect living conditions in all parts of the country and be relevant to everyone. Generally, NRK took its public service obligations seriously, with a focus on news, current affairs, talk shows (information in a broad sense), children's programmes and classical music.

Radio became an important mass medium in the 1930s. The network of transmitters was extended, and the first transmitter in the northernmost county

18 The Norwegian broadcasting history has been largely written by Hans Fredrik Dahl: Hans Fredrik Dahl, *'Hallo! Hallo!' Kringkastingen i Norge 1920–1940* (Oslo: Cappelen, 1975). Hans Fredrik Dahl, *'Dette er London!'. NRK i krig 1940–1945* (Oslo: Cappelen, 1978). Hans Fredrik Dahl and Henrik G. Bastiansen, *'Over til Oslo'. NRK som monopol. 1945–1981* (Oslo: Cappelen, 1999). A shorter version can be found in Ketil Jarl Halse and Helge Østbye, *Norsk kringkastingshistorie* (Oslo: Samlaget, 2003).

of Finnmark came into operation in 1934, and new listeners flocked to the radio. The number of licence fee payers increased from 123,000 in 1933 to 439,000 in 1940. World War Two was a temporary setback for the development of radio, but the growth continued in the post-war period. NRK had to rely on the licence fee and the stamp duty on radio receivers. The 1950s was really the 'golden age' for radio in Norway.

Norway was among the last countries in Europe to introduce television. The television service was officially opened by the king and prime minister in 1960 within the framework of NRK's broadcasting monopoly. As with radio, the main focus was on the creation of a national network of transmitters. Programme production was centralised, but the growth of the audience was steep despite limited transmission hours. In the 1950s, people had listened to radio for an average of 2½ hours per day. This declined by 30 minutes when television was introduced, and people watched TV for 1 hour 30 minutes, increasing to 1 hour 45 minutes as the broadcasting hours increased.

Table 4.2. Some key figures of the Norwegian broadcasting markets 1995-2014

	1995	*2000*	*2005*	*2010*	*2014*
Total daily radio listening (%/min.)	66% 99 min.	57% 84min.	55% 84 min.	56% 81 min.	64% 100 min.
Total daily TV viewing (%/min.)	84% 124 min.	82% 138 min.	85% 147 min.	82% 152 min.	74% 132 min.
Radio listening (%)					
- Public Service: NRK	45%	37%	34%	32%	38%
- Hybrid channels: P4, Kanal24/ Radio Norge	21%	19%	22%	26%	30%
TV viewing (%)					
- Public Service: NRK (share for NRK1 only)	62%	60%	59%	54%	48%
- Hybrid Channel: TV 2	54%	58%	54%	46%	41%

Source: TNS Gallup and MMI via MedieNorge, at http://medienorge.uib.no/statistikk/medium/radio, http://medienorge.uib.no/statistikk/medium/tv

In the late 1970s, the Conservatives proposed the dissolution of the broadcasting monopoly. This would require a change in the Broadcasting Act. In 1981, the party formed a minority government, and very soon thereafter, changes were made to the Act in order to start experiments with local radio and television. Local radio soon became a success, and in 1988 commercial television was also permitted. Since 1982, cable networks were allowed to retransmit foreign television channels from satellites and in 1988, one Norwegian and one pan-Scandinavian satellite channel (TV Norge and TV3) were also disseminated via the cable networks. In 1990, most political parties agreed on a compromise which led to the subsequent introduction of private, nationwide radio and television channels.

The second terrestrial television channel, TV 2, commenced in 1992. This channel was regulated by a licence agreement with the Ministry of Cultural and Scientific Affairs, and was given some public service obligations. The following year, a similar structure was created for radio (P4). A second, private radio channel was licensed in 2003 (Kanal24, renamed Radio Norge in 2008). With the combination of profit-oriented owners and public service obligations, these channels can be described as *hybrid channels*.[19] Today, four owners dominate the Norwegian broadcasting sector: NRK (Norwegian State), TV2 (Egmont, Danish), MTG (Kinnevik, Swedish), and Scandinavian Broadcasting System (SBS – an American company based in Europe).

The depoliticisation of the newspapers coincided with the first phases of private ownership of the broadcasting media in the 1980s. Profit-oriented investors entered into the media sector. Joint ownership of different media businesses could rationalise production and create positive synergies. Bulk purchase of newspapers took place. Two main groups have ended up with control of a large part of the newspaper industry: Schibsted (with its basis in *Aftenposten* and VG), A-pressen (with the trade unions as owner and a basis in the former Labour Party Press Association).

The new owners tend to extract far more economic resources from the media businesses than the owners prior to 1980. There is also a strong concentration of ownership. This has been of concern to several governments since the mid-1990s.[20] In order to prevent further concentration, a law was passed in 1997 (The Media Ownership Act). The Norwegian Media Authority can halt acquisition of ownership in media should such acquisition threaten freedom of expression, genuine opportunities to express one's opinions and a comprehensive range of media.

---

19 Trine Syvertsen, «Ti kjennetegn ved TV 2», in Gunn Enli, Trine Syvertsen and Susanne Østby Sæther (eds.), *Et hjem, for oss – et hjem for deg? Analyser av TV 2,* 2nd ed. (Kristiansand: IJ-forlaget, 2006), pp 34-41.

20 *St.meld.* nr. 32 1992–93 Media i tida.

Table 4.3. Major radio and television channels, 2013

Company	*Owner*	*Primary channels (distribution)*	*Secondary channels*
NRK	The Norwegian state	*Radio*: P1, P2 and P3	Several specialised radio channels
		Television: NRK1, NRK2, NRK3	NRKSuper
TV 2	Egmont (Danish)	*Television*: TV2	TV2 Zebra, TV2 Bliss, TV2 Nyhetskanalen, TV2 Filmkanalen, TV2 Sportskanalen
SBS Discovery	SBS (Scandinavian Broadcasting System) Discovery	*Radio*: Radio Norge Radio 1	
		Television: TVNorge	FEM, MAX, VOX, TLC, Discovery Channel
Modern Times Group	Kinnevik (Swedish)	*Radio*: P4	P5
		Television: TV3, Viasat4	Viasat Film, Viasat Fotball, Viasat History

Note: Radio 1 is the largest chain of local radio stations

Source: Medienorge, at http://medienorge.uib.no/statistikk/aspekt/struktur

New Media

The *Internet* has rapidly become an important media for information and entertainment. Because it is easy to establish oneself as an information provider, the Internet has been regarded as a medium with a democratic potential. But if we look at the most frequently used information providers on the Net, we find only well-established media actors. The dominant newspapers (such as *VG, Aftenposten, Dagbladet*) and the national radio and television companies (NRK, TV 2) dominate completely. One independent Internet newspaper – *Nettavisen* – was established in 1996 and became an immediate success. But the independence lasted only for three years, when it was first sold to the Swedish company Spray, then to TV 2 in 2003, and to Amedia and Egmont in 2009. Internet access has been at a relatively high level in Norway and has been increasing steadily since the 1990s. By 2014, 95% have a computer and can access the internet at home.

Table 4.4. Computer and Internet access in Norway 1997 – 2014 (%)

	1997	2000	2005	2010	2014
Computer access at home	43	71	83	94	95
Internet access at home	13	52	74	93	96

Source: SSB's media use survey via MedieNorge at http://medienorge.uib.no/statistikk/medium/ikt/

By 2012, Norwegians were spending more time on the internet than watching television, but the comparison is not really fair, as most Norwegian use the internet for work and education, while television primarily is used for leisure. Moreover, many Norwegians use the internet as a platform to access different types of media content, also from the traditional media outlets. The traditional media channels in Norway are nevertheless experiencing significant competition from the new platforms. For instance, Facebook received a higher share of daily users than the most popular TV channel NRK1 in 2013, and it is evident that Facebook and other online platforms represent fierce competition with Norwegian newspapers over ad revenues.

Interaction between media and politics

As shown above, Norwegian media have always been closely integrated into the political system. The relationship between media and politics in Norway has, however, changed substantially over the last few decades. The political role of the media has changed from being a passive channel closely tied to the political parties to a situation where it now plays an independent, yet active, role as a director of the political public sphere.[21]

The period since World War Two can be described as involving four phases. As stated in the previous section, the Norwegian newspapers were related to political parties for a long period during which we can recognise several phases. The first phase is characterised by a loyal party press. The papers constituted important links of communication between voters and parties. During election campaigns, they served as heralds for the parties, but they were also important channels for the parties between elections. The rise and heyday of radio also characterises this first phase. In this period, radio was synonymous with NRK, which had a non-partisan platform and a strategy of non-interference in the dissemination of party political messages. The role of the radio was to be a passive reporter and moderator. NRK left it to the political

21 Anders Todal Jenssen and Toril Aalberg, «Den politiske allmenningens tragedie?», in Anders Todal Jenssen and Toril Aalberg (eds.), *Den medialiserte politikken* (Oslo: Universitetsforlaget, 2007), pp. 245-264.

parties to decide the profile, form and range of election programmes.[22] In order to maintain its unbiased profile, two strategies were used. For radio programmes that focused on one party, the normal procedure was that other parties constituted a cross-examining panel. If various parties or topics were to be discussed, it was important that any form of bias was avoided. This problem was solved by allotting the same amount of time to each party, and the role of the programme leader was to ensure that each of the parties was given the appropriate amount of time.

Table 4.5. Four phases in the relationship between media and politics in Norway

Period	*Role of the media:*	*Period characteristics*
Phase I 1945–57	Channel	A loyal party press and the breakthrough of radio.
Phase II 1961–69	Arena	A loyal party press under pressure and the advent of television.
Phase III 1973–89	Actor	Dissolution of the party press and the beginning of the television era. Increased journalistic professionalization with focus on independence.
Phase IV: 1993–	Director	Television dominates. Increased focus on subjective journalism. Media intervenes in and directs the political debate. Alternative public arenas are marginalized.

Note: The beginning of these phases are related to years when national elections took place.

Source: Helge Øsbye and Toril Aalberg (2008) "Media and Politics in Norway". Chapter 5 in Jesper Strömbäck, Mark Ørsten and Toril Aalberg (eds)., *Communicating Politics. Political Communication in the Nordic Countries.* Göteborg: Nordicom.

Gradually this led to a system where collectively the media were seen as an *arena* for discussion among the parties. The radio had already started to play such a role in the first phase, but in the second phase this arena achieved a new dimension when television was introduced to the Norwegian audience.

During the 1960s, television took over as the most important medium for dissemination of political information. By 1973, 82% of the electorate had watched one or more election programmes on television during the campaign.[23] In this period, both radio and television coverage of politics followed the 'no-

22 See page 283 in Tor Bjørklund , "Election campaigns in postwar Norway (1945-1989): From party-controlled to media-driven campaigns", in *Scandinavian Political Studies,* Vol. 14 (1991), pp. 279-302.

23 Ibid., p. 285.

interference' strategy.[24] The 1960s also saw the first trend of press depoliticisation when the most dominant newspapers reduced the intensity of their partisan journalism.[25] Although the larger newspapers kept their official political labels, they reduced their direct attacks on political opponents. Some parties had lost some of their newspapers during World War Two, and this trend continued. The remaining papers tried to attract readers from all parties. Because of the close link between market position and revenues from advertising, the further expansion of newspaper sales became increasingly important, and strong partisan views would not be of much help in extending the readership. Østbye also argues that a more relaxed political climate may have contributed to the 'softer' political profile of newspapers.[26]

During the latter part of the second phase, NRK was criticized for conducting an old-fashioned form of journalism and reducing professional television journalists to passive timekeepers. The media were no longer satisfied with being an arena for other actors. They wanted to play a part themselves, and gradually TV and radio journalists started to play a more active role in Norwegian politics. By the early 1970s, even the parties agreed that the programmes should be NRK's responsibility.[27] This led to a programme format where journalists more aggressively questioned the parties about their policies or other issues which the programme leaders thought were appropriate. The split and collapse of the Liberal Party in 1972-73[28] made many of the former liberal newspapers abandon their party-political affiliation. Most non-socialist newspapers followed suit and declared themselves as independent. In this third phase, there is also an increased journalistic professionalization. The ideal is to be an independent actor based on investigative journalism. The journalists became *actors* in the political debate by demanding answers to their own questions, and questioning the answers given by the politicians.

---

24 Sigurd Allern, «Fra politikermakt til journalistmakt. Programlederroller i Fjernsynsvalgkampen 1961-2001», in Bernt Aardal, Anne Krogstad and Hanne Marthe Narud (eds.), *I Valgkampens hete. Strategisk kommunikasjon og politisk usikkerhet* (Oslo: Universitetsforlaget, 2004), pp. 141-166.

25 See page 220 in Helge Østbye, «Media in Politics: Channels, Arenas, Actors, Themes", in Kaare Strøm and Lars Svåsand (eds.), *Challenges to Political Parties: The case of Norway (*Ann Arbor: University of Michigan Press, 1997), pp.215-228.

26 Ibid., p. 221.

27 Allern, «Fra politikermakt til journalistmakt» [note 28], pp. 141-166.

28 In 1972 the pro-EEC minority of the Liberal Party, split and established a new party called the Liberal People's Party (*Det Liberale Folkepartiet*). At the time of the split, eight of the thirteen Liberal Party MPs joined the new party. At the following parliamentarian election in 1973, the Liberal People's Party only won one seat. The party's popularity declined throughout the 1980s and in 1988, it was decided to officially merge back together with the Liberal Party.

A fourth phase in the relationship between media and politics in Norway commenced in the beginning of the 1990s. The increase in the number of national and local radio and television channels led to a multitude of broadcasted election debates. In 1991, the last year with a television monopoly, NRK offered its audience only nine televised election programmes. In 1993, the Norwegian electorate was able to watch up to 32 different election programmes.[29] Television became the dominant medium and occupied a substantial amount of both politicians and voters' time. For the newspapers, this phase is characterized by a decline in readership. Much of the press coverage is also oriented toward how politicians perform in the various television programmes. During this phase, newspapers lost their leading role as the most important information channel. The major aspect of this fourth phase, however, is that the media (and especially television) starts to play the role of a *director*. Journalists, programme leaders and editors are aware of their power, and are not afraid to use it. Rather, they perceive it as their right to decide which topics to discuss and whom to invite.[30] Thus, in the fourth phase, media intervene in and direct the political debate. At the same time alternative arenas are marginalized as television companies spend more time announcing their own programmes than covering political debates organised by the parties themselves or other organizations. There also seems to be an increased focus on subjective journalism. The time and column space spent on commentaries and 'views' rather than 'news' increases. This does not however, indicate a return to a high degree of partisanship in media.

Bjørklund describes the development from one phase to the next as *cumulative*; that is when a new role is taken on and the old one remains.[31] In other words, even in the fourth phase some newspapers functioned as important channels for the parties, in spite of the fact that these channels were no longer controlled by the parties as previously. Although the Labour Party sold its shares in *A-pressen* in 1995,[32] this media corporation still has strong connections to the Labour movement as the Norwegian Federation of Trade Unions remains a major shareholder. The Labour press has always had a strong position in the northern part of Norway.[33] Troms Labour party, for instance, still owns 12 % of the shares in *Nordlys*, the region's biggest newspaper. The two other

29 Allern, «Fra politikermakt til journalistmakt» [note 28].

30 Ibid., p. 154

31 Bjørklund, "Election Campaigns in post-war Norway" [note 26], p. 283.

32 A-pressen (a mediacorporation originally established to organize Labour newspaper) bought 20% of the shares in TV 2, and the Labour party did not find it appropriate that a political party should own a national television company.

33 Østbye, »Media in Politics» [note 29] p. 218

left wing parties, The Socialist Left Party and the Red Electoral Alliance each had its own newspaper, the weekly *Ny Tid* and the daily *Klassekampen* respectively. The non-socialist parties no longer own their own newspapers, but sympathies and indirect links still remain.[34] For instance, the previous Conservative press is now regarded as independent, and newspapers in this conglomerate are based on liberal-conservative values. This holds for large newspapers such as *Aftenposten* and *Adresseavisen.* Similarly, the Centre Party no longer has formal ties to any one newspaper, but *Nationen,* which is owned by organisations and companies connected to the agricultural industry, has a profile that is close to the Centre Party. Likewise, the independent Christian newspaper *Vårt Land* shares the same value base as the Christian People's Party.

The degree of media–political elite integration is, and has been for a long time, high in Norway.[35] People moved back and forth between the political sphere and the media. According to Allern, this trend was particularly apparent within the Labour Party.[36] Several members of parliament had previously worked in the media. Press and broadcasting are important bases for the recruitment of political leaders, and several parliamentarians and cabinet members have 'retired' into leading media positions. Indeed, from the end of World War Two until 2007, all NRK broadcasting directors were leading politicians. From 1948 to 2001, the director had always had links to the Labour Party. Jon G. Bernander, who was Director General 2001-2007, was the first with a political career from a party other than Labour. In 2007, a new General Director was appointed. The new director did not have any party affiliation, and his qualifications were based solely on his long media career within NRK.

However, it is not reasonable to say that the broadcaster has been utilised for party political propaganda. Governments have appointed independent people with a clear and positive attitude to public service broadcasting ideas. The political system has had influence on the general direction of the development of NRK, but very little direct influence over programmes. In parliament, there were many heated debates, especially in the 1970s, when there were claims that the programmes were leaning towards the far left or against Christian values. Moreover, for the last ten or fifteen years, politicians more frequently 'retire' into lobbying or the PR sector than to the media. According to Allern, the PR sector experienced a significant expansion during the 1990s.[37] Allern estimates that the number of people employed in the PR industry in 2001

---

34 Allern, "From Party Press to Independent Observer?" [NOTE 16].

35 Østbye, »Media in Politics» [note 29], p. 219

36 See pages 280–281 in Sigurd Allern, «Kildene og mediemakten», in Martin Eide (ed.), *Til dagsorden!* (Oslo: Gyldendal, 2001) pp. 273-303.

37 Sigurd Allern, *Kildenes makt,*.(Oslo: Pax). 1997.

is approximately the same as that of those employed as journalists and editors in Norwegian news desks.[38]

The changing role of the Norwegian media from a passive channel to an active director also indicates that the media have gained power at the expense of the political parties. Jenssen and Aalberg describe the parties' new relationships with the media as a 'fear-based state of dependence'.[39] Not only can they no longer rely on the party press, but other important links with the voters such as party membership and party identification have also been reduced. At the same time, the parties are very aware of the effects the media may have on the public. In a survey of Norwegian members of parliament, Aalberg and Jamtøy find that the vast majority believe that the media have too much power.[40] An equally large proportion (76%) disagreed with the statement that 'The power of the mass media is overrated.' The same number stated that politicians often make use of journalists by leaking information to them, and that they have personal contact with a journalist daily or several times a week. The fear-based dependency is also illustrated by the fact that 50% of the parliamentary members declare that it is the media that determine which issues are important, and that politicians have little impact on this matter.

It is evident that the Norwegian political parties occasionally wish to avoid the 'journalistic filter' which regulates much of their current political communication so that they can regain some of the direct links they used to have with their voters. Several attempts have been made to establish such a link on the Internet.[41] But there is nevertheless reason to discuss how efficient these attempts have been. The main political function of the Internet in Norway is probably that it gives the inhabitants of the country access to a wide range of Norwegian and foreign media and other sources of information. Despite the relatively high Internet penetration into Norwegian society, political parties have not been particularly active in taking advantage of this new medium. Internet use by both parties and voters is however, increasing. Hence, there is

38 Allern, 2001, p. 278

39 Jenssen and Aalberg, «Den politiske allmenningens tragedie?» [note 25], p. 255

40 Toril Aalberg and Ann Iren Jamtøy, "*Friends, connections and enemies: The relationship between political journalists and members of parliament in Norway*". Paper presented to the 18th Nordic Media Conference, Helsinki. 2007

41 Hanne Hestvik, «Valgkampen 2004. Partier, velgere og nye medier. Ny kommunikasjon?», in Bernt Aardal, Anne Krogstad and Hanne Marthe Narud (eds.), *I valgkampens hete. Strategisk kommunikasjon og politisk usikkerhet* (Oslo: Universitetsforlaget, 2004), pp. 230-251); and Rune Karlsen, "Still Broadcasting the Campaign: On the Internet and the Fragmentation of Political Communication with Evidence from Norwegian Electoral Politics", in *Journal of Information Technology and Politics*, Vol. 8 (2011), pp. 146 -162.

reason to believe that the Internet will become a more important arena for political communication in the future.

Another more direct link, free from the 'journalistic filter', is political advertising. This is a channel the parties are using to various degrees partly based on financial research.[42] Political advertising on television is not permitted in Norway, but pamphlets, posters, boards and newspaper advertisements have been used for a long time. More recently, parties have also opened up to political advertising on the Internet. Radio advertising is also permitted, but few parties use this form of communication as they find it hard to produce good and efficient political advertising for this medium.[43] There has also been a significant discussion about whether political advertising on television should be allowed. In September 2004, important changes in the constitution were made which opened up possibilities for political and religious advertising on television. In 1996, a Freedom of Speech Commission had been formed to review and propose changes to the freedom of expression clause (Paragraph 100) in the Norwegian constitution. This paragraph had not been changed since 1814 when the Constitution was first drawn up. Among many recommendations from the Commission was a suggestion to allow political advertising on radio and television. This proposition was left out when the parliament adopted a change to the Constitution in 2004. After the parliamentary election in 2005, there was no longer a parliamentary majority in favour of political advertising on television, and the Minister of Culture and Church Affairs announced in May 2006 that he would refrain from implementing the work that his predecessor had not been able to finish.

Conclusion

In *Comparing Media Systems,* Hallin and Mancini classify Norway as representing the prototypical Democratic Corporatist Model.[44] Although this model fits relatively well with the description of the Norwegian politico-media system, there is clearly a trend away from the "ideal model" on some dimensions. The Norwegian newspaper industry and level of journalistic professionalism in Norway fit the ideal description of a democratic corporatist country.

---

42 Rune Karlsen and Hanne Marthe Narud, Organisering av valgkamp – «moderne» eller «tradisjonell»? In Bernt Aardal, Anne Krogstad and Hanne Marthe Narud (eds.) *I valgkampens hete.* *(*Oslo: Universitetsforlaget, 2004). Toril Aalberg, Toril and Therese Saur , Politisk reklame, visuelt stemmefiske. In Anders Todal Jenssen and Toril Aalberg (eds.) 2007, *Den medialiserte politikken (*Oslo: Universitetsforlaget, 2007).

43 Karlsen and Narud, «Organisering av valgkamp» [note 46].

44 Hallin and Mancini, *Comparing Media Systems* [note 1], pp 67–68)

On the other two indicators, there are factors that somewhat distinguish Norway from the ideal type. For instance, when it comes to *Political parallelism*, it took longer to sever the links between parties and the press in Norway than in most other countries. It was not until the 1970s that newspapers became more politically neutral in respect of party affiliation, and subsequently more market oriented. Many newspapers can, however, still be linked to political ideologies, and some still have close connections to specific political parties. Hallin and Mancini describe the democratic corporatist model as a system where there is strong state intervention in the *media system.* The state plays an active role in the development of the media system, and a system of press subsidies was introduced in order to maintain diversity in the press. The broadcasting system is also based on public service broadcasting ideals. Since the early 1990s, clauses in concession agreements for national private radio and television channels also emphasises the importance of diversity within each channel. However, there is a tendency for all media (including public broadcasters) to become increasingly commercial and market-oriented. This may jeopardise the diversity. Indeed, the final report of the Norwegian Power and Democracy Project pointed out that the parliamentary chain had been weakened during the last 15 to 20 years, and suggested that one of the reasons for this was that the media has become more important and independent.[45]

As in many other western and modern democracies, global enterprise and new media platforms challenge the traditional media outlets and media use patterns in Norway. For the political actors, these changes also influence their ability to communicate with voters and citizens. The new online platforms clearly provide an improved ability for direct communication and interaction, but the increased choice also enables citizens with the option of neglecting certain types of media content, that they do not like or approve of. So far however, there is little evidence of significant Norwegian echo-chambers, and the majority of Norwegians still have relatively healthy media diets, consisting of news from a number of different sources, both new and traditional.

45 Øyvind Østerud, Fredrik Engelstad and Per Selle, *Makten og demokratiet. En sluttbok fra Makt- og demokratiutredningen*. (Oslo: Gyldendal Akademiske, 2003, p. 101).

B. The Media in Slovenia*

Slovenia has a population of two million and this represents the main limit on the Slovenian media as they cannot provide a huge quantity and diversity of services that would offer attractive and/or high-quality products. The issue was raised already in the 19th century, when the small market combined with limitations of education and literacy severely obstructed the development of (independent) media and when the main motivation was a political one, led by political parties and ideologies eager to establish and support their media outlets. It was stated already in 1884 that "most of our newspapers were established by different political parties and different societies whose ownership even now includes these newspapers. But the parties and societies didn't found these newspapers to bring themselves material profit. Their newspapers were motivated only by the desire to spread the principles and ideas of these parties and societies."[46] Although the spread of education and practically complete literacy of whole population today presents different environment for the media, the limitations of small market continue to cause problems.

This is evident in the broadcasting[47] as well as the print system[48]: after the state's newly gained independence in 1991 there was a surplus of new TV programs and daily newspapers, which the market simply could not handle. The size of the market does not provide the advantages of economy of scale and the lack of business success of online media and online departments of other media. Additionally, the economic crisis has left significant effects in terms of advertising and media revenues. Due to negative economic trends, a number of media have been closed down or forced to restructure. The limits of the economic potential and economic market leave open the issue of the political interventions, whether to protect public interest or to promote particular party or ideological interests.

This chapter will present the key characteristics of the Slovenian media system. First, I shall provide an overview of the 'traditional', legacy media landscape: newspapers and print, radio and television. This will be followed by an analysis of media regulation, particularly in regards to ownership and the interplay of media and politics. This political perspective will then be complemented by an economic, market perspective and the analysis of the new digital

---

* Marko Milosavljević

46 Janez Jesenko, *Časnikarstvo in naši časniki* (Ljubljana: Narodna tiskarna, 1884), p. 117.

47 Marko Milosavljević. "Vseh šest dnevnikov najbrž ne bo preživelo. In stari so žilavi" ("All he six dailies will not survive. And the old ones are tough."). *Delo, Sobotna priloga*, 4 May 1996

48 Marko Milosavljević. "Sledi TV politiki - ali politika TV?" ("Is TV following the politics or politics following TV?"). *Delo, Sobotna priloga*, 3 July 1999.

environment and its consequences for media and politics. Finally, an overview of these developments and their consequences for media market and media policy will we added in the conclusion.

Press: Negative economic effects of the economic crisis since 2008 have been strongly felt in the Slovenian "traditional", legacy media, especially in the print media. The data on press circulation show there has been a trend of falling circulation of the daily newspapers in Slovenia since 2009. Part of this decline can be attributed to the rise of digital media, particularly online media, and part to the economic crisis. In some cases, internal problems and inadequate editorial and management responses to the challenges faced by the changing economic and media landscape were an important factor in the decline.

After the circulation figures for the last quarter of 2010 were published in February 2011, the Slovenian Advertising Chamber (*Slovenska oglaševalska zbornica*, SOZ) speculated that the negative trend of falling circulation was slowing. It pointed out that the National Readership Research (*Nacionalna raziskava branosti*) had even recorded an increase of the readership for the second time in a row, "which is very encouraging for the print media market."[49] However, the continuation of the economic crisis as well as the steady decline of circulation has led to the continuation of crisis in the press in general, including problems with the owners and their accumulated debts (in the case of for example two leading publishers, *Delo* and *Dnevnik,* and their owners, *Laško Brewery* and *DZS,* respectively).

Print media are still pointing out that their readership is still extremely large, both in print and online. In January 2012, the National Research of Readership for the first time published the combined data of newspaper readership of both print and online versions, showing how many people print media are actually reaching and emphasizing the better educational values and economic power of print media as compared to television.[50]

Today, there are eight daily newspapers in Slovenia: six national, one regional, and one dedicated to sports.[51] The total circulation of all daily newspapers is approximately 260,000 copies, accounting for a readership of 1.17

49 "SOZ: Negativni trend prodanih naklad tiskanih medijev se umirja" ("SOZ: The negative trend of falling circulation of print media is calming down"), *Dnevnik*, 25 February 2011. See http://www.dnevnik.si/poslovni_dnevnik/1042426958 (accessed 28 February 2011).

50 G. Novkovič and P. Movrin, "Milijon bralcev Žurnala24" (A million readers for Žurnal24), *Žurnal24*, 26 January 2012. See http://www.zurnal24.si/milijon-bralcev-zurnala24-clanek-146803 (accessed 26 January 2012).

51 In June 2015 this newspaper, Ekipa, has merged with the Slovenian edition of Croatian daily sports newspaper Sportske novosti, creating EkipaSN and further confirming the limitations of the market and the issue of economic sustainability of the market. MM. »Športna časopisa Ekipa in Sportske novosti združena pod imenom EkipaSN« . Marketing Magazin, 15 June

million.[52] Two of the top three dailies by circulation are owned by the same holding company, Delo: the broadsheet *Delo* ((circulation 38,500[53], readership 157,000[54]) and the tabloid *Slovenske novice* (circulation 73,700, readership 336,000). They share a number of common special-interest supplements (*Ona*, *Polet*, *Delo&Dom*, *Vikend*), while on Sunday they publish *Nedelo* (readership 157,000). Delo and its two newspapers control almost half of the market for paid daily newspapers.

Online and mobile: Online and mobile content services are increasingly popular, especially among the younger population. The 10 most popular websites in Slovenia include four sites launched by Slovenian companies and six global Internet services, including Google, Yahoo!, Facebook, YouTube, and Wikipedia.[55] The four most prominent Slovenian sites are run either by established media, such as the leading commercial television broadcaster Pro Plus (24ur.com), by the national public service broadcaster RTV SLO (Rtvslo.si), or by the biggest telecoms operator, state-owned Telekom Slovenia, which through its media and web company TS Media offers the top Slovenian search engine (Najdi.si) and one of the most-used multimedia portals (Siol.net).

The most important and popular Internet content is news. Research in 2011 showed that 77% of users aged between 10 and 75 used the Internet for news. Music and film were the second most popular type of content, with 68% of users, while 60% of Slovenian Internet users searched for information on travel. This was followed by searching for content related to sports, cosmetics, cars, food, health, and medicine.[56] With the rise of the Internet and the digitization of television, many new news providers appeared but, in most cases, only those connected to established media gained substantial audiences.

Although blogging is quite popular, most of the blogs are dedicated to personal issues (with the blog as a diary, describing personal life, personal taste,

---

2015. See http://www.marketingmagazin.si/novice/mmediji/11842/sportna-casopisa-ekipa-in-sportske-novosti-zdruzena-pod-imenom-ekipasn (accessed 18 June 2015)

52 I. Setinšek, "Recesija in oglaševanje v Sloveniji" ("The recession and advertising in Slovenia"), *Marketing Magazin*, January 2009.

53 SOZ, "RPN - Revidiranje prodanih naklad" (Revised circulation). See http://www.soz.si/projekti_soz/rpn_revidiranje_prodanih_naklad (accessed 20 June 2015).

54 NRP – "Nacionalna raziskava branosti" ("National research of readership"). See http://www.nrb.info/podatki/ (accessed 20 June 2015).

55 See http://www.alexa.com/topsites/countries/SI (accessed 12 February 2012).

56 Measurement of Website Traffic (*Merjenje obiskanosti spletnih strani*, MOSS), research by Valicon and Gemius for SOZ, January 2011. See Mi. S./STA, "Več kot tri četrtine Slovencev po novice na splet" ("More than three quarters of Slovenians go for the news to the web"), *Slovenske novice*, 10 March 2011. See http://www.slovenskenovice.si/clanek/143523 (accessed 11 March 2011).

different lifestyles or interests such as gadgets, music, etc.). There are very few blogs that are news-oriented and not many blogs by journalists writing on their own. Certain media, for example the public broadcaster RTV SLO on its website Rtvslo.si, promote blogging as a form of additional expression, either by their own journalists or by the general public (mostly by well-known Slovenes).

The comparison with Eurostat data on the attendance and participation in online communities of regular users of the Internet revealed that Slovenia was above the EU average in almost all indicators except for creating and maintaining their own blogs. This may also explain the low number of active and passive blog users (Slovenia was ranked 27th among 31 European countries).

Television and radio: Approximately two thirds of the Slovenian population use their television sets and listen to the radio every day; an average individual watches television programs and listens to the radio for approximately three hours each. As regards radio, 71% of the population between the age of 15 and 75 (1.145.000 people) listen to the radio on a daily basis.

There are two general channels of the public broadcaster RTV SLO with nationwide coverage, high production quality, and extensive news coverage—A1 and Val 202.[57] With the introduction of commercial broadcasting in the early 1990s, most commercial radio stations were granted only local or regional radio frequencies. No national commercial radio network was planned. However, as a result of changes to the Electronic Communication Act in 2006, which made possible the integration of local radio stations into radio networks covering larger territories, the Radio 1 network was created and in a few years it climbed to one of the top slots in the listenership ratings. Val 202 was the most popular radio station until 2011, when a significant change took place: the commercial Radio 1 became the most listened to on a daily basis.[58] It has 12% of daily listeners (195,000). Average daily radio consumption increased within the last ten years; it went from 165 minutes in 2005 to 192 minutes in 2009.[59]

While there was a slight and steady rise in the time spent watching television, Slovenian people are among the lighter television users, according to

57 A. Hreščak, "Že leta najbolj poslušana Val 202 in Prvi program Radia Slovenija" ("For years Val 202 and Prvi program Radio Slovenia the most popular radio stations"), *Dnevnik*, 17 July 2010. See http://www.dnevnik.si/tiskane_izdaje/objektiv/1042374363 (accessed 22 December 2010).

58 Valicon "Poročilo: Poslušanost radijskih postaj" ("Report: Radio statistics"), 10 October 2013. See http://www.akos-rs.si/files/Elektronski_mediji/Medijska_ucilnica/Raziskave_in_analize/2013-10-04-APK107-poslusanost-radijev-in-navade-poslusalcev-porocilo.pdf (Accessed 10 June 2015).

59 Radiometrija, research conducted by Media Pool for public broadcaster RTV SLO, 23 September 2010.

AGB Nielsen international figures.[60] The highest average viewership is in households with cable connections, which have a better choice of channels. Additionally, cable households have a slightly older average population, which also contributes to higher ratings, as the senior citizens spend more time at home watching television.

There are seven television channels, private and public, that can be seen by more than 90% of the population: the public channels SLO 1, SLO 2, and SLO 3, and the commercial channels POP TV, Kanal A, TV3, and Planet TV. Three of the television channels with the best territorial coverage belong to the public service broadcaster RTV SLO, while out of the other four, two are owned by an international broadcasting company: the most watched commercial television channels POP TV and Kanal A, are produced by Pro Plus, owned by Central European Media Enterprises (CME), in turn owned by Time Warner since 2013, with television stations in the Czech Republic, Slovakia, Croatia, Romania, and Bulgaria, as well as Slovenia. The third private channel, TV3, is owned by local entrepreneur without other media investments. It used to be owned by the Scandinavian company Modern Times Group (MTG) as part of its collection of commercial channels in Scandinavian and Baltic countries; however, the company withdrew from Slovenian television market in March 2012.

A fourth private channel, Planet TV, is owned by the Greek media company Antenna Group (51%) and Slovenian telecom operator Telekom (49%; Telekom in itself is majority owned by the state. However, although it was slated to be sold in 2015, yet as of July 2015 the sale had not gone through.

All in all, Pro Plus and its channels are also the most prominent commercial broadcasters in television news production. The two major channels, POP TV and Kanal A, broadcast news, with POP TV's output and ratings being the higher of the two. Based on viewer surveys, POP TV is also the most trusted television program, winning the title of a "Trusted Brand" in 2009 and in 2010.[61] In addition, Pro Plus produces several web portals: the most visited news portal in Slovenia, 24ur.com; much-visited specialist websites (e.g., Zadovoljna.si, Bibaleze.si, , Moškisvet.com, Cekin.si, and Vizita.si), and the internet community Frendi In Flirt.

Apart from public service broadcast channels, there are also around 70 private television channels, most of them niche, broadcast only on cable systems. AKOS and the Ministry of Culture granted the status of "special significance" to 10 local, regional, and non-profit television channels, which broadcast some public service content, i.e., local news and current affairs,

60 AGB Nielsen Media Research, Telemetric Summary commissioned by APEK, 2011.

61 See http://24ur.com/?section_id=610 (accessed 15 May 2012).

minority programs, children's programs, etc. This entitles them to apply for public co-funding. Others can compete for public subsidies, too, but the funds for them are not as extensive as those aimed at channels of special significance.

Commercial channels are required to comply with certain obligations in programming, including regulations on the origin of programming. These include the requirement that 20% of a station's daily programming should consist of in-house produced programs, of which at least 60 minutes must be broadcast between 6 p.m. and 10 p.m. In addition, all television channels except local ones must comply with provisions on the promotion of EU audiovisual content, requiring that EU material represents the bulk of their programming not counting news, sports events, games, advertising, and teleshopping. The Public Broadcasting Act requires that 5% of each channel's annual broadcast time must be reserved for audiovisual products of Slovenian origin.

However, commercial channels are not required to broadcast news and current affairs, as the Mass Media Acts from 1994 and from 2001, amended in 2006, had no such provisions. However, this strand seemed so important to the managers and editors of the newly established POP TV in 1995 (in order to create an image of a serious and responsible television channel) that they created daily news and weekly current affairs programs,[62] which have been broadcasted ever since. News and current affairs are among the most watched programs on the main commercial channels, POP TV and Kanal A.[63] In general, the public service broadcaster, RTV SLO—unlike some other former state television channels in other former communist countries—managed to keep relatively high ratings in general, particularly with the help of its live broadcasts of most popular sports including Olympics and winter skiing.

Liberalisation, fragmentation, and economic crisis

The main limit on the media in Slovenia is the size of the country and its population. Since Slovenia is a small country with a population of only two million, it does not have the preconditions for a huge quantity and diversity of services that would offer attractive and/or high-quality media and production.

Further, Slovenia does not share a language with any larger country that would give domestic channels and media companies the opportunity to offer content to a wider audience. This puts it at a disadvantage compared, for example, with neighboring Croatia. Croatian television channels have signifi-

62 M. Milosavljević, "Daj ljudstvu to, kar hoče – POP TV" (Give the people what they want – POP TV), *Delo-Saturday Supplement*, 23 December 1995, p. 37.

63 AGB Nielsen data from research on television trends, commissioned by APEK, 2007, 2009, and 2011.

cant ratings in neighboring Bosnia-Herzegovina, Serbia, and Montenegro, where programs in the Croatian language are fully understood. By contrast, Slovenian media have to compete in a small market.

In television broadcasting, for example, in Slovenia, unfortunately, observations made more than a decade ago still sound valid today:

> There may be some external pluralism in Slovene private broadcasting ... but there is no true, internal pluralism, pluralism of content, sources and different approaches. And there is no reason to believe that digitization will bring an end to this. For the reason mentioned above, there will probably be some increase in the number of available channels in small countries like Slovenia, but this increase will be very slight, with perhaps one or two channels more. However, recent experiences with our non-regulated commercial broadcasting indicate that the increase of available channels does not automatically mean the increase of content and source variety.[64]

In the 1990s, Slovenian society was faced with a rapid increase of broadcasting channels, but without any improvement in content plurality and diversity.[65] The development of broadcasting is taking place without a consistent media policy, as in past decades, and is left entirely to the ideas and goodwill of the most influential broadcasters themselves, RTV SLO included.

In addition, a strong economic crisis has further limited the sustainability of Slovenian media. Print media were especially struck by the economic crisis – but also by the rise of digital media, particularly free newspapers; the closures included the weeklies *Dobro jutro* and *Total tedna*, and there was also the attention-grabbing closure of the popular free daily *Žurnal24* that had a readership of 150,000.[66] It was closed down due to a decision of its Austrian owner Styria MG, stating that the wide circulation and popularity had not been enough for the economic survival of the paper. Some media have cut their content production (such as the Slovenian-licensed Cosmopolitan) or became free supplements of newspapers (such as previously independently published magazine *Mag*, which became a supplement of *Delo* in 2009 but was later on completely closed down), and there is also a growing dependence by small media on agency news

64 Marko Milosavljević and Sandra Bašić-Hrvatin, "Who will control the controllers?", pp. 253–257.

65 Marko Milosavljević, "Amerika, vendar južna: TV po slovensko " (America, but South: TV in the Slovenian style), *Delo*, 27 January 1996, p. 44; and M. Milosavljević, "Nadzor nad 'licencami za tiskanje denarja': spremembe zakona o javnih glasilih" (The control over 'the licences to print the money': changes of the mass media act), *Delo*, 28 June 1997, p. 32.

66 Lenart J. Kučič "Nauk propada časnika Žurnal: potrebujemo bolj pogumnega varuha konkurence" ("The lesson of Žurnal's failure: We need a more courageous competition watchdog"), *Pod Črto*, May 2015. See http://podcrto.si/nauk-propada-casnika-zurnal-potrebujemo-bolj-pogumnega-varuha-konkurence/ (accessed 17 June 2015).

(mostly provided by the state-owned Slovenian Press Agency (Slovenska tiskovna agencija, STA)). A number of print media have closed down completely, including the magazine *Več* and *Mag* (published by Delo), and a number of free supplements of newspapers have decreased their publication frequency, including *Polet* and *Delo & Dom* (from July 2015), both also published by Delo.

The crisis reflected also on the newspaper and magazine ownership. A number of newspapers changed owners due to their economic problems. *Delo* as the largest newspaper company in Slovenia was sold in June 2015 to the company FMR,[67] owned by a well-known Slovenian entrepreneur and businessman Stojan Petrič. The daily newspaper *Večer* was sold to the company Dober Večer in 2014, accompanied with a critique of a non-transparent and irresponsible sale processes.[68] Both were sold for only a small portion of their former value, further confirming lack of interest of investors in the daily newspapers in Slovenia: *Delo* for 7,3 million euros, compared to the price of 95 million euros that were paid for it by its former owner, the Laško Brewery (which in itself was bought by Heineken in May 2015) in 2008; and *Večer* for 1 million euros, compared to the price of 20 million euros, paid for it by the Laško Brewery in 2009.

Regulation of media ownership

Changes to the media regulations have been brought by the revised Mass Media Act, adopted by Parliament in the summer 2006.[69] It raised the ceiling on ownership to 33% for any owner, including foreigners. Before the adoption of the Mass Media Act, the task of restricting ownership was dispersed and ineffective. With the new legislation, this responsibility was assigned to the Ministry of Culture. In accordance with the Mass Media Act all media must be registered. To do that, they must provide information on all owners or part-owners owning or controlling more than 5% of shares or controlling more than

67 Klara Škrinjar "Delo prodano, novi lastnik je FMR ("Delo sold, the new owner is FMR"), Delo, 3 June 2015. See http://www.delo.si/novice/slovenija/delo-d-d-prodano-minus-novi-lastnik-je-fmr.html (accessed 20 June 2015).

68 Al. Ma. "Dober Večer kupil večer" ("Dober Večer bought Večer"), RTVSLO, 3 October 2014. See http://www.rtvslo.si/gospodarstvo/dober-vecer-kupil-vecer/347894 (accessed 20 June 2015).

69 Zakon o spremembah in dopolnitvah Zakona o medijih (ZMed-A), Uradni list RS, Official Gazette, no. 60/2006, 24 June 2006 (hereafter, ZMed-A, Uradni list RS, 24 June 2006). See http://www.uradni-list.si/1/objava.jsp?urlid=200660&stevilka=2536 (accessed 20 January 2011).

5% of voting rights (Article 17)[70] to the Official Gazette by the end of February each year, otherwise they must pay a penalty from €800 to €60,000 (Article 132).[71] There are not many breaches of this provision in evidence.

In the early 1990s, the availability of media ownership data and shareholders information was very limited. This was true not just for Slovenian companies and individuals, but also for foreign investors and their local companies: Pro Plus, which broadcasts the television programs POP TV and Kanal A, and the VOD service Voyo, is owned by CME. Although since the beginning in 1995 CME has been transparent about reporting its financial results and ownership changes, the publication of those results and ownership changes was either severely delayed or hard-to-find through either Slovenian authorities' records or the company's Slovenian public relations department.[72] Throughout the years, the situation regarding transparency in media ownership has improved, but there remain important cases of controversial ownership and control of the media including ownership and control for political purposes.

One of the cases of controversial ownership occurred only weeks before the parliamentary elections in autumn 2008: specifically, only a few issues of two new free weekly newspapers, *Ekspres* and *Slovenski tednik,* were published during that period. The articles' content was directed against left-wing parties, at the same time praising right-wing parties, particularly the Slovenian Democratic Party (*Slovenska demokratska stranka*, SDS) and its president Janez Janša. Moreover, the authorship of the articles was unclear and dubious: the authors were unspecified or using pseudonyms.

Later on the parliament established a committee, intended for an investigation of the financing of these two newspapers. It was suspected that money laundering and illegal election campaigning were among the reasons for the creation of the free weeklies. Several revelations were made before the committee: A media-buying company, Media Polis, also involved in buying advertising space for the two weeklies, admitted to having lent €120,000 (US $152,184) to the SDS. This confirmed some financial ties between the party and the newspapers.[73] In March 2011 the parliamentary committee in March

---

70 Zakon o medijih (ZMed), Uradni list RS, Official Gazette, no. 35/2001, 26 May 2001. See http://www.uradni-list.si/1/objava.jsp?urlid=200135&stevilka=2043 (accessed 4 March 2011).

71 ZMed-A, Uradni list RS, 24 June 2006.

72 Marko Milosavljević, "Slovenija kot most v vzhodno Evropo" (Slovenia as a bridge to Eastern Europe), *Delo*, 21 July 1997, p. 28; see also M. Milosavljević, "Kdo je prava motnja v sistemu?" (Who is the real fault in the system?), *Delo*, 7 February 1998, p. 30.

73 A. Delić, "Brezplačniki: Media Polis posodil SDS 120.000 evrov" (Free newspapers: Media Polis lent SDS €120,000), *Delo*, 18 January 2011. See http://www.delo.si/clanek/136869 (accessed 3 March 2011).

2011 accused the CEO of state-owned postal company Pošta Slovenija, Aleš Hauc, of false testimony before the committee regarding the financing.[74] The company was involved in some of the financing of these free newspapers as well, with possible political motivation and help for these decisions. The committee released the final report of its investigation in September 2011, in which it concluded that *Ekspres* and *Slovenski tednik* were "established and published to influence the parliamentary elections in 2008, to discredit the political competition, to help the leading party of the then-ruling coalition, SDS, and to cover up election propaganda and campaigning, and problematic funding of political parties."[75]

All in all, there are new cases of non-transparent or suspicious ownership (*Slovenski tednik*, *Ekspres*, and, according to some, also the failed *Dobro jutro*) or attempts to gain ownership of media (as already mentioned the dubious takeover attempt of the daily *Večer* by the company 3lan and later also the successful takeover attempt by company Dober Večer). These cases cast doubt over the claimed improvement of transparency of Slovenian media ownership. Although it is doubtless the case that the level of transparency is better today, it is still inadequate. Indeed, a variety of information is sometimes still completely unavailable, including financial results, ownership connections, advertising, and funding. Citizens are able to know who controls the largest media companies, but even there the transparency does not approach high levels. In general, changes of media ownership are continuous and often opaque.

Political influence and independence of media

A consequence of the former socialist regime is a distinct characteristic of the state still playing a large role as an owner, main shareholder, or important shareholder of a number of companies. "One could say that the Slovene mass media experienced complete liberalization yet only with regard to content and sanctions. In terms of ownership they are far from being liberalized."[76] Political

74 Ni. Č., "Komisija o brezplačnikih kazensko ovadila direktorja Pošte Slovenija Hauca" (The commission on free newspapers filed criminal charge against CEO of Pošta Slovenija, Hauc), *Delo*, 2 March 2011. See http://www.delo.si/clanek/142418 (accessed 5 March 2011).

75 Al. B., "Brezplačnika sta bila 'trojanska konja" (Free newspapers were Trojan horses), *Žurnal24*, 26 September 2011. See http://www.zurnal24.si/brezplacnika-sta-bila-trojanska-kon ja-clanek-136080 (accessed 10 January 2012).

76 Sandra Hrvatin in Marko Milosavljević "Media Policy in Slovenia in the 1990s: Regulation, privatization, concentration and commercialization of the media" *Eurozine*, 23 July 2003. See http://www.eurozine.com/articles/2003-07-07-hrvatin-en.html (Accessed 1 June 2015).

influence is mostly present in terms of legislation and regulatory bodies, including different agencies and offices, but also within the system of different subsidies and state-controlled or state influenced advertising. These include some of the largest advertisers in the Slovenian media (e.g., Telekom, Petrol, NLB, and Mobitel until 2011), which consequently means that state and the government or local authorities can influence a large share of the advertising income in the media. Preferential advertising by the state or by state-owned or state-controlled companies remains an important issue, often alleged by the media but difficult to substantiate in most cases. There were a number of cases where media claimed that they had ceased to receive advertising from state-owned or state-controlled companies due to their editorial policy and critical attitude toward the government (e.g., the magazine *Mag* in the 1990s in the era of liberal-dominated governments; the daily newspaper *Dnevnik* and the current affairs weekly *Mladina* in the era of a rightwing government from 2004 until 2008).

Political influence is most directly felt at the public broadcaster RTV SLO, where Parliament appoints or confirms most of the members of its programming council. It could also be seen in the July 2012 attempt to change some of the members of the RTV SLO Supervisory Council.[77] The programme council of the broadcaster on the other hand has been based similarly as was the case in Germany and included 25 members, with only five of them coming from the political sphere. But the idea of having a civil society council turned to be unsuccessful as it has been taking care of the particular interests of its members, instead of representing interests of the public and enabling depolitization.[78]

The right-wing Slovenian Democratic Party (*Slovenska demokratska stranka*, SDS), previously mentioned in connection with the ownership of two free weekly newspapers, in June 2015 announced the creation of a new radio and television media house.[79] The leader of the party and ex-prime minister Janez Janša substantiated the creation of this new media house with the argument that right-wing voices were not being heard and that the reality was being skewed by existing media. This is not a new attempt though: in the 1990s, a

---

77 The Supervisory Council consists of 11 members, five of whom are appointed by the National Assembly, in proportion to the representation of political parties in the National Assembly. See http://www.rtvslo.si/strani/introduction/3 (accessed 12 June 2012).

78 Marko Milosavljević "Propad neke ideje" ("The failure of an idea"). *Delo, Sobotna priloga*, 14. December 2002.

79 Vid Libnik. "Prihaja nova medijska hiša s podporo stranke SDS" ("A new media house with the support of SDS is being created"). 30 May 2015. See http://www.siol.net/novice/slovenija/2015/05/nova_medijska_hisa_sds.aspx (Accessed 5 June 2015).

right-wing daily newspaper *Slovenec* existed for several years but was forced to close down. It was established by right-wing Christian Democrat and then-prime minister Lojze Peterle who was also the president of Christian Democratic Party; he even provided the newspaper with state funds for its establishment, on the argument that this was needed for the pluralization of post-socialistic media environment in Slovenia. The newspaper's image was not a very positive one, due to internal political disagreements that spilled over into an open conflict, publicly expressed opinions of some journalists who worked for *Slovenec* that the newspaper should engage more in political affairs and party politics, giving priority to political factors over professional criteria when appointing top executives, absence of interest and economic nonchalance of its owners.[18] The publisher of the daily ended up with a huge financial debt.

The independence of the media in Slovenia has been further threatened or diminished in the last years by the economic crisis. It has led to cuts in the budgets of most media, the decrease of the number of journalists, and greater dependence by the media on the remaining advertisers, thus increasing the influence of these advertisers on content and editorial policy in general. Furthermore, diversity of news media and news media content has been endangered by the economic crisis due to the media's attempts to increase revenues by offering content that appeals to the broadest possible audience. This has particularly occurred with online media and even the electronic versions of traditional media (for example, print) attempt to increase the number of visitors by including more commercially attractive content, particularly entertainment, celebrities, scandals, and bizarre content, much like the practices in a number of media in Western Europe, for example. The diversity of news media is also being threatened by the increasing concentration of the Slovenian media market, where most of the actors are linked to one another in one or another area, but mostly through ownership, shared projects, and endeavors to find synergies.

For most of the media in Slovenia (and the South-East European region), the promises of a new era of market dominance and a market-based economy that followed the democratic changes in late 1980s, early 1990s and that were supposed to overthrow the previous political paternalistic model of financing the media in the 1980s and earlier have remained unfulfilled. The economic crisis on one hand and the digital disruption on the other have shown the fragility of media market in Slovenia as well as in the wider region, and emphasized the important role of the state and state interventions.

When looking at the market characteristics and potential of a particular market, we usually analyze a number of factors -- the size of the national market; GDP; the advertising market and shares and trends within specific segments, such as TV, digital, print; size/reach of the national language and emigration; equipment in terms of high-speed internet penetration and other infrastructure aspects that influence consumption patterns and potential. Unfortunately, in all of these aspects Slovenia – as well as other countries in South-East Europe which were not included in any of the categories by Hallin & Mancini – does not show much potential. Although the term "Balkanization" has a historical and political dimension, in the case of the media it provides the exact definition of the key issue in the region -- small fragmented markets that do not offer the conditions for economically strong and viable media that could use the advantages of, for example, economies of scale, and enable media companies to offer high-quality products.

Digitisation, fragmentation and pauperisation

New technological developments offer even more reasons for concern. Digitisation of media has led to an abundance of choice and media channels in many countries, and causes problems even in markets that are stronger in terms of GDP and in terms of population. This fragmentation of the media landscape is, however, even more devastating for smaller countries – in Finland for example, "the restricted size of the market makes it more difficult to introduce fresh products to the market".[80] The problem is even greater in smaller countries with weak GDPs, and Slovenia as well as all other countries in SEE can be defined as such.[81] Specifically, in all of these countries, the size of the market presented the main obstacle for media development and specialization even in the previous decades, when only a handful of media were present and when there were no digital media. Now, the fragmented landscape is presenting further obstacles for the development and survival of new businesses in media.

Warnings about the limited market potential of Slovenia (and other such small markets) were already expressed at the beginning of the digitization. "Digitization will lower certain broadcasting costs, but this doesn't mean that there will suddenly be 200 channels in Slovenia, as there are in Britain or France or Germany". And: "There will never be 200 or more channels that will

80 Katja Lehtisaari, Kari Karppinen, Timo Harjuniemi, Mikko Grönlund, Carl-Gustav Lindén, Hannu Nieminen, and Anna Viljakainen, *Media Convergence and Business Models: Responses of Finnish Daily Newspapers* (Helsinki: Communication Research Centre CRC, Department of Social Research, University of Helsinki. 2012), p. 46.

81 Apart from weak GDP, most of the countries in the region have relatively low economic/purchasing power – defined by Eurostat as GDP per capita in Purchasing Power Parities (PPPs) – and have evidenced a decrease of investments in the last five years.

cover all the niche audiences."[82] Today, there are approximately 200 channels in the Slovenian language, but the regular package of cable providers include between 120 and 180 channels and among those, there are 45 Slovenian channels and 40 channels with Slovenian subtitles (and mostly also with Slovenian advertising).[83]

An additional issue for Slovenia and all of the countries in the region is the small circulation of media in the national languages (in the absence of an international market for Slovenian-language media), hampering the economic potential of local media enterprises. Unlike other small European countries such as Austria or Ireland, for Slovenia and most of the countries in the region there is no other space where editorial products may be exported – except, in some cases, in the (economically weak) region. Although figures regarding the penetration of newspapers and magazines, for example, show these are in Slovenia frequently higher than in many other well-performing European countries, the total number (circulation) is much smaller here, ultimately posing a big challenge for media companies. This fragmentation is also causing concern for advertisers: "The market is so small that the economy of scope simply does not function… In the era of mass media, for example television, this was still possible. It is true that the reach was small, but purchases of media and production facilities were cheap as well. With everything that is brought by the modern communication this is sadly not the case."

Technological development enabled the multiplication of media channels (radio, television, online); however, economic development could not follow the pace of this fragmentation. Once the economic crisis came along, it further endangered the survival of new media outlets: revenue from advertising (which represents the majority of broadcasting and online revenue) has decreased while the number of channels has increased. This means that larger number of actors must share smaller income, leading to pauperisation of an already increasingly fragmented market. New channels therefore often developed not because of the market potential but in order to prevent the development of new competition and/or to simply re-use the existing content in an attempt to raise as much revenue from as little investment as possible. The increase of the number of channels thus does not mean also an increase in the quality of the content or even the diversity of this content.

---

82 Marko Milosavljevič, Marko and Sandra Bašić-Hrvatin, "Who will control the controllers?", in Tim Lees, Sue Ralph, and Jo Langham Brown (eds.), *Is regulation still an option in a digital universe?*, (current debates in broadcasting, no. 9) (Luton: University of Luton Press, 2000,) pp. 253-257. Milosavljević and Hrvatin, 2000: 254 and 258)

83 See for example Telemach: http://www.telemach.si/sl/zasebni-uporabniki/paketna-ponudba/paketi-gold-trojka/gold-extra-trojka.

This was also one of the main reasons for the failure of the pay television project by the TV company Pro Plus in Slovenia. The company that owns the two most popular commercial channels – Pop TV and Kanal A – launched a pay TV service Pop Non Stop in September 2011. The service included six channels: Kino and Kino 2 (movie channels), Fani (sit-com channel), Brio (women-oriented channel), Oto (kids channel) and Spot (music channel), all offered through cable providers. However, the company in March 2013 decided to close down the project due to lack of success. The programming of the channels was mostly composed of the repeats of the content already purchased and broadcasted on Pop TV and Kanal A, as an attempt to use also less-attractive content, purchased in packages from studios, that did not fit in the schedule of Pop TV and Kanal A. The lack of the original and prime content was perceived as one of the main reasons for the service failure. (However, Channels Kino, Brio and Oto continue to be offered in packages of cable operators from April 2013.)

In general, Slovenian media began attempting to find new sources of funding and new, better business models. These include paid-for content online (e.g., Piano and Voyo) and in broadcasting (e.g., POP NON STOP at POP TV), and new promotional packages, tying newspapers to new media, particularly mobile operators and tablets (*Dnevnik* with Si.Mobil in autumn 2010, Finance and Mobitel/Telekom Slovenia in March 2011, both of them in connection with an included or discounted tablet – Samsung Galaxy with the former, Apple's iPad with the latter). However, none of these attempts has brought visible results or proven to be successful, further increasing the dependence of the media on existing sources.

Indeed, there has not appeared or been developed a new source of revenue that would prove to be either successful or sustainable in terms of continuous and steady income that would bring adequate financial results to fund news production and improve the financial sustainability of the Slovenian news media. The financial resources that proved to be most helpful or sustainable were subscriptions for newspapers. In 2011, major newspaper publishers (including *Delo, Dnevnik*, and *Večer*, as well as web-only *Pozareport*) established a combined pay-wall model in cooperation with the Slovak company Piano Media. However the plans remained unfulfilled by 2015, as it became clear that there is a lack of interest for such model among users/readers, and many news companies now introduce their own paywalls or digital subscriptions either in addition to Piano or instead of it. In general, services such as Piano, or Voyo in the case of pay-tv, show that the Slovenian media increasingly focus on paid-for content and subscription models, diversifying their revenue streams, and increasingly taking into account the end users (instead of advertisers) for their financial sources and income.

Low level of internet penetration and the growth of mobile media

Another important issue is the level of internet penetration, users' habits and spending habits related to that. In most of the countries in Central and Southeast European (CSEE) region, internet penetration remains low compared to the EU average, and that includes countries that are EU members, including Slovenia. It is very often concentrated in larger urban areas. Better educated populations, living in cities and with greater spending power, are of course more interesting for advertisers, service providers or producers of different media-related products. However, in Slovenia (and most of the other CSEE countries) where we have already noted the smallness of the markets, this means that already small markets become even smaller and more fragmented, and thus less relevant and less interesting for service providers, advertisers, media companies and media producers.

The fragmentation of the already small national market due to demographic characteristics which cause the digital divide thus has serious economic consequences for the potential development of new services and products or for the potential survival of legacy media and services. The development of better internet-related infrastructure would, therefore, be not just in the interest of potential new media service providers or producers but also in the interest of the country as such. Thus, only with good Internet penetration including fast connections is Slovenia potentially interesting for investors in the field of new media, since only with excellent Internet penetration will it be able to offer a potentially attractive market for these new media services. With the rise of smartphones, mobile media are a key area of growth for news outlets. Mobile access to the internet is opening a new demographic of users and spreading the potential market. At the same time, lack of an economy of scale is seen also in the mobile market. Consequently, media publishers need to work hard at developing the UX and UI (User experience and User Interface) of their mobile offerings. Nevertheless, this is possible (economically viable) only in markets that offer enough potential – small markets again face problems as they lack the potential for the economy of scale, needed for the development of particular UX and UI or apps. This is already an issue in economically much stronger countries such as Finland. "As a small market and a small linguistic area, Finland also places its own restrictions when it comes to pioneering applications and ideas. (…) The small linguistic area means that innovations do not have the same user potential as they would get in a larger area."[84] The patterns of media consumption will of course develop and change with the proliferation

84 Lehtisaari et al,, *Media Convergence and Business Models,* p. 46.

of new platforms, devices and technologies; however certain patterns and habits will change over time, over the following years, and not overnight. Also, as seen above, personal computers and/or tablets influences the way people use the internet and the way they use the full potential of its offers and services – something that is (still) severely limited when using mobile internet, thus limiting also the economic potential of mobile internet in terms of services. The complementary role of broadband and mobile internet, personal computers and/or tablets and mobile phones is thus needed to reach the full technological and market potential of new media services.

The role of politics and the state within a limited market

Various investigations have in the past shown that market-based media financing is sustainable only in larger countries[85] and even countries with strong GDP, with positive trends in advertising revenue, and with technologically advanced infrastructure face important market limitations of small populations and language barriers with skepticism and concern.[86] In Slovenia and other countries in the CSEE region where most of the factors listed at the beginning of this chapter severely limit the economic potential of (new) media projects and entrepreneurship, it seems that a market-based model of media is even less sustainable. It is largely sustainable in catch-all media such as general television channels with national reach, strong investments, and stable ownership (for example Pop TV in Slovenia). However these same media are also blamed and attacked as »the biggest evil in the Slovenian media market«,[87] mostly because of their market power. Television is very strong in Slovenia in terms of its share of all advertising income. In particular, Pro Plus – as the parent company that broadcasts the channels POP TV and Kanal A, the pay-television package of six channels Pop Plus, the online VOD package Voyo, and a number of the most-popular Slovenian websites (including the most popular site, 24ur.com, and others such as Zadovoljna.si, Cekin.si, and Moskisvet.si) – is the strongest company in Slovenia in terms of advertising revenue. Its power in the Slovenian advertising market allows (otherwise rare) economies of scale which concentrates its power and influence on the market

85 See, for example, Ralph L. Lowenstein and John C. Merrill, *Macromedia: Mission, Message, and Morality* (New York: Longman, 1990).
Lowenstein and Merrill, 1990)

86 See Lehtisaari, et al,, *Media Convergence and Business Models*.

87 , Jože Biščak , "Zakaj je POP TV največje zlo na medijskem trgu" , (21 June 2015), at. http://www.reporter.si/iz-tiskane-izdaje/zakaj-je-pop-tv-najve%C4%8Dje-zlo-na-medijskem-trgu/53269. (Accessed on 22 June 2015)

even more, and leaves other media with even less advertising revenue (compared to its ratings in terms of broadcasting or reach in terms of print). This power was among the reasons given for the decision of Modern Times Group to abandon its Slovenian plans with its company Prva TV and its channel TV3 in January 2012 and to close down the company and channel completely.[88]

Most of the other media, including previously very profitable major newspapers (such as *Delo* and *Dnevnik*), have in the last few years seen dramatic falls in circulation and profitability. And web-only sites that are not connected to any legacy media have so far not reached the kind of adequate revenue that would provide them with stabile financial environment. It seems, therefore, that market-only media will have an increasingly difficult time in the coming years to maintain their level of production and employment. They will need financial support, be it private or public.

As far as the support coming from the private sector is concerned, in Slovenia as well as elsewhere in Central and Southeastern Europe this is still very scarce. Regional millionaires are often not willing to invest in the media, as they are not aware of the public interest, or – if they are aware of the importance and influence of the media – they see and use the media and their ownership as a tool to pursue personal business interest and/or to help personal political friends and alliances. Philanthropic investments in the media as a part of public responsibility of the richest part of the society – that is frequently seen in Western Europe or the U.S. – is not noticed in the region. On the other hand, foreign donors are not interested in the region as some parts (including Slovenia) have already joined the EU, and others are either in the process of accession, or are seen as less relevant and urgent than some other parts of Eastern Europe or the rest of the world. Foreign donors are largely shifting their help from Central and Southeastern Europe to the Middle East (ME) or other areas (such as South Sudan). At the same time, the region is not seen as adequately influential or prestigious to be relevant for, for example, Russian, Indian or Chinese billionaires who sometimes invest in media to enhance their public role and strengthen their social position, but in other, more 'prestigious' countries, such as the United Kingdom.

At the same time, there is also no strong push to develop alternative models of financing, such as foundations or consortiums founded by workers. A specific, small-scale example of such a consortium emerged in Slovenia when a free daily newspaper Žurnal24 folded in May 2014. After years of losses, the Austrian owner Styria decided to close down all its editions: daily, weekly and

88 Brankica Petkovič, "Prostora je za štiri komercialne televizije", *Dnevnik*,(10 January 2012.), at http://www.dnevnik.si/novice/aktualne_zgodbe/1042501068 (accessed 11 January 2012).

website. However, after a few months a group of former employees and contributors decided to try again, this time only with a website, and has – with permission from Styria – revived the Žurnal24 website. They are now attempting to maintain enough web traffic to attract sufficient advertising revenue for their survival. Nonetheless, this is a rare example of such an endeavour. Again, the situation in the region is not entirely specific compared to, for example, Western Europe, as in many countries new models of financing are only slowly starting to take-off or to develop, without long-term results that would prove stability of such models. Again, there are similarities in smaller countries, particularly in the Nordic countries; in Finland for example many local experts and professionals "do not seem to believe that foundations could be a vital model for financing Finnish journalism, since they do not think that Finnish foundations could secure the basics of independent journalism."[89]

On the other hand, some optimism remains and new projects (still) start even in the midst of increasing financial crisis and uncertainties. A recent example of such an effort involving new technology is Tor5 or "Torek ob petih", another project by former staff of Žurnal involving some other journalists and bloggers; it defines itself as "first mobile magazine". It started in November 2014, so its future and success remains at the time of writing unpredictable. Nevertheless, it is a – good – sign of applying new a digital reality to old journalistic models and accepting (and adapting to) new users' habits (where mobile takes more and more time and attention – and advertising income).

In general, however, for most of the media in Slovenia and the region, the promises of new era of market dominance and a market-based economy that would overthrow the previous political paternalistic model of financing the media in 1980s and earlier have remained unfulfilled. The economic crisis on one hand and the digital disruption on the other have shown the fragility of media market in SEE, and emphasized the important role of the state and state interventionism as only possible solution for maintaining a relatively diverse media. The return of the state, however, also severely limits the potential of the media in the region to become at least approximately independent in terms of political pressure and political influence. State interventions and help will probably help to maintain a larger number of media companies in each of the countries – but this does not mean that this will help to maintain the independence, plurality and diversity of views and content in those media that will survive. We are thus facing a new model of relations between media and politics, where a combination market limitations, new technologies and economic crisis severely limits the sustainability of media companies and leads to an increasingly impor-

89 Lehtisaari, et al,, *Media Convergence and Business Models,* p. 51.

tant role of the state and the state politics. Twenty-five years after the key democratic changes and the beginning of the transitions in the media system in Slovenia, but also in other countries in the region, which were shaped as "the policy of deregulation, privatization, and commercialization of the media",[90] we are again facing the limitations of the market model. In this regard, the important role of (party) politics in sustaining media environment remains relevant in a similar way as it was in Slovenia more than 130 years ago.

90 Sandra Bašić-Hrvatin and Marko Milosavljevič. *Medijska politika v Sloveniji v devetdesetih. Regulacija, privatizacija, koncentracija in komercializacija medijev. - Media Policy in Slovenia in the 1990s. Regulation, privatization, concentration and commercialization of the media* (Ljubljana: Mirovni inštitut, 2001).

Ola Svein Stugu and Peter Vodopivec

5 Narratives of the Nation History Textbooks and National Identities in Norway and Slovenia

In modernizing societies, the establishment of compulsory education systems serves several functions, one of the fundamental ones being socializing the students into officially acknowledged norms and values.[1] Because of this function, education has become one of the main integrative mechanisms in modern states, contributing substantially to the building of collective identities. In these processes, general subjects like history, literature and geography play a fundamental role. Narratives and explanations of the past have been shown to be effective tools for constructing identities, independently of whether the tales and thoughts stand the test of critical, scholarly research or not. Identifying with a past "us" against some "other", showing past grandeurs and wrongdoings against the "us" group, singling out heroes and villains, contributes to producing a sense of necessity to unite against real or perceived enemies and by this also motivates for action on behalf of the "us" group.

This function of history makes itself felt in any setting where tales of the past are being told, including schools. Credible history teaching nevertheless has to balance a value based, partisan content against a wish not to step outside the minimum requirements of scholarly history. In modern democratic societies, the teaching of history generally tries to distance itself from the biased, partisan narratives of earlier times, maintaining that history teaching of today rests upon sound and critical scholarly principles. However, even today's history education strives to find a fruitful balance between pledges to scholarly principles and the identity making functions of the subject.

The ways to meet these challenges differ between countries. A comparative investigation therefore is a fruitful way to find out not only the particularities of each country's approach to its past, but also similarities between approaches. In this way, it may also be possible to discuss history's role in identity making processes more generally, making corrections for national characteristics.

To study the identity-making narratives and processes more closely, school textbooks, above all readers and history textbooks, are well suited sources. As Rainer Ohliger has stated, "Textbooks … not only mirror the national culture of

1 The author of the introduction and conclusion of this chapter is Ola Svein Stugu.

education, but are also an essential and complex instrument for building, constructing and reproducing it."[2] Generally, textbooks are supposed to convey factual and useful knowledge of their subjects. In history this means that their narratives are based on an ideal of telling history "as it actually was"[3]. However, as a rule history textbooks do not only tell narratives about the past as such, but are also instrumental in constructing collective memories. In some societies, particularly in times of totalitarian regimes, instrumental purposes even override the pledges to factuality in ways that make the textbooks deteriorate to sheer propaganda. In open, democratic regimes a manipulative instrumentalism will have to be openly discussed against narratives that are grounded in scholarly historical research.

This, however, does not mean that a sharp, definite line can be drawn between textbook narratives based on scholarship and instrumental ones. In any society, education rests upon some kind of value-based mandate, which is more or less overtly stated in education laws, plans and curricula, and even in democratic societies it may be observed that the choice of narratives to be emphasized, tuned down or hidden in certain cases are just as well being affected by considerations of the norms to be taught as by scholarly considerations. In short, even in societies where education ideally builds upon scholarly principles, history textbooks present what may be called officially sanctioned pictures of the past, grounded in more or less explicitly stated values.

Because history textbooks become more or less overt expressions of a country's approved narrative of the past, they also become good sources to study officially sanctioned values and world views at the times when they were produced. School textbooks so to say by default express some kind of hegemonic narratives and interpretations, reflecting attitudes, mentalities and perspectives that are part of a society's official self-conception at a given time. Therefore, it also becomes fruitful to ask which kinds of narratives have been acceptable at one or another time and under a given political regime and which narratives stay hidden and are even forbidden.

Historical narratives become relevant to present day societies not primarily because of what they tell about the past itself, but because the past which they recount is always in some ways related to the present. Doing history is not only an effort to make sense of the past, but it also represents the present's perspective on what is important to remember about the past as well as what ought to be forgotten. This implies that narratives about the past also to a certain extent

---

2 Rainer Ohliger: Representing the National Other: Textbooks and the formation of ethno-national identity in Germany 1871-1945. *Internationale Schulbuchforschung* 21 (1999) pp. 103-124.

3 Cfr. Leopold von Ranke: "Wie es eigentlich gewesen", *Sämtliche Werke* Bd. 33/34, Leipzig 1885, p. 7.

reflect contemporary problems, values and attitudes, and function as more or less deliberate efforts to make sense of the present.

If the official narratives differ too openly from what is being remembered and re-told in people's everyday lives and in cases when openly contesting narratives exist within a society, the impact of the official versions will be limited. In late modern commercialized societies, media narratives may also represent serious challenges to the official ones that are being told in schools. However, when there are no openly challenging narratives, the versions of history that are to be found in textbooks have a good chance to become formative of a society's view of its own past.

The most direct encounters between the norms and values of the official school system and pupils' everyday lives take place in the classroom, but historically it is almost impossible to reconstruct oral education and encounters in the ways they were actually performed. Only selected and edited parts of these everyday situations may be reconstructed through memories that have been recorded much later. Written texts are much more easily preserved as direct sources of the period when they were produced.

As stated, textbooks have to strike a balance between adherence to scholarly based knowledge and methods and the value mandate of the educational system. These considerations obviously become much easier to reconcile where scholarly values have become parts of the explicit value system. In Norway, the current core curriculum, which was introduced in 1993, openly endorses scholarly values in several ways, e.g. under the headline "Scientific Method and the Active Pupil", where one passage reads: "Education must find [the] difficult balance between respect for established knowledge and the critical attitude that is necessary for developing new learning and for organizing information in new ways."[4]

When studying history education, it is important not to draw a too definite line between a value-based school history and scholarly history as taught and researched at universities. A basic feature of academic history research is its ability, on the basis of agreed research methods, to legitimate or dismiss certain versions of the past. Nevertheless, one of academic history's most important functions throughout the last two hundred years has been to deliver background arguments for and to legitimate certain projects of identity construction, above all of national identities. It is no coincidence that the breakthrough of professional history runs parallel to a process of strengthening and deepening national identities all over Europe. According to one of the world's leading historiogra-

4 *Core Curriculum for primary, secondary and adult education in Norway*, The Royal Ministry of Education, Research and Church Affairs, p. 15. PDF version to be found at http://www.udir.no/Upload/larerplaner/generell_del/5/Core_Curriculum_English.pdf?epslanguage=no.

phers, George Iggers, "… the new historical profession served definite public needs and political aims that made it important to communicate the results of its research to a public whose historical consciousness it sought to shape and who turned to the historians in search of their own historical identity."[5]

Methods for textbook analysis

Systematic scrutiny of history textbooks has been going on since the interwar period when the League of Nations promoted textbook revisions as a means to reduce mutual distrust and hostility. In Scandinavia, the Norden Association started investigating how the earlier arch-enemies Sweden and Denmark were described in the textbooks of the respective nations. After World War Two, UNESCO started promoting similar activities aiming at investigating and reforming stereotyped and prejudiced nationalist versions of history among former European enemies, first of all between France and West Germany, but also between West Germany and Germany's eastern neighbours.[6] A host of different methods for text analysis were employed in the studies, mostly of an eclectic character, adjusted to the particular research questions to be answered.

Only lately more systematic methods of discourse analysis have been employed also in textbook research, not least methods which stress the connections between texts and power relations which influence the production of the texts.[7] These methods have been refined in ways that are more directly applicable for historical purposes, e.g., by Ruth Wodak and a group of collaborators, for the first time in a project analysing Austrian national identity, later on in more general terms. [8]

The methods have to be applied somewhat differently to different research contexts, and whereas discourse analytic approaches seem to be of particular values in analysing the micro levels of a text, one also has to have an eye to the text's macro level and the plots and perspectives to be found there. A number of

---

5 G. Iggers 1997: *Historiography in the Twentieth Century*. Wesleyan University Press, 1997, p. 23.

6 The Georg-Eckert Institut für Internationale Schulbuchforsching in Braunschweig, Germany, has become a hub of the activities, cfr. http://www.gei.de/fileadmin/bilder/pdf/Institut/gei-past-present-future.pdf (seen 2012/11/25)

7 E.g., N. Fairclough: Analysing discourse; textual analysis for social research. Routledge 2003.

8 R. Wodak, R. de Cilia, M. Reisigl, K. Liebhart: *The Discursive Construction of National Identity*, Edinburgh University Press 1999. R. Wodak and M. Meyer: *Methods of Critical Discourse Analysis*, second ed. Sage Publications 2009, in particular M. Reisigl and R. Wodak: The discourse-historical approach, pp. 87-121. For a more particular historical discourse analysis, see A. Landwehr: *Historische Diskursanalyse*. Campus Verlag Frankfurt/New York 2008.

general questions nevertheless seem to be fruitful to take into consideration in different contexts. Among them are: Which persons and groups are included in an "us" as opposed to "the others"? On which basis are peoples and groups being included or excluded? Who personify the "us" group? Which properties do "we" possess – as opposed to "the others", and what motivates "us" for action? Who are the heroes and the villains of the texts? Which properties are being ascribed to them? What does the text say about possible divisions and conflicts within the "us"-group? Which types of historical actors and events are being highlighted in the text, which groups and events become more or less invisible? What kinds of continuous, timeless features are being ascribed to different groups? How is history being divided into periods? Are there periods and agents that are being seen as particularly glorious and heroic?

Longitudinal studies of textbooks usually reveal substantial changes in their ways of dealing with the past. Explanations for the changes may differ, but are very often to be found in one of the following categories: Changes in a nation's international status, such as the establishment of an independent Slovenia in 1991; fundamental regime changes, such as in Yugoslavia in 1945 or in South Africa in the period from 1990 to 1994; changes in scholarly interests and interpretations, exemplified by a gradually growing emphasis on economic and social history and by the shifting conjunctures of Marxist theories of history; changes in educational ideas, not at least the introduction of ideas of reform pedagogy and working school ideas from the inter-war period on.

The Norwegian history narrative

Since the year of revolutionary events of 1814, when Norway not only was founded as a modern state but also got a constitution that is still in force, changes in the country's external situation have been relatively small and gradual. This means that changes in the country's history textbooks in the main have to be explained either by scholarly or by pedagogic changes and developments. [9]

During the two centuries since 1814 two successive grand, national narratives of Norwegian history may be discerned. These two narratives have also made their mark on the textbooks of their time. The first one was retrospective

9 The most important source for this chapter is S. Lorentzen: *Ja vi elsker ...; skolebøkene som nasjonsbyggere 1814-2000* (Textbooks as nation builders), Abstrakt forlag, Oslo, 2005. The first sentence of the book's title refers to the opening line of the national anthem: Yes – we love this country.

with a clear nationalist flavour, looking back on the Viking age and the times of the medieval Norwegian kingdom as a golden age in the nation's history. The second one was progressive, highlighting the national achievements in a modern age.

The retrospective narrative was developed during the 19th Century, and by the time Norway exited its Union with Sweden in 1905 it was the uncontested narrative of the nation. As such, it was also reproduced in the history textbooks of the period. It may be summarised briefly as follows: The most heroic period of Norwegian history was the Viking age, when the Vikings made their power felt in large parts of Western Europe and sailed far afield, even reaching North America. This was also the period when the country was united and christened. The medieval kingdom grew gradually and after some decades of civil war around 1200, it peaked in the 13th Century, when the Norwegian king ruled most of the Northern Atlantic. Then followed a period of decay and loss of independence, until a long period of internal growth resulted in a resurrection and a new dawn in 1814. That year the Norwegians took their fortune in their own hands to become equal partners of the Swedes inside a loose union instead of being subjugated, as Sweden and Denmark had agreed, and the big powers had endorsed.

For the rest of the century, Norway continued defending its liberty, while at the same time becoming a modern country on equal footing with the most advanced parts of Europe. This was not only a period of growth, but also of democratisation which reached an important breakthrough in 1884 when parliamentarism was introduced and culminated in the split-up of the union with Sweden in 1905. The national heroes to be found in the textbooks during the 19th Century were above all the Viking warriors and medieval kings, but during the interwar period they were gradually supplanted and partly substituted by famous artists such as the author Henrik Ibsen and the composer Edvard Grieg and explorers such as Fridtjof Nansen, who was also a scientist and diplomat, and Roald Amundsen, the famous Antarctic explorer; all of these personalities were recognized names outside Norway. This change signalled the advent of a new narrative, turning away from ancient warrior heroes towards modern champions of culture and peaceful competition. This was a liberal democratic narrative, a kind of Norwegian Whig narrative, where farmers were assigned an important role as a progressive force in democratizing society.

Within this long period, substantial changes took place not only in Norwegian society at large, but also in its educational system. As a whole, the construction of a national Norwegian culture in the 19th century may be seen as a process of defining, refining and recirculating elements of local popular cultures within a nationally authorised and state guaranteed institutional framework, where schools played a crucial part. In 1860, a new Common Education law was introduced. For education to function as an integrative mechanism, school had to be universal, and the 1860 law was a crucial step in that direction. Some rudimentary education existed even before that time, but it was mainly directed towards teaching the knowledge and virtues necessary to live a good Christian life. In the new law, however, secular ideas of enlightenment and useful knowledge for everyday life are easily discernible. On the other hand, there was surprisingly little mention of national values and identities during the reform process, for instance in the preparatory documents of the education acts. This should not be seen as a sign that ideas of national unity and integration were unknown or irrelevant to the educators. It means rather that other aims and ideas were more imminent at the time.

The period that followed was an era of rapid economic modernisation and profound political changes towards a functioning democracy, but also of a definite breakthrough of the grand national identity-making narrative. The ideological connections are clear between the efforts to lift the population into modernity and democratic participation by help of compulsory education, and a stronger outward assertiveness, which was not at least expressed by a more outspoken nationalism in the textbooks. The ideas of Norwegianness conveyed through schools were to a large degree harmonised with ideas of democratic participation and of egalitarian ideals. It is important to note that Norwegian nationalism of the period was in the main not associated with right-wing upper classes, but with left-wing proponents of a popular national democracy.

In 1889, new school reforms followed, introducing the so-called “folkeskole”, the People’s School. The school historian Hans Jørgen Dokka sums up the intentions of the 1889 reforms like this: “The new school should influence the social structure, it should lay the groundwork for a real democracy, it should promote material growth, and it should strengthen national culture and national consciousness.”[10] History education had gradually gained ground in schools also before 1889, but only then did it become a compulsory subject in its own right.

This also introduced a new era in history textbook production. As an instrument to disperse and secure the position of the retrospective nationalist narrative, however, literature readers, which also contained engaging narratives of past times, probably played a more important part than history textbooks, which by comparison were drier and less engaging. The first general reader in Norwegian schools was P. A. Jensen’s Lesebok from 1863. However, the most widely used Norwegian reader right from the time it was published in 1892 until the time of the broad educational reforms of 1960 was the one edited by the liberal author and educator Nordahl Rolfsen. It very soon conquered the bulk of the

10 H.J. Dokka: *Fra allmueskole til folkeskole.* Oslo: Universitetsforlaget 1967, p. 409.

national market, and became a common textual reference for Norwegians of three generations.[11]

The cover drawing of the first edition shows a genuine Norwegian troll, drawn by Theodor Kittelsen, renowned illustrator of Peter Christian Asbjørnsen and Jørgen Moe's collections of Norwegian fairy tales. If this can be seen as a token of the development in Norwegian education, it shows not only that other identity markers than Christian ones had become legitimate in schools, but that they had even conquered a central position as national symbols. Nevertheless the text as a whole signals a belief in modernization as the heart and core of national liberty.[12]

The textbook's significant others or "them" during that time seemed to alternate between Sweden and Denmark, according to situation and context. During the period until 1905, when the personal union between Sweden and Norway was dissolved, there was a marked restraint in the textbooks in portraying the Swedes as the Other. However, the textbooks nonetheless included historical examples of heroes in earlier wars against Sweden.[13] Opposed to this, Denmark is seldom the villain of Norwegian history, although Danish officials – not at least the feared bailiffs, who were responsible for taxation and enforcement of law and order – are sometimes depicted as cruel and evil against Norwegian farmers. By contrast, language history has positioned itself in opposition to Danish culture and language, which became the written idiom also in Norway during the centuries of Danish rule until 1814. This is in accordance with the well-established conclusion that Norwegian nation-building was directed politically against Sweden, culturally against Denmark.

The so to say ideal typical textbook of the period shortly after the breakup of the union, is Jens Hæreid: *Norges historie fortalt for skole og hjem* (Norwegian History narrated for School and Home), which was first published in 1909. The book was marked by an all-pervasive patriotic narrative, not at least directed against Sweden, and in the decades to follow it became the most widely used textbook in Norwegian primary schools, with half a million copies sold by 1935. Its popularity not only is connected to the character of its narrative, which was well in tune with common nationalist attitudes at the time, but may not at least be explained by its lively, engaging style of writing. In the foreword to the first edition, the author stated: "The history of the fatherland

---

11 E.B. Johnsen: Nordahl Rolfsens lesebok. *Prosa* 4 (1999).

12 O. Stugu: Educational Ideals and Nation Building in Norway 1840-1900, in S. Ahonen & J. Rantala (ed): *Nordic Lights. Education for Nation and Civic Society in the Nordic Countries, 1850 – 2000*, Studia Fennica Historica 1, Helsinki 2001 pp. 107-122.

13 Tordenskiold and Anna Colbjørnsdatter in the Great Nordic War, captain Dreyer in the 1807 war.

should be told in a clear and easy way for the children. They must see and follow their people in growth and progress through the ages: feel, think, and live with the people in their everyday life, in war and peace, in dark and good times."[14]

Despite Hæreid's popularity and a hegemonic nationalist narrative, new educational ideas also found their way into history education during the interwar period, and in progressive pedagogic circles the nationalist narratives were increasingly considered antiquated and ripe for replacement by a more internationalist, peace-promoting narrative. This period thus has to be seen as the formative years of a new grand national narrative, the progressive one, which may be partly tied to progressive liberal forces, but above all to the Labour movement, which had its definitive breakthrough when the Labour party formed a stable government in 1935. In schools, everyday practice nevertheless lagged behind those signals, partly because a large proportion of the teachers had their formative years in the period before and even had received their own education under the old paradigm, but also because the economic situation of the municipalities rarely allowed for introducing new textbooks so long as the old ones might be re-used for new students.

The German occupation during World War Two seems to have provoked a reinforcement of the national patriotic narrative, stressing national independence and liberal democracy as core values and reinforcing the post-war narrative of a united people who stood their ground, with the exception of a small minority who became collaborators.[15] At this stage, however, the national narrative had to be reconciled with the new, progressive grand narrative, telling a history of society's growth towards higher prosperity, welfare and security, a development which only was secured by an active, social democratic state with the Labour Party as its main support. Historical analysis of the post-war Norwegian political regime has often made use of expressions such as "the Labour Party State" or "the Golden age of Social Democracy" to characterize the system, signalling not only the hegemonic position of the Labour Party, but also an era when social democratic ideas and principles were dominant all across the political spectrum of the nation.[16]

History textbooks were increasingly tuned into this reformed master narrative, with an increasing emphasis not only on the struggle for democratic rights,

---

14 J. Hæreid: *Norges historie fortalt for skole og hjem*, first edition, Kristiania 1909, p. 7

15 E.g. B. Stokke: *Folket vårt gjennom tidene*, 5. oppl. Cappelen, Oslo 1954, pp. 226-234.

16 Cfr. B. Furre: *Vårt hundreår*, Samlaget, Oslo 1991, R. Slagstad: *De nasjonale strateger*, Pax, Oslo 1998, F. Sejersted: *Sosialdemokratiets tidsalder,* Pax, Oslo, 2005, O. Stugu: *Norsk historie etter 1905*, Samlaget, Oslo 2012. The expression "Golden Age of Social Democracy" was coined by Sejersted.

but also on the struggle for equality and social justice. As a part of the change, the working class and the Labour movement became increasingly visible as important historical actors. The individual heroes of the textbooks in this period nevertheless continued to be men like Nansen, Ibsen, Bjornson and Grieg. No women found their way into this national hall of fame.

The narrative of growth and progress seems to have reached an apex around 1970, but it also left its mark on later textbooks. Summing up the treatment of the period between 1814 and 1905 in one of the most popular books in the period around 1990, Svein Lorentzen describes it as a narrative of fundamental changes in the conditions of life, closely tied to Norway's transition from a mainly agrarian society to a society of industry, shipping and trade, while the narrative of the 20th century until around 1970 is a narrative of changes from a society marked by hardships and toil to a modern society of prosperity and welfare, only broken by five years of war and occupation.[17]

In addition, a more research based, source critical paradigm has gained ground, and the latest textbook generations are marked not only by a far more critical, analytic approach, but also by open discussions of historical research methods, often applied on important or paradigmatic examples of sources. In addition, they are more clearly oriented to the world outside Norway, and to discussions of challenges to modern society such as environmental problems, gender, immigration and global inequalities. According to the national curricula, the students should no longer be taught patriotism and national identity as indisputable values, instead they should be able to discuss those and similar concepts and take a stand on different varieties of nationalism. Even select texts and illustrations in earlier textbooks were presented as sources of nationalism to be discussed.[18] According to Lorentzen, "To the extent that [present day textbooks] perform nation building, it is as agents for the National Curriculum's perspectives on a multicultural, globally oriented Norwegian society, focusing on processes and with a critical eye on the dark sides of the past and the present"[19]

The Slovene National Narrative in History Textbooks

In contrast to Norway, Slovenia became an independent state only in 1991, and Slovene political leaders and national ideologists of the 19th and 20th centuries –

17 Lorentzen 2005, p. 195. The textbook discussed is A. Sveen/S. Aastad: *Samfunn*, 1st edition, Cappelen, Oslo, 1987.

18 E. Lund: *InnBlikk*, historie 8, Oslo 1997, p. 143 ff.

19 Lorentzen 2005 p. 222.

except for rare exceptions with little influence – neither considered Slovene state independence nor attempted to mobilise the population with plans for a Slovene state. The authors of the first Slovene historiographic texts in the second half of the 19th century already wrote about early medieval Slovene independence at the time of the tribal alliance of western Slavs in the 7th century and the principality of Carantania a century later, but they also mentioned that the Slovenes did not have a more important state legal tradition, since from the enlargement of the Frankish state to the eastern Alps and the Adriatic at the end of the 8th century, they had lived in multi-ethnic (since the creation of modern nations, multinational) state formations: first in the Frankish state and in the Holy Roman Empire, then in the Habsburg Monarchy, from 1918 to 1941 in the Kingdom of Serbs, Croats and Slovenes (Kingdom of SHS) or the Kingdom of Yugoslavia, and from 1945 to 1991 in socialist Yugoslavia. The first books in the Slovene language were published at the time of the Reformation and the Slovene language and cultural movement began at the end of the 18 th century and continued in the 19th century. In 1848, the Slovene intelligentsia and students first formed a national political program demanding the unification of the territory with Slovene speaking population, which had until then been divided into various Austrian provinces, into an autonomous administrative political unit with Slovene language and Slovene administration. Effective national autonomy, which would grant Slovenes, included in a multinational federally regulated state framework, as much "home rule" as possible, was thereafter a national aim of Slovene politicians for almost one hundred and forty years – right up to the dissolution of socialist Yugoslavia in the course of 1990-91.[20]

The process of Slovene national formation and national political mobilisation of the Slovene speaking population was thus only at a start in 1848 and even in the second half of the 19 th century, took place relatively slowly, on the one hand through the cultural and political activity of the Slovene intelligentsia educated at Austrian universities, who were committed to enforcement of the Slovene language and its equality with German and Italian in official and public life and in education and, on the other, with the fast growing literacy of the population, which was illustrated by the increasing number of Slovene newspapers, magazines and books.

The first complete Zgodovina slovenskega naroda (History of the Slovene Nation) was published in 1866, and its author, a high school professor, ethnographer and writer named Janez Trdina, who described the Slovene "national" development from the settlement of the Slavs in the eastern Alps to the middle

---

20 Peter Štih, Vasko Simoniti, PeterVodopivec: *Slovene History, Society-Politics-Culture*, Ljubljana 2008, www.sistory.si

of the 19th century, laid the groundwork for the Slovene national historical narrative.[21] According to Trdina, three variously long periods were characteristic of Slovene history: the period of early medieval national freedom, lost in tragic circumstances; the centuries-long period of national subordination and fragmentation; and a period of gradual national emancipation and efforts towards national unification based on the idea of a national entity linked together by a common language and by centuries of unfavourable historical fate.

Although Trdina's history was already criticised by his contemporaries for being insufficiently "critical", its three-part scheme of the national past remained an integral part of the Slovene national historical narrative. Trdina maintained that the Slovenes were after two centuries of early medieval freedom struck by a "great misfortune" at the time of Charlemagne, when the Franks (Trdina equated them with the Germans) usurped their land. Seven hundred years of German domination followed until the third period began, when the Slovene Protestants "brought the Slovene language to writing and schools" in the 16th century. As a firm Catholic, Trdina did not favour the Lutheran reformers but he considered their literary work in the Slovene language to be an indisputable beginning of a new era in Slovene history. This era continued, as he put it, with the Slovene cultural movement in the second half of the 18th and in the 19th century. The Slovene national historical experience in Trdina's view was nevertheless rather sad and in this way too, he contributed to a durable Slovene national-historical self-stereotype. "Our race consists of only 1 500 000 souls and it is a miracle that we are still so many, having been oppressed by the Germans from the north, the Hungarians from the east, and the Italians from the south and west," he claimed. "All these nations have attacked us for centuries, and then there were also the Turks, who invaded our lands and sent our ancestors into slavery… Many nations that eventually disappeared completely had not been in such a danger as our nation".[22]

Trdina had considerably more difficulties with national heroes: among the more important personalities of Slovene history he mentioned the medieval Slavic or "Slovene" princes, the authors of the first Slovene books and the intelligentsia, especially poets and writers of the 18th and first half of the 19th century. He also "slovenicised" and proclaimed as heroes some nobles living on the territory with a Slovene population, who were not of Slovene birth but had become celebrated in battles with enemies of the Austrian rulers (Turks and Venetians). The answer to the question of national enemies was more indis-

21 J. Trdina: *Zgodovina slovenskega naroda* (History of the Slovene Nation), published by Matica slovenska, Ljubljana 1866.

22 Trdina, ibid. pp. 114-115.

putable. Among them the Germans were in first place, who predominated among the nobility and bourgeoisie on the majority of territory settled by a Slovene population and in the southeast there were also Italians and in the northeast Hungarians.

Trdina's three-part scheme of the Slovene past was already adopted by the authors of Slovene history textbooks in the last decades of the 19th century. The first Slovene history school textbooks were published in Cisleithania after the primary school reform in 1869 and were thereafter used (in addition to German and Italian textbooks) in schools with Slovene as the teaching language.[23] While German (and Italian) textbooks did not even mention Slovene history, Slovene ones contained a few short chapters about the early medieval Slovene independence, the loss of independence and conversion to Christianity in the 8th and 9th centuries and the hard life of Slovene peasant subjects under "foreign", mainly "German" landlords. Particular attention was paid to the beginnings of Slovene literature in the period of the Reformation and to the Slovene cultural movement after the end of the 18th century, while only some of the textbooks mentioned the Slovene political movement in 1848 and in the second half of the 19th century. Nationally zealous Slovene teachers at the end of the 19th and start of the 20th century, though, stressed that history lessons should encourage love not only of the (Habsburg) ruling house and (Austrian) homeland but also of the nation and national heroes; Austrian history curricula, however, did not mention individual Austrian nations; on the contrary: they only recommended caution to teachers in "nationally mixed" provinces in dealing with themes that could affect the "national feelings" of the population and specified that school must remain "completely intact" as concerns daily political and national party points of view.[24] In this light, even chapters on Slovene history in Slovene text-books until 1918 were for the most part taciturn, without individual commen-

---

23 From the 1880s on, only in Carniola were all primary schools in Slovene, except in the two German language islands in Kočevje and Bela peč and in the provincial capital Ljubljana. In the Littoral and Lower Styria Slovene-language primary schools predominated in rural areas. In lower Styrian towns the establishment of Slovene-language primary schools was opposed by German oriented middle classes, in Trieste and Gorizia by the Italian majority. The status of the Slovene language was even less established in the secondary schools (gymnasiums). In some of them subjects were studied in Slovene in lower classes and from the beginning of the 20th century some subjects were taught in Slovene also in the higher classes of four German-Slovene gymnasiums in Carniola. The first completely Slovene gymnasium in the Monarchy was a private episcopal gymnasium in Šentvid near Ljubljana, founded in 1905. The only state Slovene gymnasium in the Habsburg Monarchy was founded in 1913 in Gorizia. Štih, Simoniti, Vodopivec 2008, pp. 327-328.

24 Lehrplan und Instruktionen für den Unterricht an den Gymnasien in Österreich, Einzige, vom k.k. Ministerium für Cultus und Unterricht autorisierte Ausgabe, Wien 1900, pp.166-169.

tary or inserted national emphases, although some authors mentioned the violence of "Germanic and non-Germanic neighbours" against the Slovenes or even characterised Germans as "the worst enemies" who, after the loss of Slovene early medieval independence, tried to Germanise Slovenes by "force and trickery".[25]

After the dissolution of the Habsburg Monarchy and the establishment of the Yugoslav state in 1918, Slovene teachers' journals established that the "spirit ... of the old sick Austria, which was never a good mother to the Slovenes but a cruel stepmother..." must in the future be completely expelled from Slovene schools, and the study of history should "implant excellent Slavic thinking" in pupils, and focus on "Slav and South Slav history", and deal with the history of non-Slavic nations only insofar as this was urgently necessary for understanding Slavic and "national" history.[26] School instruction in the Slovene part of the new Yugoslav kingdom took place entirely in Slovene but curricula for the whole country were planned and adopted in Belgrade and, in accordance with them, the South Slavs were presented as a single nation, which history had tragically divided and which had been reunited into a unitary Yugoslav state in 1918. All the same, Slovene textbooks still treated Slovenes, Croats, and Serbs as individual nations in the 1920s and only in conditions of strong pressure towards state and national unification in the 1930s accepted the thesis of a single Yugoslav (South Slav) nation composed of three tribes living for many centuries within different state frameworks and under various foreign rulers.

History textbooks published in the 1920s thus paid much more attention to the history of Slavic and particularly South Slavic peoples (Serbs, Croats, and Bulgarians) than those published before 1918 but they also focused extensively on Slovene history and in its presentation, preserved the three-part scheme, which their authors only slightly extended by chapters dedicated to the Slovene national and Yugoslav movement in the second half of the 19th century and before World War One. The main Slovene national historical topics thus remained: early medieval Slovene independence, a millennium (until 1918) of German pressure and Germanisation, uprisings of the Slovene peasants against German landlords in the 15th and 16th centuries and the publication of the first Slovene books in the period of the Reformation, the short French rule in the time of the Illyrian provinces (1809-1813) and the Slovene cultural and polit-

---

25 J. Jesenko, *Občna zgodovina, Drugi del: Srednji vek* (General History, Part Two: Middle Ages), Ljubljana 1878, pp. 57-58.

26 I. Magerl, *Izbor učne snovi za zgodovinski,* (Selection of teaching bases for history study), Popotnik, pedagoški in znanstveni list, XL/1919, pp. 49-50. I. Dimnik, head of the first public municipality school for boys in Ljubljana 1919. Annual report of the First Municipal six class public school for boys, Ljubljana 1919, pp. 10-11.

ical movement in the 19th century. The textbook authors presented the first five centuries after the "loss of early medieval Slovene independence" as a particularly tragic period of Slovene history, when the territory populated by the Slovene speaking population, as they claimed, shrank by at least half due to colonisation by German speaking peasants, but they also emphasised that Germanisation of the Slovene population continued in the 19th century until as late as the dissolution of the Habsburg Monarchy. All the same, according to textbooks in the 19th century, the Slovenes did successfully develop into a fully formed nation and continued, together with their "South Slav brothers", to prepare for the establishment of the Yugoslav Kingdom, in which "after centuries of slavery" they finally "again saw national freedom".[27] In light of this, Slovene national heroes for the writers of Slovene textbooks were primarily the authors of the first Slovene books and poets (particularly the most important poet of Slovene romanticism France Prešeren) and writers who shaped Slovene literature and opened the way to public use for the Slovene language; some political leaders who had advocated linguistic and national equality and closer Slovene links with South Slavs in the period prior to World War One were also celebrated as national heroes.

The three-part scheme of Slovene history in the form "national independence" in the early Middle Ages – a thousand years of national servitude – and the period of gradual national emancipation after "the spring of nations in 1848" was also preserved by authors of textbooks published after 1945, in communist Yugoslavia. However, in these textbooks in accordance with communist ideological concepts the national emphasis gave way to social and "class-related" aspects and their authors shifted the focus from national "German-Slovene" relations towards social and class opposition (that is, relations among peasant subjects, landlords, workers and the middle-classes).

In this sense, even in the late 1970s, they still maintained that Slovene history from the loss of medieval Slovene independence was "almost a thousand years of the history of the Slovene peasant – serf", since the process of Slovene emancipation could only start with the struggle for the social liberation of the Slovene population and this happened only with the beginning of the workers' and socialist movement in the 19th and especially with the communist movement in the 20th century.[28] Writers of history textbooks after 1945,

---

27 A. Melik/J. Orožen, Z. Jugoslovanov. *Za nižje razrede srednjih in njim sorodnih šol* [Yugoslav History. For Lower Grades of Secondary and Analogous Schools], Ljubljana 1929, pg. 107. B. Binter/V. Štrukelj, Z. Jugoslovanov. *Za četrti razred srednjih* šol [Yugoslav History. For the Fourth Grade of Secondary Schools], Ljubljana 1939, p. 168.

28 B. Božič-Tomaž Weber, *Zgodovina 6* (History for the sixth class of elementary school), Ljubljana 1878, p. 77.

although they drew attention to the important "national awakening role" of Slovene poets (with France Prešeren at the head) and writers, proclaimed as the peasant rebels in the 14th and 15th centuries to be early national heroes, while they evaluated Slovene national leaders in the second half of the 19th century explicitly critically. They found that the Slovene national movement in the Habsburg Monarchy was relatively ineffective not only because of the relentless German pressures but also because of the opportunistic policy of the Slovene middle classes, which "accepted German dominance out of fear for their position". The situation in the Kingdom of Yugoslavia was painted in similarly grim colours: the ruling "bourgeoisie" (especially Serb, but also Slovene), according to the textbooks, had not cared about national equality and the living conditions of the population, since it had only been concerned with "its own power". National heroes were, however, mostly men: there were only a few women revolutionaries and writers mentioned and among the Habsburg rulers Maria Theresa as one of the central personalities of the Habsburg history.

After 1945, in accordance with the guidelines of the Yugoslav communist leadership, curricula in Yugoslavia for all levels of education were planned and adopted in federal units – republics – for Slovene schools in Slovenia. According to the guidelines teaching of history must educate pupils to be "conscientious fighters and builders of socialism" and show them the way "by which humanity develops to its final aim – to Communism" and, at the same time, educate them in "the spirit of brotherhood and unity of the Yugoslav nations" and "Slovene national consciousness".[29] In Yugoslavia after World War Two, there was no longer talk of a single Yugoslav nation and the Constitution adopted in 1946 proclaimed it to be a federatively arranged state community of "equal nations who, on the basis of the fundamental right to self-determination, have expressed their wish to live together in a federative state".

The authors of textbooks, too, in light of this understanding, showed the creation of the Yugoslav state in 1918 as the result of a Yugoslav movement, which had spread among "individual Yugoslav nations" before and during World War One and, although ideas about what sort of state it should be were various, they everywhere aspired to its unification. In the first two decades after World War Two, Slovene textbooks in this way presented both Slovene history and that of other Yugoslav nations (Croats, Serbs, Bosnians, Macedonians and Montenegrins) in a relatively balanced way, while later – from the second half of the sixties of last century – with the increasing autonomy of the republics,

29 *Gradivo za sestavo predmetnika in učnega načrta* (The material for the preparation of the curricula), Zavod za napredek šolstva, Ljubljana 1962, p. 49. *Osnovna šola, Vsebina vzgojnoizobraževalnega dela,* (Primary school. The contents of the ducational work), Zavod za šolstvo Republike Slovenije, Ljubljana 1973, p. 132.

the extent of Slovene history in textbooks increased and the extent of the history of other Yugoslav nations was reduced. In the same breath, from the end of the 1950s in schools in all federal republics the number of teaching hours devoted to the study of ancient, medieval and early modern history was reduced and the number of hours devoted to so-called modern history increased: the history of revolutionary movements in the second half of the 19th century and the communist movements in the 20th century and, especially, the "National Liberation Struggle and People's Revolution" during World War Two.

Writers of history textbooks in Yugoslavia after 1945 uniformly stressed that the Yugoslav Communist party during World War Two was the only political force capable of organising an all-Yugoslav resistance and leading the Yugoslav nations towards a social revolution; the National Liberation Struggle was thus also presented in Slovene history textbooks as the most magnificent, if not the only truly significant, movement in Yugoslav and Slovene history. Socialist Yugoslavia, founded on this experience could thus become after 1945, and particularly after the Yugoslav break with Moscow in 1948, the only truly democratic socialist country, which had succeeded also in ensuring the equality of all its nations. In the 1980s, some textbooks already mentioned severe economic problems and national tensions, which the Yugoslav communist regime had tried unsuccessfully to solve throughout the decades after the war. However, until the demise of the regime in 1990-91, most textbooks persisted in the claim that the Yugoslav Federation and Yugoslav "socialist democracy" as well as socialism all over the world, still had a bright future to which to look forward.

The authors of new history textbooks published after the dissolution of Yugoslavia and the communist regime thus faced a difficult task: the school narrative had to be radically transformed and cleared of the ideological formulas used in the period of communism. Furthermore, it had to be adapted to modern historiographic interpretations also in regard to the national aspect. In Slovenia, the remodelling of history teaching at the beginning of the 1990s, after Slovenia became independent, did not excite any particular political or public interest. A debate on school history education was thus initiated by the Association of Historical Societies and this, as a non-political, civic organization, formed two working groups, which produced proposals for new approaches to history teaching.[30] These, among other things, also questioned

30 For more information about history education in Slovenia after 1991 see P. Vodopivec, The Politics of History Education in Slovenia and Slovene History Textbooks since 1990. In: A. Dimou (ed.), *Transition and the Politics of History Education in Southeast Europe*, Studien des Georg-Eckert-Intituts zur Internationalen Bildungsmedien Forschung Band 124, V&R Unipress 2009, pp. 49-69.

the traditional three-part scheme of Slovene history and Slovene national historical narrative that had predominated for so long, since they rejected the transfer of modern national concepts and designations to the period when people were not defined nationally and did not yet recognise modern feelings of national affiliation.

However, the image of Slovene history in textbooks has changed slowly in the last twenty years. The majority of their authors have really modernised the national narrative as concerns the use of contemporary national designations, although there is not any noticeable transformation of the traditional three-part structure of the national past. The majority of Slovene textbooks thus continue to present as the key periods of Slovene history: the independence of "Slovene ancestors" in the early Middle Ages; the dominance of a "foreign" aristocracy and gradual diminishing of the territory populated by Slovenes after the loss of independence in the 9th century due to colonisation by German peasants; the uprisings of Slovene peasants in the 15th and 16th century and the publication of the first Slovene books at the time of the Reformation; and the beginnings of the Slovene cultural movement and gradual expansion of Slovene national awareness after the end of the 18th century.

But in the same breath, the picture of Slovene middle class politics and the Slovene middle class in the Habsburg monarchy and the Kingdom of Serbs, Croats, and Slovenes (SHS) or Kingdom of Yugoslavia in textbooks published after 1991 is much more balanced and less dark than it was in textbooks at the time of socialist Yugoslavia. The image of the Habsburg Monarchy is also no longer seen as bleak as it had been in textbooks dating back to the First and Second Yugoslavia, and Slovene development in the 19th century, despite repeated references to unfulfilled Slovene national aspirations and German nationalist pressures, is presented as fairly successful, since the Slovenes, as the authors of the textbooks write, by World War I had developed into a modern, socially structured nation with an "enviable" cultural level. Fast Slovene social, economic and cultural development, according to contemporary history textbooks, also continued in the First and Second Yugoslavia, although both states, according to the authors of textbooks, were a great disappointment for the majority of the Slovene population. The expectation that the "Slovene nation" would "achieve complete emancipation" in the Kingdom of Serbs, Croats, and Slovenes (Kingdom of Yugoslavia in October 1929) "diminished quickly" in the face of the centralist state system and pressures towards Serb-Croat-Slovene national unification, exerted especially by Serbian political parties. On the other hand, after 1945, communist Yugoslavia was a non-democratic one party state, despite the fact that after the Belgrade break with Moscow its regime was more pluralist and open than that of other communist countries and, due to this non democratic nature, it failed to solve its internal social, economic and national contradictions.

All of the textbooks written after the dissolution of Yugoslavia and the attainment of Slovene independence in 1991 agree that the majority of the Slovene population supported the resistance against the German and Italian occupiers, led by the communists after 1941, and they all condemn collaboration. However, they also point out critically that the communist leadership in Slovenia and Yugoslavia abused the struggle against the occupiers in order to ensure a "social revolution" and carried out "bloody retribution" not only against the occupiers but also against political opponents at home. The communist leadership therefore shared responsibility for the conflict between the advocates of collaboration and adherents of the struggle against the occupiers developing into a full blown "civil war".

Debates about circumstances in Slovenia during World War Two, communist Yugoslavia and its regime are still today the subject of serious political confrontations and continue to divide public opinion. This obviously also represents a problem for the authors of textbooks who, when dealing with so-called "contemporary history", keep resorting to an impersonal statement of facts and avoid making more concrete judgements and evaluations. All contemporary history textbooks also contain chapters about the emancipation of the Slovene state in 1990-91 and agree that the establishment of independent Slovenia in 1991 was a radical turning point in terms of the previous Slovene political tradition, oriented towards national autonomy in multinational states. However, they refrain from evaluating and predicting what this turning point actually meant for Slovene development and what it means for the Slovene future.

To sum up: The prevailing Slovene public and school national historical narrative is still partly rooted in 19th century national historical views and interpretations, formed in the period of strained tensions between Slovenes and Germans. This narrative, despite nationally and ideologically more relaxed historical interpretations and more balanced evaluations of Slovene development in the Habsburg Monarchy, did not significantly change during the 20th century. Unlike in Norway, as many as three radical changes took place, one after another in the Slovene national and political development in the 20th century. In the case each of them, public and school history narrative changed more or less substantially only in the evaluation of the most recent past and contemporary events. History textbooks after 1918 presented the establishment of the Kingdom of Serbs, Croats, and Slovenes in December 1918 as the final realisation of Slovene national aspirations. After 1945, this role was taken over by communist Yugoslavia and, since 1991, by the independent Slovene state. Each time, the textbooks were very critical of political circumstances, elites and leaders in the previous state context, allegedly dominated by political elites lacking national determination, political opportunists and advocates of national and political compromises. Slovene poets and writers, who shaped "Slovene culture" and strengthened Slovene national (self)awareness by writing in the Slovene language, have thus, as presented by textbook authors, been rare bright exceptions in the "dark landscape" of Slovene history. In this regard, even at the beginning of the 21st century the majority of respondents to public opinion polls referred not only to the publication of the first books in the Slovene language in the 16th century and the establishment of an independent Slovene state in 1991 but also to the alleged Slovene state of Carantania in the early Middle Ages, as the most important events in Slovene history, while the author of the first Slovene book, Primož Trubar, and the Slovene romantic poet France Prešeren were declared to be the most important Slovene historical personalities.

Conclusions

During the last couple of centuries, Norway and Slovenia have experienced very different political histories. The Norwegian state was established in its modern form in 1814, with its own constitution and independent government institutions. Since then, historical development has taken place in gradual steps within stable boundaries, with the German occupation in 1940-45 as the most dramatic rupture. The peaceful break-up of the very loose union with Sweden in 1905 was a much less dramatic event. Compared to that of most other nations, modern Norwegian history is thus mostly a history of continuity, and the nation as an object of identification in historical narratives, has remained virtually unchanged within stable borders. As a consequence, the narratives of Norwegian history textbooks have never been forced to adjust to fundamental political ruptures, and changes in contents and presentation have developed gradually and in small steps, in accordance with changes in approaches and scopes in scholarly history as well as in didactics, but also reflecting changes in the political culture, which over the years has gone through an important development in the direction of more widened democracy and more active public participation.

By contrast, Slovene history has been marked by three fundamental ruptures during the last century: the break-up of the dual monarchy of Austria and Hungary in 1918, the Second World War and the coming of the Communist regime, and the break-up of Yugoslavia from 1991. All these fundamental upheavals obviously affected the way that history was told, not only in society at large but also how it was taught in schools. This also means that present-day Slovenia appears to be a particularly well suited case to study how political changes have made their impact on education, not only at the level of prescriptions from above, but also at the reception level, asking how a population at large has received and interpreted the political changes.

As for the object of identification in Slovene textbooks, a striking feature seems to be a kind of two-level structure, with an inner core consisting of a relatively stable Slovene identity, surrounded by dramatically changing contexts not only of state belonging but also of hegemonic political ideologies. Because of the much higher frequency of ruptures and traumas in Slovene history as compared to Norwegian history, there also seems to be a higher frequency of "white spots" to be avoided in school narratives. Like other states in post-communist East central and Southeastern Europe, Slovenia has not escaped the dilemmas of creating functioning civic identities and at the same time maintaining basic national identities.[31] Fundamentally, however, there seems to be a clear convergence in Slovene and Norwegian approaches to history teaching and its textbooks: The identity making historical narratives have been gradually substituted by more scholarly approaches and a higher degree of willingness to confront more contested themes and topics, something which is a prerequisite for good history teaching in a functioning democracy.

31 W. Höpken: Between Civic Identity and Nationalism; History Textbooks in East Central and Southeastern Europe, in S. P. Ramet and D. Matic (ed.): *Democratic Transition in Croatia: Value transformation, education and media,* Texas University Press 2007, pp. 163-192.

Part Two – Gender Equality & Religion

Anders Todal Jenssen and Aleksandra Kanjuo-Mrcela

6 Gender Equality in Norway and Slovenia

This chapter focuses on the level of gender equality in Norway and Slovenia, and on the attitudes in the two countries regarding such matters as the division of domestic work, reproductive rights including abortion, and equality in the public and private spheres. According to the UNDP Gender Inequality Index, with scores for 149 countries, Slovenia is ranked as number 1 with the highest level of gender equality in 2013 and Norway as number 9. The scores reveal the extent to which national achievements in reproductive health, empowerment and labour market participation are eroded by gender inequality.

Progress with equality in political office has been uneven in both countries, with setbacks as well as improvements. But what is striking in the Norwegian case is that the proportion of women in the parliament (the Storting) and occupying ministerial positions has tended to be higher than their representation at lower levels of government and administration, while, in Slovenia, women are overrepresented in the judiciary, but underrepresented in other branches of government. In private enterprise, both countries continue to experience the phenomenon of the glass ceiling.

Attitudes about abortion are broadly similar, with clear majorities in both countries favouring open access to the procedure. On the other hand, attitudes about gender roles within the family are more conservative in Slovenia than in Norway. In both countries, there is a significant gap between women's and men' salaries, but in both cases, local feminists continue to push for legislation and other policy changes to alter this situation. The chapter ends with a brief summary of similarities and differences between the two countries in terms of gender equality.

– The Editors

A. Gender equality in Norway: Mobilization from below and economic-bureaucratic rationality from above*

The Nordic countries tend to score among the best on all international statistics related to gender equality. Women in the Nordic countries have achieved more than legal equality with men, they take part in public life, earn a living and enjoy the benefits of wealthy societies much as men do. One could argue that gender equality is a side-effect of the economic growth and generous welfare states in the Nordic countries, but that would be telling only half the story. The organized political struggle for gender equality has been important in these countries for more than one hundred and fifty years, and it was far from obvious that the welfare state would be used as an instrument for gender equality. The labour unions that pushed for many of the welfare reforms could hardly be described as a historic forerunner for gender equality. Until the 1970s, their focus was clearly on the male breadwinner. In this section, our ambition is to describe the processes that led to the present situation in Norway.

Political rights and presence of women in the elites

The Norwegian constitution from 1814 gave a large – by the standard of that time – proportion of the population the right to vote. All men twenty-five years of age with property (including farmland), public servants and priests were given full political rights. The first organization dedicated to the women's right to vote was formed in 1885 by a handful of members of *Norsk Kvinnesaks-forening*. The following year they were able - with the help of MP's from the Liberal Party – to propose a new law on an equal right to vote and eligibility to sit in the national assembly, the Storting. The proposition was turned down by an overwhelming majority, but the proposal was presented again and again in the following years, and gradually the demand gained momentum. In 1901, women were granted a limited right to vote in local elections. In the referendum on independence from Sweden in 1905, about 370,000 men (99.9%) voted for independence. Women were not allowed to take part, but the two organizations working for the women's right to vote, collected about 300,000 signatures from women demanding independence. In 1907, some women were allowed to vote in the national elections for the first time, and in 1913 all women and men 25 years of age were given the right to vote. The public statistics show only a small drop in participation in the following election, suggesting that most

* Anders Todal Jenssen

women were ready to use their new political rights. The same did not happen when all men were given the right to vote in 1898 – (the turnout dropped by twenty per cent in the following election).

It soon became clear that acquiring eligibility to hold office did not guarantee that women would be elected. The number of female representatives in the local councils rose from 1 to 3% between 1901 until 1940. The first female MP was elected in 1922. After the last election before World War Two, there was still only one female MP.

The second wave of mobilization in the electoral system started with the "women's coup" in the local elections of 1971. In one of the large suburban municipalities outside Oslo a group of female politicians started a campaign to persuade electors give their personal votes to female candidates. As a result, 27 out of the 47 elected were women. This caused a less than elegant outcry from some male politicians. Their disrespect for female politicians was displayed for everyone to see. In the following years, women all over the country organized to increase female political representation. The effect of their efforts was reduced by male politicians organizing counter-campaigns.

The use of gender-quotas within the political parties proved to be a much more effective strategy: Traditionally, women have been organized in special branches in many Norwegian parties. In many ways, this worked to isolate the women and the "women's issues" from the mainstream of party activity. When an experienced feminist politician, Berit Aas, became the first leader of the newly formed Socialist Left Party in 1975, she pushed for the use of gender quotas within the organization.[1] The Socialist Left Party became the first party to use quotas in the candidate nomination process, with alternation between male and female on the electoral lists. This system was later adopted by five of the seven parties in the Storting, and resulted in the sharp rise in the number of female MPs after 1969 (Figure 6.1).

1 Eva Kolstad became the first female party leader in Norway, when she was elected leader of the Liberal Party of Norway in 1974. She later became the world's first Ombud for gender equality in 1978.

Figure 6.1 . Proportion of female MPs elected to the Norwegian Storting 1945 – 2013

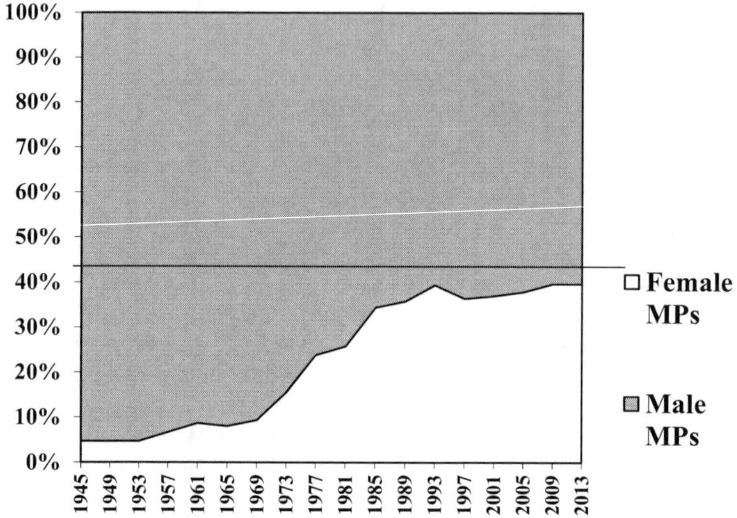

Note: Numbers fluctuate throughout election period due to replacements

Source: https://www.stortinget.no/no/Representanter-og-komiteer/Representantene/Innvalgte-fra-1945--/

When Prime Minister Odvar Nordli stepped down in 1980, Gro Harlem Brundtland was chosen to replace him and became Norway's first female Prime Minister. The Labour Party government lost the election the following year, but Brundtland returned as prime Minister in 1986, and stayed in office almost continuously until 1996. In 1986, Brundtland formed her "Women's Cabinet": eight out of eighteen ministers were women. None of the following governments – irrespective of political colour – have had less than 40% female Ministers. The "Women's Cabinet", thus, set a new standard. However, this was a revolution from above, the ratio of female to male politicians tends to decline as one moves down the ladder of political power.

It is also important to note that the proportion of women counted among the social elites does not come close to 40%. The political elite is more of an exception than the general rule. According to the Norwegian elite survey from 2001, women comprised less than 10% of the elites in the justice-sector, the Church, the business community, and the military. In a follow-up study from 2011, the proportion of women was shown to have increased in all elite sectors, but is worth noting that the change is slow in important areas as organizational elites and the media. The level is still very low in the business elite, but the change is remarkable. (We will return to this observation below.)

Figure 6.2. The proportion of females in various social elites in 2001 and 2011 (%)

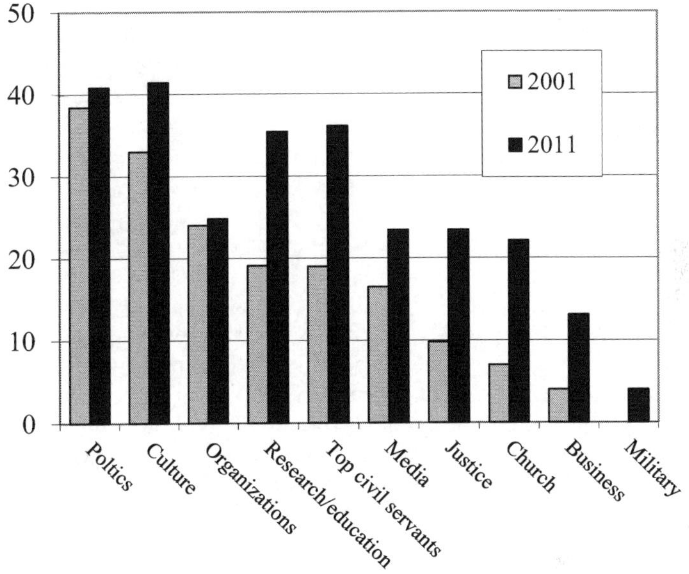

Source: The Norwegian elite survey. Marit Teigen, Norske makteliter 2001-2011. En oppdatering av posisjonsutvalget i den norske lederskapsundersøkelsen (Oslo: Institute for Social Research, 2012), pp. 4–5. Retrieved from: http://www.civilsociety.no/socialresearch.no/Publications/Other-reports/2012/2012-008

Birth control; reproductive rights

Birth control has been important for women everywhere for several reasons: reduced health risk, improved standard of living and possibility for planning a career. In 1924, the first "mother-hygiene-office" (Mødrehygienekontor) was established by women activists. Information about family planning was distributed and contraceptives were sold from these offices. They were shut down by the Nazi-occupation regime during World War Two. After the war, the Public Health Service took over these tasks, but voluntary organizations remained active. The introduction of "The pill" in 1967 had several effects. First of all, it was a more effective form of contraception than other methods, and a contraceptive fully controlled by the woman; secondly, it loosened the link between sex and reproduction. Sex before marriage became accepted in wide circles and women learned that it was normal to enjoy sex, even from traditional women's magazines dedicated to motherhood and family life.

Activists pushed for the right to abortion.[2] For the pro-choice activists on the political left the arguments were originally linked to the social and economic situation of the woman. Activists on the political right were more focused on the pro-choice argument. The law from 1960 opened up for abortion on social (for instance poor living conditions) and health grounds, but a committee of two doctors was to review each case after interviewing the woman. Many found this degrading and questioned the doctors' competence and impartiality. A study disclosed inconsistent practices across the country.[3] The present law, giving the woman the final say and ending the committee system, was passed in 1978 after 65 years of political struggle. The driving force was the activists outside and inside the political parties. In several parties the issue created internal conflicts and tensions, but in the end the parties on the left supported the law unanimously. When the parties on the left lost the majority in the 1981-election, some – especially within the Christian Democratic Party – hoped for a replay, but a new generation of feminists within the Conservative Party refused to undo the law from 1978. Without their votes, the parties on the centre and right were powerless. Public opinion was also increasingly in favour of the new law (see Figure 6.3 below) and the issue gradually faded from the political agenda in the 1990s. However, after the election of 2013, the issue dominated the public agenda again until the new right wing government realized that any change in the law would face fierce public resistance.

2 From 1687 until 1842 capital punishment was in use for abortion. From 1842 to 1902 the maximum punishment for abortion was three years of imprisonment.

3 The study was completed by Berthold Grünfeld. See Grünfeld, *Legalt svangerskapsavbrudd i Norge i tidsrommet 1965–1971*. Ph.D. Dissertation. The University of Oslo, 1973.

Figure 6.3. Changing attitudes towards abortion in Norway from 1974 until 1983

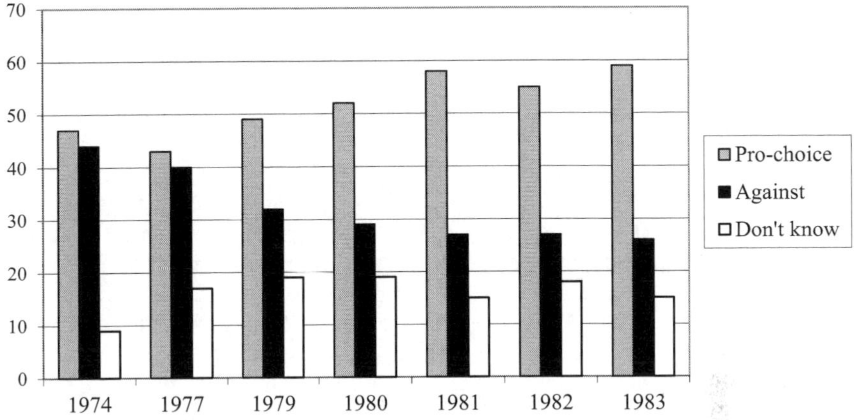

Source: Data from Bjørn Alstad (ed.), *Norske meninger 1946-93. Bind 2: Norge og nordmenn* (Oslo: Sigma Forlag Distribusjon, 1993).

The Norwegian Church (the Protestant State Church until 2012) was opposed to the new law of 1960 and even more hostile to the demand for "free abortion" as it was called by the counter-action. Before the present law was passed in 1978, the bishops made a unanimous statement (read in all churches during Sunday Mass) on the issue. The Church's general opposition to liberal attitudes (sex before marriage, sex education, availability of contraceptives, homosexuality) and abortion in particular and the widespread opposition to female priests and bishops within the Church made it a target for feminist critique. Before the 1981 election, women in Norway voted more frequently for the parties on the right, especially for the Christian People's Party. In the 1981 election and later, Norwegian women were more likely than men to vote for the parties on the left.[4] The Church's slow adaptation (the first female priest was appointed in 1961 and the first female bishop in 1993) did not help to bridge the divide between the Norwegian Church and the majority of the population with more liberal family values. The immediate effect of the weakening of the ties between the state and the Church from May 2012 may actually reverse the process toward gender equality within the Church, because with it the state has

4 See Ola Listhaug, "The Gender Gap in Norwegian Voting Behaviour", in *Scandinavian Political Studies,* Vol. 8, no. 3 (1985), pp. 187-206.

lost the final say in the appointment of bishops. The two first bishops appointed by the independent Norwegian Church were theologically conservative males. The opposition to gender equality has typically been even stronger from the smaller Churches outside the Norwegian Church, including the Catholic Church. Some of them are still banning female priests and female church leaders.

Changing family values

Data from the Norwegian Monitor[5] reveal a major shift in public opinion the last twenty-nine years (cf. Figure 6.4). This is remarkable, as prior research suggests that the attitude change may have been even stronger before 1985.[6] In 1985, 44% of the respondents stated that men and women should share the domestic work equally and have the same responsibility and right to paid work. In 2009, this group constituted 69% of the total sample. The group that argued that the woman should stay at home was reduced from 20 to 4% in the same period. The group that believes that males should remain the main bread winner and that the female should be the chief homemaker has declined as well and made up 20% in 2009. The young, the better educated and women support the "share equally" alternative more frequently than the old, the less educated and males.

During the late 1960s and 1970s, liberal views on sexuality prevailed. Sex before marriage was accepted by the majority as a normal and even a good thing. Homosexuality was no longer made invisible in public life. The new women's movement welcomed this development, and rejected the traditional view of women as sexually passive and emotionless. However, parts of the women's movement also vigorously opposed the objectification of the woman's body in pornography and parts of the popular culture. The main tabloid newspapers in Norway had developed a repertoire of ways to use images of barely dressed women on their front pages.[7] The fashion and fitness industries have put a pressure on women – especially young women – to conform to absurd and unattainable beauty standards. More recently, some of the younger self-declared

5 A comprehnsive presentation of the data can be found in Tale Hellevik and Ottar Hellevik, "Holdninger Til Likestilling", in Thomas Hansen and Britt Slagsvold (eds.), *Likestilling hjemme* (Oslo: NOVA - Norsk institutt for forskning om oppvekst, velferd og aldring, 2012).

6 A broad discussion of value change taking place in post-war Norway can be found in Anders Todal Jenssen, Hvor vil med samfunnsutviklingen? Sentrale verdier og verdiendringer i Norge. Front Cover (Oslo: Prosjekt Alternativ Framtid, 1989).

7 Margun Grønn, "Om Sex i Løssalgspressen", in Elisabeth Eide (ed.), *Narrespeil. Kjønn, sex og medier* (Kristiansand: Høgskoleforlaget, 2000).

feminists, have come to see posing in the nude in glossy magazines as the ultimate proof of the empowerment of women. More generally, women play a secondary role in the Norwegian media's image of the world: They are less often portrayed as acting, the main sources of information or persons of authority than men, and more often described as victims, or as ordinary people, or used as eye-catchers.[8]

Figure 6.4. Changing family values

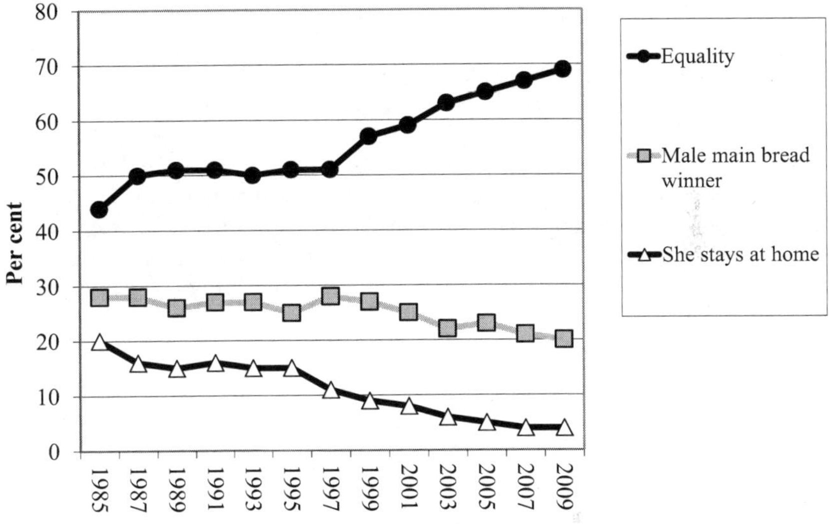

Source: Tale Hellevik and Ottar Hellevik, "Holdninger til likestilling", in Thomas Hansen and Britt Slagsvold (eds.), *«Likestilling hjemme», Rapport 8/12* (Oslo: NOVA - Norsk institutt for forskning om oppvekst, velferd og aldring, 2012), p. 17. Retrieved from: www.hioa.no/content/download/45462/674663/file/5912_1.pdf Re-traditionalization?

The Economy

The number of women working full-time outside the home has increased steadily since the 1960s. In the 1940s and 1950s, a few married women worked

8 Several researchers have contributed to this field of research for instance the contributions in the volumes edited by Eide (ed.), *Narrespeil. Kjønn, sex og medier* [note 9]; and Erika Jahr, *Kjønn og journalistikk i mediene* (Kristiansand: IJ-forlaget, 2004). Also Sigurd Allern, *Nyhetsverdier: Om markedsorientering og journalistikk i ti norske aviser* (Kristiansand: IJ-forlaget, 2001).

outside the home. It was considered proper for women to quit work, when they married or when the first child was born. Beginning in the 1960s, there was a steady increase in the number of married women with paid work. This change must be linked to the declining fertility rates in the same period.[9] In the 1960s, the four-person household became the standard, and many women were free to take up paid work when the children grew up. In the 1970s, the increase was sharpest among married women with small children. Better education motivated more women to pursue a career, but among the less educated, less paid, improving the living standard may have been just as important.[10]

In 2011, the average monthly pay for women employees was NOK 34,800 and NOK 40,800 for men. Why do males earn more than women? Three times as many women as men were working part-time in 2011. This, however, is only a partial explanation since there is a significant wage gap among full-time employees in both the private and the public sector. Three possibilities have been discussed: women and men are not paid equal wages for the same or similar work; women have problems getting through the "glass ceiling" into the top positions; and women and men work in very different sectors of the economy with very different wages.[11] The last explanation seems to be the most widely accepted and has obvious relevance due to the highly gender-segregated labour-market.[12]

---

9 For more details, see Olav Ljones, "Kvinners yrkesdeltaking i et langsiktig perspektiv", in Tor Rødseth and Kristin Dale Titlestad (eds.), *Kvinner i arbeid* (Oslo: Universitetsforlaget, 1984).

10 This aspect of the change has been discussed in An-Magritt Jensen, "Når mødre jobber - Om nødvendighet og valg", in Rødseth and Titlestad (eds.), *KvinnerilI arbeid* [note 11]; and Kari Skrede, "Family Policy in Relation to Changes in Family Structure and the Distribution of Income", in *Notat* (Oslo: Institute of applied social research, 1983).

11 The question of wage-discrimination against women in Norway has been fiercely debated, see for instance Trond Petersen, "Likestilling i arbeidsmarkedet." *Tidsskrift for samfunnsforskning,* Vol. 43, no. 4 (2002), pp. 443-78; and by the same author "Sluttreplikk: Fra tvang til valg." *Tidsskrift for samfunnsforskning,* Vol. 44, no. 3 (2003): 447-54. See also Erling Barth, "Lønnsforskjeller mellom kvinner og menn: En kommentar til Trond Petersen", in *Tidsskrift for samfunnsforskning,* Vol. 44, no. 3 (2003), pp. 427-34; Ann Nilsen and Nina Raaum, "Likestilling i arbeidslivet. En Kommentar til Trond Petersen", in *Tidsskrift for samfunnsforskning,* Vol. 44, no. 3 (2003), pp. 435-46; and Aagoth Elise Storvik, "Likestilling i arbeidslivet - Hva betyr det, og hvordan skal det studeres? En kommentar til Trond Petersens artikkel 'Likestilling i arbeidsmarekdet'", in *Tidsskrift for samfunnsforskning,* Vol. 44, no. 3 (2003), pp. 435-46.

12 For further discussion, see Gunn Elisabeth Birkelund, "Stratification and Segregation", in *Acta Sociologica,* Vol. 35, no. 1 (1 January 1992), pp. 48-49.

Figure 6.5. Monthly pay (in NOK) for men and women in 2011

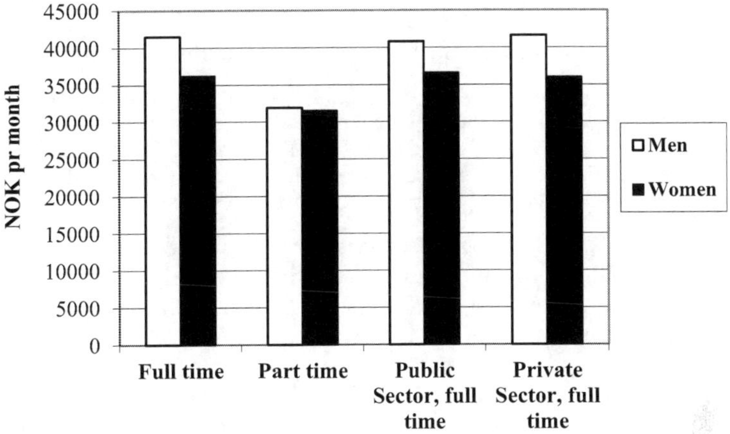

Source: Statistics Norway

More women than men work in the public sector of the economy, and the average pay is higher in the private sector. However, within each sector women dominate in some branches. In the public sector, there are more women than men in the social services, nursing, cleaning, and teaching. In the private sector, there are more women in the service sector, commodity trade, hotels, and restaurants. Usually, the branches that employ many women are characterized by lower pay compared to the branches where many men are concentrated, even when years of education are taken into consideration. Typically, the male engineer with four years of college education earns significantly more than the female nurse with four years of college education, even when they both work in the public sector. In a recent government White Paper concerning gender equality,[13] the possibility to encourage young men and women to choose educations leading into occupations traditionally dominated either by men or woman, is discussed. The idea is to use economic incentives in the form of stipends.

13 NOU, "Politikk for likestilling." Government white paper. Barne-, likestillings- og inkluderingsdepertementet (Oslo: Departementenes servicesenter, 2012), p. 15.

"State feminism"

According to Helga Hernes, the "philogynic" or women-friendly states and societies in the Nordic countries are the result of several interacting processes:

> Women have entered the public sphere from below, through the kitchen door so to speak, partly through the pull of the economic processes, partly through the push of the women's movement. Women's agitation [for] 'feminization' from below, and the official response in the form of 'state feminism from above have had lasting effects on Nordic welfare state development.[14]

One of the key elements of 'state feminism' has been to free women of many of their traditional tasks linked to childcare and care for the elderly. From the age of one, all children are guaranteed care in a kindergarten, from the age of six children are either at school or enrolled in leisure activities at school the whole day. Elderly people are guaranteed some help in their homes and care in an institution if needed. These welfare systems have made it possible for women to educate themselves and to pursue long-term working careers. Hence, the welfare systems have increased the supply to the labour-market considerably. For the women, taking up paid work has had several positive effects, like paid sick leave, the right to unemployment benefits, and much better pension schemes. But first and foremost, women earned their own money. In short, their newly won economic independence has empowered women.

Helga Hernes builds her argument on a description of the Nordic welfare state as the result of a compromise between conflicting class interests[15]: The expansion of the welfare system was necessary to avoid disruptive industrial conflict, and in turn, the expansion of the welfare systems created the demand for labour that gave women new opportunities. We would like to add to this well founded explanation that "feminization from above" may also have been driven by other political forces, motivated by human capital-reasoning.

The parties on the political right have often opposed further expansion of the welfare state, but they have appreciated the positive effects to the economy of including women in the workforce. Nevertheless, it came as a surprise when, in 2002, a Christian conservative male, Minister of Trade and Industry Ansgard

---

14 Cited from Helga M. Hernes, *Welfare State and Women Power. Essays in State Feminism* (Oslo: Norwegian University Press, 1987), p. 11.

15 The class compromise has been described in several books. See, for instance: Claus Offe, *Disorganized Capitalism. Contemporary Transformations of Work and Capital*. Cambridge, MA: The MIT Press, 1985); Walter Korpi, *The Democratic Class Struggle* (London: Routledge & Kegan Paul, 1983); Gosta Esping-Andersen, *Politics against Markets: The Social Democratic Road to Power* (Princeton, N.J.: Princeton University Press, 1985); and by the same author, *The Three Worlds of Welfare Capitalism* (Cambridge: Polity Press, 1990).

Gabrielsen suggested that 40% of the seats on the boards of publicly owned companies and privately owned publicly listed companies be reserved for women.[16] Gabrielsen argued that the discrimination against women by the "old school" male corporate leaders was a waste of talent and resources (human capital) that the country could ill afford. Despite protests both from groups within the Conservative Party and the corporate elite, the law from 2003 is still in place.

The same line of reasoning has also been important within an elite milieu with direct access to the leadership of the Labour Party, which has been in power for much of the post-war period. The so-called "iron triangle" of political-economic experts (The Ministry of Finance, the research department at Statistics Norway, and the Department of Economics at the University of Oslo) has played a major role in the economic policies of shifting Norwegian governments.[17] In their thinking, the size and competence of the workforce is among the key input factors in the Norwegian economy. In the latest report to the parliament,[18] the Ministry of Finance estimates that the effect of increased employment among women on economic growth is levelling off, but underlines that the government must increase its efforts to increase the population's reproduction rates to secure future economic growth. In other words, the welfare system must be adjusted to make it possible for both women and men to combine full-time work and a (fertile) family life.

Five dilemmas facing Norway's state feminism

When a right-wing government came to power in 2013, it challenged the previous centre-left government's policy of gender equality right away by cutting back on the parental leave reserved for fathers and by proposing to

16 See Hege Skjeie and Mari Teigen, "Political Constructions of Gender Equality: Travelling Towards … a Gender Balanced Society?" in *NORA - Nordic Journal of Feminist and Gender Research,* Vol. 13, no. 3 (2005), pp. 187-97

17 The "iron-triangle" has been discussed by several authors, for instance by the historian Runge Slagstad, *De nasjonale strateger* (Oslo: Pax Forlag, 1998), pp. 277-283.

18 A brief overview over Norway's economic policy can be found in Ministry of Finance: *Long-term perspectives for the Norwegian economy.* This document is an English summary of the Government's 2009 report to the parliament on the long term perspectives for the Norwegian economy: See http://www.regjeringen.no/en/dep/fin/Documents-and-publications/Reports/Reports/2009/long-term-perspectives-on-the-norwegian-.html?id=550473 [last accessed on 9 December 2014].

make the process of getting an abortion more trying.[19] The second proposition was hastily withdrawn due to widespread public protests, but the incidents demonstrated state feminism's vulnerability. Ideological shifts to the right may dismantle parts of the model rapidly. The right-wing parties claim that individual freedom is restricted by state feminism. For instance, they see it as interference in the family's freedom to reserve some weeks of parental leave (paid for by the state) for the fathers.

The state has applied a variety of "carrots and sticks" to improve gender equality over the years. These tools have proven more effective in the public sector than in the private, probably because the state has used its role as employer actively. Over the years a distinct pattern has emerged, gender inequality is greater in the sections of society where public policy has the least effect. In other words, the state's "toolbox is empty", when it comes to improving wages and living conditions for many women in the private sector of the economy (cf. Figure 6.5 above).

Although state feminism has increased the number of employed women, it can be accused of having created a gender-segregated labour market in the process. Relieving women of the burden of raising numerous children and taking care of the elderly was instrumental for increasing the number of women in the workforce. The result was a significant rise in the number of (mostly) public kindergartens and homes for the elderly. These new institutions were mainly staffed by women, and this pattern has proven hard to change. The public health sector is dominated by women, and the rising number of female medical doctors has contributed to the imbalance the last decade.

According to one survey, less than 2.5 percent of Norwegians are members of organizations in the women's movement.[20] The movement's political "muscles" are also restricted by internal divisions. This can partly be explained by the success of state feminism. When feminism became public policy and the state apparatus started moving, the day-to-day push from below ceased to be essential. The process has its own momentum. However, state feminism is no perpetuum mobile. In the long run, the process will halt without a renewal of the forces that put it in motion.

"Mainstreaming" has been a buzzword in the international debate on gender equality for a while. Both the EU- and the UN- bureaucracies seem to favour the integration of a gender-perspective into the existing institutions as the formula for practical reform. In the Norwegian state apparatus, main-

---

19 This reform was dropped due to strong popular opposition. The Government's ambition was primarily to help health personnel opposed to abortion, the women's movement and most parties in the opposition saw it as an attack on women's right to choose.

20 According to the survey conducted by Makt- og demokratiutredningen

streaming has been practiced for some time. One could argue that administrative mainstreaming has made the Norwegian state a rather blunt instrument in the future efforts to achieve gender equality, despite all good intentions. Making everyone in the state apparatus responsible for promoting gender equality seems to make everyone – or at least the majority of Ministries and underlying institutions – indifferent, i.e., they give higher priority to other more immediate tasks. The lack of practical results of gender mainstreaming is not a unique Norwegian experience.[21] In 2011 a group of experts presented a White Paper to the Norwegian Government,[22] suggesting the establishment of a new Directorate for gender equality to give more momentum to the policy of gender equality. So far, the suggestion has received only a lukewarm reception.

21 See Mary Daly, "Gender Mainstreaming in Theory and Practice." *Social Politics: International Studies in Gender, State & Society,* Vol. 12, no. 3 (Fall 2005), pp. 433-50;
Woodward "Too late" [note 2] ;and Ellen Kuhlmann and Ellen Annandale, "Mainstreaming Gender into Healthcare: A Scoping Exercise into Policy Transfer in England and Germany", in *Current Sociology,* Vol. 60, no. 4 (1 July 2012), pp. 551-568.

22 «Struktur for likestilling». (Government whitepaper) NOU, "Struktur for Likestilling." Government withe paper. Barne-, likestilings- og inkluderingsdepertementet (Oslo: Depertementenes servicesenter, 2011), p. 18.

B. Gender equality in (post-)socialist Slovenia*

According to international comparative data Slovenia has a relatively high level of gender equality. The Index of gender equality of Slovenia is above the EU27 average.[23] Slovenia was ranked at 1st place among 149 countries on the UNDP Gender Inequality Index[24] in 2013 with Norway at the 9th place.[25] On International Women's day 2014 the national Statistical office reported that women in Slovenia "are on average older than men, they live longer, they decide to have children later in their lives, they are ever more educated and on average earn less than men."[26]

The achieved level of gender equality should be seen as a result of different factors related to the heritage of the (socialist) past and the turbulent time of post-socialist transition and accession of Slovenia to the European Union (EU). Being the economically most successful republic at the time of the breakup of Yugoslavia,[27] Slovenia had a relatively good starting position at the beginning of the transition. Transitional changes (achieving the political independence, introduction of the multiparty political democracy and full-fledged market economic system) occurred in a society where women's access and participation in education and paid employment as well as in political and social life had been established for several post-war generations. In spite of the functioning gender contract, the socialist period in Slovenia was characterised by very

---

* Aleksandra Kanjuo Mrčela

23 EIGE, Gender Equality Index, at: http://eige.europa.eu/content/gender-equality-index (20th February 2014) [last accessed on 12 December 2014].

24 The UNDP annual reports on the Human development index (HDI) and Gender Related Development Index (GDI) take into account the Gender Empowerment Measure (GEM). Gender-related Development Index (GDI), measures achievement in the same basic capabilities as the HDI does, but takes note of inequality in achievement between women and men. The GDI is simply the HDI discounted, or adjusted downwards, for gender inequality. Gender Empowerment Measure (GEM), is a measure of agency. It evaluates progress in advancing women's standing in political and economic forums. It examines the extent to which women and men are able to actively participate in economic and political life and take part in decision-making. (http://hdr.undp.org/en/statistics/indices/gdi_gem/)

25 UNDP. 2013. Human Development Indicators and Thematic Tables available at: https://data.undp.org/dataset/Table-4-Gender-Inequality-Index/pq34-nwq7 [last accessed on 12 December 2014].

26 Statistical Office of the Republic of Slovenia (hereafter, SORS), special release on International Women's Day 2014, Thursday, 6 March 2014.

27 Yugoslav socioeconomic development after the Second World War was characterised with conflict with Stalin's Russia, overcoming of totalitarian communist regime, decades of economic orientation to both Western and Eastern markets, political and economic democratisation in 70s and rise of strong civil society movements in 80s.

important achievements – high employment of women in secure full-time jobs (making possible high economic independence) and available and affordable childcare services, generous maternity and parental leaves and various services (such as subsidised meals) which made it easier for parents, i.e., mothers to combine employment and family responsibilities. However, in spite of the declaration of equality and the achieved women's emancipation during the socialist period, the Slovenian labour market is still strongly gender-segregated (both horizontally and vertically), a gender pay gap exists, women are under-represented in the positions of political and economic decision-making, unpaid domestic and care work are highly feminised.

As happened in other post-socialist countries, Slovenia witnessed attempts at the reinforcement of patriarchy and re-domestication of women during the time of transition in the 1990s. Evidence of a backlash against women's emancipation and signs of the re-masculinisation of the gender order were observed in the Central and Southeast European region in general in the 1990s, but to different intensities in individual countries.[28] Slovenian employment and reconciliation policies, which had taken gender equality into consideration both before and after the transition, resulted in less deterioration of the position of women in the labour market and otherwise.

There are different evaluations of the impact of the politics and ideology during the socialist period on the gender equality in Slovenia. Some argue that socialist "state feminism", while enabling women to participate in paid work ("socialised housework") did not allow for full-fledged participation of women in public (if public is defined as the political space.)[29] Jogan, on the other hand, sees the presence of gender equality issues on the public agenda during the period of the "self-managing" socialist system in Slovenia as a reason for there being a better situation in Slovenia compared with some other post-socialist countries.[30] In that regard, it is important to acknowledge the influence and importance of long-lasting and diverse initiatives that contributed to the existing level of gender equality in Slovenia. We find evidence of political

---

28 Alena Křížková, Beata Nagy, Aleksandra Kanjuo Mrčela, »The gender implications of labour market policy during the economic transformation and EU accession: a comparison of the Czech Republic, Hungary, and Slovenia", in Christina Klenner (ed.), *Welfare states and gender inequality in Central and Eastern Europe: continuity and post-socialist transformation in the EU member states* (Brussels: European Trade Union Institute (ETUI), 2010), pp. 329-361.

29 See Vlasta Jalušič, »'Nove demokracije' in 'ženske študije'», in Eva D. Bahovec (ed.), *Od ženskih študij k feministični teoriji* (Ljubljana: Časopis za kritiko znanosti, domišljijo in novo antropologijo, 1993), pp. 107-118.

30 Maca Jogan, »Slovenska (postmoderna) družba in spolna neenakost«, in *Teorija in Praksa* (2004), nos. 1-2, pp. 361-376, at p. 202.

struggle for women rights of various women's societies from the late nineteenth century that were continued in different forms during the twentieth century.[31]

Political rights and presence of women in the elites

Women in Slovenia had a long-lasting struggle for their voting rights. During the time of Austro- Hungarian rule (1867-1918), some women were granted suffrage at the municipal level due to their taxpayer status, but it could have been realized only through a male representative. After fighting for it unsuccessfully in the Kingdom of Serbs, Croats, and Slovenes, and the Kingdom of Yugoslavia (as it was renamed in October 1929), Slovenian women got the active and passive right to vote for the first time on 17 May 1942 (by the decree of the Liberation Front of the Slovene People). After the war, the women's voting right was confirmed as a constitutional right. Article 24 of the first constitution of the Federal People's Republic of Yugoslavia (adopted in January 1946) stated: "Women are equal to men in all areas of the state, economic and social life. Women have the right to equal pay for equal work as men, and enjoy special protection in the employment relationship. The state especially protects the interests of mother and child, and thus sets up nurseries, children's homes and care facilities, and gives the mother the right to paid leave before and after childbirth."

Jogan reports about the proportion of women among elected holders of political power in Slovenia in the post-war period – women comprised 15.2% of the delegates to the Federal Assembly in 1963 and 6.3% in 1969.[32] After the election of 1974, women accounted for 26% of the delegates to the Republican Assembly of Slovenia and approximately the same proportion of women was maintained up to the first multiparty elections in 1990, when the share of women decreased to 18.7%; in the 1992 elections it fell further to 13.3% and in

31 Alojzija Štebi, *Demokratizem in ženstvo. Ljubljana: Slovenska socialna matica; Jeraj, Mateja. 2000. Slovenska ženska društva med obema vojnama (1918-1941)* ARHIVI XXIII ([1918], 2000), št. 2, available at: http://www.arhivsko-drustvo.si/sl/documents/18325/25923/sl+zenska +drustva.PDF (20th February 2014); and Jogan, »Slovenska (postmoderna) družba«, *passim.* Sabrina Ramet has noted that, in the 1980s, Yugoslavia was the only communist country with a developed women's movement. See Sabrina P. Ramet, *Social Currents in Eastern Europe. The Sources and Consequences of the Great Transformation*, 2nd ed. (Durham and London: Duke University Press, 1995). For the analysis of developments in the second half of 20th century and the beginning of the 21st century see Ana Kralj and Tanja Rener, "Slovenia: from "state feminism" to back vocals" in Christine M. Hassenstab and Sabrina P. Ramet, *Gender (in)equality and gender politics in Southeastern Europe: A question of justice* (Basingstoke: Palgrave Macmillan, 2015).

32 Jogan, »Slovenska (postmoderna) družba«, *passim.*

1996 it stood at only 7.8%. In the elections held in 2000, the proportion rose to the level of 1992 (13.3%) and being recorded at 12.2% in the elections held in 2004.[33] In all the governments of independent Slovenia until 2012, there were 219 ministers of whom 25 (11.4%) were women.[34] In 2013, Slovenia got its first female Prime Minister, Alenka Bratušek. After the debate on the need for more of gender equality in the distribution of political power in 1990s, the gender quota for electoral lists within political parties (at least 40 % of each sex) was introduced in 2005.

Recent data show that despite the relatively high educational attainment and economic emancipation of women in Slovenia, their vertical mobility is worse compared to men in political and business spheres and academia. Table 6.1 below shows the representation of women in Slovenia in the highest positions in different spheres. Women hold significantly lower shares of thc positions in each of these spheres with the exception of the highly feminised judicial system and members of the European Parliament.

Debates about gender equality in positions of power in the economic sphere gained more public attention in Slovenia only recently, following the initiatives from the European Commission. The topic is now on the agenda of the Government Service for Equal Opportunities, the Women's section of Slovenian Manager's association, the Women's lobby of Slovenia, and some academics. It is to be noted that the Norwegian Financial Mechanism for 2009-2014 supports some on-going projects devoted to enhancing gender equality in the economy, politics and other fields of social life in Slovenia. It is expected that the projects will encourage the introduction of various good practices from Norway, especially regarding gender equality in economic decision-making.

33 *Ibid.*; and SORS. 2005. National Assembly elections, Slovenia, 3 October 2004; Election of members of the European Parliament from the Republic of Slovenia, Slovenia, 13 June 2004 / [Zofija Savec].Results of surveys No 818/2005

34 Mateja Erčulj. 2011. *»Ženske na vodstvenih položajih v politiki, znanosti in gospodarstvu«*. Ljubljana: Univerza v Ljubljani, Fakulteta za družbene vede

Table 6.1. Share of women in top level positions in Slovenia

Positions	*Share of Women (%)*
Members of Slovenian Parliament (March 2014)	32.2
Slovenian Members of European Parliament (March 2013)	50.0
Government Ministers (March 2014)	21.4
Judges (2008) All	76.4
Local courts	81.9
District courts	74.8
Higher courts	71.0
Supreme court	39.0
Mayors (2013)	4.7
Governor and three Vice-Governors of the Central Bank of Slovenia (2009)	0
Top positions in the largest quoted companies (2013)	20
University professors (academic year 2010/2011)	36.9
Full professors	22.5

Sources: Aleksandra Kanjuo Mrčela, Barbara Lužar, and Sonja Šmuc, "Women's under-representation in top management jobs in Slovenia: new and persisting barriers for younger generations of women", in Colette Fagan (ed.), *Women on corporate boards and in top management: European trends and policy – Work and welfare in Europe* (Basingstoke and New York: Palgrave Macmillan, 2012), pp. 198-220,; Aleksandra Kanjuo Mrčela, Maša Filipovič Hrast, and Živa Humer, Vrednotenje izvajanja resolucije o nacionalnem programu za enake možnosti žensk in moških, 2005-2013: končno poročilo (Ljubljana: MDDSZ, 2013), p. 129. ; National Assembly of the Republic of Slovenia; 2014, at http://www.dz-rs.si/wps/portal/en/Home [accessed on 30 March 2014]; Government of the Republic of Slovenia. 2014, at http://www.vlada.si/en/ [accessed on 30 March 2014]; ; and Tanja .S. Pleš, Klara Nahtigal, and Angela Murko Pleš, *Ženske v politiki v Sloveniji: analiza stanja* (Ljubljana: Inštitut za družbeno kreativnost, 2013).

Trends in attitudes on gender roles in the society

Attitudes regarding gender roles are complex in Slovenia, on the one hand, the majority of population of both sexes supports the economic independence and autonomy of women (also regarding the right to decide on childbearing), but, on the other hand, there exists a strong support for the traditional division of duties concerning child care and household responsibilities.

The comparative analysis of attitudes in three post-socialist countries showed that while the traditional gender roles are continuously reproduced in Hungarian and Czech society, in Slovenia the expectation of gender equality was reflected in attitudes of the majority of women and men who accepted the active role of women in paid work as legitimate and as the basis for women's economic independence.[35] According to Slovenian public opinion surveys,[36] a large majority of respondents express (very) positive attitudes regarding gender equality in both 1992 (84%) and 2012 (81.5%). 91% respondents in 1992 and 90.7% in 2012 think that both husband and wife should contribute to family income.[37] In a 2009 Eurobarometer survey, 90% of Slovenian respondents agree that it is indispensable for a woman to have her own pay.[38] Yet at the same time, the expectations concerning priorities in division of care work are not in line with gender equality in paid work. A large proportion of respondents in the aforementioned Slovenian survey thought that women with pre-school children should stay home (28.8%) or work only part-time (45.7%).[39] And compared to the EU-27 average, gender role attitudes tend to be more traditional, with a higher proportion of the Slovenian population of the opinion that a mother must put looking after her young child ahead of her career (81% compared to 70% for the EU-27 average). Only 35% respondents in Slovenia thought that, if the father's pay is lower than that of the mother, he is the one who should give up work to look after the children, compared to the 48% EU-27 average.[40] Attitudes about the traditional division of household responsibilities are the basis of the actual overburden of women with both paid and unpaid work. According to data from the Fifth European Survey on Working Conditions on employed people who work more than 70 hours per week in EU27 (paid and unpaid work), there exists a large gender difference in both EU 27 and in Slovenia, but in Slovenia it is considerably larger as 17.3% of men and as much as 41% of women work more than 70 hours per week.[41]

According to a Slovenian public opinion survey,[42] the majority of respondents in Slovenia expressed (very) positive attitudes regarding the right to abor-

35 See Alena Křížková et al., "The gender implications of labour market policy", *passim.*

36 Toš, Niko et al. 2012. Slovensko javno mnenje 2012/1.(Mednarodna raziskava o družini in spreminjanju spolnih vlog IV.(Family, ISSP 2012).Pregled in primerjava rezultatov. Ljubljana: Univerza v Ljubljani, Fakulteta za družbene vede

37 *Ibid.*

38 European Commission. 2010. Gender equality in the EU in 2009 Report available at: http://ec.europa.eu/public_opinion/archives/ebs/ebs_326_en.pdf [last accessed on 12 December 2014].

39 Niko Toš,(Ed.)" Vrednote v prehodu III. Slovensko javno mnenje 1999-2004" Dokumenti SJM, Ljubljana: FDV IDV, CJMMK, 2004.

40 European Commission, *Gender equality in the EU* [note 16].

41 Aleksandra Kanjuo Mrčela and Miroljub Ignjatovič, *Psychosocial risks in the workplace in Slovenia* (Dublin: European Foundation for the Improvement of Living and Working Conditions, 2012). http://eurofound.europa.eu/publications/report/2012/slovenia/working-conditions/psychosocial-risks-in-the-workplace-in-slovenia

42 Toš et al., *Slovensko javno mnenje 2012*

tion in 1992 (64.1%) and even some more in 2012 (67.5%). In both years only a minority expressed (very) negative attitudes regarding the right to abortion (11.4% in 1992 and 12.1% in 2012).

The empowerment of women in the exercise of reproductive rights has since the beginning of the 1950s been stimulated by the provision of medical advice and technical assistance.[43] The Yugoslav Constitution and the Constitution of the Socialist Republic of Slovenia in 1974 legalised abortion as a right of women to freely decide on the birth of a child. This right was defended in 1991, after a fierce public debate and demonstrations in support of 55 Article on 11 December 1991 before the Assembly of the Republic of Slovenia organized by different women's groups.

Gender and the economy[44]

The employment of women in Slovenia was high already before the Second World War (for example, in 1931 in then Drava County women comprised 39.6% of all employed); after the war the share of women in the labour force rose from 33.3% (1952) to 41.2% (1970), 44.2% (1980) and 46.8% (1990).[45] In 2013, women comprised 46.6% of persons in paid employment.[46]

In 2012, the employment rate for the age group 20-64 for women was 64.6% compared to 71.8% for men (gender gap of 7.2 percentage points which is lower than the 2012 EU-28 average of 12.2. Trends regarding the gender employment gap, similar to other indicators of the position of women on the labour market should be monitored closely in times of crisis when gender equality could be marginalised and austerity measures could negatively affect employment in feminised public sectors. Female labour market participation in Slovenia is high with respect to the EU-28 average (62.3% in 2012). In Slovenia, most women choose to stay at home for one year (taking their entire maternity/parental leave, which is fully compensated) and then return to full-

43 Jogan, »Slovenska (postmoderna) družba«, *passim*

44 If it is not otherwise indicated, data in this section are derived from Aleksandra Kanjuo Mrčela, Country fiche on Gender equality and policy developments for Slovenia 1Q2013; ENEGE; prepared for and financed by European Commission, Directorate General Justice, Unit D2 "Gender Equality" in the framework of the service contract managed by FGB in partnership with IRS (2013).

45 *Ibid.*

46 SORS, special release on International Women's Day 2014, Thursday, 6 March 2014 [note 4].

time work. Since the introduction of a non-transferable right to paternity leave,[47] the majority of fathers use the fully paid part of that leave but do not participate equally in other forms of parental leave or in childcare.

However, the quality of female employment is problematic: women's employment is more precarious than men's. In 2012, 18.7% of women against 15.7% of men (a decrease of 0.8 percentage points compared to 2011) were employed on fixed-term contracts (both are higher than the corresponding EU-28 averages 14.2% and 13.3%) and the 2012 gender gap in this form of employment is -3.0 p.p., higher than the EU-28 average of -0.9 percentage points.

Generally, the indicator of full-time equivalent employment for women (age 20-64) in Slovenia is lower (60.5%) in 2012 than the employment rate 15-64 (60.5%), but it is considerably (8.1 p.p.) higher than the EU-28 average. This is due to a lower level of part-time work for women in Slovenia than the EU-28 average: in 2012, 13.1% of women against 7.0% of men. The women's rate is particularly higher than the EU-28 average (female rate 32.5% and male rate 9.4% in 2012). Gender segregation in occupations was 25.8% in 2012 and it is higher than the EU-28 average of 24.5%. Gender segregation in economic sectors at 19.9% in 2012 is also higher than the EU-28 average which is 18.7%.

The unemployment rate for women (for the age group 15-74) was at 9.4% in 2012 – higher than for men in the same age group (8.4%).

One of the important features of the Slovenian labour market is its segmentation. Secure open-ended jobs are mainly taken by older workers and highly insecure contracts are becoming common among the younger (especially female) working force. Another relevant feature of the country in relation to women's participation in the labour market is the widespread use of formal childcare, which covers more children in Slovenia than the EU-28 average in all three age groups in 2011: 37% of children under 3 years (compared to 30% in the EU-28), 92% of children aged 3 to compulsory school age (compared to 83% in the EU-28) and almost all (100%) children aged from compulsory school age up to 12 years (compared to 96% in the EU-28) in 2011. In all three cases, the majority of children are in full-time care (34%, 81%, and 73%, respectively).

The unadjusted gender pay gap stood at 2.3 % in 2011, amongst the lowest in Europe (16.2% being the EU-28 average). The Statistical Office of the

47 Since 2001, Slovenian fathers have the right to take paternal leave of 90 days (15 days are fully compensated and only social contributions are paid for the remaining 75 days). The paid part of the paternal leave was extended to 30 days by the new Law on Parental Protection and Family Benefits passed on the 3rd April 2014, but this right will be realised only when financial circumstances improve (after economic growth in the country reach 2.5%.

Republic of Slovenia shows that average monthly gross earnings of women in 2011 were 95.4% those of men.[48] SORS points out that these are average values and that the differences are due to different educational, occupational and age structure. However, the recently published analysis of matched employer-employee data examining gender differences in pay over a 15-year period (1993-2007) in Slovenia found that there was a substantial increase in gender inequality over this period, and that in the period 2003-2007 men on average earned roughly 23% more than women, and 18% more than women doing the same work for the same employer. Analysis shows that women doing the same work for the same employer earn significantly less even in the public sector.[49]

Basis and perspectives of gender equality in Slovenia

After the declaration of independence and accession to the EU, there were substantial legislative changes in Slovenia. Laws that were passed in the last two decades have improved the legislative basis for gender equality. One of the most important contributions to the equal opportunities policy framework in Slovenia was the adoption of the Resolution on the National Programme for Equal Opportunities for Women and Men (2005-2013) in 2005. The Resolution specified measures for the achievement of gender equality related aims as well as the responsible actors and indicators of the successful implementation of these measures. Analysis of the Slovenian social partners' attitudes and activities shows that the Government (mainly through the Office for Equal Opportunities) and trade unions (at least the largest confederation) were increasingly active in integrating equal opportunity into their policies and in creating internal and external EO-friendly infrastructural frameworks. Employer organisations were the least active in this respect.

Slovenia's specific transition approach was characterised by a combination of gradual reforms and some more radical socio-economic and social security system changes. In the first gradual reform phase, new legislation that was adopted in various areas (such as privatisation, commercial companies and labour relations) established a framework for reform of the old system, while social protection schemes were in place to amortize the negative economic and social consequences of these reforms. The second phase was characterised by

48 SORS, Structure of earnings statistics Statistical Office of the Republic of Slovenia, 27 September 2012, First Release

49 A. Penner, et al., "Neenakosti po spolu v Sloveniji od 1993 do 2007. Razlike v plačah v perspektivi ekonomske socilogije" [Gender inequality in Slovenia, 1993-2007; an economic sociology perspective on pay differences], in *Teorija in praksa* (Ljubljana), Vol. 59, No. 6 (2012), pp. 854-877

an attempt to implement more radical liberal reforms proposed by the right-wing government in 2005. That radical reform programme was strongly opposed by a considerable part of the public, academic community and trade unions, and political opposition. Critics objected to the radicalism of the reforms in conditions of stable and positive development in Slovenia and voiced fears that the reform package (based on the introduction of a flat tax system, privatisation of public services, increased labour market flexibility and liberalisation of the social security system) would lower the level of social security and create a polarised socially unequal society. It was argued that such a development would also have a negative impact on gender equality. As a result, there was some modification of measures foreseen by the reform programme (e.g., the controversial flat tax system was replaced by a three level progressive tax system). After several years of public debate, the pension reform that was adopted in 2012 tightened retirement conditions by raising the retirement age for both men and women to 65 years (or 60 years of age, on the basis of 40 years of service) and by extending the period for calculating the pension basis from 18 to 24 years. The equalisation of the retirement age of women and men is to be reached gradually in six years. Critiques that women will carry the major part of the pension reform burden that were raised before the reform was passed, were answered by some changes of the reform proposal. Women will be able to retire earlier – at 56 or 57 years of age if they started to work before their 18th year and if they had children for whom they took care (6 months earlier for one child, 16 months for two, 26 months for three, 36 months for four, and 48 months for five children). The proposed equalisation of retirement conditions for men and women could be additionally discriminatory toward women because of statistical discrimination as many young women get regular jobs later due to potential parenthood.

The government introduced austerity measures in 2013, while all other policies and reforms were still under debate (e.g., health reform, labour market reform, privatisation). The recent "Study on the impact of the crisis and the austerity measures on the situation of women and men and gender equality in Slovenia" shows that the government did not estimate gender specific consequences of the adoption of anti-crisis measures.[50] The analysis concludes that the austerity measures had significantly more negative effects on women than on men and endangered women's economic independence.

Although the restoration of capitalism has already changed the previously existing welfare system, and resulted in increased uncertainty in the labour

---

50 Živa Humer and Metka Roksandić, 2013. Protikrizni ukrepi in enakost spolov, at http://www.mddsz.gov.si/fileadmin/mddsz.gov.si/pageuploads/dokumenti__pdf/enake_moznosti/NVO2013ProtikrizniUkrepiInEnakostSpolov.pdf [last accessed on 12 December 2014].

market, it has not (yet) caused dramatic negative changes regarding gender equality in the social security systems and policies. It would be positive if Slovenia can sustain some of its existing advantages (such as well supported work-family balancing schemes) and does not reduce gender equality while implementing some of the EU policy-driven labour market reforms (such as, e.g., labour market flexibility). The gender-sensitive approach in the choice of future development models should acknowledge European experience that shows that in the past, the indicators of gender equality were better in countries with a social-democratic tradition (e.g., the Nordic countries) then in countries following free-market doctrines.

The existing gender equality legislative and policy framework until the end of 2013 provided a good basis for the development of gender equality in Slovenia. That framework is now changing. The new Act on Equality of Women and Men regulates the procedure of adoption and it is expected that the new strategic document will be created, based on the evaluation of the Resolution on the National Programme for Equal Opportunities of Women and Men (2005-2013). The evaluation recognized that, given the perceived lack of coherence in the implementation of the principle of gender mainstreaming, optimal implementation of a "dual" approach to gender equality policies (gender mainstreaming in all policies and execution of women targeted specific actions) should be achieved. An important purpose of the resolution remains "to improve the status of women and to ensure sustainable development in the implementation of gender equality." Despite many positive changes and steps to improve the situation of women in the Slovenian society, gender differences based on certain traditional gender roles put women in a disadvantaged position. That should be identified and addressed through appropriate policies, which does not diminish the need for addressing issues specific to men; resolution of those is complementary to solving the problems of women. Although evaluation calls for awareness of the fact that women and men are heterogeneous groups and that intersectional approach should be used to solving complex social inequalities, the Resolution as a strategic document should be primarily focused on gender equality. Focusing on gender equality is particularly important in times of economic downturn, when there are strong tendencies of marginalization or opposition to actions in this area. The evaluation stated that the existence of a strategic policy document on gender equality is even more important today than eight years ago, as it is necessary to respond to the negative responses to increasing gender equality and attempts at the re-traditionalisation of societal gender roles, which are particularly strong in circumstances of economic crisis. These trends increase the risk that normative acts are not implemented in practice. In a crisis context, ways of solving the problems associated with multiple dimensions of inequality (especially economic and gender) should be envisaged.

Similarities and differences in achieving of gender equality in two countries

In spite of the fact that the history of the development of the economic and political systems in the two countries has been different in many respects, contributing to the economic equality of women and men, many problems regarding gender equality are similar (e.g., vertical and horizontal gender segregation, unequal division of unpaid domestic and care work). A combination of factors influences gender equality in Norway and Slovenia.

Some are similar – in both countries there exists a strong gender egalitarian stance for many decades reflected in attitudes toward gender roles and rights (see Appendix I); in both countries a combination of a women's movement and strong state support influenced positively gender equality; both countries have had a strong welfare states encouraging (practically and ideologically) the high participation of women in paid employment providing for opportunities for women to combine work and family obligations; in both countries gender mainstreaming was recently introduced, practiced and proved to be a problematic method for achieving more of gender equality.

Some are different - while the Slovenian welfare state supported the two-earner model based on the full-time employment of men and women, Norwegian women mostly worked part-time (and that is, according to government plans, to be changed); a side effect of the Slovenian system (that functioned within the social environment in which primary responsibility for parenthood and home-making) was that economically independent women became overburdened; Norway is a much wealthier country[51] and the impact of the global economic crisis is weaker and issues related to it are easier to resolve; and Slovenia has gone through a rough time of multiple (political and economic) transitions.

The future developments regarding gender equality in Norway and Slovenia will be influenced mainly by the choice of models of further economic development as well as the choice of legal and institutional framework for gender equality in two countries. For gender equality in both countries, the choice of a model based on social equality, high educated and empowered workforce, development of care service and existence of policies tackling

51 The GDP (PPP) per capita of Norway in 2014 (66,937 $) may be compared to GDP per capita in Slovenia (29,658 $). Both countries invest a high and similar percentage of GDP to health (9 % in Norway and 9.1 % in Slovania) and education (6.9 % in Norway and 5.7 % in Slovenia).

gender inequalities, would be optimal and also in line with the dominant social norms and previous development.

Appendix I

Table 6.2. Attitudes on gender equality related issues in Norway and Slovenia (the European Value Survey, 1992 and 2008)

	Norway		Slovenia	
	1992	2008	1992	2008
Sharing household chores is very important for a successful marriage	33.9	34.2	34.3	38.9
Happy sexual relation is very important for a successful marriage	62.1	49.1	60.8	56.3
I think that marriage is an outdated institution	10.1	19.9	17.6	25.0
Homosexual couples should be able to adopt a child (strongly) agree	-	42.1	-	18.1
A pre-school child is likely to suffer if his or her mother works (strongly) agree	45.6	19.8	66.7	36.4
A job is alright but what most women really want is a home and children (strongly) agree	50.7	34.0	76.5	64.7
To be a housewife is equally fulfilling as working for pay (strongly) agree	53.1	47.9	62.6	59.8
Having a job is the best way for a woman to be an independent person (strongly) agree	75.1	84.2	73.4	77.9
Both husband and wife should contribute to the household income (strongly) agree	74.3	91.0	93.4	90.4
In general, fathers are as well suited to look after their children as mothers (strongly) agree	-	88.2	87.9*	90.4
Men should take as much responsibility as women for the home and children	-	96.5	-	97.2
Do you approve or disapprove of abortion in the following circumstances:				
Where the woman is not married (approve)	45.1	67.1	44.0	67.9
Where a married couple does not want to have any more children (approve)	45.9	58.1	70.4	71.8

Source: European Value Study 1999

Marjan Smrke

7 The Roman Catholic Church in Post-Socialist Slovenia: From Pride to Decapitation

According to research conducted by the few sociologists engaged in the study of religion in Slovenia, Slovene society ranks among those in Europe which are religious to an average degree, i.e., the population is secularized to an average extent. In comparison with its neighbours and other republics formerly part of socialist Yugoslavia, Slovenia is below average as regards religiosity, i.e., its secularization is above average.[1] Nevertheless - or perhaps for this very reason, religion frequently and vehemently entered public debate during the post-socialist period of transition. Not many other issues have instigated as many passionate discussions and arguments as did those pertaining to the position of the Roman Catholic Church in the new Slovene state. Such arguments pertained to the understanding of the constitutional separation of Church and state, denationalization, the nature and content of religious education in state schools, and bilateral relations with the Holy See, as well as legislation governing the religious freedom of the individual. Issues of sexual reproduction (such as abortion, artificial insemination and donor insemination of single women) as well as other general or specific political concerns (elections, the rights of children and same-sex couples) also became controversial due to the Roman Catholic Church's seeking direct involvement. To the external observer these conflicts might have seemed absurd, a waste of time and energy (which they largely were); yet from a sociological perspective they would seem inevitable.

Slovenes might not be of one mind if asked to identify which single event or issue pertaining to religion has been the most significant in the twenty years since the country's independence. Not many, however, would deny the significance of the events underpinning the recent decline in trust in the Roman Catholic Church in Slovenia, and the consequent disciplinary resignation of four archbishops (i.e., two-thirds of all elected to that position since the demise of socialism) in what was termed, by some commentators, the *decapitation* of

1 Marko Kerševan and Sergej Flere, *Religija in sodobna družba: uvod v sociologijo religije* (Ljubljana: Znanstveno in publicistično središče, 1995); Marjan Smrke and Samo Uhan, "Atheism in Post-Socialist Conditions: The Case of Slovenia", in *Teorija & Praksa,* Vol. 49, No. 3 (2012), pp. 492-515; and Niko Toš, "(De)secularisation or (Re)confessionalisation Processes in Europe", in *Teorija & Praksa,* Vol. 50, No. 1 /2013), pp. 172-204.

the Church.[2] This chapter aspires, among other things, to offer a sociological explanation for this surprising and unique unravelling of the Church's position in a post-socialist society.

Complexities of the Catholic Religious Pattern

In order to comprehend developments in relation to religion and religious organizations in the context of Slovene society, it is necessary to understand (1) the extant religious structures, their characteristics and the way they have evolved over time; (2) the general and specific historical circumstances of the social modernization of Slovenes, knowing that in Europe this process has been largely accompanied by secularization; and (3) those changes which occurred in the religious sphere during independent Slovenia's post-socialist transition.

Several authors underscore the importance that the initial religious structure has in any understanding of broader social, political, economic and cultural developments.[3] This structure is contingent upon (1) size disparities of the operating religious organizations; and (2) the character of the predominant Church or Churches.

Whether or not there is a single Church or several prevalent religious organizations makes a difference in a given society. Supply-side theory, for instance, when applied to secularization, derives its key conclusions on the basis of structure. Because they differ in character, it makes a difference whether a Roman Catholic, an Orthodox, or a Protestant Church is predominant in any given religious sphere. Churches differ with respect to their organization and have disparate expectations and demands of the individual and of society, depending on their doctrine, whilst their involvement in (or separation from) the mechanisms of state and politics reflect differently upon that society. At a dissimilar pace, and to varying extents, Churches adapt – or fail to adapt – to the evolving societies in which they operate, and through religious socialization they assert different ethoses in relation to perspectives and attitudes. Classical sociologists of religion, notably Max Weber and Emile Durkheim, researched the long-term effects of (the predominant) creed in relation to social activities.

---

2 This somewhat crude expression "obglavljenje" was introduced into the public debate by a number of Catholic theologians who considered these depositions as unwarranted, unjust and damaging.

3 David Martin, *A General Theory of Secularization* (Aldershot (England): Gregg Revivals, 1978; reprinted 1993), p. 24; Ted G. Jelen and Clyde Wilcox (eds.), *Religion and Politics in Comparative Perspective: The One, the Few, and the Many* (Cambridge: Cambridge University Press, 2002), p. 7; and Steve Bruce, *Secularization* (Oxford: Oxford University Press, 2011).

Contemporary sociologists also confirm differences stemming from religion, for instance with regard to value orientations.[4]

Europe's fundamental religious structures were established primarily during the Reformation and the Counter-Reformation, and for the most part they were the result of a violent struggle for dominance and social power.

For Slovenes, the Protestant Reformation was linked with the first budding of national consciousness.[5] In turn, the Counter-Reformation established the conditions where the religion of the ruler dictated the religion of the ruled (*cuius regio, eius religio*), thus compelling even the populations of predominantly Lutheran territories to be re-Catholicised. The Roman Catholic Church enjoyed a clearly privileged position during the centuries of Austrian Habsburg rule (which ended in 1918), and, prior to World War Two, in the albeit religiously diverse Kingdom of Yugoslavia. Slovenes lived in conditions marked by the characteristics and dilemmas of the Catholic ("Latin") religious-cultural pattern.[6]

First and foremost, this pattern is distinguished by the marked predominance of Catholicism and a religious ideology that promotes a model of obedience to the clerical hierarchy as a necessary and indeed the sole intermediary between man and God. In religious matters it allows people no freedom of choice. The individual, forever deemed immature, should obey the spiritual shepherds headed by the Pope. This is, and was, in direct opposition to the ideals and values promoted by Protestantism, such as religious exploration, the development of a personal and direct relationship between an individual and God, the rejection of irrational and superstitious practices, and unquestioning respect of hierarchies. Historically this was reflected in weaker individualism, diminished self-responsibility and a decrease in the value accorded to secular endeavour.

---

4 Ronald Inglehart and Christian Welzel, "Changing Mass Priorities: The Link Between Modernization and Democracy", in *Perspectives on Politics*, vol. 8, No. 2 (2010), p. 554; Pippa Norris and Ronald Inglehart, *Sacred and Secular: Religion and Politics Worldwide* (Cambridge and New York: Cambridge University Press, 2004; reprinted 2011); and Pippa Norris and Ronald Inglehart, *Cosmopolitan Communications: Cultural Diversity in a Globalized World* (Cambridge and New York: Cambridge University Press, 2009).

5 Crucial in this were the efforts of the Lutheran pastor and reformer Primož Trubar (1508-1586), the author of a Catechism that was the first work to be printed in the Slovene language. According to the 1995 Slovene Public Opinion Survey, Trubar is the most important historical figure in Slovenia. See Niko Toš, et al. Slovensko javno mnenje 1995/3. (Ljubljana: Fakulteta za družbene vede, CJMMK, 1995).

6 Martin, *A General Theory,* pp. 36-42)

Despite its pre-eminence,[7] the Roman Catholic Church failed to enforce absolute religious homogeneity. A number of ethnographic, historical, sociological and literary sources have identified (1) expressions of crypto-Protestantism, and (2) divergence in the form of popular piety (including traces of paganism)[8], and civil disobedience in opposition to Church politics[9], together with religious doubt and non-belief.[10]

The perceived incongruence between theory (i.e., religious ideology) and practice (i.e., habitual behaviour) of clergy and laity has been less discussed. This lack of congruity, itself typical of Catholic environments in general, reflects the unresponsiveness of Catholic ideology: unattainable ideals (such as premarital virginity) on the one side, and lax practice on the other. The sociological implication of such disparity is the far-reaching and to a great extent negative legacy which, despite the processes of secularization, maintains its grip. The adopted notion, namely, that the norm is something that can be bent, remains.

The Catholic religious pattern typically responds to the challenges of social modernization by way of social polarization[11]and division,[12] although there are exceptions. In Slovenia, this was expressed in the tensions between the pro-Church forces within society who advocated all – or at least the majority – of that which constituted the Church's notion of a perfect Catholic society (so-called integrism), and those anticlerical forces who strove for a reduction of the role of the Church in society as well as for secularization at the societal level. The open confrontation and the resulting cultural battle has been only one of the many expressions of this polarization, which left a strong mark on cultural and political life in Slovenia.[13] Marked by the Europe-wide rise of right- and

---

7 As per the 1931 census, 97% of the population on Slovene territory declared themselves to be Catholic.

8 Marko Kerševan, *Religija in Slovenska Kultura : ljudska religioznost, civilna religija in ateizem v Sloveniji* (Ljubljana: Znanstveni Inštitut Filozofske Fakultete, 1989), pp. 12-23; and Janez Trdina, *Podobe Prednikov. Zapiski Janeza Trdine iz Odobja 1870 – 1879* (Ljubljana: Univerzitetna Konferenca ZSMS, Knjižnica Revolucionarne Teorije., 1870-79; reprinted 1987).

9 Marta Verginella, *Ekonomija Odrešenja in Preživetja: Odnos do Življenja in Smrti na Tržaškem Podeželj* (Koper: Knjižnica Annales, 1996).

10 Trdina, *Podobe Prednikov.*

11 Martin, *A General Theory*, p. 24.

12 Bruce, *Secularization,* p. 8)

13 The far-reaching consequences of this division have been thoroughly discussed by Slovene sociologist Spomenka Hribar (b. 1941). She is especially critical of the role of Bishop Anton Mahnič (1850-1920) who, spurred with ideological dogmatism, incited the so-called *delitev duhov* (separation of spirits). Mahnič demanded clear differentiation between those agents

left-wing ideologies and authoritarianisms, the 1930s saw the culmination of this tension among Slovenes.[14]

Although initially only a small fraction of the anticlerical pole, the Communist Party gradually asserted its military and political power in the course of World War Two. Having won the war, it fundamentally changed the relations between the state and the Churches in Yugoslavia. This was not only spurred by Marxist ideology and its perception of religion as a sign of backwardness and false consciousness, but also grounded in the compromising fact that some of the local clerics[15] in Yugoslavia had collaborated with the Axis forces of invasion and occupation. The separation of Church and state, as it was accomplished in post-war Yugoslavia, corresponds to a conflict pattern of social secularization that Martin links mainly with Catholic and Orthodox environments.[16] According to Martin, the longer that secularization is delayed at the societal level, the more likely it will be effected in a violent manner.

Reflecting on the manner of Church-state separation following World War Two, we must bear in mind that the antagonistic agents involved were similarly rigid in terms of their ideology: at that time the Communist Party was in many aspects Stalinist and dogmatic,[17] while the Roman Catholic Church exhibited all its pre-Vatican II and anti-modernist tendencies. Both strove for control over

---

within society that acted in accord with Roman Catholic doctrine and those forces which opposed it.

14 This was not an era of moderation. Christian socialist politician, priest, journalist, and author Janez Evangelist Krek (1865-1917) was one of the few dissident voices to be heard among Slovenia's Catholic clergy during the first half of the 20th century. His advocating separation of Church and state, as well as belief that the former should be financially independent, was ultimately disregarded.

15 During World War Two, with some exceptions – including, notably, Archbishop Alojzije Stepinac -- the Croatian Roman Catholic Church was openly supportive of the government of the so-called *Independent State of Croatia* - a puppet state of Nazi Germany established across a large swathe of the dismantled Axis-occupied Kingdom of Yugoslavia; likewise, Slovenia's Catholic Church in the "*Province of Ljubljana*", and the Serbian Orthodox Church in relation to the Nedić regime in Serbia, were also more than acquiescent. In the case of the Serbian Orthodox Church, an exception should be noted for Patriarch Gavrilo (Dožić).

16 According to Martin, relations between the state and Protestant Church (the so-called Scandinavian-Lutheran pattern) cause less friction and tension due to the different character of the Protestant Church. See Martin, *A General Theory*, p. 59).

17 Following a dramatic schism within the *Cominform*, Tito's Yugoslav Communist Party tore away from Stalin's Soviet bloc in 1948. The so-called *Informbiro* period (1948–55) that followed was characterised by Yugoslavia's vitriolic quarrelling with its former communist allies within Russia's sphere of influence. Ironically this departure from the Soviet line and the exhibition of hostility towards the Soviet Union was the most Stalinist in Yugoslavia's history. It became dogmatically orthodox and repressive towards the dissidents among its own ranks.

the whole of society. This too is a reason why secularization at a societal level - i.e., the separation of Church and state - was, according to Kerševan,[18] in reality ambivalent. Kerševan reflects on those areas where socialist modernization was in fact contradictory. While the Communist Party radically introduced much of what is today considered integral to modern society (including separation of Church and state), it insisted on reserving the central role for itself, from which position it could dominate and control social sub-systems. By way of this, in reality, a pre-modern social organization was maintained. Kerševan's perspective agrees with Martin's observation that the anticlerical pole was in many aspects a counterimage of the ecclesiastical one. The dominance of the Communist Party over Yugoslav and Slovene society was an example of integrism embedded in a Marxist framework.[19] Critical sociologists at the time coined the expression "red clericalism".

We can extend this debate by asking whether or not Yugoslav socialism was, to a certain extent, a secular religion. Such an opinion was proffered by Pope John Paul II in *Centesimus Annus*[20] in relation to the recently fallen European Communist regimes. Some authors do indeed discuss Yugoslav socialism as a form of specific civil religion,[21] interpreting the 1980s, following the death of Yugoslavia's Communist President Josip Broz Tito (1892-1980), as an era of religious reinvigoration, manifested in the worship of the departed leader, followed by a gradual secularization with regard to this civil religion's dogmas and values.

Three important changes occurred in relation to religion in Slovenia during the socialist era: First, Catholicism lost its predominant position in society. Such was primarily the consequence of actions orchestrated by the political regime, although in this regard communist rule in Slovenia was markedly less restrictive in relation to religion than other Eastern European regimes. Such was, however, not entirely the consequence of politics; similar declines were identified within the processes of social modernization in a number of non-

---

Thousands of (presumably) pro-Soviet members of the Party were deported to labour camps and prisons, most notably the Adriatic island of Goli Otok, which served as a Yugoslav gulag.

18 Marko Kerševan, "L'ambivalence de la revitalisation religieuse dans les sociétés post-socialistes", in *Social Compass*, vol. 40, Issue 1 (March 1993), pp. 123-133.

19 Martin, *A General Theory,* p. 110.

20 "*Hundredth Year*", an encyclical written by Pope John Paul II in 1991 to mark the hundredth anniversary of *Rerum Novarum*, an encyclical issued by Pope Leo XIII in 1891. See Pope John Paul II.: Centesimus Annus (1991).

21 Vjekoslav Perica, *Balkan Idols. Religion and Nationalism in Yugoslav States* (Oxford and New York: Oxford University Press, 2002), p. 89; and Sergej Flere, "The Broken Covenant of Tito's People: The Problem of Civil Religion in Communist Yugoslavia", in *East European Politics and Societies*, vol. 21. Issue 4 (November 2007), pp. 681-703.

socialist Catholic environments. Contemporary sociological research at the time thus established a decline in religious belief and religious participation, together with a growing heterogeneity among Catholics in relation to Church doctrine.[22] Catholic population increasingly interlaced Catholic views with secular ones, thus the religious structure witnessed significant evolution and was no longer homogeneous. The tide of secularization was particularly evident, and public expression of religiosity fell from 67.8% in 1968 to 45.3% in 1978. The later period of desecularization somewhat reversed the trend, but the proportion of believers never again attained its former value.

Second, the party's policy toward religion evolved, as did the character of the Church. The regime gradually lessened its feisty and repressive attitude vis-à-vis religion and became more conciliatory. In the post-Vatican II era, there was a general acceptance of the separation of the Church and state as well as freedom of religion. Slovenia's Roman Catholic Church, however, soon diverged from the spirit of Vatican II, even more perceptibly than the Church in general. Both of the above, the tendencies towards secularization and the changes in the character of both protagonists, led to the establishment of the so-called post-Catholic (post-Latin) religious pattern. At the demise of socialism in Slovenia, it engendered a lesser degree of social polarisation.

Third, the 1980s saw the development of new phenomena: the rise of new age ideas, together with new religious movements and communities, variously characterized by sociologists as "religious bricolage", "pick-and-mix religion", and "do-it-yourself religion", among other terms. This return of religion[23] also manifested itself in desecularization at the level of consciousness, while the word *belief* was significantly redefined.

From Pride to Decapitation

Slovenia attained its political sovereignty in 1991 in the wake of a ten-day war which precipitated the complete collapse of the Yugoslav army on Slovene territory. This fact is of no little importance in understanding religious developments within the newly independent Slovenia. In contrast to Slovenia, other constituent republics of Yugoslavia became engulfed in long ethnic and military conflicts which engendered distinct de-secularization [24] and the disintegration of Yugoslavia itself. The fall of socialism was hastened by the rise of nation-

22 Zdenko Roter, *Vera in Nevera v Sloveniji 1968-1978* (Maribor: Obzorja, 1982); and Marko Kerševan, *Cerkvena Religioznost v Sloveniji* (Maribor: Obzorja, 1982).

23 By 1990 religious belief among Slovenes had risen to 63.8%.

24 Smrke and Uhan, "Atheism in Post-Socialist Conditions", p. 496.

alism, which in turn engendered military conflict between neighbours of different nationalities and creeds.[25] Worsening economic conditions as well as intensified social inequality in Croatia, Bosnia-Herzegovina, Serbia, Montenegro, and Macedonia contributed to a rise in religiosity and reinforced the role of each respective historically predominant Church. By contrast, Slovenia was politically stable and its relatively favourable economic situation supported a constitutionally-defined social state until the 2008 crisis.

Pluralization, at the structural level, continued: In the two decades following independence, the number of registered religious communities operating in Slovenia rose from 15 to 43; non-registered ones are believed to be at least twice this number. Typically very small in size,[26] these religious communities exhibit disparate structures and are very diverse in terms of content and character. Catholics are still by far the largest group, although in terms of numbers they account for a diminishing percentage of Slovenia's total population, falling from 71.6% in 1991 to 57.8% in 2002.[27] Internal self-differentiation among Catholics – in relation to those who are Church-faithful and autonomously-faithful (i.e., selectively religious) – continued and deepened, with those who adhered strictly to Church doctrine now representing the smallest faction of all Catholics.[28] According to some researchers, Slovene Catholic religiosity is predominantly hollow and non-binding,[29] with the greater part of the country's Catholics describing themselves as being of Christian belief. As Berger and Luckmann find typical for the modern western world "they somehow belong to the Church, yet in a non-binding manner which theologians perceive as disagreeably close to other forms of consumerism."[30] In light of the obvious interweaving of Catholic faith, secularity and new age spir-

---

25 Steve Bruce, *Religion in the Modern World: from Cathedrals to Cults* (Oxford: Oxford University Press, 1996), p. 96. Martin and Bruce recognized and theoretically assessed these factors as instrumental in desecularisation and the revitalization of religion.

26 Aleš Črnič et al. "Religious Pluralisation in Slovenia", in *Teorija & Praksa*, vol. 50, No. 1 (2013), pp. 205-232; and A. Črnič, *Na Vodnarjevem Valu* (Ljubljana: Založba FDV, 2012).

27 The most recent census (2011) no longer included religion. See Table 7.1 for data on religious adherence obtained by the Slovene Public Opinion (SJM) survey.

28 Dragoš, Srečo (2003): Katoliška Identiteta Slovencev? *Annales*, vol. 13(1), 39-54; and Niko Toš, "(Ne)religioznost Slovencev v primerjavi z drugimi srednje- in vzhodnoevropskimi narodi", in *Podobe o Cerkvi in religiji (na Slovenskem v 90-ih) 11–80* (Ljubljana: FDV–IDV – CJMMK, 1999).

29 Sergej Flere and Rudi Klanjšek, "Ali je votlost značilnost vernosti na Slovenskem?", in *Družboslovne Razprave*, Vol. 23, No. 56 (2007), pp. 7–20.

30 Peter L. Berger and Thomas Luckmann, *Modernost, pluralizem in kriza smisla* [Modernity, pluralism and the crisis of meaning], trans. from English by Suzana Cergol (Ljubljana: Nova Revija, 1999), pp. 45-46.

ituality among Catholics, one wonders how many believers would remain Catholic if they had to be so in the manner strictly prescribed by the Roman Catholic Church.

Statistical data regarding religiosity reveal oscillations in different directions. An increase in religious belief was perceived in the early 1990s, with the "conversion" of erstwhile Communists being of particular interest - a trend that was even more conspicuous in some other post-Communist states. I interpreted (a part of) such conversions as social mimicry: adaptation of one's ideological colour to the anticipated (pro-religious) change in the colour of the environment.[31] When compared to data from the early 1990s,[32] recent statistics reveal a rise in indicators of secularization, such as a decline in the importance of religion in life, a decline in the number of active believers as well as those believing in god, a decline in adherence to the Roman Catholic Church (Table 7.1), a decline in Sunday attendance at Mass (see Figure 7.1), a decline in church baptisms and church weddings,[33] a fall in the number of newly-ordained Catholic priests, fewer nuns[34] and friars. Indirect indicators, such as an increasing percentage of children born out of wedlock (57% in 2012), also point towards secularization. Over recent years, a severe decline in trust in the Church has been expressed through such indicators as the waning authority of the Church, and diminishing trust in the Church and clergy. According to Chaves, these are indicators of so-called neo-secularization.[35]

Such (neo)secularization trends reflects in part the reaction of Slovenes to the public endeavours and behaviour of Church authorities since the demise of socialism. The Roman Catholic Church entered the era of Slovene independence as by far the most powerful religious organization in the country.[36] Having survived difficult times during the socialist period, it prided itself on having considerable moral capital. Unlike in the past centuries when it was

31 Marjan Smrke, "Stare Vešče – Nova Luč: Religijske oblike družbene mimikrije v pogojih družbene tranzicije", in *Teorija & Praksa,* vol. 39, No. 2 (2002), pp. 170-181.

32 According to data obtained through the International Social Survey Programme (ISSP) and World Values Survey (WVS).

33 See Brigita Perše, (2011): "'Še-sindrom' v katoliški Cerkvi na Slovenskem zahteva novo evangelizacijo, zlasti v mestih" ["Still-Syndrome" in Catholic Church Requires New Evangelisation, Especially in Towns], in *Bogoslovni Vestnik,* vol. 71, No. 2 (2011), pp. 235 250.

34 Sonja Bezjak, "Catholic Women Religious Vocations in the Twentieth Century: The Slovenian Case", in *Review of Religious Research*, vol. 54, Issue 2 (June 2012), pp. 157-174.

35 Mark Chaves, "Secularization as Declining Religious Authority", in *Social Forces*, vol. 72, No. 3 (March 1994), pp. 749-774.

36 Adherents to the Evangelical (Lutheran) Church, itself a surviving continuation of Trubar's 16th century Protestantism, the Serbian Orthodox Church and Moslem Community together account for some 5% of the population of Slovenia.

clearly pre-eminent, the Church had been pushed to the margin of society. After World War Two, and most notably during the 1950s, many of the clergy were the victims of repression. As a consequence of deep frustrations rooted in World War Two, and particularly the bloody epilogue of the post-war executions,[37] the Church seethed with resentment toward the socialist regime. It was on this basis that the Roman Catholic Church fashioned and arrested its high expectations and demands regarding its position in the new society. In many aspects, however, the Church demonstrated a tendency to re-invoke the pre-war period when it had enjoyed ideological hegemony. The possibilities and opportunities which opened for the Church after the fall of its great historical adversary were thwarted through its regression to a pre-Vatican II guise.[38] Indeed, the Catholic Church has never considered itself a denomination, but the pre-denominational *original*,[39] in consideration of which it is easy to understand why it was ill-prepared for the post-socialist era.

Table 7.1. Which religious denomination do you belong?

	1992 (SPO 92/4)	1995 (SPO 95/1)	1999 (SPO 99/4)	2005 (SPo 05/2)	2009 (SPO 09/2)	2012 (SPO12/2)
Roman-catholic	75.0	75.1	72.4	64.5	67.5	63.1
Protestant - Lutheran	1.5	1.2	0.7	1.9	0.7	1.1
Orthodox	3.1	1.6	1.7	1.8	1.8	1.6
Other Christian	0.5	0.6	1.3	0.8	0.8	0.1
Islamic community	2.0	1.3	1.1	1.4	1.2	1.9
Other non-Christian	0.2	0.1	0.3	0.2	0.1	0.2
No adherence	15.4	17.7	16.7	20.2	23.0	30.2
Don't know: no answer	2.2	2.5	5.8	3.5	4.9	1.8

Source: Slovenian Public Opinion Surveys 1992 – 2012

37 In the months following the end of World War Two, several tens of thousands of Axis collaborators were executed in the territory of Slovenia. Some 12,000 Slovenes were put to death without trial. For the most part they were members of military formations who had collaborated with the forces of occupation, and had received ideological guidance from the Roman Catholic Church.

38 Srđan Vrcan, a prominent sociologist of former Yugoslavia, writes about the "change in methaphore" to *ecclesia triumphans, ecclesia militans, ecclessia semper eadem*: "the Church triumphant, the Church militant, the Church forever the same..." See Srđan Vrcan, *Vjera u Vrtlozima Tranzicije* (Split: Glas Dalmacije - Dalmatinska Akcija, 2001), p. 250.

39 Berger and Luckmann, *Modernost, pluralizem,* p. 45.

Figure 7.1. How often do you attend religious services?

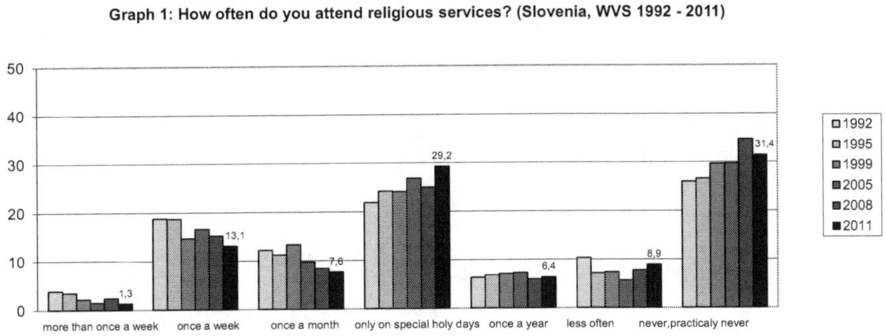

Source: Slovenia, WVS 1992 – 2011.

Such self-assured omnipotence was first articulated in the discussion of denationalization and the introduction of religious education in state schools. The Church was relentless in relation to the return of its feudal estates (most of which were acquired in the 11th century) that had been nationalized under communism. Under the terms of the Denationalization Act RS (November 1991), the Church regained all its former estates in Slovenia, much to the indignation of a substantial part of the country's population.

Asserting its ancient claim that the Roman Catholic faith is the one and only true Christian faith, and that only the teachings of the Catholic Church shall assure a moral society, the Church demanded that the catechesis be introduced into all state schools (from kindergartens to universities). It was ultimately unsuccessful in this endeavour, and Catholic teaching remained limited to the presbytery. Instead, a broader religious education - encompassing world religions - was introduced into schools, but, due to the lack of interest and the position taken by the Church, this takes place only in a small number of schools.[40]

40 Marjan Smrke and Tatjana Rakar, "Religious Education in Slovenia" in Zorica Kuburić and Christian Moe, (eds.), *Religion and pluralism in education: Comparative approaches in the Western Balkans* (Novi Sad: CEIR, 2006), pp. 9-38.

The appointment of Franc Rode as Archbishop of Ljubljana[41] in 1997 lent even more sharpness to the voice and actions of the Roman Catholic Church in Slovenia. Immediately upon his enthronement, Archbishop Rode demanded a ban on abortion, while his interpretation of Slovene history prescribed an inseparable link between the Catholic faith and the Slovene nation. He tried to persuade Slovenes, known for their respectful attitude toward the Reformation,[42] that the ultimate success of the Counter-Reformation across Slovenian lands was a fortunate development, for which they should rejoice. Regretting the occurrence of the European Enlightenment, Rode also expressed dissatisfaction with the constitutional principle of separation of state and religion, particularly with regard to the education system. He strove to picture the World War Two Partisan movement and the national liberation struggle against the occupation as negative. Archbishop Rode's public appearances and views were akin to those of a pre-war cleric believing that all spheres of society should be "permeated with the Gospel"; such was his interpretation of the new evangelization instigated by Pope John Paul II.

Many authors noticed a tendency towards integrism in Rode's public utterances, together with arbitrary deductive judgments typical of a theological style that predates the Second Vatican Council, while his assertions aimed at defaming non-religious Slovenes are certainly rebuffed by the conclusions of research. While the Archbishop asserted that Slovene atheists were unhappy and that there was no meaning to their lives, data reveal that they rank above average in both areas[43]; and while he claimed that the non-religious were less ethical than those who were religious, studies indicate that there is no significant difference between these two groups. Archbishop Rode likewise claimed that Christianity is the only assurance of humanism, despite empirical research clearly demonstrating that religious Slovenes are far more reserved and distant

41 Six men have served as archbishops in the two archdioceses of post-independence Slovenia: Alojzij Šuštar (1980-1997), Franc Rode (1997-2004), Alojzij Uran (2004-2010) and Anton Stres (2010-2013) in the Metropolitan Archdiocese of Ljubljana; together with Franc Kramberger (1980-2011) and Marjan Turnšek (2011-2013) in the Archdiocese of Maribor. Prior to his 2010 appointment as Archbishop of Ljubljana, Anton Stres served as Coadjutor Archbishop of Maribor (2009–2010). Slovenes Franc Perko (1986-2001) and Stanislav Hočevar (2001-) have also both served as Catholic Archbishops of Belgrade, while the Vatican's papal nuncio in Russia Ivan Jurkovič is a Titular Archbishop who has served in several countries.

42 31st October - Reformation Day - is the only new national holiday introduced in independent Slovenia which pertains to a religious event.

43 See Marjan Smrke, "Brezbožni in srečni: A/teizem in srečnost v medevropskih primerjavah", in Brina Malnar and Ivan Bernik (eds.), *S Slovenkami in Slovenci na štiri oči* (Ljubljana: FDV-IDV, 2004), pp. 233-252.

towards minority groups than the non-religious and atheist Slovenes.[44] Such was further confirmed in the public discussion of the so-called Family Code,[45] legislation intended, among many other things, to broaden the family rights of gays and lesbians. The Roman Catholic Church actively pushed for a referendum[46] which ultimately prevented the Code's adoption.

Slovenia's Catholic Church has consistently and successfully prevented the introduction of any legislation governing religious communities that would not be in its favour. It certainly lent its political support and tried to prevent expert public discussion of the 2007 Religious Freedom Act RS drafted by Slovenia's then Justice Minister Lovro Šturm, a member of the Roman Catholic lay-religious Order of the Knights of Malta.[47] Said Act provides the Roman Catholic Church and other larger religious organisations with concessions, but introduces fresh requirements for the registration of a religious community (including at least ten years of operation and at least one-hundred members), thus hindering the institution of smaller congregations. Only one new religious community has been registered in Slovenia since the law came into force. In 2010, the Constitutional Court established that two of the Act's articles, including the one addressing registration, were incongruent with the constitutional provision on separation of Church and state. The law is now being amended.

A specific *modus operandi,* which I believe serves as a mode of social mimicry, is discernible in the activities of the Catholic Church during the post-socialist era. Its clergy routinely play the victim, and express discontent with the position of their Church in society, while everything that opposes the Church's interests is presented as the vestiges of Communist oppression. Any criticism regarding the behaviour or actions of the clergy is portrayed as an assault on Christianity – if not Jesus Christ himself. Indicative is the difference in the respective assessments as to the situation regarding religious freedom in Slovenia as expressed by Anton Stres, the former Archbishop of Ljubljana, and

---

44 See Marjan Smrke and Mitja Hafner-Fink, "(Ne)religioznost in socialna distanca do izbranih družbenih manjšin v postsocialistični Evropi", in *Teorija & Praksa,* Vol. 45, Nos. 3-4 (2008), pp. 285-300.

45 The 2011 Family Code bill enacted by Slovenia's parliament extended the rights of registered same-sex couples to a degree equal to married couples, save for adoption, but allowing the adoption of one partner's biological child by the other same-sex partner. The law also expanded provisions protecting the rights of children.

46 In the 25 March 2012 referendum, 54.55% of voters rejected the Code, although voter turnout was a mere 30.31%. The Evangelical (Lutheran) Church did not join the coalition of conservative religious communities led by the Roman Catholic Church, which vehemently opposed the Code's adoption.

47 Črnič *Na Vodnarjevem Valu,* p. 253.

Bishop Geza Erniša, who heads the Evangelic Lutheran Church in Slovenia. Stres compares Christians in Slovenia to a "*game anyone can hunt with impunity*" [48] Erniša's assessment is distinctly more objective:

> Despite some difficulties and problems which occasionally appear between religious and secular spheres, the level of civilization we have attained is high enough to preclude any significant intolerance towards the religious. /.../ Personally, I am not aware of any instance of intolerance towards believers. Many people of faith hold important offices. If they were in any way discriminated against on the basis of their belief, this would signify that we have failed at all levels of inter-human relations".[49]

Despite having attained many of its goals following the demise of the one-party system in Slovenia, the Roman Catholic Church, still dissatisfied with its achievements, sought to reinforce its social power by building a financial foundation for its realm. This ambition was very much in accord with the position expressed by some of its hierarchy in the 1990s, who opined that the Church's social power would correspond to its wealth. This perspective found its anthropological expression in public statements of Archbishop Anton Stres, who portrayed man as a material as well as a spiritual being. Gradually, the (arch)diocese of Maribor[50] set about building a financial empire. It was to provide the financial basis for a Catholic university, media, and hospitals. In other words, the Church set about the construction of a Catholic social pillar which, if successful, would lead to the political-denominational segregation of society[51] - so-called pillarisation.

The project commenced in the mid-1990s through the Church's collection of ownership certificates which had been issued to the public as part of the privatization process of socially-owned enterprises; it ended between 2008 and

48 See "Druženje z nadškofom je nenormalno" (interview with Archbishop Stres), *Družina* (Ljubljana), 13 January 2013, p. 8, at http://www.druzina.si/icd/spletnastran.nsf/all/CF68DE82ACA9DAE5C1257AEE0032C728?OpenDocument [last accessed on 2 December 2014]. Reports on religious freedom, such as the International Religious Freedom Report issued annually by the US Department of State don't come anywhere near to confirming any such assertion.

49 Geza Erniša, "Anketa: Kateri so hujši, beli ali rdeči?", in *Dnevnik* (Ljubljana), 5 July 2013, p. 2, at http://www.dnevnik.si/slovenija/v-ospredju/kateri-so-hujsi-beli-ali-rdeci [last accessed on 8 September 2013].

50 The Catholic Church operates two archdioceses in Slovenia: the Metropolitan Archdiocese of Ljubljana, with suffragan diocese in Koper and Novo Mesto, and, since 2006, the Metropolitan Archdiocese of Maribor with suffragan diocese in Celje and Murska Sobota.

51 This goal, in itself, is by no means unlawful or illegitimate; however, its social justification remains questionable.

2010 with an attention-grabbing financial scandal.[52] The Church's financial investments, aggregated under the *Zvon 1* and *Zvon 2* holding companies, were controlled by the Archdiocese of Maribor. A debt of some 800 million euros, heavily mortgaged Church property, some 65,000 bamboozled small investors and a swathe of companies whose futures were now imperilled were left stranded in the wake of its total collapse. The *holy crash* – as it was dubbed – was the greatest financial meltdown in the history of independent Slovenia, as well as the largest loss experienced by a local Roman Catholic Church in the modern era. The warnings that had been expressed by a critical public had been ignored.

The tale of the Church's financial empire is one brimming with unlawful activities and violations of European and Slovene legislation, as well as canon law. In addition to the anticipated consequences of still pending court actions, the most resounding outcome of the scandal has been the disciplinary resignation of the three implicated archbishops: Franc Kramberger of Maribor in 2011, Anton Stres of Ljubljana (who was also president of the Slovenian Bishops' Conference) in 2013, and Kramberger's successor Marjan Turnšek, also in 2013. The Holy See required they resign under the terms of the second paragraph of Canon 401[53] of the Code of Canon Law. Added to these is also the 2009 resignation and exile to Trieste of the former Archbishop of Ljubljana, Alojzij Uran, supposedly in relation to rumours surrounding his having fathered illegitimate children. By way of these resignations, Slovenia's Roman Catholic Church lost two-thirds of its post-socialist archbishops,[54] further to which it had badly squandered a great deal of that trust which the Slovene public had accorded it.[55] The Church is now perceived by a large number of Slovenes as a greedy and morally suspect organization which disguises its thirst for power behind religious pretexts.

52 See Marjan Smrke, "Učinki "svete polomije" na zaupanje v cerkev", in *Teorija & Praksa*, vol. 49, No. 1 (2012), pp. 9-31; and M. Smrke, "Impact of the 'Holy Crash' on Trust in the Church in Slovenia", in *East European Politics & Societies,* Vol. 28, Issue 1 (February 2014).

53 "*A diocesan bishop who has become less able to fulfil his office because of ill health or some other grave cause is earnestly requested to present his resignation from office.*"

54 Some believe that Archbishop Franc Rode's elevation to the Roman Curia as Prefect of the Congregation for Institutes of Consecrated Life and Societies of Apostolic Life (2004-2011) and his elevation to the cardinalate in 2006 was, in reality, a way of removing him from Slovenia; namely *promoveatur ut amoveatur* - let him be promoted, so that he be removed.

55 Smrke, "Holy Crash", p. 129.

Perspectives of Catharsis and Deliverance

It will be interesting to observe the future implications of the financial scandal and the consequent decapitation of Slovenia's Catholic Church by the Vatican. The three main areas to keep an eye on are: (1) future trends in religious belief and religious structure, (2) changes in the character of the Slovene Church, and (3) the evolution of the Church's political relations, particularly with the state.

First, given the conditions of a relatively open religious market, significant changes in the structures of religious adherence and belief are possible; such have, however, remained fairly stable in the post-independence era. Although, in the wake of this crisis, there may be no significant long-term drop in the overall number of Slovenia's Catholic faithful, a further distancing of believers from their Church can be anticipated, as can a rise in conversions to alternative suppliers.

Second, is the Catholic Church in Slovenia capable of catharsis? Can lost trust be regained? The initial reactions of prominent clergymen in Slovenia to the Vatican's purge do not give any impression that they realize the seriousness of the reasons that forced this reprimand. The new president of the Slovenian Bishops' Conference, Bishop Andrej Glavan, who is also the apostolic administrator of the Archdiocese of Ljubljana, blamed the financial collapse on "satanic forces" and the "red dragon" (communists).[56] Some clerics, clearly displeased with the removals of the archbishops, have criticized Pope Francis for his alleged lack of knowledge as regards the situation in Slovenia. Likewise, they perceive the disciplinary resignations as wrongful. At the same time, however, some critical clerics are also demanding radical change, and perhaps the new bishops will be selected from among these. Renewal of Slovenia's Catholic Church in the spirit of the Second Vatican Council and current social teaching would no doubt aid its better coexistence with contemporary society. Yet this alone might not be enough. Much shall depend on the leadership of the Church, which is in crisis the world over.[57]

Third, the current situation, in which the Catholic Church is on the defensive, facilitates political opportunism and the taking of more confident positions in relation to it. The political left, which one would expect to be far more consistent in its promotion of disestablishmentarianism, has arguably been too

---

56 See Andrej Glavan, "Nagovor škofa Andreja Glavana pri maši na praznik Marijinega vnebovzetja" (2013), at: http://katoliska-cerkev.si/nagovor-skofa-andreja-glavana-pri-masi-na-praznik-marijinega-vnebovzetja-2013 [accessed on 10 September 2013].

57 In the meantime Franciscan Stane Zore was appointed the new Archbishop of Ljubljana (October 4, 2014), while Jesuit Alojzij Civkl was appointed as the new Maribor Archbishop (March 14, 2015).

lenient in its allowances regarding the interests of the Church. The political right – a traditional ally – has found no way of curbing the Church's ambitions. As a result, the state and its citizens will have to pay for the Church's mistakes and the harm which has been incurred. Having squandered its reputation, right-wing parties might not seek the support of the Catholic Church so uncritically in the future.

For these reasons, the future seems open for beneficent change, such as a reduction of the role of the Roman Catholic Church in society, and consequently a release of the spasm in which Slovenes have been caught since the Counter-Reformation.

Christine M. Hassenstab, with Sabrina P. Ramet[1]

8 The Norwegian Church: From the Reformation to Partial Disestablishment

On 21 May 2012, there was applause in the gallery of the Norwegian parliament as the country's constitution was amended, mandating a separation of its national Church (DNK, Den norske kirke) from the Norwegian state.[2] The constitutional amendment was not unforeseen and was, in fact, a bipartisan effort wherein the result was never really in doubt.

But, at the same time, outside the Parliament, there were prayers and religious songs by various opponents of the separation as they circled the building while the vote took place. Rather than being challenged by the state Church itself, the separation amendment attracted opposition from three basic groups. The first were individuals involved in anti-Islamic organizations such as the Organization to Stop Islamization of Norway and the Norwegian Defense League. The second were anti-abortion groups. Both of these groups had campaigned vigorously against this change to the 1814 Eidsvoll Constitution.[3] The third group could be categorized as those who feared that the somewhat progressive goals and attitudes within the Lutheran Church, as a state Church, would deteriorate as the state surrendered its right to veto episcopal appointments and as grassroots "populist" groups would begin to try to steer the Church in a more conservative direction. The fears of this third group would prove to be well-founded.

There were six major changes initiated by the constitutional amendment. One change was that the Church itself would name bishops and deans without the government giving its final approval to the appointments, as had been done previously. In the future, there would be no Church advisor at the ministerial level and also no need to have a majority of the ministers-of-state as members of the DNK. In addition, the Minister in charge of Church Affairs need not be a

1 We are grateful to Kristen Ringdal and members of the Writers' Circle (Jennifer Bailey, Thomas Berker, Torbjørn Knutsen; and Priscilla Ringrose) for helpful comments on an earlier draft of this chapter and to Kristen Ringdal for preparing Tables 8.1 and 8.2.

2 *Aftenposten* at http://www.aftenposten.no/nyheter/iriks/Staten-koblet-kirken-fra-staten-6833318.html [last accessed 13 September 2012].

3 *Nationen* (20 May 2012), at http://www.nationen.no/2012/05/21/politikk/kommentar/grunnloven/kirken/skilsmisse/7442093/ [accessed 13 September 2012]. Organisasjonen Stopp islamiseringen av Norge (Sian) og Norwegian Defence League (DNL)

member of the Church. The King, however, does need to be a member of the Church. Other changes included a name change from The Norwegian Church (DNK, Den norske kirke) to The Norwegian People's Church (NFK, Norges Folkekirke). The Constitution was also changed to reflect the fact that the foundations of the state rest on *both* Christian and humanist traditions. These changes were supported by the Church itself and had been reflected in an agreement among all parties in the Parliament as early as 2008.

One unusual feature of the legislation is that the government continues to finance the Church from its state budget, including the payment of the salaries of all Church employees. As before, the government subsidizes *all* legally established denominations based on the number of registered members, but does not pay the salaries of non-NFK employees. This begs the question of exactly how much of a separation this actually was and this question is analyzed below.

We will begin our analysis by discussing secularization theory, using the theory developed by Steve Bruce to discuss the changes between the state of Norway and the DNK. We also discuss some of the social and cultural changes in Norway that brought the Church and the state to the resolution of 21 May 2012.

Secularization Theory

The central purpose in this chapter is twofold: first, we shall argue that the manner in which secularization has unfolded in Norway has resulted in the emergence and development of a civil religion closely linked to the Norwegian Lutheran Church; and second, we shall show that, as the state has offered services which were earlier reserved exclusively to the Church (such as marriage and funeral services) and has passed laws accepting same-sex partnerships and abortion, the Church has accommodated itself to these developments, in the process becoming, in itself, highly supportive of the principle of tolerance.

Before pursuing this any further, it would be advisable to state what we shall mean by *secularization* and by *civil religion*, as these terms have been defined in diverse ways by scholars. For example, Liv Taule has pointed to three alternative ways of understanding secularization: secularization as a process of differentiation, whereby the hitherto hegemonic Church loses its monopoly; secularization as a weakening of religious belief and reduction in religious practice; and secularization as the privatization of faith, in which individuals decide for themselves what to believe and what not to believe.[4] For the purposes of this chapter, *secularization* will be defined as the process by which a formerly hegemonic religious institution loses its religious monopoly and is forced to retreat on several fronts, as the state takes over functions previously reserved for religious institutions, and whereby some members of the religious institution start to accept religious doctrines selectively, rather than *in toto*.[5] There are a number of competing theories about secularization, but here we shall follow Thomas Luckmann, in holding that secularization begins "when the originally homogeneous view of the world splits into different layers." As a consequence, religion loses (at least some of its) control over various spheres of life. This leads directly to privatization, a process defined by "people [being] compelled to shift back and forth daily between different social spheres, each of which demands of them superficial allegiance but functions according to an interpretation of the world incompatible" with those of other spheres, resulting in individuals ending up constructing their own "private" understandings of religion, morality, and the world.[6] The chief camps among scholars writing about secularization are the functionalists (e.g., Talcott Parsons, Robert Bellah, and Niklas Luhmann), the phenomenologists (e.g., Peter Berger and Thomas Luckmann), and a group of scholars who stand outside these two camps (e.g., Bryan Wilson, David Martin, and Richard Fenn). As Pippa Norris and Ronald Inglehart point out, most scholars have abandoned the original, naïve view that religion would gradually die out over time[7] – a view most closely associated with Karl Marx. Yet it is clear enough, as they note, that there is a direct correlation between poverty and high fertility on the one hand and high rates of religiosity on the other, just as there is between affluence and low fertility on the one hand and low or declining rates of religiosity on the other (although the USA is an exception to the latter correlation).[8] Indeed, Gallup reported in 2010 that there was "a very strong correlation between religiosity and poverty" and that "the poorest countries…are the most religious."[9] Furthermore, consulting

---

4 Liv Taule, "Norge – et sekulært samfunn?", in *Samfunnsspeilet* (2014), no. 1, p. 10.

5 See Fujio Ikado, "The Search for a Definition of Secularization: Toward a General Theory", posted at http://www2.kokugakuin.ac.jp/ijcc/wp/cimac/ikado.html [accessed on 7 July 2015].

6 Thomas Luckmann, as summarized in Olivier Tschannen, "The Secularization Paradigm: A Systematization", in *Journal for the Scientific Study of Religion*, Vol. 30, No. 4 (December 1991), p. 398.

7 Pippa Norris and Ronald Inglehart, *Sacred and Secular: Religion and Politics Worldwide* (Cambridge: Cambridge University Press, 2004), pp. 3-4.

8 *Ibid.*, p. 6.

9 "A correlation between poverty and religiosity", Gallup Poll (4 September 2010), at https://whyevolutionistrue.wordpress.com/2010/09/04/a-correlation-between-poverty-and-religiosity/ [accessed on 8 July 2015].

U.S. statistics for the years 1776-1976, one finds that during periods of war and/or economic depression, religious interest and participation rise, while during periods of peace and prosperity, people prove to be less interested in religion. One key to understanding Norwegians' relaxed attitude about religion, thus, is precisely Norway's economic prosperity.

Although the concept of *civil religion* was first outlined by Jean-Jacques Rousseau (1712-1778) in his *Social Contract,* contemporary sociologists tend to take their cue, at least to some extent, from a landmark article by Robert Bellah, published in 1967.[10] Here he defined civil religion as the "public religious dimension…expressed in a set of beliefs, symbols, and rituals," adding that this civil religion "provides a transcendent goal for the political process."[11] Although he noted that the concept of God, albeit variously understood, remains a central symbol in civil religion in the USA (and, for our case, in Norway as well), he added that "[t]here is no formal creed in the civil religion."[12] In a subsequent essay, Bellah clarified that civil religion should be understood as "the subordination of the nation to ethical principles that transcend it and in terms of which it should be judged."[13] We shall follow Bellah in discussing civil religion.

It is well known that secularization theory as applied within the sociology of religion is in flux, or may even, as Jean Bethke Elshtain has said, have "… failed, and failed spectacularly."[14] We find a more nuanced rendering in Gorski and Altinordu who write that it "appears to be entering a new phase."[15] Whatever this "new phase" is, it is clear to them "how much the terms of the secularization debate have shifted since the late 1960s."[16] These two scholars compare secularization theory to "a Frankenstein monster, stitched together, as it is, from the remnants of long-dead debates – Augustinian theory, canon law, the Henrician Reformation, positivist philosophies of history, and so on."[17] But monster

10 Robert N. Bellah, "Civil Religion in America", in *Daedalus,* Vol. 96, No. 1 (Winter 1967), pp. 1-21.

11 *Ibid.,* p. 4.

12 *Ibid.,* p. 15.

13 Robert N. Bellah, *Beyond Belief: Essays on religion in a post-traditional world* (New York: Harper & Row, 1979), p. 168, as quoted in Ronald C. Wimberley, "Testing the Civil Religion Hypothesis", in *Sociological Analysis,* Vol. 37, No. 4 (Winter 1976), p. 341.

14 Jean Beth Elshtain, "Religion and Democracy" in *Journal of Democracy,* Vol. 20, No. 2 (April 2009), p. 16.

15 Philip S. Gorski and Ateş Altinordu, "After Secularization?" in *The Annual Review of Sociology*, Vol. 34 (August 2008), p. 55.

16 *Ibid.,* p. 57.

17 *Ibid.,* p. 71.

or not, secularization theory still continues to be used as an analytical tool, to one extent or another.

The question is, how to determine that "extent". In this respect, we find Steve Bruce's reaffirmation of secularization theory useful, insofar as it relates to the West European experience. In fact, one of the main criticisms of Bruce's retrenchment of the theory is that it is too "Eurocentric". That said, it would thus easily apply to the Norwegian case.[18] As Steve Bruce and Tony Glendinning write,

> ...[T]he sociological tradition that leads from Karl Marx, Max Weber and Emile Durkheim, via Bryan Wilson and Peter Berger, lists as compound causes [of secularization] the rationalization, religious diversification and increasing egalitarianism and individualism that have accompanied industrialization, democratization and economic growth.[19]

Adding to this already long list of causes is the fact that different religions play "differing roles in preserving national identity and representing it to the other parts [of the nation]."[20] Moreover, "putatively secularizing forces" will impact groups defined by "class, gender, occupation and educational background" differently.[21]

In his 2002 book entitled *God is Dead: secularization in the West*, Bruce cites a 1987 article by J. K. Hadden which claims that secularization theory comprises "a hodge-podge of loosely employed ideas rather than a systematic theory."[22] Bruce goes on to say that he agrees with this evaluation, but insists that this is a "virtue" and we find his reasoning persuasive. He argues that, with so "large a phenomenon", any "systematic theory" would become so abstract "as to be worthless."[23] So, in summary,"[t]here is no secularization theory. There is a cluster of testable explanations that cohere as well as anything in the social sciences. That they are sometimes 'loosely employed' is neither here nor

18 Victor Roudemetof, "Secularization: In Defense of an Unfashionable Theory", Book Review in *Social Forces*, first published on line 9 May 2012, at http://sf.oxfordjournals.org/, last accessed 19 September 2012.

19 Steve Bruce and Tony Glendinning, "When was secularization? Dating the decline of the British churches and locating its cause", in *The British Journal of Sociology,* Vol. 61, Issue 1 (March 2010), p. 108.

20 *Ibid.*

21 *Ibid.*

22 Steve Bruce, *God is Dead: secularization in the West* (Oxford and Malden: Blackwell Publishing, 2002), p. 39.

23 *Ibid.*

there."[24] What matters is that they can be employed rigorously. We agree that, at this point, secularization theory is in flux and that it is not dead. The "cluster of testable explanations" is still useful, especially as they relate to a historical study – such as this. Nonetheless, it is also clear that new paradigms are becoming visible and old definitions are in need of revision.

Here, we may refer to the three main "broad structural traits" typifying a modern society, which are

> [t]he demise of segmental localism and the mobilization/inclusion of a whole population in to the national centre/nation-state…the overall differentiation of institutional spheres…[and] the spread of individualization from the elite to the non-elite level.[25]

It is these three general traits that will be used here to discuss the Church-state relationship in Norway throughout its history. In addition, we will use the "rationalization, religious diversification and increasing egalitarianism and individualism that have accompanied industrialization, democratization and economic growth", mentioned above, to create the structure for our discussion. Finally, we discuss how the "ethos" of Lutheranism in Norway continues in new and varied ways despite evidence for secularization.

We will divide our analysis of Norway into four historical periods. The first period begins with the Reformation and ends with Norway's independence from Sweden, covering the years 1527-1905. The second runs from the completion of the process, begun in 1814, of consolidating the independence of Norway (1905) until the end of World War Two (1945). This involves a span of only 40 years and in terms of socio-structural modernity, we would do well to remember that a great deal of Norwegian institution building had already been done while Norway had been in a "personal union" with Sweden from 1814 to 1905, during which time it shared the same monarch but had its own parliament and laws. The third period runs from 1945 to 1970 and saw the development of a "civil religion" in Norway in the light of sweeping cultural changes initiated in the 1960s. And the fourth period runs from 1970 to the present, with Norway moving from its splendid, but relatively poor, homogeneous isolation closer to being a multi-cultural and extremely wealthy state.

---

24 Ingrid Storm, *Secular Christianity as National Identity: Religion, Nationality and Attitudes to Immigration in Western Europe,* Ph.D. dissertation, University of Manchester, 2011.

25 Nicos Mouselis, "Modernity and the Secularization Debate", in *Sociology*, Vol. 46, No. 2 (April 2012), p. 207.

Church and Religion in Norway, 1527 – 1905

Until the early sixteenth century, the religious establishment in Norway was in communion with Rome. This began to change in 1527, when King Fredrik I (1471-1533) adopted an official posture of neutrality in the ecclesiastical sphere and, in August of that year, declared that the *Christian* faith was free in Denmark and that neither Catholics nor Lutherans should have to fear the suppression of their faith. But by 1530, all the major towns in Denmark had been affected by the Reformation, with some towns already fully reformed. Then Frederik changed the balance of forces by having some "surplus" Catholic churches demolished, while turning over the monastic churches to the Evangelicals. There were violent clashes between Catholics and Evangelicals in those days in Copenhagen, Malmø, and elsewhere.[26] In Norway, the Evangelicals did not find much support among ordinary people, although some of the leading noble families in Norway converted to Lutheranism between 1527 and 1529. In the years that followed, civil war broke out, initially pitting Catholic forces against Protestant forces although, by 1534, both sides – one side loyal to Fredrik's predecessor as king, Christian II, now imprisoned, and the other side swearing allegiance to Fredrik's son, Christian III (1503-1559) – were Protestant. By 1534, Christian III had won the war and in 1536 he imprisoned all but one of the Catholic bishops; the sole bishop to escape imprisonment did so by agreeing to help to set up the Lutheran Church in Norway. In effect, thus, 1536 marked the adoption of Lutheranism as the state religion in Norway, but this was made official only in 1537, when King Christian III signed a new Lutheran state ordinance and declared himself head of the Church.[27] The King also expropriated all property which had belonged to the Catholic bishops along with considerable parts of what had formerly belonged to the cathedral chapters.

With the dismissal and imprisonment of the Catholic bishops, Lutheran 'superintendents' were appointed to take their places. The first generation of Lutheran superintendents in Norway consisted entirely of Norwegians. Later in the century, however, most of Norway's bishops (with the restoration of the traditional title) were Danes. Converting the population to Lutheranism took time and involved, among other things, the eradication of beliefs in saints, purgatory, and indulgences, and the elimination of the use of the rosary. In 1614, Lutheranism became the only official acceptable doctrine in Denmark

26 See Bernt T. Oftestad, Tarald Rasmussen, and Jan Schumacher, *Norsk kirkehistorie* (Oslo: Universitetsforlaget, 1993).

27 "Church of Norway – a brief history", *Church of Norway* (16 February 2015), at https://kirken.no/nb-NO/church-of-norway/about/brief-history/ [accessed on 1 November 2015].

and Norway. Sixty-one years later, in 1685, this hard stance was modified, with the issuance of an edict of tolerance for adherents of the Reformed (Calvinist) Church over the bitter opposition of the kingdom's Lutheran bishops. Pietism spread from Germany and Denmark to Norway in the early eighteenth century. Pietists criticized the state Church for being lethargic and impure, and there were boycotts of Church sacraments, peaking in the 1740s.

During the Napoleonic Wars (1803-1815), Denmark took the side of Napoleon and, when the French side lost, Denmark was punished by being forced to give up Norway, under the Treaty of Kiel, signed in 1814. After a short war with Sweden, Norway agreed to a personal union with that country, meaning that the King of Sweden would also function as King of Norway, and that the two countries would have a common foreign policy.

Here, it is also important to remember some essential concepts inherent in the Reformation. Martin Luther's theology included two important doctrines – the doctrine of vocation and the priesthood of all believers. The first implicitly argues for the right to a job and we see this as an explicit belief of the Norwegian welfare state today. Political parties emerged already during the phase of Norway's dynastic union with Sweden, with the Liberal Party (*Venstre*) in 1884 followed by the Conservative Party (*Høyre*); in 1887 came the establishment of the Labour Party (*Arbeiderpartiet*). The right to a job had entered the Norwegian culture much earlier through Reformation theology. On 17 May 1814, Norway adopted the Eidsvoll Constitution, which made Lutheranism the state religion. In this Constitution, we read,

> § 2. The Evangelical Lutheran religion is the official state religion. All inhabitants professing it are bound to bring up their children the same. Jesuits and monks must not be tolerated. Jews are forbidden access into the kingdom.[28]

The ban on Jews was lifted in 1851 and the one on monks in 1897. The Parliament debated the ban on Jesuits in 1897, 1925, and 1926, and finally lifted it in 1956 in response to the Norwegian ratification of the European Convention on Human Rights. Despite these two prohibitions, there was what was considered to be a "general rule of religious freedom" in the 1814 Constitution.[29]

---

28 Storting, *Grunnloven fra 1814,* at http://www.stortinget.no/no/Stortinget-og-demokratiet/Lover-og-instrukser/Grunnloven-fra-1814/ [accessed on 18 October 2012]. Translation from original: Den evangelisk-lutterske Religion forbliver Statens offentlige Religion. De Indvaanere, der bekjende sig til den, ere forpligtede til at opdrage sine Børn i samme. Jesuitter og Munkeordener maae ikke taales. Jøder ere fremdeles udelukkede fra Adgang til Riget.

29 Ulrik Sverdrup Thygeson Jr., "2/2010 – Grunnlovens forbud mot jesuitter og munkeordener" in *Rettshistoriske studier*, No. 21, 2010 at http://www.jus.uio.no/ior/forskning/publikasjoner/skriftserien/rettshistorie/02-2010.html [last accessed on 19 October 2012].

The 1820s saw the appearance of the *sterktroende* (or firm believers). Led by Knud Kittelsen Spødervold (1791-1848), a farmer and lay preacher from Bjerkreim near Egersund in southwest Norway, the firm believers launched a crusade against the pietists who, they said, were preaching "justification by works". The firm believers gave Martin Luther's teaching of justification by faith alone a simple-minded interpretation, denouncing the pietists' emphasis on stringent moral standards as "un-Christian legalism" and declaring ethics to be secondary to doctrine. The firm believers became virulent anti-clericals. There was yet another religious current at this time: the Haugeans – followers of Hans Nielsen Hauge (1771-1824), who wanted to reinvigorate spiritual life in Norway. Hauge was arrested 10 times and imprisoned from 1804 to 1811. A farm boy from Tune, he grew up resentful of the Lutheran clergy, whom he accused of "having attended school in a synagogue of Satan."[30] But Hauge was no separatist and he urged his followers to remain within the established Church. A final current which shook the religious firmament in the nineteenth century was Grundtvigianism, a tendency associated with Danish theologian N. F. S. Grundtvig (1783-1872), who was ordained in 1811 and who argued that the souls of sinners could be saved even after death. His ideas spread to Norway.[31]

In 1741, in response to the pietist movement, the Danish-Norwegian government had adopted the Conventicle Act, which prohibited lay-led meetings. In 1836, the Storting (the Norwegian parliament) voted unanimously to repeal the Conventicle Act of 1741, only to see the government veto the bill. The Storting voted twice more for its repeal in the years 1837-1841, only to be overruled both times by the government. In 1842, the Storting voted for a final time for repeal: this time the government accepted the repeal, which had the result of legitimating lay-led religious meetings, which had been a fact of Norwegian religious life for some decades, albeit in violation of the now-repealed edict. Meanwhile, in 1833, Søren A. W. Sørenssen (1793-1853) of Kristiania (as Oslo was called at that time) submitted a bill to the Storting to insert into the constitution a paragraph providing for freedom of worship for all Christian denominations. The campaign for religious toleration was revived toward the end of the decade, when some pastors joined Sørenssen. The Department of Ecclesiastical Affairs now turned to Claus Winther Hjelm (1797-1871), a professor of law at the university in Kristiania, to draft a counter-proposal. The document which Hjelm published in 1840 defended the

30 F. Hale, "Transatlantic Norwegian religion and ethnicity", in *Fides et Historia,* Vols. 17-18 (1984), p. 13.

31 See A. M. Allchin, *N. F. S. Grundtvig: An Introduction to his Life and Work* (Aarhus: Aarhus University Press, 1997).

existing order, praised the notion of a culturally homogeneous state, and specifically criticized the American model. Hjelm proposed to ban the public practice of any religion except that of the state Church, with fines and imprisonment for those violating the ban. Ironically perhaps, Hjelm's polemic was probably decisive in shifting public opinion toward a more pro-tolerance stance. In particular, Jens Lauritz Arup (1793-1874), a deputy in the Storting who would be appointed Bishop of Kristiania in 1846, wrote an article for *Morgenbladet* in 1840, in which he opposed Hjelm's heavy-handed approach.[32] A month later, the same newspaper carried an article by Christian Juell Sandberg, in which he stated, "It is clear from Christian doctrine that violence and force should not be used to compel people to confess the holy faith; that kind of action violates the entire spirit of Christianity."[33] Three years later, the government appointed a commission to investigate the question of regulating religious dissent; after a year and a half of work, the commission presented to the Storting a law concerning Christians not belonging to the state Church, granting them full legal status. In June 1845, after several days of stormy discussion, the Storting adopted a modified version of the commission's proposal, granting any Norwegian at least 19 years of age the right to withdraw from the state Church, merely by informing the parish pastor and signing a form. This law is known as the Dissenter Law.

In the decades that followed, first Mormon missionaries and Methodist missionaries and later also Baptist and Seventh Day Adventist missionaries came to Norway and won converts. Some members of the state Church began to regret that the Dissenter Law had ever been passed but there was no effort to repeal it. The Norwegian Church was also shaken by the anti-clerical rhetoric of Marcus Thrane (1817-1890), the socialist father of the labour union movement in Norway, and repercussions from the excoriation of institutionalized Christianity by Danish philosopher Søren Kierkegaard (1813-1855) in a series of articles published in the last two years of his life.[34] Meanwhile, in the last decades of the nineteenth century, the Norwegian Church was afflicted by declining attendance, declining participation in communion, growing anticlericalism, and a widening clergy-to-lay ratio.

---

32 *Morgenbladet* (27 October 1840).

33 As quoted in Frederick Hale, *Norwegian Religious Pluralism; A Trans-Atlantic Comparison* (Lewiston: Edwin Mellen Press, 1992), p. 23.

34 See Frederick Hale, "Anticlericalism and Norwegian Society before the Breakthrough of Modernity", in *Scandinavian Studies,* Vol. 52, No. 3 (Summer 1980), pp. 253-255 and 257-259.

Norwegian Church and State, 1905 – 1945

Differences between liberal and conservative theologians and clergy flared in the years 1905-1940. Curate Carl Konow made a contribution to stoking polemics in a series of public lectures he presented in Bergen in 1906-1907. In these lectures, Konow rejected the Church doctrines of the Virgin Birth, Jesus' pre-existence, and his bodily resurrection, and called for higher standards in Biblical exegesis. A pastoral conference in Bergen voted unanimously to request Konow's resignation, a request backed by the state Minister for Church Affairs; but Konow refused to resign (eventually a compromise was found when an additional pastor was appointed to "assist" him). But theological liberalism had growing numbers of adherents and, in 1913, liberal pastors organized an association called "The Progressive Norwegian Ministerial Group". The conservative counterpart, the "Brotherhood of Pastors Loyal to the Church's Confession", was founded in 1919. The conservatives used the Apostles' Creed to define orthodoxy, offering the liberals a truce if they would accept the Apostles' Creed word for word. Speaking for the liberals, Professor Lyder Brun rejected the offer, noting that liberals "...refuse, as historically thinking evangelical Christians, to identify faith with a fixed complex of historically conditioned sentences."[35] An attempt at reconciliation between the two camps was made in September 1919, when the conservative but peace-loving Bishop Jens Tandberg (1852-1922) brought the two sides together for a dialogue at Drammen. Although both conservatives and liberals sat on the organizing committee, conservative Professor Ole Hallesby (1879-1961) attacked the project in extreme terms in newspapers, and all the conservatives except Tandberg withdrew, explaining that they had not intended to recognize the liberal position in any way.[36] Subsequently, Tandberg, hitherto chair of the board of directors of the conservative Faculty of Theology, failed to be reelected.

Then came the publication, of a series of newspaper articles by Kristian Schjelderup, an assistant lecturer in theology at the university and an advocate of radical theological revision. These articles were later collected into a book published in 1924 under the title, *Who Jesus Was and What the Church has Made of Him.*[37] The thrust of Schjelderup's argument was that Jesus of

35 As quoted in Einar Molland, *Church Life in Norway, 1800-1950,* trans. from Norwegian by Harris Kaasa (Westport, Conn.: Greenwood Press, 1978; reprint of a 1957 edition published by Augsburg Publishing House), p. 105.

36 See Dag Kullerud, *Ole Hallesby. Mannen som ville kristne Norge* (Oslo: Gyldendal Norsk Forlag, 1987), p. 163.

37 Kristian Schjelderup, *Hvem Jesus var – og hvad kirken har gjort ham til* (Oslo: Gyldendal, 1924).

Nazareth was a religious genius, but not a god. Liberals led the attack on Schjelderup, whose conclusions embarrassed them, while conservatives smugly noted where liberal theology had led. Liberal-conservative frictions continued, but after 1930, with the celebration of the 900th jubilee of the Battle of Stiklestad, relations became calmer and the 1930s were by and large devoid of any dramatic incidents. Significantly, in 1938, the Norske Kirke approved the ordination of women (earlier than Denmark (1947) or Sweden (1958)).

Norway was occupied by German forces from 9 April 1940 until 8 May 1945. While the DNK was slow to react during the early days of the occupation, it eventually committed to a full scale refusal to cooperate with the regime, named after the infamous Vidkun Quisling (1887-1945). Bishop Eivind Berggrav (1884-1959) is a good example of this progression. At the outset, he suggested to Lutherans that they "refrain from interference" in the war and refuse to "mix themselves up in the war by sabotage or in any other way."[38]

It is noteworthy that the war enabled conservatives and liberals to set aside their differences and effect a partial reconciliation. Specifically, in summer 1940, Bishop Berggrav, a liberal, extended an olive branch to his chief nemesis, the conservative Ole Hallesby, and the two of them achieved a sufficient degree of reconciliation to be able to organize a common resistance to the occupation. Already at the beginning of 1941, the Norwegian bishops sent a letter to the Kirkedepartement to protest violations of human rights. The letter was also read aloud from pulpits around the country.[39] Nonetheless, a few theologians and pastors began to interpret the Scriptures in the light of pre-Christian Nordic traditions.

Matters came to a head on 24 February 1942, when the bishops met and declared that they would henceforth refuse all cooperation with the occupation authorities, and would refuse to accept state salaries. The Kirkedepartement responded by "suspending" the bishops and by banning them from any spiritual work. At this point, Berggrav was told by Quisling that he should have had him killed when he had a chance; Berrggrav replied "Here I am."[40] In response to Nazi interference with religious education in schools, Berggrav orchestrated a mass resignation of all Lutheran bishops and priests. At Easter 1942, some 805

38 Norwegian Biographical Lexicon at http://snl.no/.nbl_biografi/Eivind_Berggrav/utdypning, [last accessed on 29 November 2012].

39 Oftestad et al., *Norske Kirkehistorie,* p. 267.

40 As quoted in D. M. Yeager, "God, Church, and Country: Berggrav's Leadership in the Norwegian Resistance" in *The Journal of Lutheran Ethics*, Vol. 6, Issue 5 (May, 2006). JLE is a computer journal and can be found at http://www.elca.org/What-We-Believe/Social-Issues/Journal-of-Lutheran-Ethics/Issues/May-2006/God-Church-and-Country-Berggravs-Leadership-in-the-Norwegian-Resistance.aspx [last accessed on 22 November 2012].

of the 854 pastors of the Norske kirke resigned, henceforth refusing state salaries and refusing to perform weddings for occupation authorities, but otherwise continuing their pastoral work. The other 49 pastors, along with newly ordained collaborationist pastors, agreed to work with the wartime authorities. The NS authorities now consecrated their own bishops. Churches were empty as Norwegians refused to attend the few services still held by priests who were prepared to cooperate with the regime. Berggrav was arrested in April 1942 and, until the end of the war, he was held in a concentration camp outside Oslo, from which he still managed to work with the Norwegian resistance.

Population and Church Membership

In 1900, Norway had a population of between 2.23 and 2.24 million people. In 1945, the population reached 3.09 million, an increase of 1.14 million in 45 years. In terms of both religion and population, the country was extremely homogeneous. There were non-Lutherans in Norway in 1900, but their number (52,714) comprised only 2.36% of the total population.[41] Aside from the group of "dissentere" who espoused no religion (13,279), the largest group of non-state Church members were members of the Lutheran Free Church (12,618), followed by the Methodists (10,286).[42]

Economic Development and the Social Welfare State, I

Steve Bruce's secularization paradigm[43] shows a clear, unobstructed path from the Protestant Reformation (PR) to the Protestant Ethic (E1) to Industrial Capitalism (E2) to Economic growth (E3).[44] Economic Growth then divides into two different pathways, Social Differentiation (S1) and Structural Differentiation (S2). Simply described, when societies become wealthier, they become more "internally varied and specialized."[45] Industrialization forced economic activity out of the house, out of the "private" sphere into the public sphere where increased specialization secularized the schools, healthcare, and welfare

41 Thygeson, "2/2010 – Grunnlovens forbud" [note 29], p. 24

42 *Ibid.*

43 Please see from the flow chart in Steve Bruce, *Secularization: In Defence of an Unfashionable Theory* (Oxford: Oxford University Press, 2011), p. 27.

44 *Ibid.*, p. 27.

45 *Ibid.*, p. 29.

– all of which had earlier been the province of the Church.[46] Even where Churches may have remained a "conduit" for these services, "secular standards and values" gradually became the norm.[47]

Social differentiation occurs alongside structural differentiation. Economic growth created diverse jobs unknown in earlier eras; it also stimulated social mobility and fragmented the hitherto single moral understanding. But the relationship between economic growth and religion is a two-way street, if not a multi-lane superhighway with several variables at work. In recent years, another school of thought has entered the arena alongside the secularization thesis: this is the "market", "supply-side" or "rational choice" theory of religion which "downplays the role of economic development and other 'demand factors'…and focuses instead on competition among religion providers."[48] This is not the place to assess either; but we do take note of which theory – or theories – may seem applicable to the case of Norway.

If we consider the "supply-side" theory of religion we can see that between 1900 and 1945, in terms of the national economy, Norway was poor. It relied on fishing, timber, and farming and an impressive international merchant fleet as sources of income. In 1900, the Norwegian GDP per capita, adjusted by purchasing power parity, had been about 69% of that of Sweden.[49] After having climbed to about 90% in 1920, by 1945, during a period of postwar recession, the GDP was *below* what it had been in 1900 (about 60%). This would obviously change later with the flow of oil revenues.

During this time period, the national social welfare model was established, not without great effort. In 1842, Norwegian miners first received Workmen's Compensation from the government, well before Bismarck's national insurance policy, introduced in the 1880s.[50] Somewhat earlier, in 1837, the Norwegian state had devolved some of its power to local councils, making them part of the state public administrative apparatus as well as being an "instrument of the local population's wishes and needs expressed through free elections."[51] What this did was to open up for reform the then current "poor laws" from the liberal

---

46 *Ibid.,* p. 30.

47 *Ibid.*

48 Robert J. Barro and Rachel M. McCleary, "Religion and Economic Growth across Countries" in *American Sociological Review*, No. 68, No. 5 (October 2003), p. 761.

49 Eurostat, please see Governor Øystein Olsen, *The role of oil in the Norwegian economy* (Norges Bank, 5 April 2011), at, http://www.norges-bank.no/pages/85389/nhh_foredrag_til%20olsen_english_110405.pdf [accessed 29 November 2012].

50 Please see Stein Kuhnle, "The Nordic Approach to General Welfare", 1998 at http://www.nnn.se/intro/approach.htm [accessed 28 November 2012].

51 Øyvind Bjørnson, "The Social Democrats and the Norwegian Welfare State: Some Perspectives", in *Scandinavian Journal of History*, vol. 26, No. 3 (November 2010), p. 198.

machinations of farmers who were the dominant political force at this level at this time.[52]

Unlike in Great Britain, where social issues were raised against the backdrop of the industrial revolution, in Norway, social issues were raised simultaneously as industrialization unfolded.[53] Although the Labour Party was a force to be reckoned with from about 1910 onwards, it did not achieve parliamentary power until 1935, having to be content instead to work at local levels. The first public welfare legislation in Norway was passed in 1843, but changed in 1863 and 1900; it remained in force until 1964 when it was supplanted by the Social Care Act.[54] The 1863 law pertained to only orphans and the mentally ill; the elderly, disabled or indigent, i.e., those without the help of family, could receive social welfare only in cases of extreme need.[55] This scheme was largely underwritten by local taxes.

Because of the coincidence of industrialization and social issues, it was easier to determine a nexus between social need and risky work conditions, especially in the fishing industry and among seasonal workers. Morally abhorrent laziness did not enter into the equation. Thus, entire groups of workers received state compensation based on the German and British models. One group and social issue after another then became the focus of debate. Old age pensions, accident insurance and factory inspection debates all took place in the late 1800s. Life gradually became better after 1935 and again after the occupation. The Labour Party formed a majority government between 1945 and 1981, excluding three short intervals of no more than a year in each case. The largest single leap in the growth in Norway's real GDP, to date, took place during the period 1914-1973. The GDP growth from 1914 to 1945 was recorded at an average annual rate of 2.28%, while the average annual rate of growth of GDP per capita was 1.55%.[56]

During the years 1843-1875, Norway had experienced significant economic growth matched by few other countries. High productivity in agriculture and the adoption of new technology contributed to this growth.[57] This period of economic boom was followed by about two decades of relative depression but, after 1905, when Norway severed its loose connection with

52 *Ibid.*
53 *Ibid.*, p. 198 – 99.
54 *Ibid.*, p. 199.
55 *Ibid.*
56 Ola Honningdal Grytten, "The Economic History of Norway", in EH.net at https://eh.net/encyclopedia/the-economic-history-of-norway/ [last accessed on 8 July 2015].
57 *Ibid.*, p. 4 of 12.

Sweden, a serious program of industrialization got underway.[58] The economy was somewhat volatile during the interwar years, 1918-1939. During the years 1940-1945, the German occupation forces constructed or expanded airfields, railway lines, a military telecommunication system, and other objects relevant for the occupation. Of course, overall, the German occupation was damaging in many ways, including for the Norwegian economy.[59]

Religiosity during this Period

Bruce's secularization paradigm posits a direct link between the Protestant Reformation (PR) and Individualism (RO1).[60] The Reformation divided the theological landscape into those who believed in one immutable way to salvation and others who were more flexible, allowing for any number of paths to salvation. Previously, the Vatican had decided everything; but Lutherans, Reformed Christians (i.e., followers of John Calvin), and other Protestants rejected the authority of the pope, and the rest is a history of competing Churches and sects. The priesthood of all believers' theology "inadvertently caused a major change in the relative importance of community and individual."[61] In rejecting the "transfer of merit" (e.g., Masses for the dead, indulgences) by a privileged priesthood, Reformers developed the idea that we are all severally equal before God, not just jointly equal. Equally sinful and equally responsible soon mutated into equal rights.[62] When combined with economic growth and mobility, this made it possible to distinguish between the person and his or her social role.

Bruce also theorizes that from Social Differentiation (S1) flows Social and Cultural Diversity (S3) leading to Religious Diversity (RO4). This creates the Moderation of Sects and Churches (RO5), finally leading to Relativism (CS2). While it is clear that his thread has led to RO5, in some contexts, and while the following discussion may lead some to believe that Relativism is the next step in the secularization paradigm, we are not convinced; this will be discussed in our conclusion.

Religiosity as we understand it today was not a matter of research in the early 20th century. Indeed, it is extremely difficult to find figures for church

---

58 *Ibid.*, p. 5 of 12.

59 Harald Espeli, "Economic Consequences of the German Occupation of Norway, 1940-1945", in *Scandinavian Journal of History,* Vol. 38, No. 4 (2013), pp. 504, 507, 510.

60 Bruce, *Secularization* [note 43], p. 27.

61 *Ibid.*

62 *Ibid.*

attendance during that era. However, we have the benefit of some longitudinal studies which include Norwegians born and educated during that time period.

In summary, during the foundational stage of the state of Norway we see a very small, homogeneous population with a relatively low annual per capita income. DNK-related employees accounted for about 0.13% of the total population; clergy were drawn from the middle and upper classes. Late industrialization made it possible to create a social security network for workers, a net which was then extended to society at large during the 1930s; this was, in part, due to an ethos based on religious doctrine inherited from the Reformation. Religiosity consisted of belief in Lutheran dogmas and there was agreement on the universality of right and wrong based on these doctrines.

Norwegian Church and State, 1945 – 1970

After the war, Norwegians set about to reclaim their culture, institutions, and economy. But the influence of the occupation was strong and had an impact on Norway's civil religion. Inger Furseth found a continuing impact among the middle class, members of DNK, and the religious lay movement until late in the 1950s.[63] This civil religion, however, was found in a "low key", i.e., a fairly latent phenomenon, within society. Using data from national rituals, celebrations, and debates in the Parliament, she found that this flirtation with religion was activated during the Nazi occupation in Norway and not equivalent to the state Church, although religious groups were organizational vehicles for this civil religion.[64]

Population and Church Membership. In terms of religion and ethnicity, the state continued to be relatively homogeneous. By 1946, the number of non-DNK members totalled 120,106.[65] Given that the population in 1946 was 3,127,000, this reflected 3.84% of the population, an increase of only 1.48% from the previous period. In 1970, the population of Norway was 3.87 million, an increase of 0.75 million in 25 years. In 1960, 96.3% of the population were

---

63 Inger Furseth, "Civil Religion in a Low Key: The Case of Norway", in *Acta Sociologica*, Vol. 37, No. 1 (1994), pp. 39 – 54.

64 *Ibid.*, p. 51.

65 Asle Rolland, *Statistikk om religion, tro og livssyn – en behovsanalyse* (Oslo: Statistisk sentralbyrå, 2011), https://www.ssb.no/a/publikasjoner/pdf/notat_201107/notat_201107.pdf [accessed on 6 November 2015], p. 26.

members of the Norwegian Church; the figure stood at 87.9% in 1999.[66] Those espousing no religion numbered 23,058.

One striking change, however, was that other faith communities, which had not been seen in 1900, became very visible by 1946. The highest number of "dissentere" (30,036) in 1946 could be found in the Pentecostal Church, a Church which had not even been mentioned in the 1900 rolls. This religious body had a higher membership in relation to those claiming no religion (21,985) and even in relation to the Church which had had the highest "dissenting" membership in 1900, the Evangelical-Lutheran Free Church; in 1946 the Evangelical-Lutheran Free Church membership was 18,185. The Methodist Church had 11,186 members in 1946.[67]

Economic Development and the Social Welfare State, II

Economic growth and prosperity are relevant to considerations of religiosity because of the well-known correlation between prosperity and detachment from religion. To put it a bit differently, and as already mentioned, people tend to participate in greater numbers in liturgy and to go to church more often during hard times, and to pay less attention to religion during times of relative affluence.[68]

Although there was also damage to the economy, including to the merchant fleet, during the war and occupation, post-war reconstruction proceeded apace and, in the years 1945-1973, GDP grew at an average annual rate of 4.73% (with GDP per capita growing at an average annual rate of 3.81%).[69] This robust growth was achieved, thus, even before the discovery of oil in the Ekofisk field in 1969. The 1960s saw an effort to decrease poverty as well as increase and guarantee social welfare, as more capital was put into public trust, especially during the Gerhardsen government, 1963-1965. The public sector grew at a fast pace and progressive taxation was introduced.

Norway's solid economic growth and convincing prosperity meant that there were now more opportunities for people to get higher education, more outlets for recreation, better social welfare, and less crime and violence than in poor societies.

---

66 Harald Hegstad, *Kirke i forandring. Felleskap, tilhørighet og mangfold. Den norske kirke* (Stavanger: Luther Forlag, 1999), pp. 37-38.

67 Rolland, *Stastikk om religion* [note 65].

68 See Phil Zuckerman, *Society without God: What the Least Religious Nations Can Tell us about Contentment* (New York: New York University Press, 2008).

69 Grytten, "Economic History" [note 56], p. 2 of 12.

Religiosity during this Period

After World War Two and until the 1970s, DNK enjoyed a relatively unfettered position when compared with other Norwegian state institutions. It is at this time that we find the transition from the middle group of the RAMP study (a survey of religious attitudes in the Nordic countries, explained below) to the youngest group. Religiosity changed significantly as a result of challenges to social norms during the 1960s, and one factor that demonstrates this is the large decline, beginning in this period, of the number of couples who married rather than simply cohabitated to begin a life together. Norwegian Church dogma prior to the 1960s had emphasized marriage within the Church.[70] Between 1966 and 1970, the annual average number of marriages throughout Norway was 29,055. By 2011, this number was 23,135.[71] The number of marriages dissolved by divorce between 1961 and 1965 was 2,452. Between 2006 and 2010, 10,300 marriages ended in divorce.[72] In 1988, 79.4% of newborn infants were being baptized.[73]

By the 1950s, one of the most important debates between liberals and conservatives had to do with the ordination of women; liberals were in favour, with conservatives opposed. In 1961, the state entered on the side of the liberals, appointing the country's first female priest. In the 1990s, the first female bishop was appointed. In the meantime, the Church became involved in three major debates: concerning abortion, homosexuality, and the Church-state relationship itself.

Concerning abortion, already in 1960 the Storting adopted a law allowing women to obtain abortions when certain social/medical conditions were satisfied. This law was passed in spite of opposition from the Norske kirke.[74] The Church soon reconciled itself to this new legal situation and, in 1971, issued a statement allowing that abortion might be justified under some circumstances. But there were pressures for further liberalization of the law on abortion. The Church put up fierce resistance but to no avail and, in spring 1975, the legaliza-

70 Natalie Rogoff Ramsøy, "Non-marital Cohabitation and Change in Norms: The Case of Norway", in *Acta Sociologica*, Vol. 37, No. 1 (1994), pp. 23 – 37.

71 SSB data at, http://www.ssb.no/ekteskap_en/tab-2012-08-23-01-en.html [last accessed 30 November 2012].

72 SSB data at http://www.ssb.no/ekteskap_en/tab-2012-08-23-08-en.html [last accessed 30 November 2012].

73 Hegstad, *Kirke i forandring* [note 66], p. 38.

74 See Christine M. Hassenstab, *Body Law and the Body of Law; A Comparative Study of Norm Inclusion in Norwegian and American Laws* (Berlin/Munich/Boston: De Gruyter, 2014), pp. 214-215; and Oftestad et al., *Norsk kirkehistorie,* p. 284.

tion of abortion as a decision taken by a woman herself ("selv-bestemt") was set in law. Finally, in 1978, ignoring the Church's misgivings, the Storting liberalized the law still further, giving women full rights to an abortion during the first 12 weeks of pregnancy.[75]

Concerning homosexuality, in 1977 the civil unions of same-sex couples also became a reality, although anyone in such a union could not serve in a clerical position in the Norske kirke. Yet the Norwegian Church has become gradually more liberal. One sign of this was the agreement by Norway's 11 bishops, in March 2000, to go back to school for *sex education!* Again, in February 2001, the Norske kirke consented to allow homosexual couples to adopt children.[76] But the question of whether persons living in homosexual partnerships might be employed in Church positions, whether as pastors or as deacons, remained divisive.

In 1995, the General Synod of the Norske kirke met and voted 58 to 21 to stand by the traditional practice of excluding homosexuals from positions in Church employment. That same year, at the episcopal conference, eight of the country's 11 bishops voted in favour of maintaining traditional practice. But, in February 1999, Bishop Rosemarie Køhn (b. 1939) of Hamar reinstalled Siri Sunde in her chaplaincy after some controversy over Sunde's lesbian relationship. Thereupon, the NK National Council asked the bishops to clarify their views. Eventually, a doctrinal commission was appointed, which completed a three-year study of this question in 2003. However, the only point on which the commission could agree at that time was that the disagreement was straining the unity of the Norske kirke. What is striking, however, is that during the commission's deliberations, it became clear that six of the 11 bishops wanted the Church to abandon its traditional teaching on this question and to allow same-sex co-habitants to hold consecrated office.[77]

Concerning Church-state separation, this issue will be discussed in concluding section of this chapter.

75 See Hassenstab, *Body Law and the Body of Law,* pp. 228-237.

76 Rev. Trond Bakkevig, chair of the Commission for Church-State Separation, in interview with SPR, Olso, Spring 2002.

77 "Church of Norway doctrinal commission split on homosexuality", *Church of Norway* (24 January 2006), at http://www.kirken.no/english/news.cfm?artid=74390 [accessed on 24 January 2006]; and *Aftenposten* (Oslo), 20 May 2006, updated 22 May 2006, at http://www.aft enposten.no [accessed on 8 August 2006].

Norwegian Church and State, 1970 – 2015

An important fact that defines this period is the discovery of gas and oil off the coast of Norway. This small country experienced a "rags to riches" phenomenon, taken directly from the pages of a Scandinavian fairy tale. One can debate whether the resulting changes in society and culture are an advantage, but the economic phenomenon is real. In addition, since the Ekofisk discovery in 1969, other oil/gas fields have come "on stream"; in 2012, Norway's petroleum production capacity was 2.6 million barrels per day, making it the 7th largest petroleum producer in the world – a standing it still held in 2015.[78]

Population and Church Membership. Between the years 1970 and 2015, the population of Norway made a dramatic increase of nearly 1.3 million, rising from 3,875,000 to 5,165,802 inhabitants; the fertility rate of 2.5 in 1970 declined to 1.76 by 2014, but this remains one of the highest fertility rates in Europe.[79] Members of Christian communities other than DNK numbered 266,834 in 2011; of the 17 minority religious communities surveyed, the three largest were the Roman Catholic Church (83,018), Pentecostal Congregations (39,599) and the Evangelical-Lutheran Free Church of Norway (19,614).[80] As of 1 January 2011, 10% of the Norwegian population or 484,500 were members of minority (i.e., non-NFR) religious communities, which represented an increase of 37,700 over 2010.[81] Half of the 484,500 were in Christian communities, 84,500 were in "life stance" communities, with Islamic communities representing 22% of this number, while Buddhist, Sikh, and Hindu communities amounted to 3%, 1.2% and 0.6% respectively.[82]

---

78 U.S Department of State, Diplomacy in Action website at http://www.state.gov/r/pa/ei/bgn/3421.htm last accessed 30 November 2012; and Government.no – Old and Gas, a https://www.regjeringen.no/en/topics/energy/oil-and-gas/id1003/ [accessed on 4 July 2015].

79 *Population Pyramids of the World from 1950 to 2100: Norway 1970,* at http://populationpyramid.net/norway/1970/; Statistik sentralbyrå, at https://www.ssb.no/en/befolkning/statistikker/folkemengde; and Lars Dommermuth, Rannveig Kaldager Hart, Trude Lappegård, Marit Sønsen, and Kenneth Aarskaug Wiik, *Kunnskapsstatus om fruktbarhet og samliv i Norge* (Oslo: Statistisk byrrå, 2015/31), p. 9, at https://www.ssb.no/en/befolkning/artikler-og-publikasjoner/_attachment/232700?_ts=14e299bfeb0 [all three sources accessed on 4 July 2015].].

80 *Statistics Norway,* at http://www.ssb.no/trosamf_en/tab-2011-12-06-03-en.html [accessed 26 November 2012].

81 SSB at http://www.ssb.no/trosamf_en/ last accessed on 20 November 2012. SSB began to use the term "life stance" in its reports from 2006. We have not been able to find a definition of this term in SSB's materials.

82 *Ibid.*

Although it is true that 74.9% of the population in Norway were registered members of DNK in 2013,[83] this statistic is misleading for a number of reasons. First, a Norwegian is automatically registered as a member of DNK unless one re-registers him- or herself outside the Church. In the past, this process was difficult, but it has been made easier recently.[84] Second, only about "2% attend church regularly, according to 2009 and 2010 data."[85] Third, a study done by "Gustafsson and Pettersson in 2000 revealed that 72% of Norwegians 'do not believe in a personal God.'"[86]

Economic Development and the Social Welfare State

Until the aforementioned discovery of oil (and gas), the country was at the margins of Europe in many respects. The discovery of oil in the northern basin of the North Sea, the huge Ekofisk oil field, by Phillips Petroleum could be said to have accelerated the modernization of the Norwegian state and society.[87] The rather stable growth in the number of employed during the 1970s is an important reason why the number of unemployed stayed at a rather low and stable level in those years. Lower growth in employment at the beginning of the 1980s contributed to an increase in unemployment which reached a temporary peak of 3.4% in 1983. The strong growth in the job sector in the period 1985 to 1987 caused the rate of unemployment to fall again, but in the period 1988 to 1991, the rate of unemployment increased once again, reaching 5.5% in 1991.[88]

In 1981, the Conservative Party formed a government and proceeded to cut taxes and pursue a policy of deregulation. This was followed by an economic crisis in 1986 as speculation in kroner ultimately forced an increase in taxes and the Conservatives were forced out of office. But low-skilled manufacturing became unfeasible and it could not maintain its competiveness; many govern-

---

83 *Klassekampen* (Oslo), 29 March 2014, at http://www.klassekampen.no/article/20140329/ARTICLE/140329946 [last accessed on 5 July 2015].

84 "Norway abolishes state-sponsored Church of Norway", *Digital Journal* (15 May 2012), at http://digitaljournal.com/article/324906 [accessed 13 September 2012].

85 "Norway makes another step in the long road to separating church and state", *National Secular Society* (5 May 2012), at http://www.secularism.org.uk/news/2012/05/norway-shows-the-way-by-separating-church-and-state [last accessed on 1 November 2015].

86 *Ibid.*, summarizing Gärab Gustafsson and Thorleif Pettersson (eds.). *Folkkyrkor och religiös pluralism – den nordiska religiösa modellen* (Stockholm: Verbum, 2000).

87 James Bamberg, *British Petroleum and Global Oil 1950 – 1975: The Challenge of Nationalism* (Cambridge: Cambridge University Press, 2000), p. 202.

88 Nils Martin Stølen, "Wage Formation and the Macroeconomic Function of the Norwegian Labour Market", *SSB Social and Economic Studies* Vol. 89 (1995), p. 12 at http://www.ssb.no/histstat/sos/sos_089.pdf, last accessed 30 November 2012.

ment-subsidized industries were closed during the 1980s. But Norway continued to prosper through the 1990s and into the new millennium until today it is virtually debt free, devoid of the worst forms of poverty, and, as of 2011, had around 530 billion US dollars in overseas investments, a portfolio exceeded only by the Abu Dhabi Investment Authority.[89]

One of the most discussed treatises on the welfare state, entitled *The Three Worlds of Welfare Capitalism,* by Gøsta Esping-Andersen, was published in 1990.[90] His ideal types of the welfare state – conservative, liberal, and social-democratic – had their origins in different histories and economic forces. By 1997, Esping-Andersen defended these ideal types, in spite of the fact that each country presents as a mix of the types, because it was a way to "see the forest rather than the myriad of unique trees."[91] Today, although Norway can still be classified as "social democratic" according to the Esping-Andersen model, there are stressors within society that will provide for interesting developments and perhaps a few more unique trees. Some of these stressors are actually produced by the flow of money from the oil industry, which is creating significant social and cultural changes.

The State of Religiosity Today and the Triumph of Civil Religion

Research has been conducted on generational differences in religiosity in Norway. Between 1998 and 1999, the so-called RAMP (Religion and Moral Pluralism) study was conducted in several European countries, including Norway. Roughly 1,700 Danes, Finns, and Norwegians alongside 1,000 Swedes between the ages of 18 and 79 were interviewed in their homes. Altogether a total of 2,700 respondents from Denmark, Norway, Sweden, and Finland were involved.[92] Researchers who published the results from this survey focused on two interview questions, specifically: "Would you say you are a religious person?" and "Whether or not you think of yourself as a religious person, would you say that you have a spiritual life – something that goes beyond a

89 "Norway's economic riddle", *NEWSinENGLISH.no* (13 May 2011), at http://www.newsinengli sh.no/2011/05/13/norway%E2%80%99s-economic-riddle/ [accessed 28 November 2012].

90 Gøsta Esping Andersen, *The Three Worlds of Welfare Capitalism* (Cambridge: Polity Press, 1990).

91 Wil Arts and John Gelissen, "Three worlds of welfare capitalism or more? A state-of-the-art report" in *The Journal of European Social Policy*, Vol. 12, no. 2 (May 2002), p. 139.

92 Pål Ketil Botvar, "The Moral Thinking of Three Generations in Scandinavia: What Role Does Religion Play? ", in *Social Compass*, Vol. 52, No. 2 (June 2005), p. 189.

merely intellectual life?"[93] Within the Norwegian/Scandinavian setting, the words "religious" and "spiritual" have different connotations. "Religious" connotes a more orthodox acceptance of actual dogmas and being involved in a Church, whereas "spiritual" connotes less dogmatic and open reflections on morality and what matters in life without the benefit of organized religion.

The oldest generation (65 to 79 years old) scored 3.8 on "religiosity", while the youngest generation (28-34 years old) scored only 2.9. The middle generation (40-49 years old) scored 3.3. With regard to the youngest and oldest groups and "spirituality", the reverse was true. The youngest group scored 3.8 and the oldest 3.6; the middle group scored 3.7.[94]

Respondents in the RAMP survey were also asked two questions that dealt with how they made moral decisions. On a scale of 1 to 7, with 7 meaning "influences me strongly" and 1 meaning "has no influence at all", they were asked to what extent they were influenced by A. my conscience, B. What others will think of me, C. My upbringing, D. The law, E. My religion, F. What makes other people happy, and G. What make me happy.[95] The oldest cohort's highest score (6.0) was the answer A. My conscience. followed by D. The law and C. My upbringing. This generation's lowest score (3.0) was B. What others will think of me. By contrast, the youngest generation's highest score (5.9) was A. My conscience followed by G. What makes me happy. In third place, two answers both received a score of 5.3; these were C. My upbringing (for the youngest generation only) and F. What makes other people happy (for both the youngest and oldest generations).[96] Scores on this question from the middle generation were somewhere between the two other generations. For example, the score for E. My religion from the middle group was 3.3, while the older group scored 4.0 and the younger group scored 2.6.[97]

In a similar fashion, and using the same methodology, the three groups were asked "Some people think that what is good and what is bad depends entirely on the circumstances. Other people think that rules about what is good and bad apply at all times, whatever the circumstances. Which is closest to your opinion?"[98] The oldest group emphasized the universality of what is good and bad (4.1), while the youngest group emphasized the circumstances (3.3), with the middle generation closer to the oldest (3.9). Botvar rightly questioned whether the situational ethic among the youngest group would remain so

93 *Ibid.*, p. 190.
94 *Ibid.*
95 *Ibid.*, p. 192.
96 *Ibid.*
97 *Ibid.*
98 *Ibid.*

throughout their lives, or whether or not they might move closer to universal principles as they grew older. He summarized the study by noting that the youngest and the oldest groups understood morality in different ways and tended to confront moral dilemmas in different ways.[99] However, the data did not support the idea that the youngest group had no moral values; first, they "simply have *other principles*..." and second, the morality of the youngest group was "not a function of a non-religious world-view."[100]

The point to be made here is that the members of the oldest group in this study were born between 1919 and 1933. What the RAMP study demonstrated is that this group derived a moral sense from the acceptance of moral doctrines and that these were universal in their nature. There is the possibility that they developed these attitudes late in life, but the date of attitude formation within a person's life was not investigated. It may be that this older group had held quite opposite attitudes as young people; however, given their responses to how they made moral choices, we suspect they are representative of the time in which they grew up.

According to the aforementioned RAMP study, we now see the decrease in standard indicators of religiosity; young people are opting for spirituality and for a contextualized morality. Christian discourses, even within the traditionally most conservative regions of Norway are less polarized than during the 1960s.[101] From the Hodne Study from 2005 of Agder (a southern region), which used qualitative methods, we find that more stress is placed on emotions, a sense of community, and experiential religion rather than on anything that resembles religion in the other two periods.[102] Helje Sødal conducted a study of three conservative Christian youth organizations in this area (Kristiansand) and found that the image of God that is used by these members is one of being both a "close friend" and "almighty".[103] She coined the expression "the cosy majesty" for this idea.

The European Social Survey also included questions about religious adherence in Norway (see Table 8.1) and religious affiliation among minority religious associations (see Table 8.2).

---

99 *Ibid.*, p. 193

100 *Ibid.*

101 Pål Repstad, "A softer God and a more positive anthropology: Changes in a religiously strict region of Norway", in *Religion*, Vol. 39, Issue 2 (June 2009), p. 128.

102 *Ibid.*, p. 127.

103 Helje Kringebotn Sødal, "Forandring fryder? Endringer i tre kristne ungdomsgrupper i Kristiansand 1984-2004", in Pål Repstad and Jan-Olav Henriksen (eds.), *Mykere kristendom? Sørlandsreligion i endring* (Bergen: Fagbokforlaget, 2005), as cited in *Ibid.*, p. 128.

Table 8.1. Religious adherence during the years 2002-2012 (a summary of six surveys)

	%
Yes	53.4
No	46.6
Sum	100.0
Number of respondents	10260

Note: Question to the respondents: "Do you consider yourself as belonging to any particular religion or denomination?"

Source: European Social Survey 2002 – 2012

Table 8.2. Religious affiliation during the years 2002-2012 (a summary of six surveys)

	%
Roman Catholic	2.7
Protestant	88.8
Eastern Orthodox	0.6
Other Christian denomination	2.9
Jewish	0.1
Islamic	2.5
Eastern religions	0.8
Other non-Christian religions	1.4
Sum	100.0

Note: Question to the respondent: "To which religion or denomination do you belong?"

Source: European Social Survey 2002 – 2012

Norway's Lutheran Church is slowly declining in importance. This can be measured in several ways. First, there is the fact of the relative decline in its registered membership – dropping from 86.3% of the population in 2001 to 74.9% in 2013.[104] And the trend continues: according to official statistics, more than 11,000 persons withdrew from membership in the Church in 2014.[105] Second, there has been a decline in participation in certain Church rituals, including a decline in the number of marriages being contracted in church.[106]

104 *Klassekampen* (29 March 2014), [note 83].

105 *Klassekampen* (2 July 2015), at http://www.klassekampen.no/article/20150702/NTBI/1309886178 [accessed on 5 July 2015].

106 *Ibid.*

On the other hand, it is also true that, in the years 1977-2008, attendance at Mass remained "fairly stable".[107] And third, there are tendencies toward the privatization of religion, with an estimated 15% of members of Norway's Church rejecting such central Christian doctrines as life after death and the existence of heaven and hell, while being more inclined to believe in angels and demons than in God.[108] Moreover, already by the end of the 1980s, some 50% of Norwegians said that religion had no meaning for them, and, while 15% declared that they were active in the Church, 18% of the population said that they believed in astrology and 12% in reincarnation.[109] According to a poll conducted in February 2002, 42% of Norwegians favoured the separation of Church and state, with only 28% opposed; 30% had no opinion or refused to answer.[110] The following month, the Commission for Church-State Separation filed its report, recommending the disestablishment of Lutheranism as the state religion and the elimination of all constitutional clauses on religion, except those guaranteeing freedom of religion and the equality of all religions.

At the same time, the Lutheran Church remains the historic Church of the country, symbolized by the fact that the King of Norway is required, as already mentioned, to be a member of that Church. The celebration of St. Olav Haraldsson (995-1030) as the country's national saint is important, but it is worth stressing that the St. Olav Festival Days (Olavsfestdagene), held every summer in Trondheim, are an overwhelmingly secular event, at which merchants sell their wares and at which there is a traditional jousting between equestrian knights in full armour. Two things follow from the evolution of the Church from a strict, doctrinally oriented institution into a symbol of the country's history and vehicle of its civil religion. First, we witness the steady growth of Christian communities other than the Lutheran Church – a growth not opposed by the formerly state Church (see Table 8.3, below).

107 Kristin Strømsnes, "The Importance of Church Attendance and Membership of Religious Voluntary Organizations for the Formation of Social Capital", in *Social Compass,* Vol. 55, No. 4 (December 2008), p. 479.

108 *Dagbladet* (Oslo), 22 July 2013, at http://www.dagbladet.no/2013/07/22/kultur/meninger/hovedkommentar/kirka/folkekirke/28321083/ [last accessed on 5 July 2015].

109 Oftestad et al., *Norsk kirkehistorie,* p. 298; and Knut Lundby and Ann Kristin Gresaker, "Religion i mediene – omstridt og oversett? ", in Inger Furseth (ed.), *Religionens Tilbakekomst i Offentligheten? Religion, politick, medier, stat og sivilsamfunn i Norge siden 1980-tallet* (Oslo: Universitetsforlaget, 2015), pp. 70, 89, 91, 93-100.

110 *Dagbladet* (Oslo), 16 February 2002, at http://www.dagbladet.no/nyheter/2002/02/16/313543.html [last accessed on 6 November 2015].

Table 8.3. Members of Christian communities outside the Church of Norway (2005, 2013)

	2005	2013
Adventists	5,567	4,841
Free Evangelical Congregations	3,653	3,443
Evangelical-Lutheran Free Church	21,140	19,552
Finnish Evangelical Lutheran	3,504	3,440
Icelandic Evangelical Lutheran	3,395	6,634
The Christian Church	6,054	7,259
The Orthodox Church	5,028	12,959
The Roman Catholic Church	43,118	121,130
Evangelical Lutheran Church	3,410	3,209
Norwegian Baptist Union	9,549	9,589
Church of Norway Mission Covenant	8,505	9,091
Jehovah's Witnesses	14,502	12,049
The Christian Community	2,472	2,544
The Methodist Church	11,981	10,744
Pentecostal congregations	42,744	39,412
Swedish Margareta Congregation	7,267	20,901
Other Christian communities	19,937	25,035
Totals	215,090	266,834

Note: "Other Christian communities" includes the Christian centers, not listed separately in 2005.

Source: Statistics Norway, at http://www.ssb.no/a/english/kortnavn/trosamf_en/tab-2011-12-06-03-en.html and http://www.ssb.no/149605/members-of-christian-communities-outside-the-church-of-norway.per-1-january -- both accessed on 7 July 2015.

Second, we find that "religious involvement is positively associated with… social trust and tolerance"[111] – again, earmarks of and features associated with strong civil religion. Kristin Strømsnes points out that

> Significantly *fewer* active members of religious voluntary organizations feel that immigrants, Christian fundamentalists and people with criminal records should be *refused* permission to arrange meetings. They also have significantly less aversion [than persons who are not active members of religious voluntary organizations] to having neighbours who are homosexuals, immigrants, Christian fundamentalists, Islamic fundamentalists or people with criminal records.[112]

111 Strømsnes, "The Importance of Church Attendance" [note 107], p. 478.

112 *Ibid.*, p. 490.

Moreover, Norwegians who are active in religion are significantly more tolerant than nonbelievers when it comes to having as neighbours persons of non-white racial groups, immigrants, left-wing extremists, Christian fundamentalists, and Islamic fundamentalists, and somewhat more tolerant than nonbelievers, in this regard, where homosexuals, drug addicts, right-wing extremists, and persons with criminal records are concerned. The only group which active religious believers were less inclined than nonbelievers to tolerate as neighbours were racists, but not by a significant margin.[113]

Conclusion: Facts in Search of a New Paradigm

In many respects, the relationship between Church and state in Norway is a compressed and fast-paced summary of what has taken place in many other European countries over a longer period of time. Norway, as a case study, should be simple enough since it has had a relatively small population, it was ethnically homogeneous, and the Lutheran Church enjoyed a virtual monopoly over the population. Under these conditions, people might have believed that a separation of Church and state would be next to impossible. And, to an extent, they were correct, since the definition of "separation" is extremely blurred by the fact that – even after "separation" – the state of Norway still pays the salaries of all DNK (now, the "NFK") bishops, priests, and employees. Through public financing, the state will continue to be responsible for Lutheran churches and burial sites. As Ulla Schmidt writes, there is no "linear process of disestablishment" in Norway between Church and state.[114] And, the changes which have taken place have been, at best, "modest and somewhat reluctant."[115]

But what accounts for these changes? The 2012 separation was the result of a process in which both state and Church were willing participants, and which began well before the 2008 parliamentary accord. Because of its history and the deep ethos of Lutheranism in Norway, today it is closer to what Schmidt calls a "cultural religion" where there is "less weight [placed] on personal conviction and commitment, and more on creating and sustaining identities by providing connections with a 'passive cultural heritage'."[116]

In Norway's early, foundational period, before the Labour Party became an important factor in the parliament, the Church was responsible for the social

113 *Ibid.*

114 Ulla Schmidt, "State, Law and Religion in Norway", in *Nordic Journal of Religion and Society*, Vol. 24, No. 2 (2011), p. 149.

115 *Ibid.*

116 *Ibid.*, p. 150.

safety network, although this was in combination with the local city council ("kommune"). And as the social welfare state took shape within a relatively short period of time, more structural differentiation took place. Social differentiation increased with economic growth. All of the components of Bruce's model are present but, as we reach the present time, his model becomes less convincing when details are examined.

After World War Two, and a short flirtation with civil religion, Norway's next major change with respect to religion grew out of the 1960s. All things sexual, which had been controlled by religiously-based morality and societal norms, were on the table for debate and change. As we have seen, these issues included abortion and homosexual unions, divorce, and cohabitation.

Evidence from the most recent period indicates a deep and continuing religious ethos based in Lutheranism. Lejon and Agnafors rightly point out that

> [A] society can have [a] religious ethos, or religious character, while many of its citizens nevertheless profess to be atheists (and vice versa). While the religious convictions of a population are a part of the society's ethos and certainly play a role in shaping the society, the primary vehicle for change and societal design, leading to prosperity, is the public expression of the ethos itself through norms, values, policies, and laws.[117]

If this is true, then Norway continues to be a "Lutheran" state, despite its recent Church-state separation, although it is also a "secularized" nation, within some new meaning of that word.[118]

There is currently a basic problem with the secularization paradigm. While Steve Bruce's paradigm may hold – in general terms – in relation to Norway up until the last time period described above, Ulla Schmidt writes that, for Norway today, "it is necessary to take into account that religion…is too multifaceted [a] phenomenon [for] one theory alone…[to] describe it satisfactorily."[119] Nonetheless, she adds that even though the concept of secularization is too narrow, it is

117 Kjell Lejon and Marcus Agnafors, "Less Religion, Better Society? On Religion, Secularity, and Prosperity in Scandinavia", in *Dialog,* Vol. 50, Issue 3 (2011), p. 303.

118 For a different perspective, see Ultike Popp-Baier, "From Religion to Spirituality – Megatrend in Contemporary Society or Methodological Artifact? A Contribution to the Secularization Debate from Psychology of Religion", in *Journal of Religion in Europe,* No. 3 (2010), pp. 34 – 67.

119 Ulla Schmidt, "Religion i dagens Norge: Sekulisert? Privatisert? Pluralisert? in Pål Ketil Botvar and Ulla Schmidt (eds.), *Religion i dagens Norge: mellom sekularisering og sakralisering* (Oslo: Universitetsforlaget, 2010), p. 204. «Det er nødvendig å ta høyde for at religion i dagens Norge er et for mangesidig fenomen til at en teori alene kan beskrive den tilfredsstillende.»

through its ambiguity that one can still "capture some of the most striking and dominant tendencies" in the religious sphere today.[120]

Religion still plays a major role in Norwegian society, despite the 2012 "separation" of Church and state. Indeed, in 2014, 58.9% of Norwegian parents had their newborn children baptized in church, in spite of the fact that, already in 1985, only 38% of Norwegians said that they believed in God, versus 38% who did not, and 24% who were unsure.[121] Is this *religion* or is it an entirely different phenomenon? This is why the fact of Norway's "separation" continues to cry out for a sociological theory of secularization.

In this discussion of secularism and Church-state relations in Norway, we have often referred to Steve Bruce's paradigm. While relativism could be inferred from his model, we prefer to give the final word to Inger Furseth, who sees a more dynamic and more intricate model of secularism developing in Norway. She sees ecumenical cooperation in various settings and institution-building outside what one would normally consider the religious sphere, as the basis for a new upsurge in religious sentiment and activity. Nonetheless, she questions the extent to which the weakening of ecclesiastical bonds necessarily entails what has come to be called the privatization of religion.[122]

---

120 *Ibid.* "Men selv om begrepet sekularisering alene er for snevert til å gi en dekkende forståelse av de mangesidige og motsetningsfylte ved religion i Norge, er det likevel flertydig nok til å fange inn noen av de mest iøynefallende og dominerende tendensene. "

121 "Like mange som tror og ikke tror på Gud", in *Dagen* (31 March 2015), at http://www.dagen.no/Nyheter/nyheter/Like-mange-som-tror-og-ikke-tror-p%C3%A5-Gud-184971 [accessed on 6 November 2015].

122 Inger Furseth, "Religionens tilbakekomst, nedgang eller økende kompleksitet?", in Furseth (ed.), *Religionens Tilbakekomst* [note 109], p. 181.

Part Three – The Economy & the Environment

Jože Mencinger and Jonathon Moses

9 Economic developments in Slovenia and Norway

Although Slovenia and Norway are both young nation-states (but old countries!), their economies are remarkably different. This is understandable, in that the Norwegian economy appears as stable and developed, while Slovenia is a new country undergoing many systemic changes. This chapter describes the varying sorts of concerns facing these two different countries. In Slovenia, our emphasis is on describing the country's economic development from "the success story" to the Troika. In Norway, our focus is aimed at describing how the country has managed an admirable record with regard to unemployment, poverty reduction and public ownership.

Both countries are relatively small; Norway has a population of 5 million and Slovenia of 2 million people. Norway's GDP (393 billion euro in 2013)[1] is nearly eleven times Slovenia's (36.1 billion), and Slovenian GDP per capita, corrected for purchasing power parity, reaches only 43% of the Norwegian. While Slovenia has been, similarly to other countries in the EU, constantly facing budget deficits, Norway has experienced unique budget surpluses, reaching or exceeding 10% of GDP. This is due to Norway's general government revenues of 54.7% of GDP (in 2014) and expenditures of 45.7% of GDP, while in Slovenia the figures are 45.0% and 49.8%, respectively. Slovenia has been looking for a way out of the current crisis by increasing its exports; hence it managed a current account surplus of 5.8% of GDP in 2014, while a current account surplus of nearly 10% is a constant feature in Norway. The population of Norway is younger than that of Slovenia (average age in Norway is 39 years, average age in Slovenia 42.5 years) and grows faster (with 1.12% a year while the population in Slovenia grows at only 0.11% a year) which is to a great extent due to very high net immigration rate in Norway (0.77%) and low in Slovenia (0.02%). While the Slovenian unemployment rate is slightly below the EU average, reaching 10.1% in 2013, the Norwegian rate is much lower, only 3.5%. This is due to a very high employment rate of 78% in Norway, in Slovenia it is 70%; 52% of the population in Norway is active, only 44.5% in Slovenia. There is only one field in which Slovenia is similar to Norway; its

1 All the data are from Eurostat and relate to 2013 or 2014.

equality in income distribution (see Figure 9.5 for Gini coefficients) and net earnings in both countries are approximately 78% of gross earnings.

Slovenia

The Yugoslav Heritage

Between World War One and 1991 Slovenia was a part of Yugoslavia and shared its specific features: self-management and social property. Indeed, Yugoslavia after World War Two served as the one example of a socialist market economy. The features were summarized by Bićanić [2] who enumerated the differences between the centrally planned system and socialist market system as follows: social ownership of the means of production as opposed to the state ownership, reliance on the market mechanism for the allocation of goods and services as opposed to the administrative mechanism, increased use of financial instruments as opposed to adoption of simple administrative rules, free distribution of available income by workers councils as opposed to administratively fixed wages, decentralized and functional budgeting at all administrative levels as opposed to an all embracing state budget, the rehabilitation of consumer sovereignty as opposed to the treatment of personal consumption as residual, and the acceptance of independent farmers as opposed to compulsory collectivization.

The actual economic system, however, was not very stable and Yugoslav post-World War Two systemic development can be divided into four distinct periods: administrative socialism (1945-1952), administrative market socialism (1953-1962), market socialism (1963-1973), and contractual socialism (1974-1990).[3] The major goal of "administrative socialism" was to transform the underdeveloped, predominantly agricultural, capitalist society into an industrial socialist society, modelled after the Soviet pattern. However, after 1950,

2 R. Bićanić,"Economic Growth under Centralized and Decentralized Planning: Yugoslavia - A Case Study" in *Economic development and cultural change*, Vol.5 (1957), 63(c)74.

3 The demarcation of the periods is normative, four post-war constitutions (in 1946, 1953, 1963, and 1974) form the periods; the starting year of each period is the year in which a new constitution was passed. The demarcation is also closely related to the normative allocation of decision-making in the economy. Such demarcation, based on constitutional rules for the functioning of the economy, is open to criticism. First, it creates the perception of abrupt changes, which did not occur. Second, some far-reaching institutional changes preceded the constitutional changes, others were introduced after them. Third, the gaps between the ideology represented by a constitution, the actual normative setting, and reality were always wide. Fourth, some economic policy changes had greater impact on the actual economic development than systemic changes.

Yugoslavia began to move away, step by step, from centralized economic planning by reducing administrative constraints and by giving enterprises a more independent role in decision-making. Nevertheless, up to the early sixties, self-management was rather limited even in a normative setting; two of four basic economic decisions, namely the decision on income distribution and the savings/investment decision, remained under government control, while what to produce and how to combine productive factors was to be decided upon on the markets by consumers and producers. Systemic changes occurring during the sixties increased the autonomy of economic units; income distribution and capital allocation were, at least formally, transferred to independent enterprises. However, by the early seventies, new institutional changes were introduced; they were the blueprints for the so-called associated labour concept by which the market character of the Yugoslav economy became questionable.

The systemic development raises the question of what were the reasons for changes. If a rather mystical "development of productive forces" is not accepted, the question is reduced to a simpler one, namely, whether the reasons for systemic changes were inspired predominantly by economic or by political considerations. One can argue that political factors prevailed in the abandonment of the Soviet-type system in the early fifties and in the adoption of the associated labour concept in the seventies, while the reforms in the sixties were triggered predominantly by economic considerations.[4]

According to "official beliefs", the changes in the fifties can be explained by the ideas of Yugoslav political leaders long before the split between Tito and Stalin. However, the overwhelming nationalization in 1948, and the strongest pressure for forced collectivization in agriculture after the split, indicate that immediately after the split Yugoslav communist leaders wanted to demonstrate that they were better communists than Soviet communists. They failed and began the search for a new form of socialism – a socialist market economy was discovered. The motives for the changes in the seventies were again political, though they can be partly attributed to worsened economic performance in the late sixties accompanied by even less desirable developments in the social domain. However, it was the concentration of power in the hands of managerial

4 The pillars of the system, theoretical and actual performance of the Yugoslav economy are described in many articles, among others in: Horvat, Branko, "Yugoslav Economic Policy in the Post-War Period: Problems, Ideas, Institutional Developments" in *American Economic Review (supplement)*, Vol. 61 (1971), No. 2, 71-169; Joze Mencinger, "Theoretical and Actual Performance of the Worker-Managed Economy" in *Economic Analysis,* Vol. 13 (1979), 253-265; Jaroslav Vanek, "The Macroeconomic Theory and Policy of an Open Worker Managed Economy" *in Economic Analysis,* Vol.6 (1972), 255-269; and Benjamin Ward, "The Firm in Illyria: Market Syndicalism" in *American Economic Review,* Vol. 48 (1958), 566-589.

elite-technocrats (though predominantly members of the Party) which threatened to deprive the Party bureaucracy of political control. Institutional changes therefore emerged as inevitable if the political power of the Party was to be upheld. The new "contractual" socialism was again shaped by Slovenian politician Edvard Kardelj.[5] In a few years, every single part of the economic system was affected, and an entirely new and awkward terminology was introduced. Although a divergence between practice and legal doctrine was the rule rather than the exception in Yugoslavia, the breakdown of the system introduced by institutional reforms in the seventies can hardly be questioned. In short, the blueprints of the system were either inoperative or produced undesirable results. Both required corrective government interventions and incessant changes in legislation; the system gradually acquired characteristics of the administrative systems: rigidity, slowness, inconsistency, distrust, and application of non-economic means for the implementation of economic goals. Macroeconomic performance in the period of "contractual socialism" was characterized by the break in 1980, when acute difficulties began. When the supply of foreign credits became inadequate to cover the current account deficit, deterioration turned to stagflation and, after 1983, to a kind of hyper-stagflation. This prompted attempts to a new reform. The Long Run Stabilization Program, which can be considered the reform of the eighties, tried to increase economic efficiency by introducing the tools of capitalist market economies, while at the same time retaining social property and the Party's political monopoly. Yugoslavia suddenly appeared unable to move in any direction; the country reached the point at which any economic reforms unaccompanied by political reforms could only increase the inconsistency between the economic and political system. While Party ideologists and economists speculated about other types of socialism, the government, maintaining its inability to deal with economic problems within the existing economic system, launched a new reform in 1988. The proposals commenced from the premise that ownership of the means of production constituted the essence of Yugoslav economic problems, and urged abandonment of the so-called non-property philosophy of social property, by which everybody and nobody is the owner. They insisted, instead, that "the subject" of social property be determined and that the principle according to which management was given to labour only be replaced by the principle according to which those who provide capital are entitled to management and profit sharing. Indeed, one could say that socialism was abolished well before its formal abolition.

---

5 The systems and their changes were indeed dominated by three Slovenian politicians in federal authorities: Boris Kidrič, Boris Kraigher, and Edvard Kardelj.

During 1986-1988, the economic situation worsened and it became clear that the federal government was unable to control fiscal and monetary policy. Before the end of 1988 the government of Branko Mikulić resigned. It was succeeded by a new government led by Ante Marković who eagerly continued economic reform and launched a new "shock therapy" stabilization program. A fixed exchange rate, tight monetary policy, and wage controls were to be its pillars. In fact, initial overvaluation of the dinar, the weakness of wage controls, and fiscal overhang existed from the very beginning. In the first two quarters of 1990, economic performance was satisfactory; in April 1990, the rate of inflation was even negative. In June, fatal mistakes were added to those in December 1989 which made price stability unsustainable; policy makers began to pump money through selective credits and nearly doubled the wages of federal employees. The program was thus left without consistent built-in nominal anchors except for the fixed exchange rate. In the last two quarters of 1990 prices jumped up again. Severe monetary restrictiveness that followed in the last quarter pushed the economy into critical illiquidity, large scale bartering, and recession without deflation. With the exchange rate fixed at a highly overvalued level, dinar exports were left without support, imports were pushed up and the trade deficit started to grow. In October, a speculative attack on foreign exchange deposits started. Finally, foreign currency reserves, the last resort of the stabilization program, started to vanish. The collapse of the economic reform and stabilization programs, which had been launched in conditions of acute economic crisis and carried out during political crisis, was unavoidable.

The federal government tried to stop deteriorating economic performance but the attempts were blocked by the republics, which led to the break-up of the country. In autumn 1990, Yugoslavia actually ceased to exist as an economic entity; taxes were not collected, money was "printed" elsewhere, tariffs and special levies were introduced for "imports" from other republics. In addition, the republics started to build up their own economic systems, which differed considerably.

Despite the failure of systemic change and macroeconomic stabilization on the federal level, former constituent parts retained many advantages for economic and social transition compared to other East European countries. Most of the so-called essentials for economic transition: decentralization, price reform, openness to the outside world, and diversification of ownership were at least partly met before its political and ideological collapse.

Creation of a Country

The proclamation of the country's independence on 26 June 1991 coincided with unresolved disputes over custom duties. Yugoslav federal authorities intervened in an attempt to grab control of the borders. The army was, however, badly surprised by the resistance. After a week of fighting between the Yugoslav army on one side and Slovenian territorial defense and police forces on the other, a ceasefire was signed at Brioni. In accordance with it, Slovenia had to defer the implementation of independence activity for three months. On 8 October 1991, the moratorium expired and Slovenia introduced its own currency - the Slovenian Tolar (SIT); the country became "fully independent". This ended tense and uncertain political and economic developments in the eighties and, definitely so, in 1990[6] when the political future of Slovenia was not yet firmly established and the shape of the future arrangement within Yugoslavia was unknown. Consequently, the new Slovenian government, installed after elections in April 1990, began cautious preparation for a likely collapse of Yugoslavia by gradually acquiring control over economic policy and the economic system.

The early economic performance of the new country was satisfactory and the social costs of transition were rather low. The reasons for that can be found in two major factors: the initial conditions and the patterns of transition. First, many essentials of a market economy had been created before 1989; enterprises were autonomous, basic market institutions existed, and the government could use many standard economic policy tools. Second, Slovenia, the richest of the former socialist countries in Central and Southeastern Europe, could afford to implement macroeconomic stabilization cautiously with pragmatism and risk aversion while refusing the patronage of international financial institutions and foreign advisers.

Gradualism versus Shock Therapy

Slovenia has been often considered "a success story" of transition. However, after two decades, the country has found itself in an economic, social, political, and moral crunch which has no end in sight. It is thus proper to reconsider the events that had a decisive impact on the current situation. Would there have been better paths than the one actually chosen? When was Slovenia straying

6 For a comprehensive review of political, social, and economic development of Slovenia see: Mojmir Mrak, Matija Rojec, Carlos Silva-Jauregui, eds. *»Slovenia – From Yugoslavia to the European Union«,* The World Bank, 2004.

from the path which would bring the country closer to the romantic expectations of two decades ago? Or maybe it was just a time for illusions?

There are many who claim that gradualism is to be blamed for the recent crunch. However, gradualism was, in a sense, a natural legacy of previous systemic changes. It was embodied in the country's initial economic conditions and consistent with soft changes occurring in the political sphere, the pillars of which can also be found in the process of pre-1989 democratization. Already in the 1970s, the League of Communists in Slovenia evolved into a sort of a conglomerate of bureaucratic elites; most of their members only pretended to believe in socialism and could easily adapt to and turn to any ideology. At the end of the 1980s, a basic consensus on democratization was achieved without any formal negotiations between the new political actors and the existing political elite; the members of the existing elite became an ally in the emerging battle with federal authorities. The existing economic elite (i.e., managers) retained or strengthened its position, as well. The coalition of these two elite groups ensured the exchange of economic and political support and enabled both to be the survivors (or even the winners) in the transition process.

Slovenia, as a part of Yugoslavia, shared the latter's advantages and disadvantages compared to other socialist countries in Eastern Europe, in particular its openness, and a rather unique economic and political system based on social property and self-management. Owing to a decades-long series of reforms during Yugoslavia's existence, many of the essentials for a successful transition were at least partly met before 1989: enterprises were autonomous, basic market institutions existed, and the system of macroeconomic governance made possible the use of standard economic policy tools. Slovenia itself had additional advantages: the country was the richest part of Eastern Europe, with an ethnically and socially homogeneous population, a diversified manufacturing sector, a predominantly private agriculture, a partly privately owned services sector, well-established economic links with Western markets, and a good geographic position. Slovenia was also not fully integrated into Yugoslavia; it was quite autonomous in infrastructure, with its own access to the sea as well as its own pipelines, railways, telecommunications, and electrical grid; the trade patterns with the rest of Yugoslavia resembled trade patterns with the rest of the world.

The privatization issue caused a major controversy within the government, divided politicians, and became the root of political instability. The controversy was political rather than economic, the root of the matter being who should control the economy. Adoption of the gradual and decentralized approach in privatization would presumably have allowed control to remain in the hands of existing managers, thus in the hands of the former elite, whereas the shock therapy and centralized approach would have transferred control to the government and thus to the new political elite. The controversy resulted in a stalemate. After a year and a half of maneuvering and debates, the controversy was resolved by the adoption of The Ownership Transformation Act, passed in November 1992, which was a compromise combining decentralization, gradualism, and diversity of privatization methods of the gradualist approach with the free distribution of vouchers called for under the shock therapy.

Establishing the monetary system involved a choice between a fixed and floating exchange rate. The search for monetary independence began in June 1990 and concentrated on three issues: the consequences of unilateral decisions for the functioning of the financial system and for the relations with other countries and international institutions; the possibilities of a monetary system in a confederation which was at a time considered a viable political solution for Yugoslavia; and the prospects of eventual monetary independence.[7] While economic theory does not provide a definite answer as to which is preferable, a majority of experts supported the view that a fixed exchange rate system would suit a country in transition better, or they proposed a crawling peg or currency board as appropriate possibilities. The exchange rate regime and ensuing macroeconomic stabilization patterns were therefore, beside privatization, fields of heated controversy. The "pegging versus floating" issue also reflected two opposite approaches to transition: a radical one and a gradualist one. The "shock therapists" supported by foreign advisers suggested an overwhelming package encompassing price stabilization, a fixed exchange rate, a balanced budget, administrative restructuring of the manufacturing and of the banking system, and centralized privatization be part of the package of measures for independence. The gradualists suggested that economic policy remains funded on a gradual construction of market institutions and on the separation of political independence from macroeconomic stabilization. There would be no formal stabilization program and the government would play only an indirect role in privatizing and restructuring the economy. The economic policy instruments of this approach would be a firm but flexible wage policy, restrictive government spending enhanced by a budget deficit, if required, a monetary policy enabling tolerable liquidity, flexible exchange rate regime, reliance on foreign equity capital, and concessions for investments in infrastructure. It was

---

7 Actual developments between June 1990 and October 1991 reveal uncertainty and confusion. Already in October 1990, nameless provisional notes were secretly printed, and the debates shifted to the pattern and the most appropriate moment for the introduction of the Slovenian currency. After the so-called "break in" of the Yugoslav monetary system by Serbia at the end of 1990, Slovenia hastened in preparing acts for its own monetary system; all crucial acts were prepared in spring of 1991. For more information see "Slovenia: From Yugoslavia to the European Union". [note 6]

argued that such a policy would result in a smaller loss in product and lower unemployment on the account of higher inflation. Gradualists, who gathered in the governing board of the central bank, prevailed. However, Slovenia chose floating for a very practical reason; fixed exchange rate could not be preserved. First, the new central bank had no foreign exchange reserves to defend the fixed rate. Secondly, monthly inflation in October 1991 was 21.5 per cent! A moderate initial devaluation would therefore be overridden by inflation immediately while a large devaluation would stimulate inflation and again endanger the fixed rate. Thirdly, it was impossible to determine the starting equilibrium exchange rate in a new country. Pegging would, in such circumstances, hinder accommodations of the equilibrium real exchange rate to a newly required volume of trade and trade patterns. Slovenia thus established a system of managed floating; the experiences which followed proved that the managed floating exchange rate was the right choice.

Four periods in the development of the country

Four periods can be distinguished in a brief economic history of the country: a short period of transitional depression (1991-1992), a decade of balanced economic and social development (1993-2004), the “gambling” period (2005-2008), and the crisis period (2009-). In1993, Slovenia reached the bottom of the transitional depression. After two years, the benefits of secession appeared to prevail over its costs. While the costs of reorienting trade from protected to competitive markets were significant, the secession intensified economic restructuring, pushed for sound economic policy, and enabled the creation of a "normal" economic system. GDP grew at more or less constant rate of 4% annually, inflation and unemployment were gradually lowered, the state budget was nearly balanced, public debt amounted to only 30% of GDP, a surplus in trade of services outweighed the deficit in trade of goods, and foreign exchange reserves more than matched foreign debt. Social cohesion was retained.

Figure 9.1. Economic development of Slovenia (index, 1990=100)

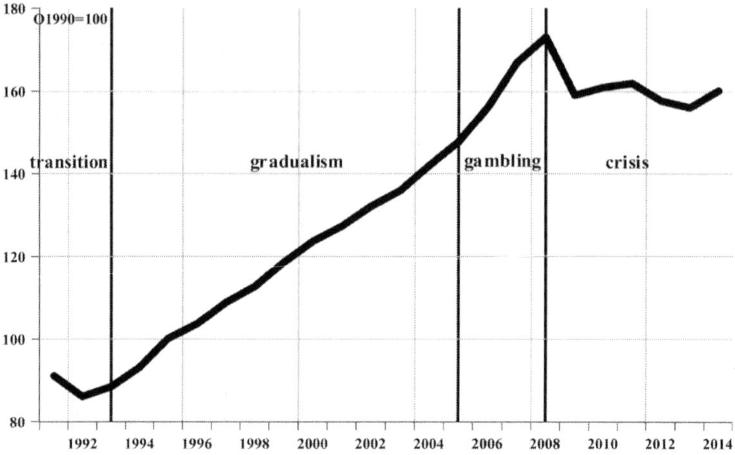

Source: Eurostat

"Back to Europe" was a slogan of the last decade of the 20th century and the ultimate goal of all former socialist countries in Central and Southeastern Europe, Slovenia included. A new "emergency exit" appeared with a delay but continued rather smoothly. In 1999, the country began preparations for joining the EU and EMU which required changes in economic policies, particularly the opening of the capital market. Upon entering the EU in 2004, Slovenia had already fulfilled four of the Maastricht criteria and immediately assumed ERM2 status. In February 2005, the national master plan for the introduction of the euro was formally adopted. Contrary to hasty and uncertain procedures in conversion from the Dinar to the Tolar in 1991, the procedures in the conversion from the Tolar to the Euro were precisely scheduled and the changeover on 1 January 2007 was smooth. However, in the process of accepting the EU "aquis", Slovenia was gradually losing control of its economic policies. By entering the EU in May 2004 and the ERM2 in July 2004, Slovenia also formally lost control of its monetary policy and surrendered a large part of its fiscal policies. In a decade, a newly born national economy turned again to a regional economy.

Slovenia´s experience after the euro area entry could serve almost as a textbook example of possible outcomes. For example, the rounding up of prices and the correction of relative prices which had been under control before conversion to euro contributed to inflation which was, however, pushed upwards also by the increase of world oil and agricultural products prices. The previous constant growth in the Slovenian share of exports in the EU exports turned to a stagnation of the share, which could be a consequence of the disappearance of exchange rate policy. An unprecedented increase of the current account deficit which followed the entry can be explained by the relaxation and replacement of an "old fashioned" philosophy that one can succeed by working hard with a "modern" philosophy, by which wealth can be most efficiently created by »financial deepening«, looking for "opportunities", and buying securities at home and abroad; savings turned to speculations. GDP growth strengthened to 7% per year due to 15% growth in the construction and financial services sectors. This was enabled by credits growing at the rate of 30% per year, and after entering the euro area, at the rate surpassing 40% per year. The banks were enthusiastic to cooperate in the "gambling" by borrowing cheap money in the EU or acquiring it from their mother banks; the inflow of capital in 2007 reached 12% of GDP; half of it was used for buying securities abroad. Net foreign debt increased from 0 € in 2005 to 10 billion € at the end of 2008 when the crisis hit. "The success story" became questionable. Indeed, after years of steady convergence towards EU average in terms of GDP per capita, the country's small and very open economy was severely hit by the global financial crisis. The imbalances from the gambling years, growing political instability, and social discontent have also severely hindered recovery.

Figure 9.2. Gambling (financial deepening, creation of virtual wealth and foreign indebtedness) in Slovenia

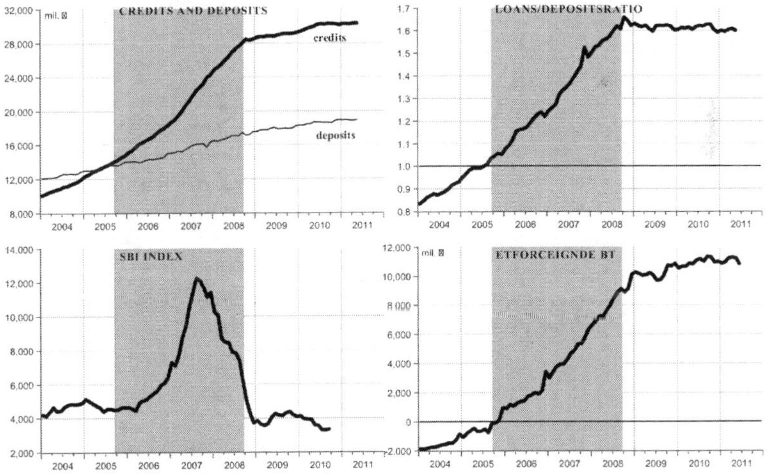

Source: Banka Slovenije and Ministry of finance

The Crisis and the Stalemate

The global financial crisis did not affect Slovenia until the end of 2008. But when the financial and economic crisis deepened, the very open Slovenian economy was unable to avoid the decline. Manufacturing companies were hit by the drop of foreign demand, crippled investments congested construction activity. In 2009, the GDP fell by 7.8%, exports by over 15%, gross fixed investments by more than 30%. Active use of fiscal policy helped to make the fall in GDP in 2010 less than it would otherwise have been; the costs were a high general government deficit level and a large increase in public debt. The crisis in domestic demand deepened in 2011, when government consumption declined alongside the contraction in investment and household consumption. The only contribution to GDP growth came from a net trade surplus created by export-oriented manufacturing industries and weaker domestic demand for imports. In 2012, economic activity in Slovenia declined again much more than in the euro zone. The decline was the result of an accelerated contraction in domestic consumption, caused by government austerity measures, difficult access to financing, and a high level of uncertainty. Yet a more significant drop in GDP was again prevented by the positive contribution of net exports; the large current account surplus was largely a result of the narrowing of the merchandise trade deficit. After five years of financial crisis, the Slovenian economy slid into deeper recession again in 2013; the reasons for the second wave were over-leveraging in the non-financial companies and austerity measures. Improvements first appeared at the end of 2013 and continued in 2014 and 2015.

A large increase in the budget deficit and public debt level was an inevitable consequence of the contraction of economic activity and the need for the socialization of losses of banks, by which the government prevented a collapse of the financial system. Indeed, while indebtedness of the "private" sector (banks) abroad decreased, indebtedness of the public sector increased. The financial turmoil badly affected Slovenian banks which had borrowed abroad extensively during the "gambling period"; the effects on the non-financial companies were enhanced by their high banking orientation, financed almost entirely via bank loans. By the crisis, the virtual wealth that had been created by "gambling" was devastated, while credit obligations remained to be served. Due to the drop of economic activity, more and more non-financial companies became unable to serve their obligations, more and more loans turned to bad loans. Banks, open-handed and imprudent during the gambling period, became thrifty and prudent or could not provide credits because of their own indebtedness. Regulators who were also lenient before the crisis became hard-hearted. Foreign banks began to squeeze credit by reducing liabilities to their mother banks, while large domestic banks faced three problems: repayment of loans abroad, tougher rules on capital adequacy by the regulators (EBA, ECB and BS),[8] and very attractive political demagogy against "tycoons" which frightened the bankers from restructuring credits; it was safer to do nothing.

The imbalances from the gambling years, growing political instability and social discontent, incompetent governments and their unreasonable submission to the "guidance" of the European Commission produced a stalemate. Public confidence in the parliament, the parties, state institutions, and politics in general which was gradually weakening – disappeared totally amidst real and virtual corruption scandals often connected to privatization attempts by managers in the "gambling" years when they were buying "their" companies by easily acquired credits and when these actions were considered desirable symbols of proper capitalism. Austerity measures, suggested by the European Commission (immediate fiscal consolidation, reduction of the public sector, and privatization) and hasty implementation of new stricter capital adequacy rules for banks, deepened the crisis. Social cohesion, a pride of the country, worsened considerably, a rather robust Gini coefficient increased from 22.7 in 2009 to 24.4 in 2014, the inequality coefficient enhanced from 3.2 to 3.6. Many considered that the "assistance" of troika was unavoidable[9], and that Slovenia should become a proper capitalist economy. Indeed, the government and the parliament agreed on forced ideological privatization similar to ideological nationalization in 1948. This should finally put an end to a rather specific development and to what is called "national interest", and bring Slovenia back where it "deserves" to be, i.e., among other former socialist economies, where the fate of which is more or less decided by the owners of multinational corporations, especially banks, and international financial institutions.

Can current economic and social problems, revealed by the crisis, be linked to the socialist heritage, gradualism or "national interests" i.e., resistance to selling productive assets to multinationals as often suggested by younger economists? Can the existing stalemate be explained by a lack of hardship before and during the transition which made Slovenians rather spoiled as suggested by some foreign observers? Can we blame greedy tycoons and systemic corruption as believed by a disillusioned population constantly bombarded by real and virtual corruption scandals? The tycoons are the first popular choice. However, the loans to them to buy "their" companies were provided by banks, which could not resist enormous amounts of cheap money

8 European Banking Association, European Central Bank, Bank of Slovenia.

9 Acquiring finances outside the EU enabled the government of Mrs. Alenka Bratušek to refuse the "assistance" of "troika" in the beginning of 2013.

which became available after the entry of Slovenia into the EU and the euro area. Securing loans by shares of purchased assets and repayment of loans with new loans were generally accepted practices. This was considered proper by auditors, monetary authorities, rating agencies, state authorities, lawyers, and economists. Above all, this was allowed by law. Then, practically overnight, everything changed; what had been considered praiseworthy capitalist behaviour, became a criminal offense. Previously good loans became bad loans, not because they would be different, but mainly because the rules or their perception and application had changed. Politicians, who have been engaged with demagogic hypocrisy on "tycoons persecution", have overlooked that the "persecution" by cutting credits to firms owned by tycoons would spread and stop the whole economy. Claiming that criminal acts were not present, would be pointless, but if the unwanted behaviour becomes common, one should look into the economic system, therefore to the lawmakers who created the rules and who, when the crisis came, began to alter them in a reckless and panicked manner. Also the Bank of Slovenia has contributed by constantly creating new "equations" for various risks thus increasing uncertainty and instability. The law makers along with the public prosecutors and courts turned into a kind of inquisition to find the perpetrators. Yet, the most important reason for the stalemate has been a paranoid atmosphere created in the country rather than the communist or "socialist self-managing" legacy. In such a mistrustful situation, doing nothing is the only safe act, doing anything carries the risk that one will sooner or later become a crook.

Norway

Since the beginning of the 1990s, Norwegian economic developments have remained relatively constant. Although Norway has experienced some significant changes in its external economic relationships—most prominently, the signing of a European Economic Agreement (EEA) with the European Union in 1992[10]— Norwegians have continued to manage their economy in a way that has allowed them to secure full employment and broad-based economic security. As a result, Norway is one of the richest, but also one of the most egalitarian, countries in the world.

This section will focus on three important elements in this effort at economic management: Norway's admirable full employment record; its relatively low levels of poverty; and the country's willingness and capacity to

10 For more information on Norway's relationship to the EU, see Chapter 12 in this volume: "Relations with the EU", by Damjan Lajh and Jonathon Moses.

sustain a high level of state ownership throughout the entire period. While it is common to explain Norway's economic bounty with reference to its significant resource wealth, this sort of argument is misleading. Norway's enviable economic record was secured despite its resource wealth, not because of it.[11] While the Norwegian economy remains a market-based, capitalist economy, it is also characterized by a high level of organization, regulation, and state activity. It is these characteristics, more than its petroleum wealth, that best explain how the country has secured such an enviable economic record.

Unemployment

Norway is a country which has jealously guarded its economic sovereignty (remaining outside of the European Union and its Eurozone),[12] and long embraced the logic and utility of economic management, but of a type that differs significantly from pre-1990 Slovenian-style socialism (as described above). As a small state dependent on the international economy, Norwegians recognize the need for active management and social corporatist strategies in order to adjust quickly to exogenous shocks.[13] As a prominent economic historian in Norway, Einar Lie, noted recently (with reference to the post-war period):

> The belief that the state now had control over economic development, and that it could pursue an industrial policy that was better than a more market-oriented economy could produce, and that it was able to combat economic crises and economic downturns, was stronger in Norway than in most, perhaps *all* other western countries.[14]

This affinity for economic management is usually explained with reference to political ideology—as a reflection of the Labour Party's dominant role in Norway's post-war electoral history. Indeed, the Labour Party led a coalition government (along with the Socialist Left and Centre Party) from 2005 to 2013, i.e. for most of the period covered in this chapter. The country is currently governed by a Right-wing (Conservative and Progress Party) minority govern-

11 We're referring to the literature on the so-called resource curse, or paradox of plenty. See, for example, Terry Lynn Karl, *The paradox of plenty: Oil booms and petro-states* (Berkeley and Los Angles: University of California Press, 1997).

12 Having said that, the Norwegian economy is still tightly bound to the European market (and European regulations) via the European Economic Agreement (EEA).

13 For a description of the historical roots to this recognition, see Peter Katzenstein, *Small States in World Markets* (Ithaca: Cornell University Press, 1985).

14 Einar Lie, *Norsk økonomisk politikk etter 1905* (Oslo Universitetsforlaget, 2012), p. 99. Emphasis his, translation ours.

ment, but it continues to follow the same basic framework of economic management. Furthermore, it is necessary to point out that Norway's embrace of economic management stretches beyond the count of Labour Party voters. There has long been a strong desire, deeply anchored in Norwegian political mores and traditions, for managing the Norwegian national economy, and for ensuring, at least in theory, an equitable distribution of its bounty.

The effect of this economic management has been a remarkably low level of unemployment among Norwegian citizens, through the entire post-war period. Full employment was secured by a number of changing policy instruments, as the country constantly found itself adjusting to changes in the international context.[15] A central element of the Norwegian economic management strategy has been its reliance on a highly regulated and organized labour market, where representatives of employers and workers work together to secure moderate (read internationally competitive) wage and investment developments. In contrast to most of the OECD, the level of union organization in Norway has remained stable over the last several decades, allowing organized labour to maintain a strong (and largely unified) voice when enunciating its demands. This highly organized labour market, combined with a political climate that prioritizes "work for all", helps to secure Europe's lowest level of unemployment—as evidenced in Figure 9.3.

Figure 9.3. OECD unemployment rates (2012)

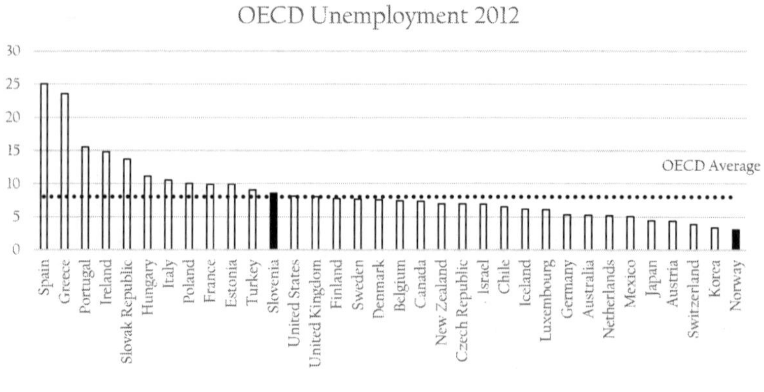

Source: stats.oecd.org

15 For a description and analysis of Norway's postwar economic management strategies, see Jonathon W. Moses, *Open States in the Global Economy* (Houndmills, Basingstoke, Hampshire: Macmillan, 2000).

The best way to protect people from poverty is to help them find secure, well-paid jobs. It is in large part because of Norway's full employment policies that the country suffers from relatively little abject poverty. Those Norwegians who are not able to secure full employment find protection from poverty in a developed welfare system that provides basic support (health, education, social security) and which is designed to retrain them for quick re-entry into the labour market.

As poverty is a relative concept, the difficulty of comparing different levels of poverty (within countries, across countries, over time) is enormous and already familiar to academics and policymakers. Absolute indicators of poverty, such as the ability to live on under one or two US$ per day, make little sense in a wealthy country like Norway. After all, a simple (.33 litre) bottle of water costs over two US$ in a Norwegian store. For this reason, Norway is not usually included in the international poverty rankings, for example by the World Bank (http://data.worldbank.org/topic/poverty).

Indeed, Norway is one of the wealthiest countries in the world, when measured in terms of GDP/capita. Figure 9.4 ranks OECD countries in terms of GDP per capita, using constant prices in USD (ppp). To give the foreign reader an idea of the scope of this wealth, the average manufacturing wage in Norway is about €50.00 an hour. A pint of beer in a local pub now trades for about €10. This high cost of living is affordable to a workforce that remains (almost) fully employed, as we already saw in Figure 9.3 (above).

Figure 9.4. GDP per capita, OECD, 2013

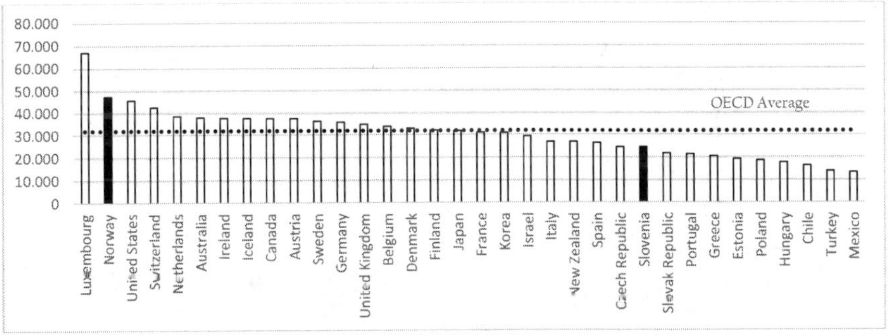

Note: USD, constant prices, 2005 PPP

Source: stats.oecd.org

Norway's relative wealth is usually attributed to the country's petroleum reserves, but the explanation is surely more complicated than that. As a general rule of thumb, countries with vast petroleum resources tend to have great difficulty in sustaining broad-based economic growth. The wealth generated by resource wealth is usually squandered in a way that undermines the competitiveness of the surrounding economy. Norway has largely avoided this so-called Dutch Disease by the active management of its petroleum wealth (by investing most of that wealth abroad, and by letting relatively little of it affect the domestic economy), and because its economy enjoys a high level of organization and coordination, to protect against the wage inflation that often occurs with natural resource wealth.[16] In short, many of the instruments that the country uses to secure full employment have also been deployed to protect the economy from the most costly side-effects of natural resource wealth.

Norway's economic glory is not limited to full employment, of course, but the other indicators trail in its wake. During the recent economic crisis, Norway's GDP continued to grow (except in 2009), under conditions of low inflation, a surplus in the current account, its government budget in surplus.[17] Norway has incurred no net debt.[18] Just as importantly, these economic outcomes are secured for a broad swath of the Norwegian public. Indeed, as shown in Figure 9.5, the level of income inequality in Norway's is remarkably low: ranking seventh best in the OECD (as measured by gini-coefficients). While this is itself impressive, the distribution of net income in Norway is even more egalitarian after taxes and transfers are taken into account: Norway then rises to third in the class (behind Slovenia and Denmark). This is the effect of Norway's famous welfare state.

16 See Jonathon W. Moses, "Foiling the Resource Curse: Wealth, Equality, Oil and the Norwegian State", in Omano Edigheji (ed), *Constructing a Democratic Developmental State in South Africa: Potentials and Challenges* (Cape Town: HSRC Press, 2010), pp. 126-145.

17 OECD, *OECD Economic Surveys. Norway*. February (Paris: OECD, 2012), p. 13.

18 In the official accounts, Norway does report annual debt figures, but these are used to ensure that the government has a certain liquidity reserve in order to be able to cover daily payments. For the central bank's full explanation of why Norway reports debt, while its assets far exceed its debt, see Norges Bank, "Why does the Norwegian government hold debt?" 9 January 2013 update. http://www.norges-bank.no/en/price-stability/government-debt/why-government-debt/

Figure 9.5. Inequality Index

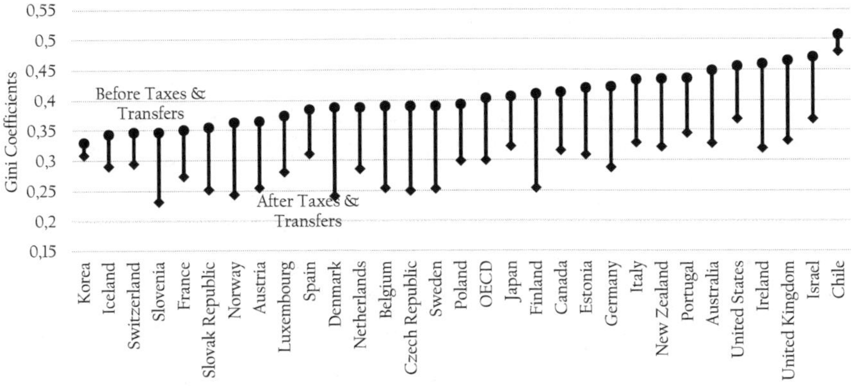

Source: *OECD Economic Surveys. Norway*, 11; and I. Joumard, M. Pisu and D. Bloch, "Less Income Inequality and More Growth – Are They Compatible? Part 3: Income Redistribution via Taxes and Transfers across OECD Countries," *OECD Economics Department Working Paper*, No. 926 (Paris: OECD, 2012).

It is Norway's generous provision of public services that secures the country a leading position on the UN's annual Human Development Indices, which rank countries in an index comprised of life expectancy, education, and income records; for the past five years, Norway was ranked first.[19] Similarly, Norway is ranked 3rd (after Switzerland and Australia) in the Economist Intelligence Unit's 2013 "Where-to-be-Born" index.[20] Norway's high scoring on these indices provides evidence of the opportunities available to the broader Norwegian population—opportunities generated by a well-managed economy and an extensive public network of services and support.

Public Ownership

In the 2005 parliamentary elections in Norway, voters witnessed a lively debate over the shrivcling size of Norway's economic toolbox. The impetus for this debate was a decision by Norske Skog to close its Union paper mill in Skien, laying off over 350 employees—even though the factory was still realizing a

19 UNDP "Table 2: Human Development Index trends, 1980–2012." http://hdr.undp.org/hdr4press/press/outreach/figures/HDI_Trends_2013.pdf.

20 *The Economist*, "The Lottery of Life." 21 November 2012. http://www.economist.com/news/21566430-where-be-born-2013-lottery-life?fsrc=scn/tw/te/tr/thelotteryoflife.

profit. The local community protested the closure, and the resulting debates generated a broad political consensus that the state should somehow ensure that a profit-making employer of such magnitude be kept in business.

The incoming (Red-Green) government included a strong public ownership model as part of its coalition platform,[21] and the incoming Minister of Industry, Odd Eriksen, promised a parliamentary report to detail the opportunities that still existed for supporting Norwegian industries and jobs in an increasingly liberal European and international economy. Although the resulting report was a disappointment,[22] it flagged the rise of a new, rather ad hoc,[23] instrument of economic management: Norwegian government ownership of shares in private companies.

As a result of this political debate, ownership is recognized as one of the few tools that the government has at its disposal for conducting an autonomous industrial policy. Rather than trying to encourage state-ownership outright, or to facilitate special advantages for national producers, the government promised to use its voice as a major shareholder to secure influence in important sectors. Indeed, when describing its ownership role, the government distinguishes between explicitly business-oriented objectives and more political objectives (e.g., ownership of the state liquor stores (*Vinmonopolet*).[24] The catch-phrase for this new tool is: "active ownership" (*aktivt eierskap*).

Although the government argues that it can play an active ownership role when these firms make decisions that affect local markets, in practice it fears the consequences of intervening in the market (as its share values will decline if the firm is seen to be responding to political pressure, at the expense of its bottom line). Despite the political rhetoric, the Norwegian government's owner-

21 In particular, the governing coalition's Soria Moria declaration promised to: "secure strong public and national ownership in order to obtain important political objectives and to secure a return and income for the community" (our translation).

22 The promised white paper did not arrive before Eriksen had resigned. His replacement, Dag Terje Andersen, eventually delivered the report—St. meld. nr. 13 (2006-2007) *Et aktivt og langsiktig eierskap*—but it was a clear disappointment: almost all of the tools considered and discussed during the national debate were found to conflict with EEA (and other international legal) obligations.

23 We say ad hoc, as the way in which the government gained stock in these companies was not the result of any long-term strategic plan. Rather, the government's extensive ownership portfolio had been collected through a number of pressing circumstances over time (e.g., the privatization of the national telephone company (Telenor); the confiscation of German shares after WWII (Norsk Hydro); the privatization of once state-owned companies (Statoil); the need to bail out irresponsible banks in an earlier banking crisis (DnB); etc.).

24 See St. meld. nr. 13 (2010-2011*) Et aktivt eierskap – norsk statlig eierskap i en global økonomi* (Oslo: Stortinget), pp. 10-11.

ship role is remarkably passive; its objective is simply to maximize returns on these investments (and sometimes ensure that the main headquarters of a company remain in Norway).

While this strategy generates a good deal of political capital, the financial returns are less than inspiring—at least with regard to the needs of economic management. On the one hand, the size of the government's share of ownership in Norwegian firms is impressively large (estimates suggest is to be about 33% of the estimated value of all Norwegian firms in 2003, or 2,700 billion kroner),[25] especially when the indirect ownership forms are taken into consideration, as shown in Figure 9.6.

Figure 9.6. Estimated market value of Norwegian firms, by ownership type

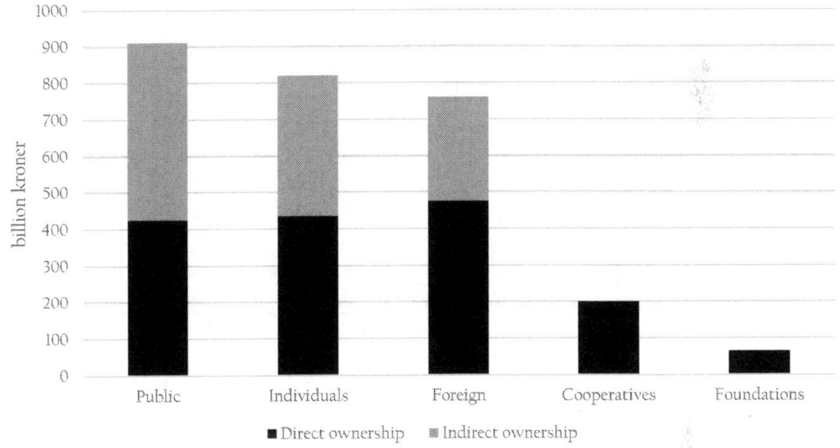

Note: data from 2003. Public figures do not include the government's interests in the SDØE (the state's direct economic engagement in offshore petroleum activities) or the GPF (Government Pension Fund).

Source: Jakobsen and Grünfeld, *Hvem eier Norge?*, p. 67

On the other hand, the actual size of the economic return from these shareholdings is miniscule, when compared to the government's other forms of revenues

25 See Erik W. Jakobsen and Leo Grünfeld, *Hvem eier Norge? Eierskap og verdiskaping i et grenseløst næringsliv* (Oslo: Universitetsforlaget, 2003). Subsequent analyses by the Ministry of Industry and Trade reveal that the ownership structure of firms listed on the Oslo Børs is fairly similar, or around 35%. See St. meld. nr. 13 (2010-2011): 8-9.

(e.g., taxes). For example, in the 2013 budget, returns/dividends on government-owned shares were estimated to be about 28 billion kroner (or about 1.6% of total government revenue for that year).[26] You cannot hire a lot of nurses with that kind of money.

Conclusions

Norway relies on a market economy, but is a highly organized and regulated market economy, which is managed in a way that maximizes employment, and minimizes poverty. These priorities are held by governments of all hues (both left and right), over a long period of time. Norway's high level of employment and low level of poverty cannot be attributed to the country's petroleum wealth (although it probably helps!). Rather, these results are secured by the country's long-term political commitment to secure work for all, and its willingness to protect the weakest in Norwegian society (by way of a strong welfare state).

Due to changes in the surrounding (international) political and economic context, the tools that Norway has used to secure these objectives have necessarily changed over time. As many of its more traditional tools of industrial policy have been taken away by the EEA Agreement (and other international obligations), the Norwegian state has come to rely increasingly on public ownership of firms to ensure political control, and to discourage the threat of capital (and jobs) flight.

This public ownership provides political cover for elected officials, and has managed to keep some jobs in the country—but the economic benefits of this ownership (in the form of dividends paid) is relatively small. It is the large corporatist groups that organize the Norwegian labour market (the LO, representing labour, and the NHO representing capital), and their willingness to cooperate with the government to secure mutually beneficial economic outcomes, that best explains Norway's enviable economic position.

Given their very different historical legacies, we should not be surprised to find that Slovenia is very different from Norway. While Norway is proud of its "socialism" (the country's long-term political commitment to secure work for all, its willingness to protect the weakest, and the increasing reliance on public

26 In particular, NOK 13,887,000 from Statoil dividends, and NOK 14,837,555 from all other ownership shares, totaling NOK 28,724,555 (which comes to just under 1.6% of total government revenue). See Norwegian Ministry of Finance, "Forslag til vedtak om statsbudsjettet for budsjettåret 2013: Oversikt over utgifter og inntekter i statsbudsjettet for budsjetterminen 2013," Prop. 1 S (2012–2013) Gul bok (Statsbudsjettet 2013). http://www.regjeringen.no/nb/dep/fin/dok/regpubl/prop/2012-2013/prop-1-s-20122013--20122013/12.html?id=703464.

ownership of firms) and independence, Slovenia is retreating on both fronts. Though joining the EU was a kind of emergency exit for Slovenia after the break with Yugoslavia, the EU was admired and full membership in the EU and euro zone was a kind of a sacred goal from the very beginning of transition. Political democracy and a social market model with high standards of living were understandably attractive. However, by the time Slovenia joined the EU, many features of the widely admired European social market model were no longer there. Furthermore, the EU showed very little interest in promoting the social market model in transition countries. The void created by the fall of socialism was filled by American advisers promoting a pure "shareholders value" type of capitalism and the neoliberal paradigm was immediately adopted by many "Marxists" who turned immediately to "neoliberals". Furthermore, Slovenia has become a province of the EU, losing all economic attributes of sovereignty. The country's political elite, right or "left", is ashamed of the legacy of a socialist market economy. Since the crisis, Slovenia has been constantly pushed by the EU authorities to "privatize" which in the current situation implies selling everything to foreign multinationals. This would bring Slovenia in line with other former socialist countries of Central and Eastern Europe that Slovenia was avoiding for two decades of independence. Norway, through its EEA obligations, has also lost some of its policy independence, but it has retained an autonomous monetary policy and a model of economic management that allows it to pursue a more social democratic and autonomous line of policy.

Matej Knep

10 Slovenia: An Evironmental Leader, a Laggard or Both?

Slovenian territory is characterised by a diverse and relatively well-preserved natural environment. The contributing factors are not only its geographical position and extraordinary examples of natural heritage but also the characteristics of its socio-political development. Late industrialisation, extensive farming practices, early examples of sustainable forest management and protective policy measures, as well as engaged enthusiasts and an organised civil society, are all factors which have contributed to the state of the natural environment. It is no surprise that the natural environment plays an important role also in the collective identity of Slovenes. A lively history of nature preservation in Slovenia and cultural references to nature do not add to the efficient problem solving of some pressing environmental issues, however. When it comes to environmental pollution or to cross-cutting environmental issues, Slovenia lags behind the most environmentally advanced nations.[1]

---

1 One of the popular environmental scoreboards, the Environmental Performance Index, developed by the Yale Center for Environmental Law and Policy and the Center for International Earth Science Information Network at Columbia University, put Slovenia's overall environmental performance in 2014 in 15th place among 178 countries. Angel Hsu, Jay Emerson, Marc A. Levy, Alex de Sherbinin, Laura Johnson, Omar Malik, Jason D. Schwartz, and Malanding Jaiteh, *The 2014 Environmental Performance Index* (New Haven, Conn.: Yale Center for Environmental Law and Policy, 2014), at http://www.epi.yale.edu [last accessed on 11 December 2014]). However, as its critics point out (see R. Andreas Kraemer and Henrike Peichert, *Analysis of the Yale Environmental Performance Index (EPI)* (UBA-Texte 09/08) (Dessau: German Federal Environment Agency, 2007), at http://www.umweltbundesamt.de/sites/default/files/medien/publikation/long/3429.pdf [last accessed on 11 December 2014]), while it measures general environmental problems with widespread significance, it does not take into account the environmental idiosyncrasies of states and regions. More comprehensive environmental performance analyses, such as the OECD's "Environmental Performance Review" (Organisation for Economic Co-operation and Development, *OECD Environmental Performance Reviews: Slovenia 2012* (OECD Publishing, 2012) and the European Environment Agency's *The European Environment – State and Outlook. Country assessments: Slovenia* (2010), at http://www.eea.europa.eu/soer/countries/si [last accessed on 11 December 2014]), reveal many weaknesses in the environmental performance of Slovenia. Among them are the non-implementation of environmental legislation and poor performance in cross-cutting issues such as the land use, waste management and climate change mitigation.

This chapter tries to explain why Slovenia is facing this shortfall in the environmental performance of different environmental policy domains. To do so, the concept of 'policy paradigm' is applied. After defining the principal environmental policy paradigms, the chapter turns to the analysis of environmental policy paradigms in Slovenia. The analysis is based on the available literature review, a review of relevant normative documents and research findings from ongoing research into the open method of coordination,[2] interest group politics[3] and green political parties in Slovenia,[4] conducted within the Centre for Political Science Research, at the Faculty of Social Sciences, University of Ljubljana.

Environmental policy paradigms and policy paradigm shifts

Environmental policies around the globe have undergone rapid development in the last forty years, although early environmental measures predate this period. If early environmental measures concerned the protection and conservation of nature, today environmental policies address a wide array of issues, and environmental concerns are becoming a guiding principle in an increasing number of policy fields, such as the economy and labour, development and foreign policies, finance and others. The study of environmental policies rarely grasps this complexity. Instead, it focuses on selected elements of environmental policies, such as specific environmental issues,[5] the use of policy instruments, or the changing modes of environmental governance.[6] This chapter applies the concept of policy paradigm[7] to study environmental policies in Slovenia. The

2 Basic research project "J52030: The Open Method of Coordination: An Analysis of Its Policy and Political Consequences", headed by Danica Fink-Hafner and financed by the Slovenian Research Agency.

3 European Collaborative Research Project in the Social Sciences (ECRP) – "ECRP VI (2010), Comparative research on interest group politics in Europe" (INTEREURO): project leader David Lowery; head of the Slovenian research team Danica Fink-Hafner; financed by the European Science Foundation and the Slovenian Research Agency.

4 Research programme "Political science research", headed by Danica Fink-Hafner and by the Slovenian Research Agency.

5 In the study of international relations, the concept of environmental regimes is often used.

6 Within this strand of literature, macro-level (state-society relations) and meso-level (interest-intermediation) approaches are common (see, e.g., Paul Fawcett and Carsten Daugbjerg, "Explaining Governance Outcomes: Epistemology, Network Governance and Policy Network Analysis", in *Political Studies Review,* Vol. 10. No. 2 (2012), pp. 195–207.).

7 Thomas Kuhn, *The Structure of Scientific Revolutions,* 2nd ed. (Chicago: International Encyclopedia of Unified Science, University of Chicago Press, 1970), at http://www.f.waseda.jp/sidoli/

concept "has emerged [...] as a useful tool for analysing and comprehending the interactions between ideas, institutions, and organized actors engaged in political and administrative processes".[8]

A policy paradigm is understood as a set of values, norms and underlying assumptions that frame the definition of policy problems and appropriate solutions to solve them as well as legitimise the policy actors, who negotiate in a distinctive polity structure. Carson and his collaborators have pointed out that the architecture of a policy paradigm comprises not only the cognitive-normative complex but also the socio-structural and organisational complex (see Table 10.1).[9]

Table 10.1 . Architecture of a policy paradigm

Cognitive-normative complex	Social-structural and organisational complex
– values and underlying assumptions – framing and conceptualisation of policy problems – framing and conceptualisation of appropriate solutions	– agents (policy actors) and their relationships – procedures of deliberation and decision-making – place and time

Source: Adapted from Carson, Marcus, Tom R. Burns and Dolores Calvo (eds) (2009). *Paradigms in Public Policy. Theory and Practice of Paradigm Shifts in the EU.* Frankfurt am Main, Berlin, Bern, Bruxelles, New York, Oxford, Wien: Peter Lang, p. 144.

We believe that such an analytic device is useful in explaining the variations in policy outcomes of contemporary environmental policies. It allows us to understand contemporary environmental policies holistically, as a combination of its internally coherent parts, each defined by a distinctive set of underlying assumptions, set of rules and institutional structures. Changes to environmental policies cannot be seen only as an incremental development, because profound changes in scope, institutions and the involved policy actors have occurred. Today, three environmental policy paradigms co-shape environmental policies,

Kuhn_Structure_of_Scientific_Revolutions.pdf [last accessed on 11 December 2014]; Peter A. Hall, "Policy Paradigms, Social Learning, and the State: The Case of Economic Policymaking in Britain", in *Comparative Politics,* Vol. 25, No. 3 (1993), pp. 275–296; Marcus Carson, *From Common Market to Social Europe? Paradigm Shift and Institutional Change in European Union Policy on Food, Asbestos and Chemicals, and Gender Equality* (Acta Universitatis Stockholmiensis) (Stockholm: Almqvist & Wiksell International, 2004); and Marcus Carson, Tom R. Burns, and Dolores Calvo (eds.), *Paradigms in Public Policy: Theory and Practice of Paradigm Shifts in the EU* (Frankfurt am Main: Peter Lang, 2009).

8 Carson et al., *Paradigms in Public Policy,* p. 11.

9 *Ibid.*, pp. 141–155.

but unlike in several other policy fields, they do not exclude and replace each other. To a certain extent, they complement each other; thus, it is possible to see environmental policy paradigm additions rather than paradigm shifts.

Not every policy innovation can be considered a new policy paradigm. In his study of economic policymaking in Britain, Hall describes the policy paradigm shift as a "third order change", characterised by a radical change in settings of policy, hierarchy of goals and set of policy instruments in relation to the shift in the locus of authority.[10] To effectuate a policy paradigm shift (or, in our case, establish a new policy paradigm) it is not enough that a new set of underlying assumptions emerge or that new actors gain power to effectuate change. The combination of dissatisfaction with problem solving (policy failure), the emergence of new values and underlying assumptions, as well as a transformed constellation of policy actors, are all prerequisites of a policy paradigm shift.[11] In addition, the policy paradigm shift does not necessarily occur radically; it is more likely that a new policy paradigm is established over an extended period.

Looking at contemporary environmental policies from a global perspective, the earliest established environmental policy paradigm is what we call the *conservationist environmental paradigm* (Table 10.2). This emerged in the nineteenth century in different (nation)-states and later spread at a transnational level. It is based on values of "deep ecology",[12] the underlying assumption being that nature has an intrinsic value, thereby advocating an eco-centric worldview of the relationship between humans and nature. Public policies deriving from the conservationist environmental paradigm are concerned typically with the preservation of the natural environment and a view to limiting any human intervention. Establishing natural parks or protecting desired life-species are examples of environmental policies based on the conservationist environmental paradigm. Examples that are more recent include the preservation of habitats, genetic diversity, etc. The most common policy instruments here are typically top-down regulatory interventions.

After World War Two, rapid industrialisation and the increased use of chemicals and potentially toxic substances shifted public concern towards public health issues. Pollution trends helped to crystallise what we call the *modern environmental paradigm*, which gradually broadened the scope of then-

10 Hall, "Policy Paradigms, Social Learning", pp. 279–281; 283–284.

11 See *Ibid.*, pp. 279–281; and Carson et al., *Paradigms in Public Policy*, pp. 382–391.

12 See Andrew Dobson, *Green Political Thought,* 4th ed. (London and New York: Routledge, 2007).

existing environmental policy measures. Concerned individuals,[13] later joined by environment-oriented "new social movements", started to raise public awareness in the most industrialised states about the dangers posed by industrial production and mass consumption to human health and the adverse effects they had on the environment.[14] This represented a radical change in the value base, because environmental protection was not aimed at protecting nature for its intrinsic value but to protect human health and to prevent the destruction of the environment in order to allow for its continued use to cater to human needs. It was thus based on an anthropocentric worldview of humans' relationship with nature or a "shallow ecology".[15] Typical environmental policies based on the modern environmental paradigm include pollution prevention measures, such as emission limits, prescribed technologies for industrial processes and regulation of the use of chemicals, which often take into account the principles of environmental liability of polluters and the need for precautions. With the advent of the modern environmental paradigm, powerful economic actors acquired a stake in environmental decision-making processes, which in turn affected the choice of policy instrument mix, with economic instruments becoming more important.

Such environmental concerns were raised to a transnational level, where it was soon clear that governments around the globe were dealing with policy failures. Global awareness and international recognition of environmental problems paved the way for the establishment of a new environmental policy paradigm, which we call the *sustainable environmental paradigm*. Its appearance did not stem from a change in the way humans' relationship with nature was viewed but rather with the policy failures and the changes in the perception and understanding of nature itself. The advances in space exploration and the famous "Blue Marble" photograph popularised the perception of the interconnectedness and fragility of Earth's natural environment, helping to advance the idea of planetary limits,[16] to which we are all inevitably bound. Environmental degradation was attributed to different paths of (economic) development. Environmental policies based on the sustainable environmental paradigm are typi-

13 An exemplary manifestation was the book *Silent Spring*, by Rachel Carson, in which she described the adverse effects of pesticide use. It was published in 1962 in the USA.

14 In major urban centres and early industrialised nations, policy measures to reduce pollution (e.g., limiting air pollution) were adopted much earlier.

15 Dobson, *Green Political Thought,* see the section on Anthropocentrism, pp. 42–46.

16 Among the first instances of public presentation of this thesis, then radical, were the report *The Limits to Growth*, written by Donatella Meadows, Dennis Meadows, Jørgen Randers and William Behrens, and the environmental text *A Blueprint for Survival*, published in a special issue of *The Ecologist,* both in 1972.

cally cross-sectoral and address "environmental-megatrends". They often take into account the principle of the mainstreaming of environmental concerns in all policy fields and decision-making processes. Because of the changed perceptions, the sustainable environmental paradigm expanded the range of policy actors beyond the established policy arenas, including many actors traditionally not concerned with environmental matters. This raised the level of conflict, which in turn accelerated the transition of environmental decision-making processes to less hierarchical modes of governance.[17] The trends leading to changes in governance structures were reinforced by a parallel process of neo-liberal indoctrination in international organisations and public administrations, which widened the use of voluntary decision-making processes (such as industry-wide voluntary agreements on environmental standards) in the field of environmental protection.

Table 10.2. Architecture of environmental policy paradigms

Elements of environmental paradigms	Cognitive-normative complex			Social-structural and organisational complex		
	Values and assumptions	*Policy problems*	*Policy solutions*	*Policy actors*	*Decision-making processes*	*Time and place*
Conservationist	Eco-centric	Danger of destroying wild nature	Protection and conservation	Nature enthusiasts and state	Hierarchies	(Nation-) state since 19th century
Modern	Anthropo-centric	Danger to human health	Technological solutions	NSMs, industry, state	Market in shadow of hierarchy	(Nation-) states in post-WWII world order
Sustainable	Interdependencies	Danger of crossing planetary limits	Environmental integration	Various	Networks	Transnational (since 1972)

17 This shift is evident from, on the one hand, the declining number of (legally binding) multilateral environmental agreements (and EU environmental laws), falling drastically since the year 2000 (see Ronald B. Mitchell, *International Environmental Agreements Database Project*, Version 2013.2 (2002-2014), at http://iea.uoregon.edu/ [last accessed on 11 December 2014]), and the rise in less institutionalised/less hierarchical forms of governance and decision-making processes, such as the Partnerships for Sustainable Development instituted at the World Summit on Sustainable Development in Johannesburg in 2002. See Matej Knep and Danica Fink-Hafner, *Eksperimentalna vladavina na področju zelene politike: slovenske okoljske politike na razpotju* (Ljubljana: Faculty of Social Sciences, University of Ljubljana, 2011).

Policy trajectory and policy paradigm shifts: Slovenia

Conservationist environmental paradigm. In Slovenia, too, environmental policies based on the conservationist environmental paradigm have the longest tradition. At the beginning of the twentieth century, nature enthusiasts and organised civil society started to call for the protection of valuable parts of nature or rare animal and plant species. In 1920, the Department for the Preservation of Nature and Natural Monuments within the Museum Society for Slovenia published a Manifesto,[18] considered the first blueprint of a conservationist environmental paradigm in Slovenia. Addressed to the government, it pointed to nature preservation policy developments in contemporary European countries and demanded, among other things, the establishment of a natural park, protection of plant and animal species and protection of caves. An important achievement stemming from this effort was the establishment of the Alpine Park in the valley of Triglav Lakes in 1924, which today remains the only national park in Slovenia. However, stormy political conditions did not allow for more systematic nature preservation policy development until 1970, when the first Law on Nature Protection was adopted. The law represented a major milestone because it was the first modern and comprehensive environmental act. Its primary aim was to preserve natural areas and typical landscapes. Under the influence of the UNESCO Convention Concerning the Protection of the World Cultural and Natural Heritage, a new Law on the Protection of Cultural and Natural Heritage in 1981 replaced the first Law on Nature Protection. It coupled the preservation of nature with cultural heritage protection and placed greater emphasis on the latter, marginalising nature preservation. It was only in 1999, under the pressure of EU accession negotiations, that the normative arrangements of nature preservation were modernised in the form of a new Nature Preservation Act.[19] This reintroduced a comprehensive and integrated approach to nature preservation but brought little policy innovation because it assumed mostly restrictive regulatory measures.

Civil society played an important role in establishing the conservationist environmental paradigm in Slovenia. It not only placed it on the political agenda at an early stage but also was crucial in establishing the administrative structure of nature preservation. When the first public offices dealing primarily with environmental issues were formed after World War Two, they closely cooperated with civil-society organisations and incorporated their human resources, such as those from the Institute of Hydro-meteorology and Geodynamics at the University of Ljubljana and from the Museum Society. However,

18 In Slovene, *Spomenica Odseka za varstvo prirode in prirodnih spomenikov*.

19 The act was amended several times until 2004, when Slovenia gained full EU membership.

under the socialist political system, the functioning of civil-society organisations was controlled by the ruling political elites. Because of a lack of federal competence over environmental matters and because Slovenian communists were more moderate than those in other Yugoslav republics were, environmental civil-society organisations were allowed to function, albeit with a limited amount of freedom. In 1971, they established an environmental umbrella organisation, the Community for Nature Protection in Slovenia, within which environmental efforts could be effectively coordinated among its members.[20] It was also important because it ensured the continued existence of environmental civil-society organisations. After the independence of Slovenia, the Community for Nature Protection in Slovenia was functionally dissolved but some of its core members are among the most powerful environmental civil-society actors in the field of nature preservation.[21]

Today's administrative settings for nature preservation resemble those established in 1970. Administrative responsibilities are divided among the ministry and parliamentary committee for policy formulation and public institutes and local communities for implementation and enforcement of environmental preservation policy measures. While nature preservation was first coupled at the ministerial level with urban and spatial planning, and only later with other fields,[22] the core nature preservation institute,[23] the Institute of the Republic of Slovenia for Nature Conservation, was coupled with cultural heritage protection from its inception, becoming independent from its cultural counterpart in only in 1999.[24] The parliamentary committee and the local

20 The Community for Nature Protection in Slovenia was not a typical environmental umbrella civil-society organisation. It had public administration bodies and businesses among its members.

21 The Nature Preservation Act of 1999 gave special status to civil-society organisations that function in the public interest in the field of nature preservation. There are 30 such organisations, among them the fishermen, mountaineers and hunters' associations, speleological and mycological associations and bird-watching associations.

22 From 1970, the law coupled nature preservation with spatial planning; from 1981, it coupled nature preservation with culture; in 1990, the ministry responsible for nature preservation was coupled again with spatial planning; in 2012, the ministry for the environment was coupled with agriculture; since late 2014 the ministry for the environment has been coupled again with spatial planning. These relatively frequent administrative changes represent one of several indicators which point to a weak political interest for environmental matters in Slovenia.

23 The core implementation and law enforcement institute in the area of nature preservation is the Institute of the Republic of Slovenia for Nature Conservation, which is complemented by natural parks administrations.

24 The Institute for the Protection and Scientific Study of Cultural and Natural Heritage was established in 1945 as an independent body (See Mladen Berginc, Jelka Kremesec-Jevšenak and Jana Vidic, *Sistem varstva narave v Sloveniji* (Ljubljana: Ministrstvo za okolje in prostor,

communities are mostly less visible players, although the parliamentary committee is a primary target of lobbying when the issues are highly politicised.

When it comes to nature preservation, Slovenia is undoubtedly one of the most successful countries in Europe. It has, for instance, the largest share among EU member states of protected territory (35.5%) under the EU's nature and biodiversity policy [25] and one of the thickest, sustainably managed forest covers in Europe, with large sections of primeval forest.[26] It is also home to exceptional geomorphological and biological diversity. Slovenes, at least at declaratory levels, place great value on the natural environment.[27] Although there is an ongoing controversy over the protection regime in the Triglav National Park, it remains heavily protected. Civil-society organisations have long been successful in preventing large infrastructure projects, such as wind farms, from being installed in the preserved natural environment.

Modern environmental paradigm. Under international influences, the modern environmental paradigm was introduced in Slovenia in the early 1970s. The first blueprint was the *Green Book on the Threats to the Environment in Slovenia*, which was published in 1972 by a group of activists and experts.[28] The authors stressed that the environmental problems in then-socialist Slovenia were the same as in the industrialised countries with capitalist economies. The book presented scientific evidence of environmental pollution. This prompted the adoption of some sporadic normative measures to curb pollution,[29] but the introduction of a comprehensive environmental policy based on the modern

---

2006). However, the 1981 act subordinated the institute to the executive secretariat responsible for culture. The act adopted in 1999 separated the institute into nature preservation and cultural heritage sections, both subordinated to their respective sectoral ministries.

25 See European Commission (EC) (2011), *N2000 Sites "Snapshot" of January 2011,* at http://ec.europa.eu/environment/nature/natura2000/barometer/docs/n2000.pdf [last accessed on 11 December 2014].

26 See, for example, FOREST EUROPE Liaison Unit Oslo, the United Nations Economic Commission for Europe (UNECE) and the Food and Agriculture Organization of the United Nations (FAO) (2011), *State of Europe's Forests 2011: Status and Trends in Sustainable Forest Management in Europe* (Oslo: Ministerial Conference on the Protection of Forests in Europe, 2011), at http://www.foresteurope.org/docs/SoEF/reports/State_of_Europes_Forests_2011_Report_Revised_November_2011.pdf [last accessed on 11 December 2014], p. 288.

27 See Danica Fink-Hafner, Matej Knep and Meta Novak, *The Slovenian Greens: From Quick Success to Long-Term Failure* (Ljubljana: Faculty of Social Sciences, University of Ljubljana, 2015).

28 See Stane Peterlin (ed.), *Zelena knjiga o ogroženosti okolja v Sloveniji* (Ljubljana: Prirodoslovno društvo Slovenije; Zavod za spomeniško varstvo RS, 1972).

29 Examples include measures related to air, noise and waste.

environmental paradigm was possible only after the social, economic and political changes of the late 1980s and early 1990s. A major milestone was the Law on Environmental Protection, adopted in 1993, which introduced major policy innovations, including modern environmental principles, strategic planning and the gathering of and public access to environmental information and environmental impact assessments. This was partly modelled on EU environmental legislation, although it was replaced by a revised law in 2004 that had to comply with EU environmental regulations. On the basis of the 1993 law, the first National Programme for the Protection of the Environment[30] was adopted in 1999, and many environmental policy areas, including industrial pollution, were normatively regulated in more detail. Today, in normative terms, the modern environmental paradigm is heavily influenced by EU regulation.

Civil society played a crucial role in introducing the modern environmental paradigm in Slovenia. Environment-oriented new social movements, which emerged during the 1980s, put the environment on the political agenda during the socialist period. After their institutionalisation as the Green political party in 1989—which joined the winning coalition in the first multi-party democratic elections in 1990—they were able to establish normatively the modern environmental paradigm in Slovenia at an earlier stage than movements in other post-communist countries.[31] Rapid modernisation of environmental policies continued in the decade prior to EU accession. This was also possible because of the pressure exerted by the new environmental non-governmental organisations, modelled after ENGOs, anchored in the liberal-democratic traditions of Western Europe. Under pressure from the European Commission, the Slovenian government supported environmental civil-society organisations in the period of accession and formally included them in environmental decision-making. In this period, such organisations increased in number and scope.[32] The enhanced cooperation with civil society in the field of environmental protection lasted until Slovenia presided over the Council of the EU in 2008, during which time

---

30 *Nacionalni program varstva okolja* (NPVO) (1999), Uradni list Republike Slovenije, No. 83/1999.

31 The new environmental social movements established the Greens of Slovenia political party in 1989, which joined the oppositional (anti-communist) political forces to form the Democratic Opposition of Slovenia (DEMOS) coalition. The coalition won the first multi-party elections in 1990, which enabled the Greens to exert significant influence over modernisation of environmental policies until 1993.

32 Matej Knep and Meta Novak, *Environmental Interest Groups in Slovenia*, Presentation for the workshop on interest group research, Faculty of Social Sciences, University of Ljubljana, 30 August 2012.

one of the priorities was EU energy-climate policy,[33] which was loudly advocated by these organisations. However, after 2008, they seem to have become less well integrated into the environmental decision-making processes,[34] especially when it comes to emerging modes of governance over environmental matters.[35] Moreover, the introduction of modern environmental paradigm was met with a strong opposition from economic interests.

One consequence of introducing the modern environmental paradigm was the establishment of a new kind of administrative body to enforce, monitor and finance policy measures. The most important in this regard was the reorganisation of several environmental bureaus to form the national Environment Agency before accession to the EU and the establishment of a financial mechanism in the form of a public fund, financed using environmental taxes, at the beginning of the 1990s. After EU accession, most of the decision-making took place at the EU level, where Slovenia in the environmental field and otherwise is regarded as a policy-taker.

When it comes to the modern environmental paradigm, the most pressing problem is the problem of non-implementation. This is not only recognised by domestic policy actors, but it is also subject to sanctions in the context of the EU political system.[36] Additionally, public opinion on environmental matters

33 The EU environmental laws adopted during the Slovenian presidency of the Council of the EU were related to waste, mercury, environmental quality standards in the field of water policy, inclusion of aviation activities in the emissions trading scheme and the protection of the environment through criminal law (see more on the Slovenian presidency of the EU 2008 web site, available through: http://www.eu2008.si/en/News_and_Documents/Press_Releases/June/0630SVEZdosezkid41d.html? [last accessed on 11 December 2014].

34 Such an assessment is based on several opinions of Slovenian ENGO representatives and public officials who were interviewed within the context of the basic research project "The Open Method of Coordination" and the "Intereuro" European collaborative research project.

35 The emerging modes of governing in the context of the EU political system are usually referred to in the political science literature as the open method of coordination. For more on this issue, see Danica Fink-Hafner, Damjan Lajh and Tomaž Deželan, "The Open Method of Coordination in the Global Context of Policy Cooperation," in Danica Fink-Hafner (ed.), *The Open Method of Coordination: A View from Slovenia* (Ljubljana: Faculty of Social Sciences, University of Ljubljana, 2010) pp. 17–34.

36 In 2009, Slovenia was sued before the Court of Justice of the European Union because of its failure to transpose the Community law on environmental liability with regard to the prevention and remedying of environmental damage. In 2010, Slovenia was sued again because of its failure to transpose the Community law on integrated pollution prevention and control. In 2011, Slovenia was sued for failing to fulfil its obligations on limit values for concentrations of PM10 in ambient air. In 2014, Slovenia was sued for its failure to comply with the requirements of EU waste legislation. In addition, the European Commission has initiated many more infringement procedures against Slovenia, the vast majority related to measures stemming

concerning modern environmental paradigm (i.e., perception of environmental threats) is periodical, with periods of high support (i.e., after Chernobyl explosion) but also with periods where environmental matters become marginal (i.e., in circumstances of economic crises). The domestic political and public attention to environmental issues decreased sharply after the break out of economic and financial crisis of the late 2000.[37] This influences on the political agenda, and although the potential exists,[38] it seems that the parliamentary political parties do not embrace that potential to put forward new environmental measures and enhance implementation.

Sustainable environmental paradigm. The first attempts to introduce the sustainable environmental paradigm were made after Slovenia participated as an independent state in the United Nations Conference on Environment and Development (UNCED) in 1992.[39] The Law on the Protection of the Environment of 1993 included among its main aims sustainable development as formulated by the World Commission on Environment and Development (WCED).[40] Its subsequent amendments and changes to the law placed extended definitions of sustainable development among the guiding principles of the national environmental protection policies.[41]

---

from the modern environmental paradigm, which may result in legal action before the Court of Justice of the EU in future.

37 See Fink-Hafner, Matej Knep and Meta Novak, *The Slovenian Greens.*

38 One example is an international environmental civic movement, Let's Do It!, which, following a one-day action in Slovenia in 2012, attracted (comparatively) the largest share of the population among participating countries (12.93% of total population) that volunteered to clean up litter and illegal landfills (DEBM 2012; Let's Do It Web Site (2013). *Slovenia: Statistics,* at http://85.204.235.17/country/slovenia [last accessed on 11 December 2014].).

39 Previous work in preparatory committees at the UN, in which Slovenes participated as representatives of Yugoslavia (an example was Janez Stanovnik as a member of the World Commission on Environment and Development), had very little effect on national policies.

40 Among the definitions of purposes in Article 1 of the Law on the Protection of the Environment from 1993 was also the WCED definition of sustainable development: *Meeting the needs of the present generation must take into account equal opportunities for meeting the needs of future generations.* Later, national reports on the implementation of Agenda 21 to the United Nations Commission on Sustainable Development indicated the inclusion of policy measures promoting the commitments made at the UNCED in several strategic documents and relevant policy sectors, but these efforts had little effect in practice. See United Nations Commission on Sustainable Development (UNCSD) (1997). *National Implementation of Agenda 21: Slovenia* at http://www.un.org/esa/earthsummit/slove-cp.htm [last accessed on 11 December 2014].

41 Later, the Law on the Protection of the Environment included the principle of integration of environmental concerns into all decision-making processes regarding economic and social development.

Under the pressure of the accession to the EU, the EU sustainable development frame replaced the UN frame, according to which the sustainable development goals were added to development strategies and certain policy strategies. Different aspects of the sustainable environmental paradigm, such as environmental integration into sectoral policies and climate change mitigation, were added to the first National Programme for the Protection of the Environment in 1999 and reinforced in the renewed environmental strategy of 2005. The National Development Strategy of 2005 was the first to include sustainable development goals explicitly,[42] although it included very few concrete and coherent measures to promote the sustainable environmental paradigm.[43] After it was clear that the core development strategy of the EU, namely the Lisbon Strategy, had failed, Slovenia adopted additional economic strategies with sustainable development goals, as promoted at the EU level.[44] From 2009, a process of adapting a new National Development Strategy was initiated, but the recent economic crisis, social turmoil and political instability are retarding this process.[45] In addition, several sector-wise strategies and regulations have included aspects of sustainable environmental paradigm, mainly as a conse-

42 Some aspects of sustainable development were added to previous national economic strategies See Tomaž Deželan, "Sustainable Development in Slovenia: Cooperation in Vain?", in Danica Fink-Hafner (ed.), *The Open Method of Coordination: A View from Slovenia* (Ljubljana: Faculty of Social Sciences, University of Ljubljana, 2010), pp. 81–108.

43 Although one of the declared goals was the integration of environmental concerns into other sectoral policies, related measures only partially supported this. Out of 14 sustainable development indicators (monitoring progress of related policy measures set in the National Development Strategy), eight concerned the environment, among them two measuring emissions, two concerning the energy sector, two relating to agriculture and forestry, one relating to transport and one relating to the measurement of environmental taxes. Most place Slovenia as an underachiever. Exceptions (until 2011) are environmental tax revenues as a percentage of GDP (high taxes on energy use), which was mirrored in increasing subsidies for renewable energy; above-average percentage of eco-farmers, which can be explained by the small/low-intensity farm structure in Slovenia; and the high share of abated wood used for energy purposes compared to use for further processing, which could be explained by the composition of the wood industry (interest balance) in Slovenia. For details on indicators, consult the Institute's for Macroeconomic Analysis and Development web page (http://www.umar.gov.si/en/).

44 One example was the Reform Programme for Implementation of the Lisbon Strategy in Slovenia, adopted in 2008. It included priorities concerning sustainable development in the fields of spatial planning and climate change mitigation, with an emphasis on energy-related recommendations.

45 In August 2013, the Ministry for the Economy launched a public consultation process on the Proposal for the National Development Strategy 2014–2020 (*Strategija razvoja Slovenije 2014–2020, osnutek* (2013). Ljubljana: Ministrstvo za gospodarstvo. Available at: http://www.mgrt.gov.si/fileadmin/mgrt.gov.si/pageuploads/EKP/Drugi_dokumenti/SRS_09_08_2013.pdf

quence of EU pressure.[46] Although the aforementioned additions are expanding the list of environment-related goals and measures in development strategies and policy programmes, they do not represent a paradigmatic change, either in developmental policies or in environmental or other policy sectors; rather, they are an addition of policy measures to existing public policies.

The role of civil society in the process of introducing the sustainable environmental paradigm in Slovenia has been reactive. As a direct consequence of the UNCED, the Slovenian government sponsored a nationwide consultation process among ENGOs that resulted in the adoption of the proposal for Agenda 21 for Slovenia in 1995,[47] but little action followed. It was only in 2007, as a reaction to the Resolution on National Developmental Projects for the Period 2007-2023, that a group of ENGOs established a non-governmental network named "Plan B for Slovenia", with the purpose of promoting sustainable development.[48] Among their members are some of the most influential NGOs in the field of environmental protection. Since the 1990s, an increasing number of new ENGOs supporting the sustainable environmental paradigm have been established, and with support from the European Commission, they are increasingly active in consultations with ministries and governmental agencies. They are becoming professionalised and are significantly funded by the Slovenian and the EU governments. Nevertheless, there exists sparse evidence of their direct influence on government decisions.[49]

The first administrative body to deal directly with sustainable development issues was the Council for Sustainable Development, established in 2003 as a consultative body of the Slovenian government. Although representatives of

---

[last accessed on 11 December 2014]), which is expanding the sustainable development priorities to new policy fields, such as agriculture and tourism.

46 Examples include action plans for energy efficiency and renewable energy, programmes for development of environmental infrastructure and for reduction of greenhouse gases and regulation of green public procurement.

47 *Agenda 21 za Slovenijo, prispevek nevladnih organizacij* (Ljubljana: Umanotera, Slovenska fundacija za trajnostni razvoj, 1995). This document, prepared by civil-society actors, suggested inclusion of environmental concerns into many policy areas and was very broad in scope (suggested policy areas were consumerism, education, strengthening of civil society, environmental legislation enforcement, use of economic policy instruments, environmental considerations in industry, energy, urban planning, transport, tourism and agriculture sectors and strengthening of nature conservation).

48 The network has nine working groups, on climate change; eco-farming; sustainable energy; sustainable transport; financing of non-governmental organisations; green development; environmental law enforcement; efficient use of resources and waste; and government monitoring and elections.

49 Knep and Novak, *Environmental Interest Groups*.

civil society were among its members, its work was carried out under the auspices of the government office responsible for European affairs within the Cabinet. Since 2014, it has worked under the auspices of the ministry responsible for the environment. The administrative body intended to deal with climate change mitigation across policy sectors, the Government Office of Climate Change, which was established in 2009 within the Cabinet, was abolished in 2012 and its tasks were transferred to the ministry responsible for the environment. The Agency for Energy Efficiency, established in 1995, was also abolished and its tasks were transferred to various ministries.[50]

Overall, and in contrast to previous environmental policy paradigms, the sustainable environmental paradigm in Slovenia is still in the phase of policy experimentation and is not yet consolidated. It has had no genuine Slovene formulation; rather, it is diffusing from the international level and being imposed by the EU. It is slowly emerging from a process of uncoordinated inclusion of elements of the sustainable environmental paradigm into development strategies and policy programmes. Civil society remains weak in this field. The trend of transferring the tasks of partially independent coordinative administrative bodies dealing with various aspects of environmental sustainable paradigm to ministerial-level bureaus is hindering the systematic implementation of the sustainable environmental paradigm, not the least because of the administrative culture in Slovenia, which impedes efficient cross-sectoral coordination.

Evaluating Slovenia's response to environmental challenges

When assessing environmental challenges facing Slovenia today and the government interventions to deal with the environmental challenges, it seems appropriate to evaluate them according to the underlying environmental policy paradigm employed. Even if more general assessments place Slovenia among environmental leaders, this analysis shows that Slovenia lags behind the most developed when dealing with contemporary environmental challenges. The poor environmental performance of Slovenia is evident especially when it comes to the (non-)implementation of anti-pollution measures and to its (non-systematic) approach to switching to environmentally sustainable development.

50 Tasks of the Agency for Energy Efficiency were transferred, first to the ministry responsible for the environment, then to the ministry responsible for the economy and are now the responsibility of the ministry responsible for infrastructure.

Table 10.3. Architecture of environmental policy paradigms in Slovenia

Elements of environmental paradigms	Cognitive-normative complex		Social-structural and organisational complex		
	Blueprint	*Establishment of normative arrangements*	*Role of policy actors*	*Decision-making processes*	*Time and place*
Conservationist	*Spomenica* from 1920	Fragmented policy measures until the adoption of the first Law on Nature Protection from 1970	Active civil society; important national and local governments	Hierarchies – protective regulation	Since early 20th century, civil society, followed by state actors
Modern	*Zelena knjiga* from 1972	Some policy measures since second half of 1980s; Law on Environmental Protection from 1993	Active civil society, including conflict with economic actors; important EU governance	Hierarchies – regulation; and market – labelling, certifying, voluntary compliance, economic policy instruments	Since early 1970s, national level, later integrated in EU political system; civil society inspired by capitalist countries
Sustainable	*Agenda 21 for Slovenia* from 1995 inspired by government activities	Fragmented policy measures (i.e., National Programme for the Protection of the Environment from 1999; National Development Strategy from 2005)	Weak civil society; weak national administration; important international organisations (UN) and the EU	Networks – consultative bodies, usually non-binding decisions (action plans, strategies, etc.)	Since early 1990s, government initiatives, diffusing from international organisations

Table 10.3 summarises the core features of the architecture of environmental policy paradigms in Slovenia. It reveals that a combination of factors determines environmental performance today. The conservationist environmental paradigm is well established in its cognitive-normative complex and is coherent and less contradictory in its social-structural and organisational complexes. By contrast, the modern environmental paradigm is normatively well established and strongly integrated into the EU environmental *acquis* but is more contradictory in its social-structural complex, where it seems that economic interests cooperate closely with national government to avoid a strict implementation of the EU rules. The sustainable environmental paradigm is weak both in its cognitive-normative complex and in its social-structural and organisational complexes.

While the immediate challenges for better environmental performance by Slovenia are the stricter implementation of the modern environmental paradigm, the building up of a genuine and coherent blueprint for the sustainable environmental paradigm, the strengthening of civil society and the building of administrative capacity to implement sustainable environmental measures, in the longer term the balancing out of the different environmental policy paradigms will be crucial for better environmental performance.

Espen Moe

11 Environmental Issues in Norway

Norway as a frontrunner on all things environmental and Norway as a particularly clean, progressive and environmentally conscious nation has long been part of the Norwegian national identity. Several governments have issued programmatic statements referring to Norway's perceived frontrunner status. The frontrunner argument was very much part of the campaign against Norwegian EU-membership in 1994 (anti-EU campaigners hailing Norway as "the different country", high levels of environmental protection being part of this self-proclaimed differentness), and the fact that former Prime Minister Gro Harlem Brundtland was Chairman of the 1987 World Commission's Report on Environment and Development certainly boosted Norwegian environmental egos, among other things making the phrase sustainable development (*bærekraftig utvikling*) part of household Norwegian vocabulary.[1] To some extent the frontrunner belief is justified. Norway does well in international environmental rankings.[2] 96-98% of electricity production is generated by hydropower.[3] This is one of the highest percentages in the world. CO_2 emissions per unit of GDP are dropping, in a country that is already highly energy efficient.[4] Norway is a leader in addressing climate change internationally, and it is implementing ambitious nature diversity legislation domestically. Air and

1 John S. Dryzek, David Downes, Christian Hunold, David Schlosberg and Hans-Kristian Hernes, *Green States and Social Movements: Environmentalism in the United States, United Kingdom, Germany, & Norway* (Oxford: Oxford University Press, 2003); Marit Reitan, "Norway: a case of 'splendid isolation'", in Mikael Skou Andersen and Duncan Liefferink (eds.) *European environmental policy: The pioneers*, (Manchester: Manchester University Press, 1997), pp. 287-330; Liv Astrid Sverdrup. "Norway's institutional response to sustainable development", in *Environmental Politics*, 6(1), pp. 54-82 (1997).

2 Norway is for instance second (out of 146 countries) in Yale's 2005 ranking of environmental results, see Anders Haug Larsen, *Söta storebror – en komparativ studie av Natuskyddsföreningen og Naturvernforbundet*, Political Science Master's thesis (Trondheim:NTNU, 2013).

3 OECD, *OECD Environmental Performance Reviews: Norway 2011* (Paris: OECD Publishing, 2011), p. 22.

4 By 16% between 2000 and 2009, see *OECD Environmental Performance Reviews: Norway 2011*, p. 15.

water quality is high, and compared to most other countries, relatively few species are threatened by extinction.[5]

At the same time, there are major and persistent challenges remaining. Greenhouse gas (GHG) emissions dropped quite sharply in 2009, but this was because of the worldwide recession, and the effect was only temporary. Norway's Kyoto commitments limit Norway to a 1% increase in GHG emissions since 1990. At 2.4% in 2014, Norway was not close to achieving this, despite emissions dropping somewhat since peaking in 2007.[6] That means that the cuts, including a unilateral commitment to a 9% overall reduction (i.e., a 10% reduction beyond what was mandated by the Kyoto Protocol), have to be implemented through the purchase of emission permits. Extending from this, one of the main reasons for the increase in Norway's GHG emissions is the increased pace of oil and gas extraction. Herein also lies one of the bigger, but ultimately completely predictable, paradoxes of Norway's environmental status, i.e., the persistently tricky and tenuous relationship between energy and environment. By virtue of being a major petroleum producer, Norway is the third largest energy exporter in the world, behind Russia and Saudi Arabia only.[7] The pace of petroleum extraction and the fact that petroleum, at roughly 15% of GDP and half the export value, is the biggest Norwegian industry , has obvious consequences for Norwegian energy policies. It has given Norway less of an incentive (economy- and energy-wise) to invest in renewable energy (beyond hydro). There are very strong industrial and institutional interests in Norway working for the perpetuation of the petroleum paradigm, to the extent that we can almost speak of a Norwegian petro-industrial complex.[8] Thus, the Norwegian energy infrastructure and energy institutions make it very hard for Norway to implement anything along the lines of structural change in its energy production and consumption, despite harbouring a very significant wind power potential onshore and even more offshore. Also, nature conservationists and local interests have opposed wind power as often as they have not. Thus, when we

---

5 Larsen, *Söta storebror*; OECD, *Environmental Performance Reviews*; and *SABIMA*, 2013. "Naturmangfoldloven", at http://www.sabima.no/Naturmangfoldloven (accessed on 12 December 2014).

6 *Statistics Norway*, "Emissions of greenhouse gases, 1990-2014, final figures" (18 December 2015), at http://www.ssb.no/en/klimagassn (accessed on 18 January 2016).

7 IEA, *Energy Policies of IEA Countries: Norway, 2011 Review* (Paris: OECD/IEA, 2011), p. 7.

8 *Norwegian Petroleum*, "Economy: Revenues & spin-off effects", at www.norskpetroleum.no/en / (accessed on 18 January 2016); Espen Moe, "The Norwegian Energy-Industrial Complex: The Rise of Renewables, or All About Oil?", in Gunnar Fermann (ed.), *Political Economy of Energy in Europe: Forces of Integration and Fragmentation*, Berlin: Berliner Wissenschafts-Verlag, 2009), pp. 337-364.

shift the focus away from purely environmental policies and toward energy and environment, Norway's record is considerably more checkered.

Recurring environmental themes

The first major Norwegian environmental legislation was the 1910 Nature Preservation Act (revised in 1916), inspired by Sweden opening its first national park the year before, by the 1872 foundation of Yellowstone National Park in the US, and probably even further back in time the British nobility that started venturing into the Norwegian mountains already in the 1820s. The Nature Preservation Act protected species and restricted areas and specific objects of nature. It very clearly represents one of several recurring themes in Norwegian environmental policy; that of defining and conserving parts of nature both as a source of recreation and for its intrinsic value. As early as 1921, motions were made to have the mountainous area of Jotunheimen declared a national park, but the first Norwegian national park was not established until 1962 (Jotunheimen national park was not opened until 1980), and in 1964 another 16 areas were singled out. Still, this was more than half a century behind Sweden. In-between this, other nature protection acts were introduced, as the 1954 Nature Conservation Act, which expanded upon the 1910 act in several ways, and the 1957 Open-Air Recreation Act, which ensures the rights of everyone of access to and passage through uncultivated land, including privately owned areas. As of today, 16% of the Norwegian land area is protected.[9]

Another recurring theme has been that of conservation versus hydropower. Conservation interests have frequently bumped up against economic interests, with industrialization and economic growth a top priority of most Norwegian governments. Early Norwegian industrialization was to a major extent founded on the exploitation of waterfalls for hydroelectric power. From 1905 onwards,

9 Ole Kristian Fauchald and Lars H. Gulbrandsen, "The Norwegian reform of protected area management: a grand experiment with delegation of authority?", in *Local Environment: The International Journal of Justice and Sustainability*, Vol. 17, No. 2 (2012), p. 207; Alf-Inge Jansen and Per Kristian Mydske, 1998. "Norway: Balancing environmental quality and interest in oil", in Kenneth Hanf and Alf-Inge Jansen (eds.), *Governance and Environment in Western Europe* (Harrow: Longman, 1998), pp. 181-207; OECD, *Environmental Performance Reviews*; Hilde Reinertsen and Kristin Asdal, *Fra naturfredning til klimakamp: Norges Naturvernforbund 1914-2014* (Oslo: Senter for Teknologi, Innovasjon og Kultur, 2010), at https://www.sv.uio.no/tik/forskning/publikasjoner/tik-artikkelserie/ReinertsenAsdal.pdf (accessed on 12 December 2014); and Reitan "Norway: a case".

the battle over who has the rights to Norwegian waterfalls became one that has essentially lasted until the present. The first large dam for regulating freshwater for hydropower production was constructed as early as 1906. The first major conflict was that over the Rjukan waterfall, where a power station was built between 1911 and 1915. And the first law regulating the exploitation of watercourses came in 1917. While industrialization and economic growth were obvious priorities, nature conservation had its victories, for instance with the 1924 protection of the Vettis waterfall.[10] However, by 1962 between a third and a half of all Norwegian waterways had been regulated. Yet, by now conservationist voices were growing stronger. In 1973, when the first Water Conservation plan was approved in the parliament, 95 watercourses were permanently protected. This may sound considerable, but the reality is that neither of these had much potential in terms of hydropower in any case, and that the plan was biased by the fact that it was conceived by the Ministry of Industry, and not the Ministry of the Environment. In 1980, another 51 watercourses received protection. Yet, one of the recurring criticisms was the lack of a comprehensive plan and that regulation was piecemeal and arbitrary. A comprehensive plan, worked out by the Ministry of the Environment and with conservation concerns ranked far more favourably than in previous conservation plans, was finally approved in 1985. By 1993, when Water Conservation Plan IV was approved, the general consensus was that further hydropower expansion would contribute little to the Norwegian electricity supply. In 2001, Prime Minister Jens Stoltenberg in his New Year's speech declared the end to major hydropower expansions.[11]

The more general relationship between conservation and growth is another recurring theme. It is probably fair to say that up until the 1960s, for most of the main Norwegian political actors, nature was a resource to be harvested for economic gain, rather than something that should primarily be preserved. The attempt at squaring the circle has been to stress how growth and environmental protection both need to and can coexist, or "growth with conservation".[12] Several government White Papers stressed this in the 1960s and 1970s. The "polluter pays" principle was established in the early 1970s.[13] And when the

---

10 In addition to this, the concession laws, enacted in order to prevent foreign capital from acquiring all of Norway's natural resources put a significant brake on waterway exploitation, see Jansen and Mydske, "Norway: Balancing environmental quality".

11 Jansen and Mydske, "Norway: Balancing environmental quality"; Reinertsen and Asland, *Fra naturfredning til klimakamp*; Reitan, "Norway: a case"; and Jens Stoltenberg, *Statsministerens nyttårstale 2001*, at http://www.regjeringen.no/nb/dokumentarkiv/Regjeringen-Stoltenberg-I/smk/Taler-og-artikler-arkivert-individuelt/2001/statsministerens_nyttarstale_2001.html?id=264461 (accessed on 15 July 2013).

12 Jansen and Mydske "Norway: Balancing environmental quality", p. 196.

13 Dryzek et al. *Green States and Social Movements*; Reitan "Norway: a case".

World Commission made the term *sustainable development* a household linguistic item, according to Sverdrup, the notion was already well-established in the Norwegian environmental policy community, and quite in harmony with *growth with conservation*.[14] Work to establish a specific ministry with the responsibility for administering Norway's natural resources had been underway for many years already when the Ministry of the Environment was founded in 1972. One of the suggestions made by a government-appointed committee had been to create a Ministry of Resources. This ministry was supposed to have responsibility for all the nation's physical resources and be the primary repository of ecological and biological expertise in the same way as the Ministry of Finance controlled economic resources and was the locus of economic expertise. The Ministry of Finance was not overly enthusiastic about this, and within other ministries the notion that their concerns should be subordinated to ecological concerns was strongly resisted. The end result was a Ministry of the Environment that would only coordinate and harmonize, not overrule. It has the responsibility for initiating, developing, implementing and the monitoring of environmental measures.[15] Thus, the Ministry of the Environment also ended up being an institution very much in the spirit of coexistence of growth and environmental protection. And so, it is still the Ministry of Finance that coordinates work on sustainable development.[16]

As climate concerns have risen, sustainable development and the relationship between growth and conservation have to an ever greater extent dominated the environmental scene. This does not, however, mean that conservation issues have fallen by the wayside. Thus, originating from initiatives from the early 2000s, 2009 saw the approval of the Nature Diversity Act. It is an ambitious act that seeks to provide better management of Norwegian biodiversity, and it makes three key principles part of the legislation: First, any pressure on an ecosystem should be assessed based on present and future environmental effects on the ecosystem. Second, costs associated with preventing damage to biodiversity from a project should be carried by the project owner. And third, there is the precautionary principle.[17] Protected areas have increased considerably and the Act has also been followed by the revision of sectoral laws as well as the enacting of new laws in order to strengthen biodiversity protection. In many areas the Diversity Act goes further than EU directives, for instance introducing the concepts of *priority species* and *habitat types*. Priority species

14 Sverdrup, "Norway's institutional response", p. 56.

15 Reinertsen and Asdal, *Fra naturfredning til klimakamp*.

16 OECD, *Environmental Performance Reviews*.

17 OECD, *Environmental Performance Reviews*, p. 143

are protected and their habitats regulated if necessary.[18] If a habitat type is threatened and given priority status, then all plans involving land use change and development needs to take the habitat into account. What this means for practical purposes is not always clear, but there is little doubt that the Act is a major step forward. It has met with considerable expectation domestically, and it has drawn attention internationally. Yet, as of 2010 Norway had protected less of its land area than the EU average (16 and 18% respectively) and only 2.5% of its forest area.[19] Reform has also led to the delegation of authority of protected areas to local management boards, with the consequence that more than 75% of the total protected land area is now subject to local management regimes. While this is in line with developments in a number of other countries, it is not clear to what extent this will alter the balance between long-term environmental interests and local use interests. There are concerns, primarily with respect to "its failure to develop regulatory and institutional frameworks to ensure fulfilment of environmental conservation objectives."[20] The fear is that local boards will cater to landowners, resource users and tourist businesses, as well as more easily tolerate violations of regulations.

The Nature Diversity Act also applies offshore. It is worth noting that the two major fish stocks inside the Norwegian exclusive economic zone, cod and herring, are in good shape, and in better shape than 10 years ago, among other things because of the 2009 Marine Resources Act. Aquaculture may be a bigger concern. It has grown rapidly, and while a highly profitable industry, its continued growth has had negative impacts on water quality and coastal water biodiversity, as well as led to local cases of eutrophication. A more general criticism that has been ventured at the Diversity Act is that beyond 12 nautical miles the Act provides less protection for species and underwater habitats. In the 2004 proposal, the same principles were applied both to the 12 nautical miles zone and to the exclusive economic zone. In the final version of the Act, this, however, did not carry through, possibly because of resistance from the

18 The amount of threatened species is low compared to most other countries. Still, more than 20% of the 18,500 monitored species are threatened, mainly because of changing land use and infrastructural developments, with more than 10% critically endangered. 12 species are considered for selection as "priority species". Of the four large carnivore species (bear, lynx, wolf, wolverine) none has a population large enough to be viable, and the protection of these is politically sensitive as it clashes with animal husbandry interests, see OECD, *Environmental Performance Reviews*, pp. 142-146.

19 Fauchald and Gulbrandsen "The Norwegian reform", p. 207; Larsen, *Söta Storebror*, p. 4; OECD, *Environmental Performance Reviews*; SABIMA, "Naturmangfoldloven".

20 Fauchald and Gulbrandsen, "The Norwegian reform", p. 218.

petroleum industry.[21] If so, this is testimony to the fact that, while environmental conservation ideals may be held high, there is a continuously ongoing battle with industrial and energy interest, interests that represent some of the strongest actors in the Norwegian political economy.[22]

There is also a strong international dimension to Norwegian environmental policies. Norway has pushed for internationally binding commitments on GHG emissions both with the Kyoto Protocol and during subsequent climate change meetings. During the 2007 climate change negotiations in Bali, Norway initiated the International Climate and Forest Initiative. Tropical forests are amongst the planet's biggest carbon sinks. Deforestation and forest degradation account for roughly 17% of annual man-made carbon emissions. With the Climate and Forest Initiative, Norway is allocating up to NOK 3 billion a year to reduce GHG emissions from deforestation in developing countries.[23] In addition to this, Norway has been active in promoting multilateral and bilateral (in particular with Russia on both fish and pollutants in the Barents) cooperation with selected partners in specific issue areas. Protected areas have also been actively internationalized. One of the Norwegian UNESCO World Heritage sites is a natural heritage site and Norway has proposed four new natural heritage sites to the list.[24]

That said, it has often been in Norway's national interest to look for international rather than national solutions. Just over two decades ago (1993 figures), when acid rain was the primary Norwegian environmental concern, more than 90% of acid precipitation originated from abroad, with Norway probably the most exposed of all OECD countries.[25] But it has also long been acknowledged that the costs of environmental regulation are higher in Norway than in other countries. Thus, the principle of cost-effectiveness has been a governing principle of Norwegian environmental policy, which has also provided the Ministry of Finance with quite an important role. Norway is one

---

21 Ministry of Fisheries and Coastal Affairs [MoFCA], 'Ny havressurslov', *Regjeringen.no* (8 May 2008), at https://www.regjeringen.no/nb/aktuelt/ny-havressurslov---et-tidsskille-i-forva/id510832/ (accessed on 17 December 2014); OECD, *Environmental Performance Review*; SABIMA, "Naturmangfoldloven"; *WWF*, "Naturmangfoldloven – vårt viktigste naturvernverktøy", http://www.wwf.no/dette_jobber_med/miljopolitikk_og_lovverk/naturmangfoldloven/ (accessed on 17 December 2014).

22 See, for example Moe, "The Norwegian Energy-Industrial Complex".

23 Ministry of the Environment [MoE], *The Government of Norway's International Climate and Forest Initiative* (2012), at http://www.regjeringen.no/upload/MD/2011/vedlegg/klima/klima_skogprosjektet/Infohefte__kos_nov 2012.pdf (accessed on 17 December 2014), p. 3; OCED, *Environmental Performance Reviews*, pp. 110-112, 137.

24 Fauchald and Gulbrandsen, "The Norwegian reform", p. 207.

25 Reitan, "Norway: a case".

of the countries that has put the strongest emphasis on the flexible mechanisms and joint implementation of the Kyoto Protocol. Norway has actively sought to create arrangements that enable it to reduce GHG emissions where it is cost effective, hence typically abroad rather than domestically. This is a strategy that fits a country abundant in energy-intensive industries, and a country with so much hydropower that an increase in the production of emissions-free energy can only come at a high financial cost. The tropical forest initiative is part of such a strategy.[26]

Dryzek and his collaborators state that, while Norway early became an environmental leader, it is "unlikely to improve upon a solid record."[27] Among the reasons for this statement are the weakness of Norwegian civil society and the organization of the Norwegian environmental sector. Norway is a state with strong corporatist elements. For our purposes, this means that environmental interests have been institutionally integrated, with environmental groups working in close relationships with the state as well as to a large extent being dependent on funding from it. And while this funding does not come with particular strings attached, and while environmental groups do not feel controlled by the state because of this,[28] by default funding strengthens those groups that receive it at the expense of those that do not, thus rewarding cooperation over confrontation. Environmental groups will typically also be invited into numerous committees. This participation is based on expertise and not on environmental groups representing alternative viewpoints, it takes place behind closed doors, and it encourages compromise.[29] While it provides environmental groups with some influence (possibly more influence than other interest groups in other sectors), it also makes the process distinctly top-down, and it crowds out and marginalizes more radical organizations and initiatives, of which there are far more in other countries.[30]

Maybe because of this, Norwegian environmental groups have far lower membership numbers than other Scandinavian groups.[31] And so, genuine

26 Moe "The Norwegian Energy-Industrial Complex"; Reitan, "Norway: a case".

27 Dryzek et al., *Green States and Social Movements*, p. vii.

28 Apart from project grants, which specify what the money should be used for, see Dryzek et al. *Green States and Social Movements*, pp. 22-27, 75-78.

29 Dryzek et al.,*Green States and Social Movements*; Reitan, "Norway: a case".

30 The counterargument to this is that environmental lobbying in the parliament is both considerable and on the rise, and that the environmental movement is focused as much on pluralistic channels of influence as on corporative, see Larsen, *Söta storebror*.

31 In Norway, the largest environmental organization is the Norwegian Society for the Conservation of Nature. Membership peaked at 40,000 in 1991, but currently stands at marginally above 20,000. In comparison, the Swedish and Danish equivalents have nearly 200,000 members. See Dryzek et al., *Green States and Social Movements*, p. 24; Larsen, *Söta storebror*, pp.

bottom-up protest in Norway has been limited to (previous and largely unsuccessful) ad-hoc based campaigns against the damming of rivers and waterfalls and more recently (and more presently and successfully) against the erection of wind farms. Bottom-up activism against for instance industrial pollution – so widespread in other countries – has not been a dominant feature of the Norwegian environmental scene, and limited mainly to the 1980s and to actions against hazardous waste.[32]

Thus, in either case, Norwegian bottom-up protest has been *against* projects that in most other countries would have been embraced for their ability to deliver more or less emissions-free energy. Dryzek and his collaborators thus conclude that, while Norway is the most inclusive country in their study (which also consists of the US, the UK and Germany), it also has the most anemic environmental movement, possibly for that same reason.[33] In the 1990s, when sustainable development and a Norwegian frontrunner position on climate change started interfering with the principle that Norwegian policy should not be to the detriment of the competitiveness of Norwegian industry and commerce, it also became clear that in Norway there is a dearth of strong actors or social movements that seriously object to the basic structure of the Norwegian political economy. Green taxes were introduced (another victory for the cost-effectiveness agenda, and for the notion that growth and protection must coexist), but a number of key industrial actors were exempt for competitiveness reasons. The argument that it is important for Norway to keep its energy-intensive industries (aluminum, oil and gas) because no country has more efficient energy-intensive industries, and that on a global basis this leads to reduced GHG emissions, is frequently heard. Thus, the point made by Dryzek and his collaborators, that Norway's leadership position is unlikely to endure ultimately rests on the lack of willingness to undertake serious ecological restructuring of

---

61-62; Reinertsen and Asdal, *Fra naturfredning til klimakamp*. It should however be noted first that because of government support, the Norwegian organization is far less dependent on its members as a source of funding than its Swedish counterpart, and second, that Norway has quite a large number of environmental organizations, and if we include their membership numbers, the relative difference between Norway and Sweden becomes quite small. In *Söta storebror*, Larsen does however also conclude that the greater size of the Swedish organization to a greater extent enables it to push more ambitious environmental policy.

32 Reitan, "Norway: a case". It should be mentioned that this activism was taken seriously by the political establishment. A Pollution Control Act had been approved already in 1981, but it was only towards the end of the decade that implementation and enforcement was given due attention. Thus, controls became more frequent and penalties more severe, among other things due to a doubling of the budget of the Ministry of the Environment. See Reitan, "Norway: a case".

33 Dryzek et al., *Green States and Social Movements*, p. 162.

the Norwegian political economy.[34] The weakness of the civil sector and the lack of radical environmental movements (Norway has for instance not until very recently had a major Green party, instead environmental issues have been incorporated into all the regular parties) pushing major reform onto the political agenda have certainly contributed to this lacking willingness.

Energy and environment

What the above boils down to is that, especially in a country such as Norway, it is completely impossible to see environmental policy as distinct from energy policy. This is because the growth of Norwegian industry in so many ways is also the growth of Norwegian energy production, energy production that has been based on exploiting the comparative advantages of the Norwegian geography and of Norwegian natural resources. Even today, 96-98% of Norwegian electricity consumption comes from hydropower.[35] This puts Norway in a very fortunate situation of being able to provide almost all of its required electricity by renewable means. However, this is not energy production that has come about in altogether frictionless manners. As ever more Norwegian waterfalls and rivers were regulated, the conflict between nature conservation and industrial and political pressures for more energy production became ever more obvious.

The first major example of this conflict was the 1970 Mardøla action concerning the regulation of the Mardøla waterfalls, easily some of the finest remaining waterfalls in Norway at the time. However, the most spectacular manifestation of the conflict between conservation and energy production, leading to two acts of civil disobedience, was the Alta controversy in the late 1970s and early 1980s in the Norwegian far north, as the Norwegian parliament in 1978 approved the regulation of the Alta River. The consequence of regulating the river would be the creation of an artificial lake on large areas of land up until then used by Sami people for reindeer herding and fishing. This, in 1978 led to the formation of a popular movement against the development of the Alta-Kautokeino watercourse. In 1979, as work was about to begin, protesters sat down in front of the machines in order to prevent construction work from commencing, whereas in Oslo several Sami activists went on a hunger strike outside the parliament. As construction re-started in 1981, more than a thousand protesters chained themselves to the ground. They were eventually removed, but at one stage as much as 10% of the entire Norwegian police

34 Ibid.

35 OECD, *Environmental Performance Reviews*, p. 22.

force was stationed in Alta to deal with the riots. Conservation interests eventually lost out, as the Supreme Court ruled against the protesters.[36] The power station, with a maximum capacity of 150MW finally opened in 1987.

When Prime Minister Stoltenberg in 2001 stated that the time for major hydropower developments had passed, this was both because of the built-up controversy surrounding every major new regulated waterway and because after a century of hydropower expansion, there simply were not that many rivers and waterfalls with major hydropower potential left to exploit. Stoltenberg's sentiment was reiterated by newly elected Prime Minister Kjell Magne Bondevik (2001-05) later that same year.[37] This however had consequences in other areas. As the need for energy has been steadily increasing, in combination with a few years with little rainfall (thus, running down the water levels in Norwegian reservoirs), the 1990s were a decade when energy security became more tenuous than in the past. In the absence of hydropower expansions, electricity would have to be generated elsewhere. In 2000, Bondevik's first government – a centrist minority coalition (1997-2000) – fell because of this. The two most likely candidates to fill the power gap were renewable energy and gas. The Bondevik government refused to go for gas, but faced a majority against it in the parliament. Upon demanding a vote of confidence, it was ousted from power, with Stoltenberg forming a Labour Party government (2000-2001) in its place. In declaring the end to major hydropower expansions, he implicitly also gave the go-ahead for gas. Concessions were given for several gas power plants that same year. Stoltenberg most likely preferred gas over renewables for several reasons. First, gas does not have intermittency issues. Second, at the time the government did not foresee much of a potential for wind power in Norway. And third, it may also be that concerns about a decrease in demand for Norwegian gas from Europe (partly triggered by a perception that in Europe (but not in Norway), wind power would be expanding rapidly) was part of the deliberations that led to gas being preferred over wind.[38]

---

36 Dryzek et al., *Green States and Social Movements*; Reinertsen and Asland, *Fra naturfredning til klimakamp*; Reitan, "Norway: a case". Although not completely: As early as 1974, the project had been scaled down, so as to limit the destructive effects of the construction work, which originally would have partially flooded parts of the nearby village of Masi.

37 *Aftenposten*, "Mange bekker må i rør" (10 February 2001), at http://www.aftenposten.no/fakta/innsikt/Mange-bekker-ma-i-ror-6335149.html#.UdLvBvn0GLo (accessed on 16 July 2013).

38 Bernt Blindheim, "Implementation of wind power in the Norwegian market; the reason why some of the best wind resources in Europe were not utilised by 2010", in *Energy Policy*, Vol. 58 (2013), 337-346; Caroline Persson Hager, "Skiftende bris? En casestudie av de største endringene i norsk vindkraftpolitikk i perioden 1990 til 2012". *FNI*-rapport, 6/2014 (Oslo: Fridtjof Nansens Institutt, 2014).

What this means is that in terms of energy policy there has been quite a lot of resistance to policies that would make Norway environmentally more sustainable. Norway is one of the biggest petroleum exporters in the world, and bridging the gap between sustainable and environmentally friendly policy and wealth-generating extraction of major GHG-emitters has been inherently troublesome. The petroleum sector in 2014/15 accounted for 26% of annual investments, 15% of GDP and 46% of Norwegian exports,[39] and the Norwegian petroleum company Statoil, owned 67% by the Norwegian state, is the country's biggest company. This makes for a heavy concentration of very powerful industrial interests – interests that are very well entrenched within the political institutions of the state.

Thus, whereas Norway in many ways has been a frontrunner with respect to environmental policy, its history is far more checkered, and far more dominated by strong industrial interests, when it comes to energy. Norwegian efforts in new renewables, like wind power, have been feeble. At 856MW of installed capacity (2014), Norway finds itself far behind most other European countries (Germany has 39GW of installed capacity and Denmark around 5GW) despite having a high technical potential for wind power. The 1999 goal of 3TWh of wind power by 2010 – adopted at a time when electricity consumption was expected to increase and where wind and gas were thought of as the main contenders to meet a potential electricity shortage – was never fulfilled and has now been abandoned. 2014, which has so far been the best year for Norwegian wind power, yielded roughly 2.2TWh, or about 2% of the Norwegian electricity supply. In comparison, hydropower delivers roughly 120-130TWh of electricity every year.[40] Furthermore, in terms of government support for wind power, the subsidy that was approved in 2006 at 8 øre per kWh (roughly €0.01) of produced electricity was the third lowest in Europe at the time (EREF 2007). For any serious number of installations to be built,[41] the subsidy would prob-

39 *Norwegian Petroleum*, "Economy".

40 76 TWh/year as opposed to only 29TWh/year for for instance Denmark, according to Jørund Buen. "Danish and Norwegian wind industry", in *Energy Policy*, Vol. 34 (2006), pp. 3887-3897. In addition to this comes a potential 18-44TWh of off-shore wind power, see Anne Therese Gullberg, "The political feasibility of Norway as the 'green battery' of Europe", in *Energy Policy*, Vol. 57 (2013), pp. 615-623; Blindheim "Implementation of wind power"; Energilink (2013) "Vannkraftproduksjon (Norge)", http://energilink.tu.no/leksikon/vannkraftproduksjon%20norge.aspx (accessed on 22 October 2013); IEA, *Energy Policies of IEA Countries: Norway 2005 Review* (Paris: OECD/IEA, 2005); *Vindportalen*, "Vindkraft i Norge", http://www.vindportalen.no/ (home page) (2015), (accessed on 8 July 2015).

41 *Teknisk Ukeblad*, "Vindkraft tar av – men ikke i Norge" (20 February 2008), at http://www.tu.no/energi/article137812.ece (accessed on 17 July 2011); *Teknisk Ukeblad*, "Nå er vindstøtten tilbake" (21 April 2008), at http://www.tu.no/energi/article154598.ece (accessed on 17 July

ably have needed to be at least doubled. The subsidy was seen almost as an affront to the industry and as something that could not be taken seriously. The consequence was that a number of actors more or less just gave up on wind power.[42] However, in 2012 a green certificate system in cooperation with Sweden was introduced instead. There are a number of reasons for the policy change. First, there had been talks about certificates for more than a decade. 2005-06 saw negotiations between Norway and Sweden, with Norway withdrawing at the last minute. Thus, the present joint Norwegian-Swedish green certificate market is a resurrection of an already fairly mature idea. Second, and probably more importantly, as an EEA (European Economic Area) member, Norway is committed through the EU Renewable Energy Directive to increasing its renewable energy share of electricity production from 58% (reference year 2005) to 67.5% by 2020.[43] The joint certificate market, through which Norway and Sweden will fund a total of 26.4TWh of green electricity production annually by 2020 (split 50-50 between the two), is the main policy instrument by which this target will be reached. Third, it happens somewhat out of necessity, as ESA (the EFTA Surveillance Authority) did not approve the Norwegian feed-in system for wind power. And fourth, the opposition parties at the time (now in government), as well as a number of nature and environmental organizations have fought for it.[44] While this is a system for the phasing in of renewable energy rather than a system for the phasing in of wind,[45] the fact that between 2002 and 2007 talks and negotiations over a certificate system with Sweden triggered concession applications for between 5 and 7GW (as opposed to the accumulated capacity of only 856MW installed by 2014),[46] suggests that

2011); *Zero*, "Sverige gjør det Norge ikke klarer: 3TWh vindkraft innen 2010" (9 August 2009), at http://www.zero.no/fornybar-energi/sverige-gjoer-det-norge-ikke-klarer-3-twh-vindkraft-innen-2010 accessed on 17 July 2011.

42 Ane Brunvoll of environmental organization Bellona states that this led to 9 out of 10 wind power projects being cancelled, see *Teknisk Ukeblad*, "Latterlig satsing på fornybar energy", 33, pp. 34-5 (2007).

43 Blindheim, "Implementation of wind power"; Europaportalen, "Fornybardirektiv 2", https://www.regjeringen.no/nb/dokumenter/fornybardirektiv-2/id522812/?regj_oss=10 (accessed on 17 December 2014).

44 Gullberg, "The political feasibility of Norway"; Hager, *Skiftende bris?*

45 A large part of the Norwegian 13.2TWh will probably come from hydropower rather than wind. The NVE has estimated that new hydropower has a potential of 33TWh of production whereas concessions, notifications and applications for wind power accounts for a total of 43TWh. See Gullberg, "The political feasibility of Norway", p. 618.

46 Hager, "Skiftende bris?" Blindheim states that in 2005, the application volume was a little over 3GW, corresponding to 7TWh. While this is a lower figure than that reported by Hager the

there is a potential for growth and considerable optimism in the business as long as framework conditions are stable and conducive to growth.

Nevertheless, behind petroleum and hydro, new renewables in Norway have been treated as an afterthought up until very recently. The first obvious reason for this is that Norway already had a vested energy interest in hydropower. Prior to the rise of the petro-industrial complex, the 1950s and -60s saw the rise of a hydro-industrial complex, resulting from the state's political priority on cheap electricity. This could only be done by going extensively against the market and systematically over-investing in electricity production. And despite fulfillment of the political goals, the sector kept expanding, accompanied by cost overruns and weak oversight from close ties between government institutions, hydropower and energy-intensive industry.[47] Thus, renewable electricity was already at a level that until recently made other types of renewables redundant.

However, in addition to hydropower, Norway has what we can easily label a petro-industrial complex. For a number of reasons, policy is biased away from energy and environment and towards energy, which in this case means oil and gas at the expense of renewable energy. It made sense for the state to support the rise of a Norwegian petroleum industry in the 1970s. Norway identified the petroleum sector as one with enormous growth potential and did a good job of setting up an institutional structure that would cater to its needs. However, institutional structures often take on a life of their own, and there is little doubt that in Norway, the institutional structure, comprising the Ministry of Petroleum and Energy (MoPE) and the Norwegian Petroleum Directorate (NPD) is a major bias in favour of petroleum to the at least partial detriment of renewables. These to a large extent are allies of oil and gas. The industry recruits from the bureaucracy, and the bureaucracy tends to look for people with industry connections. Careers frequently start at the MoPE, gather pace within the industry, before ending back in the bureaucracy. Many NPD employees consider it their task to promote the interests of petroleum and stomping actors that side against it.[48] The notion that MoPE should play a

---

main point stands, namely that this would by far have been enough for Norway to reach its 3TWh/year target, see Blindheim, "Implementation of wind power".

47 Atle Christer Christiansen, "New renewable energy developments and the climate change issue", in *Energy Policy*, Vol. 30 (2002), pp. 235-243; Atle Midttun, "The Negotiated Political Economy of a Heavy Industrial Sector", in *Scandinavian Political Studies*, Vol. 11, No. 2 (1988), pp. 115-143.

48 Elin Lerum Boasson, "Klimaskapte beslutningsendringer", *FNI-rapport* (Oslo: Fridtjof Nansens Institutt, 2005); Interview with Marius Holm, telephone interview, 2007; Helge Ryggvik, "Oljekomplekset", *TMV-senteret*, nr 102 (1996); Helge Ryggvik and Ole Andreas Engen, "Den skjulte dagsorden, rammer for en alternativ oljepolitikk", *SAFE* (2005).

major role in promoting renewable energy seems distant. In 2006, as feed-in tariffs were being discussed, the impression was one of facing a wall of MoPE bureaucrats, none of which had any belief in wind power. Upon asking a senior MoPE bureaucrat if a change of government would make a difference, Øyvind Isachsen of Norwea was told that it would not, as the bureaucrats would ensure that policies remained stable.[49]

Institutions that one would expect to speak on behalf of renewables – the Ministry of the Environment (MoE) and The Norwegian Climate and Pollution Agency (NCPA) – are far less influential and tend to be overruled. In an interview with the newspaper *Aftenposten* back in 2006, the previous head of NCPA, Håvard Holm lamented the fact that whereas the climate section of NCPA has 10-12 people and less than NOK 1 million (€125,000) a year for independent analysis and investigations, the MoPE, the NPD, Petoro,[50] the Norwegian Water Resources and Energy Directorate (NVE), and the oil companies have staffs of hundreds of highly qualified people. Further, neither the MoE nor the NCPA have traditionally been strong on climate policy. These were institutions erected at a time when climate change was still a fanciful theory. Their expertise has rather been on toxins and pollutants.[51] Steps have been made to rectify this. Thus, in July 2013, the Climate and Pollution Agency merged with the Norwegian Directorate for Nature Management into one big agency, known as the Norwegian Environment Agency.[52] Still, in terms of turning the Norwegian energy production in an environmentally friendlier direction, these have traditionally not been very powerful players.

The NVE, mentioned above, is the institution in charge of the concession process. This is another reason why renewables have struggled. It takes renewables far longer to get a concession application through the bureaucracy than it does oil and gas. An average wind power application takes the NVE one to two man-years. The NVE has three to five man-years to its disposal on wind-, gas- and coal power put together. Thus, the shortage of staff means that it takes an average of four years to get a wind power concession through (2007 figures) (add to this that planning, purchasing and construction takes another two-three years).[53] At current rates, it will take 40 years to get the wind power applica-

49 Hager, "Skiftende bris?"

50 Petoro is owned by the Norwegian state, and manages Norwegian offshore petroleum properties and the State's Direct Financial Interest on behalf of the government.

51 Boasson, "Klimaskapte beslutningsendringer"; Interview with Marius Holm.

52 *Miljødirektoratet*, "Norwegian Environment Agency", at http://www.miljodirektoratet.no/english/ (accessed 17 December 2014).

53 Blindheim, "Implementation of wind power".

tions currently in the system through.[54] The problem lies however not exclusively with the NVE. Those four years are on average split 1.5 years between the NVE and 2.5 years with the MoPE. This is because most concession application (84%, 2009-13) are appealed to the MoPE, which then has to oversee the appeal. For Norway's most recent wind farm (Raggovidda), planning started in 2003, the concession application was approved in 2010, in 2013 the decision to invest was made, and in 2014 the farm finally provided the grid with electricity.[55] The time that it uses for this is indicative of the lack of enthusiasm for renewables in the MoPE. That the 2010 3TWh goal was unachievable was clear as early as 2007, and a major part of the reason for this was that the MoPE itself constituted one of the biggest bottlenecks, both in handling the appeals and in not adequately staffing the NVE.[56]

What should also not be neglected is the language of cost-effectiveness, which permeates every main government ministry. Even the MoE has adopted a language of cost-effectiveness in order to be taken seriously.[57] This has been a strong influence on Norwegian policy. It may indeed seem like a good compass, but it inevitably plays into the hands of the already established industries, as these are the ones that have had the time to actually become cost-effective. The present-day willingness to support projects long-term in scope is markedly less than in the past and linked to the influx of economists in government departments and the requirement that projects be viable from day one. And while wind power is not viable from day one, simply waiting for the technology to improve and costs to come down effectively means missing out on great opportunities. Technological thresholds must be crossed, and this does not just happen by itself.[58] The cost-effectiveness bias, and how it has affected energy-political decisions in Norway, is something that has been pointed out by a number of studies.[59]

---

54 *Teknisk Ukeblad,* "50 urørte vindkraftsøknader" (7 December 2007), at http://www.tu.no/energi/article126511.ece (accessed on July 17, 2011)

55 *E24*, "Her reises Norges nyeste vindpark" (12 September 2014), at http://e24.no/energi/her-reises-norges-nyeste-vindpark/23294469 (accessed on 19 January 2016); *Teknisk Ukeblad*, "Det kan ta opptil 11 år å få konsesjon til et vindkraftverk" (14 January 2014), at http://www.tu.no/kraft/2014/01/14/det-kan-ta-opptil-11-ar-a-fa-konsesjon-til-et-vindkraftverk (accessed on 19 January 2016).

56 Blindheim, "Implementation of wind power".

57 Boasson, "Klimaskapte beslutningsendringer".

58 Gard Hopsdal Hansen and Markus Steen, "Vindkraft til havs", *CenSES-rapport* 1/2011 (Trondheim: NTNU, 2011); Moe "The Norwegian Energy-Industrial Complex".

59 For example Blindheim, "Implementation of wind power"; Boasson, "Klimaskapte beslutningsendringer"; Hager "Skiftende bris?"; Jøran Solli, *Kalkylenes retorikk*; PhD dissertation (Trondheim: NTNU, 2004).

The Norwegian climate change approach is also grounded in the notion of cost-effectiveness. It advocates the flexible mechanisms and joint implementation schemes of the Kyoto protocol. Reducing emissions at home rather than abroad would put undue strains on Norwegian industry, and on the Norwegian petroleum sector. By all means, the petroleum sector is subject to a carbon tax (introduced in 1991), but most of the Norwegian energy-intensive industry beyond petroleum is exempt (only about 60% of the CO_2-emissions are covered). Combined with technological initiatives on Carbon Capture Storage (CCS), this provides for an industrial future where Norway sticks with its existing industrial structure, but at a slightly lower environmental cost. Oil and gas was not happy about CCS, thus this political battle was fought and lost. Yet, for the industry this was a smaller evil than a steep carbon tax, which was the perceived alternative. For renewables, the implication is an unwillingness to see energy and industry as linked and no recognition of a need for structural change. It preserves the existing structure, but makes it slightly more efficient, pushing structural change ever farther into the future. The consequence has been an inability and a lack of political will to create a stable and fruitful framework for renewable energy. This lack of stability has been pointed out both in outside reviews, like the IEA (2005), and from Norwegian windpower actors.[60]

But part of the irony is that it is not just strong industrial interests and institutional biases that have led Norway along a path that implies the indefinite perpetuation of the existing oil and gas regime at the expense of more ambitious renewable policy. Public opinion, in particular local nature protection agencies, has been skilled at lobbying against wind power, sometimes creating the impression that wind power is ruining huge chunks of pristine wilderness. Gullberg quotes the following February 2011 statement from The Forum for Nature and Outdoor Life: "We have enough energy in Norway. The potential for energy efficiency and energy recycling is vastly under-utilised… In the future climate measures will pose a greater threat to the natural environment in Norway than climate change". Amongst the environmental organizations, Friends of the Earth Norway is skeptical both of hydropower and windpower.[61] Others, like Zero and Bellona, are more positively inclined. Hager sees a clear divide between what she labels conservationists (*naturvernere*) and climate warriors (*klimaforkjempere*).[62] The conservationists comprise amongst others the Norwegian Society for the Conservation of Nature, the Norwegian Trekking Association, WWF, and the Norwegian Hunting and Fishing Association, and

60 Blindheim "Implementation of wind power"; IEA; *Energy Policies of IEA Countries*; Moe, "The Norwegian Energy-Industrial Complex"; Reitan, "Norway: a case".

61 Gullberg, "The political feasibility of Norway", p. 619.

62 Hager, "Skiftende bris?"

in general they are against both hydropower and windpower, their primary point of view being that energy problems should be solved by energy conservation rather than an increase in energy production. She does, however, also point out that in the 1990s, as the perceived choice stood between gas and renewables, conservationists lobbied for renewables, with the climate warriors, rather than against them. Thus, while there is a strong conservationist bent against wind power, at least locally, on the national level resistance has weakened. However, as Blindheim notes, one of the reasons why wind power applications take such a long time, is that pretty much every application is appealed.[63] Both Buen and IEA list a lack of social and local acceptance as a significant problem in Norway.[64] The fact that other countries (such as Denmark) have been far more successful with respect to the siting of windmills, and as a consequence suffer far fewer local complaints, is worth noting, and an indication that it is possible to create contexts in which local communities are the main supporters and not the main opponents of renewable energy.

Conclusion

We are left with the paradox that in Norway the most die-hard conservationists are also the ones that are the most hardline with respect to their opposition against the expansion of renewable energy. This for all practical purposes means that, while it is true that in Norway a lot of work has gone into creating a thorough and well-developed framework for nature conservation, if we expand our discussion to include climate and energy, the lines become blurrier. Here, environmental standards are under threat both because of strong industrial interests and strong institutional biases pointing Norwegian energy interests in the direction of more petroleum (the previous Norwegian Minister of Petroleum and Energy also explicitly declared that off-shore wind power is too expensive[65]) augmented by CCS, and because conservationists and local interests are not overly enthusiastic about alternative modes of power. Instead, it may easily be external factors, such as the implementation of the aforementioned EU directive on promoting the use of energy from renewable sources (Directive 2009/28/EC of the European Parliament and of the Council) that will provide impetus and direction to future Norwegian efforts in this area.

---

63 Blindheim, "Implementation of wind power", pp. 341-342; *Teknisk Ukeblad*, "Det kan ta opptil 11 år…"

64 Buen, "Danish and Norwegian wind industry"; IEA, *Energy Policies of IEA Countries*.

65 *Teknisk Ukeblad*, " –For dyrt med vindmøller til havs" (17 March 2011), at http://www.tu.no/energi/2011/03/17/-for-dyrt-med-vindmoller-til-havs (accessed on 16 July 2013).

Part Four – Foreign Relations

Damjan Lajh and Jonathon Moses

12 Relations with the EU

This chapter investigates Norway's EU-skeptic and Slovenian EU-enthusiastic relations with the European Community/European Union.[1] While a remarkably stable percentage of the Norwegian population wants to keep Europe at arms' length, Slovenia's transition to democracy was closely linked to its joining the European integration processes. In this sense, Norway's experience with the European Community, and subsequently the European Union, can be seen as an inverse image of Slovenia's. While Slovenia's relationship to the European Union can be described as dynamic, Norwegian attitudes toward EU membership have been remarkably stable (and skeptical). While Slovenia's economic development and integration with the world economy brings it closer to Europe; Norway's growing economic strength complicates her economic (especially monetary) relations with Europe. Finally, while Slovenia's transition to democracy is closely linked to the European integration process, Norwegians see membership in a political union with powerful neighbouring states as a constraint on their independence, secured only in 1905. By comparing the Slovenian and Norwegian experiences, we can test many of the most common arguments for why Norwegians continually oppose membership in the European Union. After all, both countries share features which are often used to explain Norwegian exceptionalism with respect to EU membership: small and peripheral countries, suppressed by large neighbours.

The chapter is divided into two major sections and proceeds as follows. The first section surveys Norway's relationship to the EU in terms of its growing political and economic muscle. It begins by describing the remarkably stable nature of Norway's relationship to Europe over the past forty years: Norwegian elites and urban dwellers have always tended toward stronger relations with the European Community/Union, but her people have been reluctant

---

1 Today's European Union has evolved from three separate Communities based on the three founding treaties: the Treaty of Paris, which in 1951/1952 established the European Coal and Steel Community (ECSC), and the Treaties of Rome, which in 1957/1958 established the European Economic Community (EEC) and the European Atomic Energy Community (EURATOM). A merger of the three Communities into a single European Community took place with the signing of the Treaty on European Union in Maastricht in 1992. For consistency, in this chapter we will use the term European Union (EU) for the description of the EEC, the EC as well as the EU.

to follow suit. This attitude will not be swayed as long as the legitimacy and strength of Norwegian political and economic institutions continue to rise, while those of the EU fall. The second section surveys the evolution of Slovenia's relationship to the EU. It begins by describing the key physiognomies of Slovenia's accession to the EU, i.e., relatively smooth integration into the EU with only a few problems, marked by a strong pro-EU orientation on the part of the Slovenian political elite as well as of citizens since the country's independence. It then focuses on the main challenges in the period of full membership in the EU, and concludes by discussing Slovenia's future position within the EU, taking into account especially the financial and economic crisis. The third section synthesizes the main comparative findings.

Norway's relationship to the EU

Good fences make good neighbours

Norway's relationship to an expanding European Community has been almost constant over the past 40 years: a remarkably stable percentage of its population wants to keep Europe at arms' length. Since the 1960s, Norway's economic and political elites have dreamt of playing in the European league. In the 1960s, along with Ireland, Denmark, and the United Kingdom, Norway twice applied for membership in the European Economic Community (once in 1962, again in 1967), but the hopes of its elites were dashed both times by France's willingness to veto the UK's membership application. When Charles de Gaulle left office, however, French resistance to British membership in the EEC softened. Britain again sought membership; once again, Ireland, Denmark and Norway followed in tow.

After completing its membership negotiations in January 1972, the Norwegian (Conservative-based coalition) government prepared an advisory referendum to decide whether Norway should join the EEC. The referendum date was set for 25 September 1972. During the campaign, pro-Europe supporters (Norway's political and economic elites, huddled mostly in Oslo) painted a bleak picture of Norway's economic future if Britain and Denmark joined the EEC, but Norway didn't. The Labour Party, Norway's dominant post-war party, strongly backed Norwegian membership. In opposition, Norway's fishermen and farmers gathered under a banner claiming "Norway is not for sale!", arguing the need to maintain local control over farming and fishing grounds which were unlike those on the continent.

The result of the referendum (53.5% opposed membership, 46.5% supported) landed a strong blow to Norway's elites. The sitting government was forced to resign, and the Labour Party was decimated in the 1973 parliamentary elections—losing 1/3 of its voters. Many anti-EEC members left the party and joined the Socialist Left Party. A new coalition government (headed by Lars Korvald) was left to negotiate a trade agreement between the EEC and Norway which came into effect in June 1973.

For the next 15 years, the EEC was kept off Norway's political radar. It wasn't until the 1990s that Norway's elites were again willing to broach the subject.[2] In October 1992, a significant majority (130 votes to 35) in the Norwegian parliament adopted the Agreement on the European Economic Agreement (EEA[3]), which replaced the free trade agreement signed in 1973. The government had introduced the EEA as an independent alternative to EU membership, hoping to divide opposition to EU membership--both within the Labour Party, and beyond.[4] The EEA came into effect on 1 January 1994.

Already in April (1992), it had been revealed that the government intended to apply for EU membership again. In its justification to Parliament, on 16 November 1992, Prime Minister Gro Harlem Brundtland argued that a changing world already made the newly-ratified EEA inadequate for Norway's needs.[5] She wanted Norway to again consider membership in the EU, and proposed another referendum to decide the matter in 1994. Once again, the country was split apart in a divisive campaign;[6] and once again the result of the referendum was largely divided along elite and geographic lines: 52.2% against; 47.8% in support of EU membership.

---

2 The impetus for this was the so-called Oslo Declaration from 15 March 1989, where six EFTA member states (Norway, Sweden, Finland, Iceland, Austria and Switzerland) declared their desire to sign an agreement with the EU in support of the EU's new attempt to facilitate the free movement of goods, services and capital. The resulting negotiations lead to the EEA. See Dag Seierstad, "EØS—en kritisk vurdering" *De Facto Rapport* 2: 2012 for a critical introduction.

3 The Norwegian acronym is EØS: Det europeiske økonomiske samarbeidsområde.

4 Hege Skjeie, Lars Langengen, and Libe Rieber-Mohn, "'Aldri mer' 1972", in "Behandlingen av EU-saken i Arbeiderpartiet", in *Tidsskrift for samfunnsforskning,* Vol. 36, No. 31 (1995), p. 53.

5 In particular, she focused attention on three particular changes: the end of the cold war; the establishment of the EU internal market from 1 January 1993, and that Sweden and Finland had already applied for membership. See Anders Todal Jenssen, "Ouverturen." In Anders Todal Jenssen and Henry Valen (eds.), *Brussel midt imot: Folkeavstemningen om EU* (Oslo: ad Notam, 1996), pp. 13-29, at p. 14.

6 For analyses of these cleavages, see the many contributions in Jenssen and Valen (eds.) *Brussel midt imot,* as well as Jonathon Moses and Anders Todal Jenssen, "Nordic Accession: An Analysis of the EU Referendums", in Barry Eichengreen and Jeffry Frieden (eds.), *Forging an Integrated Europe* (Ann Arbor: University of Michigan Press, 1998), pp. 211-246.; and Anders Todal Jenssen, Kristen Ringdal, and Jonathon Moses, "Bridging the Micro-Macro Gap: A Multilevel Approach to Voter Behavior in the Nordic European Union Referendums", in *Tidsskrift for Samfunnsforskning,* Vol. 45, No. 2 (2004), pp. 215-243.

Since then, Norway's relationship to the European Union has been channelled through the EEA, which requires that Norway implement and follow legislation relevant to the functioning of the common market.[7] Born in 1992, the EEA today includes only three non-EU states (the other EFTA states having joined the Union, or refused to sign): Norway, Iceland and Lichtenstein. Tellingly, the agreement does not cover the EU's common agriculture and fisheries policies, the customs union, the common foreign and security policy, justice and home affairs or monetary union. But the areas covered remain extensive, and there exists a set of surveillance institutions (e.g. the EFTA Surveillance Agency (ESA) and the EFTA Court), which ensures that the signatories respect their obligations.

Norway enjoys the possibility of vetoing any directive coming out of the EU, but—until recently—it had been afraid to employ that veto for fear of the retributive consequences. As the number of directives being passed by Brussels (and quietly adopted by Norway) increased, and as the EU's regulatory hand began to reach deeper into Norway's political norms, the rank and file in Norway's Labour Party revolted against its leadership and demanded that the EU's third postal directive be vetoed. In 2011, for the very first time, Norway reclaimed the sovereignty it was said to have protected in opposing EU membership.

Since that time, the offensive has been with the anti-EU movement in Norway. In a recent (July 2012) survey, only 17.2% said they would support Norwegian EU membership (74.8% would oppose).[8] In January of 2012, the foreign ministry published an enormous (911 page!) review of the various options available to Norway,[9] both inside and outside of the EU (NOU 2012: 2) —but the report itself generated much critical discussion and a backlash of alternative, much more critical, reports.[10]

7 In addition, Norway signed the Schengen convention. Since 2001, passport controls between Norway and the then 14 (now 26) Schengen countries have been abolished.

8 "Norge: 74,8 pct. nej til EU", *Folkebewægelsen mod EU* (23 July 2012), at http://www.folkebevaegelsen.dk/spip.php?page=print-soren&id_article=4917 [last accessed on 7 December 2014].

9 NOU (2012: 2) "Utenfor og innenfor: Norges avtaler med EU." Utredning fra utvalg oppnevnt av Utenriksdepartementet 7. januar 2010 (Europautredningen) Avgitt til Utenriksdepartementet 17. januar 2012, at http://www.regjeringen.no/pages/36797426/PDFS/NOU201220120002000DDDPDFS.pdf [last accessed on 7 December 2014].

10 See, e.g., Seierstad, «EØS—en kritisk vurdering»; and "Nei til EUs høringsuttalelse til NOU 2012:2: Utenfor og innenfor (Europautredningen)" Online at: http://www.neitileu.no/om_nei_til_eu/fokus/alternativer_til_eoes/nei_til_eus_hoeringsuttalelse_til_nou_2012_2_utenfor_og_innenfor_europautredningen [last accessed on 7 December 2014].

In short, Norway's relationship to the European Union has been relatively stable over the past 40 years, with a small majority of the population consistently opposing EU membership (while a broad majority of its political and economic elites have consistently supported EU membership). Only in the past few years has this balance been disrupted, with a much larger, and growing anti-EU sentiment taking root in the population.

Explanation

What can explain Norway's consistently skeptical relationship to the European Community over the last forty years? If we keep our focus trained on the national level of analysis,[11] then two arguments are most commonly forwarded: one political, the other economic.

Union is a dirty word

Dominated by foreign powers for centuries, and truly independent only since 1905, Norway is not ready to cede its young and hard-earned sovereignty. There can be little questioning the intensity of Norwegian national pride (witness any 17th of May parade—Norway's constitution day). But we need to consider whether Norway's colonial past is unique enough to explain its skepticism to EU membership.

Hilary Allen makes the historical argument cogently:

> History and geography had combined to make 'no' a natural reaction for many Norwegians. Centuries of foreign domination had given the anti-marketeers' slogan of selvråderett (sovereignty) a profound emotional appeal. Their recent independence, intense patriotism, small numbers, and peripheral location had also injected a proud, touchy defensiveness into many Norwegian's reactions to anything, be it neighbouring states or foreign economic interests, which might possibly infringe this independence.[12]

Norway is a country rich in natural resources and with a long and fertile coastline, but it is sparsely populated and (until recently) relatively underdeveloped. This combination of characteristics makes Norway a prime real estate target for neighbouring powers. Norwegian waters are filled with fish; its forest filled with trees and waterfalls; its coastline offers a million nooks and crannies for

---

11 A good argument can be made that this level obfuscates as much as it clarifies. Indeed, the strongest empirical analyses of union support tend to be run at lower levels of aggregation. Still, nation-level analyses are most common in the media, and in political discussion, and they offer convenient means of comparisons, as here with Slovenia.

12 Hillary Allen, *Norway and Europe in the 1970s* (Oslo: Universitetsforlaget, 1979), p. 161.

hiding, leaving and entering. As a consequence, Norway's relationship to neighbouring powers has always been an exploitative one, with Norway feeling the hard end of the stick.

Norway's history of political subservience can be traced back to 1389, when the three Scandinavian kingdoms (Norway, Denmark and Sweden) were united in what is known as the "Union of Kalmar". The actual terms of the original union are disputed, and a certain degree of Norwegian sovereignty may have been protected,[13] but it is common to recognize that Norway lost its political autonomy in practice to the Union's common monarch (especially with respect to foreign policy).

The Kalmar Union was formally dissolved in 1523, when Sweden broke out and re-established its independence under Gustav Vasa. Norway remained connected to Denmark for nearly another 300 years. In 1536, Denmark's King Christian III made Norway fully subservient to the Danish Crown and a new constitution (in 1660) provided the Danish monarch with absolute power over Norway.

This state of subservience lasted until the end of the Napoleonic Wars, when Denmark (having allied itself with Napoleon) was forced to surrender Norway as booty to the Swedish king (Carl Johan). For the next 91 years (1814-1905), Norway fell under Swedish tutelage, although Norway had its own parliament and was autonomous in domestic affairs. The Treaty of Kiel proclaimed Norway a kingdom in its own right, but it was formally united with Sweden in a personal union, and never obtained the right to its own representation abroad. This state of affairs lasted until 1905, when Norway finally gained true independence.

This independence was short lived. While Norway remained neutral in the First World War, and sought neutrality in the Second, she was invaded and occupied by yet another neighbouring power (Germany) for most of the Second World War (9 April 1940 until 8 May 1945).

In short, in the 623 years since 1389, Norway has experienced just 102 years free of foreign domination—the most recent experience was but a generation (67 years) ago. For most of this period, membership in a political union was associated with domination by powerful neighbours—hardly the association that the European Union wanted to convey when attracting voters in the 1994 referendum.

---

13 T. K. Derry, *A History of Scandinavia* (Minneapolis: University of Minnesota Press, 1979), p. 73.

Affording democracy

The second popular argument for explaining Norwegian reticence to join the European Union has to do with Norway's impressive wealth. This argument can be easily exaggerated, as Norway's wealth has grown significantly since the 1960s (it would have been a much more difficult argument to make in 1962).

What *has* mattered is that threats made earlier (about the cost to Norwegians in staying outside of Europe) never materialized. Indeed, Norway's economy has enjoyed remarkable growth since it first rejected EEC membership, and the wealth that this growth has generated is used to help defend the lifestyles of small farmers and fishermen along the coast. In effect, the country's economic growth allows it to afford the costs of maintaining traditional (and inefficient) sectors.

Norway's capacity to remain economically viable, outside the European Community, is based on two things. First, Norway has always enjoyed free trade relationships with its neighbours, regardless of EU membership, via the EFTA. Already in 1960, Britain had established the European Free Trade Association (EFTA), where Austria, Britain, Denmark, Norway, Portugal, Sweden, and Switzerland created a rival free trade zone (minus the ambitions for political union) to the EEC. As mentioned above, in the wake of the first referendum, the Norwegian government worked quickly to establish a free trade agreement with the European Union, and this was later fortified by the EEA agreement (as well as parallel GATT, and subsequent WTO, agreements). The result has been strengthening EU trade relationships over time, despite staying outside the EU, as illustrated in Figure 12.1.

The second reason is the most commonly cited: oil. At the time of the first referendum, Norway was still exploring the potential for developing its offshore oil capacity. By the time that oil was tapped, OPEC had jacked up its price significantly, and Norway began to swim in money. This affects Norway's relationship to Europe in two ways. First, because of Norway's wealth, she contributes a great deal of money to the EU program budget in exchange for open access to the European Union (in 2008, the figure was €188 million) and to reduce economic disparities across the EEA (between 2009-2014, Norway provided almost €1.8 billion toward this objective; see Figure 12.2).[14]

---

14 Norwegian MFA [Ministry of Foreign Affairs] (2009) "Norway and the EU—partners for Europe." Publication number E-853. Online at http://www.regjeringen.no/upload/UD/Vedlegg/eu/Norway%20and%20the%20EU.pdf [last accessed on 7 December 2014], p. 4.

Figure 12.1. Norwegian trade to the EEC/EU (exports plus imports/GDP)

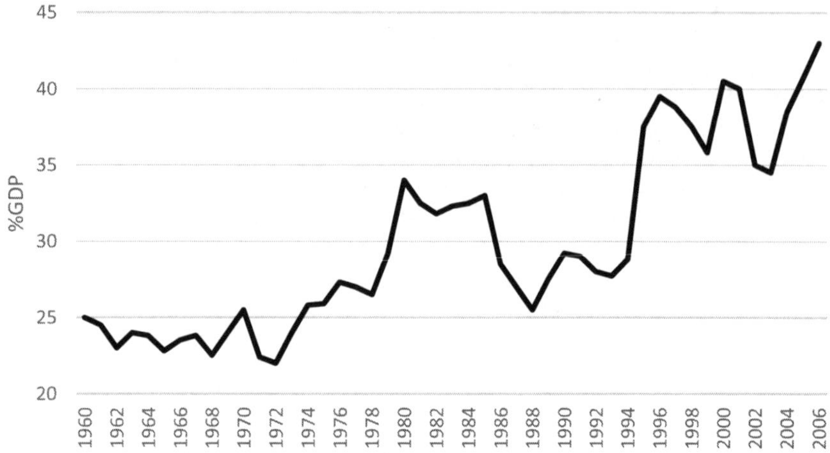

Note: European countries include: Denmark, Belgium, Luxembourg, France, Greece, Ireland, Italy, Netherlands, Portugal, Spain, Great Britain, (W) Germany.

Source: Statistics Norway: historical statistics, on-line

Figure 12.2. Norwegian transfers to the EU

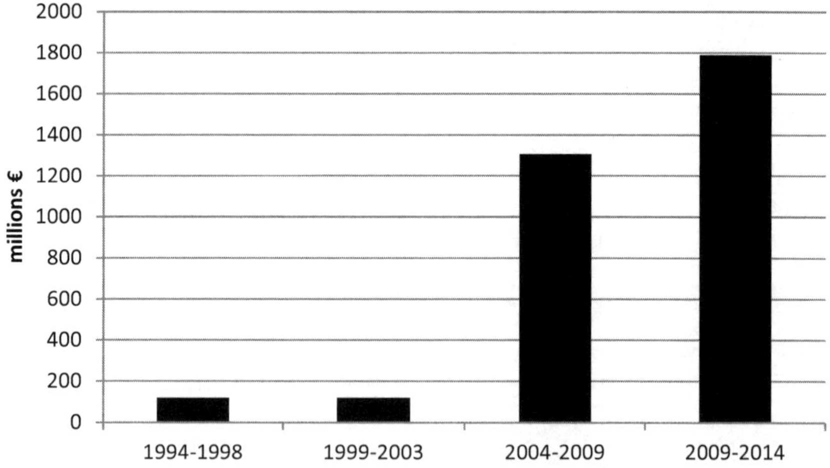

Source: NOU 2012:2, http://www.regjeringen.no/nb/dep/ud/dok/nou-er/2012/nou-2012-2/25.html?id=669800

More significantly, the wealth generated by oil places the Norwegian economy on a different growth path from the rest of Europe. When the price of oil goes up, this is a good thing for Norway (and usually a bad thing for the rest of Europe). This means that Norway has very different needs with respect to monetary policy, and its economy often has different needs from economies on the continent. As a consequence, EU membership which includes membership in a common monetary union would be very problematic for Norway (not that it is working all that well for Europe, either!).

In short, Europe needs Norway more than Norway needs Europe. Rightly or wrongly, Norwegians fear that many of their most cherished political institutions and newly-won independence will be threatened if more and more decisions are made in Brussels (as both opponents and supporters of EU membership point out: this is happening anyway). Norway's strong economy allows it a great deal of political leeway, and this leeway has been used to secure policies which benefit the broader Norwegian population, more than those of its political and economic elites.

Slovenian relationship to the EU

Knocking on the door of European integration

The end of the 1980s brought tectonic changes to the political and economic arrangement of the European continent, when (post-)socialist countries of Central and Eastern Europe started applying for membership in West-European organizations. With the collapse of the military and political division of Europe, the disintegration of economic boundaries between formerly divided blocs of the continent, pressures of democratization of post-socialist Central and Eastern European countries,[15] and as a result of economic pressures of "old" Member States to expand the common market to the East, the EC/EU has opened its doors to new members.[16] In the summer of 1993, the European Council in Copenhagen decided that post-socialist countries from Central and Eastern Europe could enter into the EU under certain criteria, which have entailed in particular: a) institutional stability, which should ensure a democratic and constitutional order and the protection of human rights and minority rights

15 Damjan Lajh and Danica Fink-Hafner, "Institucionalno prilagajanje slovenske izvršne oblasti povezovanju Slovenije z ES/EU: mednarodno primerjalni pogled," in *Teorija in praksa,* Vol. 39, No. 6 (2002), p. 976.

16 Damjan Lajh, "Twenty years of relations between the Republic of Slovenia and the European Union", in *Studia Historica Slovenica,* Vol. 12, No. 1 (2012), pp. 125–146.

(*political criterion*); b) the establishment and development of a functioning market economy, which should be capable of surviving openness to and competition within the European common market and given market forces (*economic criterion*); and c) the ability to take over the obligations arising from full EU membership, together with a commitment to achieving the aims of political, economic and monetary union (i.e., all prospective members must enact legislation in order to bring their laws into line with the body of European law built up over the history of the EU).[17] This led to the largest enlargement in the history of the EU when, in May 2004, ten new countries joined the EU, including Slovenia.

The process of Slovenia's independence in the late 1980s and early 1990s was heavily marked by the idea of inclusion in Euro-Atlantic integration processes. Slovenian membership in the EU was recognized[18] as the country's main foreign policy goal even before the formal declaration of independence, and as an important step towards a democratic, economically-successful and internationally-recognized country.[19] Accession into the EU ran relatively smoothly, with only a few problems that the young Slovenian state faced shortly after the establishment of its first relationships with the EU – both in the process of negotiating the European Agreement as well as in the phase of its implementation.[20] The most obvious problems[21] were questions related to the purchase of Slovenian real estate by foreigners, initiated by Italy,[22] and the problem of the closure or transformation of duty free shops, which was raised

---

17 Hanns D. Jacobsen, "The European Union's Eastward Enlargement," in *European Integration Online Papers,* Vol. 1, No. 14 (1997).

18 In this respect, the reformed Slovenian League of Communists had for example adapted to civil society's demands at the end of the 1980s so much that it adopted the document "Europe now – for the European quality of living", prepared for its congress in autumn 1989 and it decided to use almost the same slogan ("Europe Now!") for the first multi-party and democratic elections held in spring 1990.

19 Danica Fink-Hafner and Damjan Lajh, *Proces evropeizacije in prilagajanje političnih ustanov na nacionalni ravni* (Ljubljana: Fakulteta za družbene vede, 2005), pp. 53–54.

20 Lajh, "Twenty years of relations" [note 16], pp. 125–146.

21 At this point we can observe the genealogy of relationships of neighboring countries in the context of the enlargement policy and the use of the principle of conditionality. Namely, after achieving full membership in the EU, Slovenia was occasionally criticized for the "exploitation" of the status of EU Member State for the purposes of solving bilateral disputes with Croatia in the context of the latter's accession to the EU.

22 See Irena Brinar and Marjan Svetličič, "Enlargement of the European Union: the Case of Slovenia," in *Journal of European Public Policy,* Vol. 6, No. 5 (1999), pp. 810; and Fink-Hafner and Lajh, *Proces evropeizacije in prilagajanje političnih ustanov na nacionalni ravni* [note 19], pp. 55–56.

under pressure from neighbouring countries Austria and Italy.[23] In spite of these challenges, the process of Slovenia's integration into the EU represented a consensually adopted national goal of the political elite. Naturally, in this period some differences in the political parties' views on specific "European" issues appeared, but, with the exception of only one parliamentary party, the Slovenian National Party led by Zmago Jelinčič, all other parties clearly agreed and supported the country's entry into the EU. Moreover, at the beginning of July 1997, leaders of all the parties represented in the parliament, except the Slovenian National Party, even signed a unique (*vis-à-vis* other countries applying for EU membership) special agreement on cooperation during the process of Slovenian integration into the EU.[24] Additionally, the entire period of Slovenia's integration into the EU was characterized by a very high level of public support for European integration. This was shown especially in the referendum on joining the EU, when accession into the EU was confirmed by a "plebiscitary majority" (almost 90%) of Slovenians.[25]

The Slovenian political system is thereby marked by the absence of any (real) Eurosceptic parties. In this way only a few parties tried to take advantage of the gap between the EU-supportive politics of practically all parliamentary parties and that part of the public which has not been in favour of the EU; one such party has already been mentioned, the Slovenian National Party, represented in the National Assembly until early elections in 2011. Two small, non-parliamentary parties, New Party and Democratic Party of Slovenia, have also been critical of EU accession. Some minor efforts to mobilize the electorate on this had been seen in the Slovenian National Party and in the New Party already in 1996, but the question became more salient in the next few years and especially at the 2000 parliamentary elections. However, they were neither very extremist nor successful, whereas the Slovenian National Party even softened its position and described itself as "Eurorealist". At the 2000 parliamentary elections[26] both parties together attracted only 5.0% of the total vote (the first

23 See Danica Fink-Hafner and Damjan Lajh, "Lessons from Managing Conflict Situations in the EU Accession Negotiations: the Case of Slovenia," in *Central European Political Science Review,* Vol. 5, No. 15 (2004), pp. 52–73.

24 Fink-Hafner and Lajh, *Proces evropeizacije in prilagajanje političnih ustanov na nacionalni ravni* [note 19], p. 56.

25 See Alenka Krašovec and Damjan Lajh, "The Slovenian EU Accession Referendum: A Cat-and-Mouse Game," in *West European Politics,* Vol. 27, No. 4 (2004), pp. 603–623; and Danica Fink-Hafner and Damjan Lajh, *The 2008 Slovenian EU Presidency: A New Synergy for Europe?* (Stockholm: SIEPS, 2008), p. 24.

26 Pretty much the same situation can be observed at the first elections to the European Parliament held in June 2004, where the campaign was again marked by a lack of any Eurosceptic parties. The only two parties that were not in favour of full membership (they called them-

one received just 0.6% while the second one won 4.4%).[27] Therefore, Eurosceptic standpoints in Slovenia have (at least so far) not been rewarded by the electorate.

Directly prior to the onset of Slovenia's full EU membership, there were two important adaptations of the political system which have to be mentioned here: first, the amendments to the Slovenian Constitution in 2003,[28] which set down the relationships between the national political system and the EU political system by allowing the delegation of execution of a part of sovereign rights to international organizations; and second, in late March 2004, a more detailed legislative definition of the relationships between the National Assembly and the Government as regards the decision-making on EU affairs, adopted in March 2004.[29] This arrangement defines the executive as the agent representing and arguing for the positions of the Republic of Slovenia in the EU institutions, whereas the National Assembly cooperates in the formulation of the standpoints of Slovenia on EU matters, which would fall under its jurisdiction according to their substance, Slovenian Constitution and the law.[30] Fink-Hafner and Lajh[31] maintain that Slovenian experience of Europeanization effects on the national political system confirm the thesis that, with European integration, national institutions, processes, traditions and politico-cultural context rather undergo gradual adaptation than experience radical change. Therefore, in general, it can be argued that the adaptation of the Slovenian political system to European integration has been predominantly pragmatic and flexible. This means that during the phase of entering the EU (i.e., the pre-accession period

---

selves "Eurorealist" rather than Eurosceptic parties) – the (parliamentary) Slovenian National Party and the (non-parliamentary) Democratic Party of Slovenia – together received just 5.3% of votes.

27 Alenka Krašovec and Damjan Lajh, "Specialisti za zadeve Evropske unije in njihova vloga v volilnih procesih," in Alenka Krašovec (ed.), *Volitve v Evropski parlament 2009* (Ljubljana: Fakulteta za družbene vede, 2010), pp. 117–140.

28 The constitutional amendment, represented by Article 3.a, allows for the delegation of execution of a part of sovereign rights to international organizations, provided that: a) these international organizations are based on the observation of human rights and fundamental freedoms, democracy and the rule of law; and b) that the international treaty which sets down this delegation is ratified by the National Assembly of the Republic of Slovenia by a two-thirds majority vote (see Constitutional Act amending Chapter 1 and Articles 47 and 68 of the Constitution of the Republic of Slovenia, *Official Gazette of the Republic of Slovenia*, No. 24/2003).

29 See Act on Cooperation between the National Assembly and the Government in EU Affairs (*Official Gazette of the Republic of Slovenia*, No. 34/2004, No. 43/2010, No. 107/2010).

30 For a more detailed analysis of the aforementioned political system adaptations see Fink-Hafner and Lajh, *Proces evropeizacije in prilagajanje političnih ustanov na nacionalni ravni* [note 19], pp. 82–86.

31 *Ibid.*

and the time of negotiations) Slovenia established an institutional structure which adjusted to the adoption of the EU *acquis* and the common EU policies, while in the period of full membership it had to rearrange its institutional setup to meet the demands of the processes of formulating common EU policies.[32]

Challenges of the full membership in the EU

The first decade of Slovenia's membership in the EU can be divided into two parts. The first part was marked by a lot of EU-enthusiasm and includes a clear vision of Slovenian goals within the EU: the adoption of the common currency the *Euro*, entry into the Schengen Area, and holding the Presidency to the Council of the EU. The second part involved the emergence of a financial and economic crisis, which hit Slovenia particularly hard, accompanied by the absence of a clear strategic orientation concerning Slovenia's position, role and interests within the EU. Generally speaking, one of the main challenges throughout the whole decade has been its small public administration, which has been encountering a lack of EU cadres for purposes of fully and efficiently taking part in EU policymaking processes.[33] Additionally, it is worth mentioning that an important part of this EU cadre has moved either to EU institutions or to the Permanent Representation of the Republic of Slovenia at the EU in Brussels.

First half of the first decade in the EU: graduation performed with distinction brought "awards" for the best student in the class

Among the post-socialist states that joined the EU in 2004, Slovenia was one of the most EU-enthusiastic countries and at the same time it was also perceived as a "good pupil" in the socialization processes.[34] For this reason, as a kind of "reward", Slovenia was the first newcomer allowed to adopt the Euro, and to assume the presidency over the Council of the EU. These – along with the entry

32 Danica Fink-Hafner, "Europeanization in Managing EU Affairs: Between Divergence and Convergence, a Comparative Study of Estonia, Hungary and Slovenia," in *Public Administration*, Vol. 85, No. 3 (2007), pp. 805–828.

33 Fink-Hafner and Lajh, *Proces evropeizacije in prilagajanje političnih ustanov na nacionalni ravni* [note 6], p. 92; Fink-Hafner, "Europeanization in Managing EU Affairs" [note 32], pp. 805–828; and Krašovec and Lajh, "Specialisti za zadeve" [note 27], pp. 117–140.

34 Damjan Lajh, "The executive co-ordination of the Slovenian EU Presidency: an honest broker," in Petr Drulák and Zlatko Šabič (eds.), *The Czech and Slovenian EU Presidencies in a comparative perspective* (Dordrecht: Republic of Letters Publishing, 2010), p. 111.

into the Schengen Area – were also the most important policy changes,[35] accomplished after the entry into the EU when viewed from the citizens' point of view. Upon its accession to the EU in May 2004, Slovenia also entered the Economic and Monetary Union (the EMU).[36] Two and a half years later, after having met all the Maastricht convergence criteria, Slovenia became the thirteenth Eurozone Member State on 1 January 2007, and the first new (post-socialist) EU Member State to adopt the Euro. In this manner, Slovenia ceded its sovereignty in monetary and currency exchange rate policy to the supranational level.[37] Prior to the introduction of the Euro, Slovenian citizens had had the greatest knowledge of the common European currency when compared with citizens of other then-new EU Member States[38] and also displayed a high degree of trust in it. According to the Political Barometer survey, undertaken in March 2007,[39] which occurred practically simultaneously with the introduction of the euro, the common European currency was trusted by 61% of respondents, which was also the highest recorded degree of trust in any institution of the system. More than five years later, in December 2013,[40] the common European currency was still trusted by 35% of survey respondents. Obviously, the trust of Slovenian citizens decreased between the introduction of the Euro and the end of 2013; yet it remained relatively high compared to the degrees of trust in other institutions of the system.[41] Interestingly, Slovenian citizens have expressed a higher degree of trust in the Euro than in the EU: in March 2007,

---

35 Like other states, Slovenia is a "Europeanization hybrid", as Europeanization has varying degrees of influence on individual public policies. Clearly, the extent of this influence is primarily dependent upon the characteristics of the policy field in question: its arrangement at the supranational level in terms of the extent of nation-states' ceding of sovereignty to the supranational level and the resulting existence of legally (non-)binding legislation in a certain field ("hard" versus "soft" law). However, in this chapter we do not focus to individual policy fields (for more about that, see Sabina Kajnč and Damjan Lajh (eds.), *Evropska unija od A do Ž* (Ljubljana: Uradni list RS, 2009).

36 Accession to the EMU is compulsory for new EU Member States, which obviously includes Slovenia. On their entry to the EU, these states committed themselves to adopting the common European currency when they were ready, i.e. when they met the Maastricht convergence criteria (for a more detailed account of these criteria see Vladimir Lavrač, "Ekonomska in monetarna unija," in Kajnč and Lajh (eds.), *Evropska unija od A do Ž* [note 35], pp. 52–53.).

37 *Ibid.,* pp. 52–53.

38 See Flash Eurobarometer 191. Introduction of the Euro in the New Member States Analytical Report. European Commission.

39 CJMMK, Politbarometer 03/2007 (Ljubljana, 2007).

40 CJMMK, Politbarometer 11/2013 (Ljubljana, 2013).

41 According to the "Politbarometer" public opinion poll, in December 2013, Slovenian citizens included in the survey expressed the same trust as in the euro only to the President of the Republic of Slovenia, while the trust to all other institutions of the system has been lower,

the EU was trusted by 40% of respondents,[42] whereas in December 2013, the respective share was 19%.[43]

If the year 2007 began with the introduction of the common European currency for Slovenia, it ended with the accession to the vast area within the EU that has no internal borders: on 21st December 2007 Slovenia became a part of the Schengen Area. This meant the abolition of border control on internal borders of Schengen Member States (in the case of Slovenia, on the borders with Italy, Austria, and Hungary). At the same time, accompanying measures were introduced to enable the abolition of internal border controls, especially those concerning cooperation in the fields of police and justice relating to criminal affairs. For Slovenia, admission to the EU also brought about the obligation to set up an appropriate EU regime on its external border (the Slovenian border with Croatia represents a segment of the EU's external border), meaning that Slovenian customs and inspection bodies have been performing customs, veterinary and phytosanitary controls for all EU Member States since Slovenia's accession to the EU.[44]

In the first half of 2008, Slovenia held the Presidency to the Council of the EU. The Slovenian Presidency represented a symbolic peak in the country's social and political transformation. Indeed, for a country such as Slovenia, which for a long time had lived within the borders of several multinational states along with other predominant nations, holding the EU Presidency meant a qualitative challenge to the mainstream collective psychology of such a small nation.[45] As the first former socialist country and also the first Slavic country to hold the Presidency, it had to respond constructively to certain prejudices and doubts about its ability to deal with this exposed and important position at the EU level and in global international relations. For this reason, and due to various other challenges during its term in the Presidency, Slovenia behaved cautiously, making sure that EU policy-making processes ran smoothly and in a problem-free way.[46] Nonetheless, at the very start of its term in the Presidency, some parts of the minutes of the talks between Slovenian and American diplomats were published in the Slovenian newspaper *Dnevnik,* giving rise to controversy. The article, entitled "Slovenia receives a secret list of demands for its

---

including for example health care, the education system and the media (CJMMK, Politbarometer 11/2013 (Ljubljana, 2013)).

42 CJMMK, Politbarometer 03/2007 (Ljubljana, 2007).

43 CJMMK, Politbarometer 11/2013 (Ljubljana, 2013).

44 Radica Nusdorfer, "Območje svobode, varnosti in pravice," in Kajnč and Lajh (eds.), *Evropska unija od A do Ž* [note 35], p. 258.

45 Fink-Hafner and Lajh, *The 2008 Slovenian EU Presidency* [note 25], p. 6.

46 *Ibid.*, pp. 10–11.

Presidency to the Council from the US", published parts of documents containing the latest information, statements and assessments of diplomats that had not been intended to be seen by the public, but which had been intended to serve as the basis for the direction and political decisions of Slovenia. Although with some exceptions this diplomatic awkwardness did not attract significant attention abroad, it did spark controversial debates in Slovenia,[47] while at the same time revealing the weaknesses of Slovenia's lack of experience in diplomacy that later on also appeared several times.[48] All in all, we can claim that Slovenia took on the fairly "traditional role" of a small country holding the EU presidency, managing "a good presidency" for the EU, whereas it probably deserves also some criticism for "being shy".[49] Last but not least, it must be mentioned that, during its Presidency, Slovenia strongly represented its "natural linkage" to the post-Yugoslav region by fulfilling the "genuine" Slovenian priority within the framework of the European perspective on the Western Balkans.

Financial crisis and missing identity within the EU

After being the most economically developed post-socialist country in Central and South-eastern Europe, during the last few years Slovenia transformed into a seriously indebted country, with economic stagnation, increasing unemployment, and a very deprived banking sector.[50] While the pre-accession period had provided strict guidance and a blueprint for systemic reforms, Slovenia failed to impose enough initiative and self-discipline in its "adolescent" post-accession period.[51] Although Slovenia was the fastest growing Eurozone member, in 2009 its export-driven economy was badly hit by the global financial crisis and

47 Damjan Lajh, "Slovenia", in Lisa Mootz (ed.), *Nations in transit 2009: democratization from Central Europe to Eurasia* (New York and Budapest: Freedom House, 2009), p. 489.

48 The most recent diplomatic scandal emerged in July 2015 as part of the Slovenian–Croatian border arbitration process, after the Croatian newspaper *Večernji list* published excerpts from a leaked tape in which Slovenian judge Jernej Sekolec discussed the case, the probable outcomes and strategy with Simona Drenik, who represented Slovenia's Foreign Ministry before the court.

49 Fink-Hafner and Lajh, *The 2008 Slovenian EU Presidency* [note 25], p. 64.

50 Damjan Lajh, "Slovenia", in Sylvana Habdank-Kolaczkowska (ed.), *Nations in transit 2013: democratization from Central Europe to Eurasia* (Budapest and Lanham, Md.: Freedom House and Rowman & Littlefield, 2014), pp. 535–552.

51 Anže Burger and Andreja Jaklič, "Economic policies and development of the Slovenian economy after EU accession", in Damjan Lajh and Zdravko Petak (eds.), *EU public policies seen from a national perspective: Slovenia and Croatia in the European Union* (Ljubljana: Faculty of Social Sciences, 2015), *passim*.

shrank by 8%.[52] Access to financial resources for the state thus became limited, whereas in the banking system, the deterioration of assets at home and abroad continued. At the end of 2013, results from the banking stress tests were presented, which showed a capital shortfall of eight banks in the amount of 4.7 billion Euros. Slovenia's public debt has been rising just as steeply, which is still well below the average of the Eurozone and the EU, although it has already exceeded 60% of GDP, which is the upper limit set by the European budgetary rules of the Stability and Growth Pact.[53] Yet despite poor public finance conditions and ever increasing public borrowing, Slovenia, too, had to issue financial guarantees to states in greater financial distress (i.e. Greece, Ireland and Portugal) so as to help with the provision of financial stability across the entire Eurozone. This, of course, sparked a lot of criticism among Slovenian citizens.

In March 2012, the countries of the Eurozone agreed to adopt a so-called "fiscal rule," an agreement under which participating countries' expenditures should not exceed their revenues. In the same year the government wanted to inscribe the rule into the Constitution in order to send a strong signal to international financial markets that Slovenia was taking serious measures to counter the financial crisis, but the motion was blocked by the opposition, weakening international confidence in Slovenia's economy. At the end of May 2013, after long efforts at reconciliations and numerous difficulties in finding the necessary two-thirds majority, deputies of the National Assembly finally confirmed the introduction of a fiscal rule in the Constitution.[54] After the adoption of several structural reforms in 2015, Slovenia again recorded positive economic growth.

During the most recent years, it seems that Slovenia has been missing a clear strategic orientation of its position, role and interests. After achieving its major goal – full membership in the EU, and three sub-goals – adoption of the Euro, entry into the Schengen zone and fairly holding the Presidency of the EU, the future direction of functioning within the EU became undefined. In EU policymaking, Slovenia plays a rather passive role, in the majority of cases just following Commission proposals. The same situation can be observed in the slow and unsuccessful implementation of EU legislation. For instance, the introduction of stricter environmental standards imposes certain implementation costs and (consequently) implementation deficit(s) on EU Member States.

52 "Izvoz poganja okrevanje Slovenije po krizi", *Izvozno okno* (17 March 2011), at http://www.izvoznookno.si/Teme_tedna/Izvoz_poganja_okrevanje_Slovenije_po_krizi_14798.aspx [last accessed on 23 August 2015].

53 Damjan Lajh, "Slovenia", in Sylvana Habdank-Kolaczkowska and Zselyke Csaky (eds.), *Nations in transit 2014: democratization from Central Europe to Eurasia* (Budapest and Lanham, Md.: Freedom House and Rowman & Littlefield, 2015), pp. 589–590.

54 Lajh, "Slovenia" [note 50], p. 540.

In this respect, the European Commission has filed several lawsuits before the Court of Justice of the EU against Slovenia, because of its non-compliance with environmental legislation.[55] In March 2009, Slovenia was for the first time faced with charges before the Court of Justice of the EU in Luxembourg, because it had failed to transpose a directive on environmental liability to its national legislation by the specified deadline. As an interesting fact, for the first time in the history of the Court the original judgement was written in Slovenian and the language of the proceedings was Slovenian. In the beginning of 2014 the European Commission again took Slovenia to Court for its failure to comply with the requirements of EU waste legislation. The Commission's concerns related to two illegal landfills containing hazardous waste, one near the centre of Celje, and another in nearby Bukovžlak. Although Slovenia had agreed to address the problem, the slow progress led the Commission to call Slovenia before the Court.[56] In July 2015 the Court upheld the Commission's file against Slovenia.

Finally, the general public sometimes might also get the impression that the only interest the political elite (or one part of it) has in EU politics is well-paid jobs at the EU level; this confirms for example the struggle for the Commissioner post in 20014 or in-party rivalry for the best position at the party lists for elections to the European Parliament. For this reason, it is not surprising that, ten years later, the trust of Slovenian citizens in European integration has started decreasing markedly. While, in March 2007, the EU was trusted by 40% of respondents, in June 2014 the corresponding share dropped to 19%. However, although the trust of Slovenian citizens in the EU decreased, it still remained relatively high compared to the degrees of trust in some other institutions of the system: for example, according to the same opinion poll the government is trusted only by 4%, the National Assembly only by 2%, and political parties only by 1% of respondents. While a "plebiscitary majority" expressed satisfaction with that development on joining the EU in 2003, ten years later only 44% of respondents said that they would vote again for Slovenian accession to the EU now, while 43% of respondents would vote against accession.

Over the last quarter of a century, the EU has undoubtedly played an important role in the formation of the young Slovenian state. It intervened into

55 See, e.g., Case C-49/10: 29 January 2010 – European Commission v Republic of Slovenia; Case C-365/10: Action brought on 22 July 2010 – European Commission v Republic of Slovenia.

56 See the *European Commission Press Release*: "Environment: European Commission takes Slovenia to Court for pollution problems from waste disposal" (Brussels, 23 January 2014), at http://europa.eu/rapid/press-release_IP-14-51_en.htm [last accessed on 23 August 2015].

the operation of the latter's political system as well as into the regulation of individual policy domains. Slovenia has become a capitalist economy with a political system ever-more integrated into EU politics. However, at the same time it has moved from the position of a socio-economic leader in the Balkan region (part of the "Second World") with a rather high level of westernization, toward a peripheral position within the "First World" (the EU) in economic and political terms. In this way, Slovenia has had to re-define both its relations with its former domestic region (the post-Yugoslav region), and, as a newly-established independent state, has also had to search for its space within the EU political system as well as in broader international relations.

However, since the process of Europeanization does not merely flow one-way, the EU, in turn, has itself significantly changed and is now certainly not the same regional association that it used to be in the late 1980s and early 1990s. These changes have undoubtedly been profoundly influenced by the accession of thirteen new (mostly post-socialist) states to the integration and the developments in global economic markets at the beginning of the 21st century.

Conclusion

Despite being small countries on the margins of Europe, Norway and Slovenia have remarkably different relationships with the European Union. On the one hand, the Norwegian people (if not always their elites) have maintained a steady dose of euro-skepticism for over 40 years. In the doing, Norwegians have underscored their desire to maintain sovereign and democratic institutions, even under the threat of significant economic costs. Those threats proved to be exaggerated, and the Norwegian economy has surely not suffered from staying outside the European Union. The Norwegian oil-based economy is on a different trajectory from the rest of Europe's, and the lure of a future union has shrunk along with the reputation of the European Union and its crisis-prone euro.

The situation in Slovenia is almost the inverse: the country has embraced the European Union and its Eurozone with gusto. EU membership offered Slovenia an opportunity for rapid political and economic transition to development, and the EU has played a significant role in influencing the nature of contemporary Slovenia and its politics. As a result, there has been strong and wide-spread support for Slovenia's strong relationship to the European Union. Although faith in European solutions has been challenged by recent developments, the country's fate is now clearly linked with developments in Brussels.

Torbjørn L. Knutsen and Zlatko Šabič

13 Norwegian and Slovenian Foreign Policy

They praise his seamanship and navigation and knowledge of the sea…
[But] they have no idea that the true navigator must study the seasons of the year,
the sky, the stars, the winds and all the other subjects
appropriate to his profession if he is to be really fit to control a ship…
Plato, *The Republic*

Introduction

Foreign policy is concerned with relationships between a sovereign state and actors external to it – in particular other states. To more fully appreciate the nature of foreign policy it is useful to recall, first, that all states are sovereign and stationary actors.[1] Second, there is a distinction between Foreign Policy and International Relations: whereas Foreign Policy tends to concern individual states, International Relations concerns the entire international system.

No two states are alike. States differ vastly in terms of size, wealth, climate, culture, governance and governability. This enormous variance, together with the habit of scholars to focus on the behaviour of specific countries, is a challenge for comparative foreign-policy analyses. Is there a way to make a comparative study of two countries that differ so widely in size, wealth, location and history as Slovenia and Norway? Yes, the best way to approach such a comparison is to identify a few general features – a few core concerns – that preoccupy virtually all countries in their daily foreign-policy practice. This chapter proceeds from the assumption that there are at least four concerns that preoccupy virtually all governments as they seek to navigate their ships of state through the currents, shoals and eddies of the international system:[2] security,

1 International law defines "a"state" in terms of three properties: A) a demarcated territory B) a sizable group of permanent inhabitants and C) an effective government. A fourth property is usually added: D) recognition by other states in the international system. Again, it is useful to recall that states are stationary in the sense that they occupy a closely defined area of the earth's geography, and that they are sovereign in the sense they the exercise authority over the people who inhabit that area and over the resources with which the area is endowed.

2 The allusion to the state as a ship and foreign policy as maritime navigation, is first elaborated in Plato's *Republic* – see esp. book VII, chapter 3.

welfare, autonomy, and the prestige of the state.[3] Various states might emphasize these concerns differently – some states may be more concerned with only one or two of them;[4] others may supplement these four basic concerns with other preoccupations.[5] But security, welfare, autonomy, and prestige are the most basic and most sustained foreign-policy goals of modern governments.

This chapter will discuss the foreign policy of Norway and Slovenia along these four basic goals. Such a systematic discussion will allow these two countries to be readily compared. However, in order to make a systematic comparison, it is necessary to substantiate these four goals:

Security refers to a state's ability to defend its territory and survive as a unit in the international community of states. This is often described as a country's "defence policy" or "security policy". Virtually all states maintain military forces and commit some proportion of their national wealth to maintain internal and external security forces.

Welfare refers to a state's ability to take care of its citizens – to provide employment and a sound economic base for the nation. It involves the ability to manage the resources with which its territory and its inhabitants are endowed, put them to a productive use, ensure a reasonable rate of economic growth and engage in trade with other nations. An important task for every government is to find a proper role for the country in the international division of labour. This activity, then, is often referred to as a country's "trade policy".

Autonomy refers to a state's ability to shape its own destiny – to freely formulate its own political goals and define political priorities. All governments strive to command the destiny of their respective countries. They guard the sovereignty and the independence of the state. They seek to ensure that political decisions are made by actors and institutions internal to the nation and to prevent procedures of key political decision-making from being lost to external actors.

Prestige refers to the state's international reputation. It involves the ways in which other states perceive the state – the degree to which other states respect it or hold it in high regard. This is sometimes referred to as a country's "cultural policy", although prestige involves much more than traditional culture. This

3 Ole Holsti, (1992) *International Politics*. Englewood Cliffs, N.J.: Prentice-Hall

4 Costa Rica and Iceland seem to be no longer concerned with security, as they no longer have military forces of their own.

5 States which rank other goals above the four basic goals of security, welfare, autonomy and prestige are often in a particular predicament, Thus, the island-state of the Maldives is particularly concerned with global warming because an increase of the ocean level would threaten the very existence of the state,

aspect of a country's foreign policy is more important than commonly perceived.

Norway and Slovenia are small, European states – Norway is a country of about five million inhabitants; Slovenia of about two.[6] Both were long members of larger unions – Norway was an integrated part of Denmark for several centuries, while Slovenia was part of the Habsburg Empire; Norway was joined in a union with Sweden many decades prior to independence, while Slovenia was part of the Socialist Federated Republic of Yugoslavia (SFRY). Both are relatively new states; but both have had a growing sense of separate nationhood within their respective unions before becoming sovereign states – Norway in 1905, Slovenia in 1991.

There are many similarities between these two countries. But there are also profound differences. To identify the similarities and differences of foreign policy and begin to explain them, it is necessary first to identity their foreign-policy outlooks and trajectories. This chapter will first do this along the four major foreign-policy goals of security, welfare, autonomy, and prestige. It will then identify some of the major differences and chart some of the key similarities of the foreign policies of the two countries.

Norway's Foreign Policy Tradition

Only sovereign states have a foreign policy, in the strict sense of the term. Thus, Norway had no foreign policy during early modern history, as it was an integral part of Denmark. In the wake of the Napoleonic wars, the Great Powers of Europe broke Norway loose from Denmark, and transferred it to Sweden – to punish Denmark and reward Sweden for their respective roles in the war against Napoleon.

Historical Background

In spring of 1814, a few weeks before Norway was transferred to Sweden, Norwegian politicians formed a constitutional assembly and an independent legislature (the Storting). When the transfer took place, both the new Norwegian constitution and the legislature were accepted by the Swedish king.

6 It may be added that Slovenia's territorial area is slightly over 20,000 km^2, whereas Norway's is well over 15 times larger (about 325,000 km^2). The differences in population density is, in other words, significant. Slovenia is a maritime nation, with direct access to the Mediterranean Sea. The length of its coastline is about 47 km. By contrast, Norway commands a maritime area which is 7 times larger than the size of its mainland, emphasizing its maritime character.

Because of this acceptance, Norway and Sweden were joined in a personal union by the fact of having a common monarch.[7]

With a constitution of its own, Norway was, for all practical purposes, a self-governing country. The major exception was in matters concerning diplomacy and security affairs; such matters were decided by a circle of ministers around the king in Stockholm. Thus, although Norway was granted self-rule in domestic matters, it could make no dispositions in foreign affairs. During the entire 19th century, then, Norway was not a sovereign state. It had no independent foreign policy.

This changed in 1905. In the wake of international changes that originated with Russia's defeat in the war against Japan, the Norwegian Storting broke with the Swedish monarch and proclaimed Norway a sovereign and independent state. The Norwegian Storting, then, appointed a government which immediately launched several foreign-policy initiatives: First, it appointed a foreign minister and began to establish a ministry of foreign affairs. Second, it initiated negotiations with the Swedish authorities in order to prevent the tense situation between the two countries from erupting into war. Third, it began a diplomatic process to gain recognition from the Great Powers of Europe. And, fourth, it began to search for a new head of state – a new king for Norway's vacant throne.

The government appointed Jørgen Løvland as the Norway's first Foreign Minister in the late summer of 1905. Løvland's first task was to placate the Swedish authorities and establish a truce. His second task was to make a speech to the Storting, and propose the basic principles for an independent foreign policy. This speech is important for several reasons. The first of these is its analysis, which established Norway's basic foreign policy course: viz., that Norway ought to trade with all, but establish military alliances with none. The proposal was partly a continuation of an established foreign-policy orientation. But it was also based on the common recognition that maritime trade was the foundation of Norway's national wealth and welfare,[8] and that this trade was predicated on friendly relations with Great Britain, the primary maritime power of the age.[9]

---

7 Norway's union with Sweden after 1814 was thus very different from the tight, political union with Denmark before 1814.

8 Around 1905, Norway was the third largest shipping nation of the world, after Britain and France.

9 Roald Berg, (1995) *Norge på egen hånd.* Oslo: Universitetsforlaget; and Trond Bergh, Even Lange and Helge Pharo (1983) *Norge fra u-land til i-land. Vekst og utviklingslinjer 1830-1980.* Oslo: Gyldendal norsk forlag, pp. 106ff.

Løvland's speech was whole-heartedly supported by the members of the Storting at the time. His analysis was widely shared. And it provided a stable keel for Norwegian foreign policy for the decades that followed.

Løvland and his colleagues were much concerned with making Norway an economically viable state. Concerns of shipping and trade were foremost in their minds when they set out to perform their other important task in the summer and fall of 1905: inviting the Great Powers of Europe to recognize Norway as a sovereign monarchy.

When the Norwegians broke with the Swedish king, they agreed that it would be unwise to proclaim Norway a republic; for, if they did this, the monarchs of Europe would perceive the proclamation of sovereignty as an affront and might not recognize the new state. It was especially important to gain recognition from Great Britain, upon whose goodwill Norway depended for both security and welfare. So those who privately favoured a republic form of government kept wisely mum, and the Storting proudly proclaimed Norway a monarchy.

When the Norwegian Storting searched for a royal prince who was free and willing to assume the vacant throne, their eyes immediately fell on Crown Prince Carl of Denmark. He would be a good choice, not only because he was close at hand and familiar with Scandinavian politics, but also because he was married to Maud Charlotte Mary Victoria, Princess of Wales – the youngest daughter of the British king Edward VII. When Crown Prince Carl accepted the Norwegian invitation to become King of Norway (and assumed the name Haakon VII), his wife Maud became Norway's new queen.

Security

Thus, an important dynastic link was established between Norway and Great Britain. This eased British recognition and cemented the British goodwill Norway needed to carry out its lucrative shipping business.

In 1905, Norway was a liberal trading state. Its concern for welfare and security were tightly interconnected. Great Britain was not only one of Norway's most important trading partners, its Royal Navy was also the preeminent master of the world's oceans, upon which Norwegian vessels sailed and upon which Norway's national economy so crucially depended. Norway's security polity was designed to protect the trade and the merchant fleet whose vessels earned foreign exchange for the new nation. Ensuring peace and order on the seven seas would provide conditions for maximizing trade. War was seen as a destructive intrusion and in violation of Norwegian national interests.

Thus, it was reasonable to base Norway's foreign policy orientation on the principles of neutrality in peace time and non-alignment in times of war.[10]

When the conditions of world affairs changed, however, this doctrine proved hard to maintain. When World War One broke out in 1914, it soon became evident that it was nigh-impossible for Norway to conduct a neutral foreign policy and at the same time be on good terms with Britain. Norway was invariably pulled towards favouring Britain, upon whose goodwill Norway's national interests so tightly depended.

As a response to the untenable situation, Norway seized an opportunity that presented itself in the wake of the war, basing its security policy on the new principle of collective security: In 1921, Norway joined the League of Nations. This Norwegian move meant the end to the policy of neutrality, as collective security is inconsistent with one based on neutrality.

In the longer run, however, the League of Nations did not live up to its promise. The League grew paralyzed by increasing great-power rivalries and could provide no security to its members. This became apparent when it could not contain the expansionist policies of Italy, Japan and Germany. Norway, together with several other small European states, began to re-think their association with the League. In the early fall of 1939, Nazi Germany struck the sparks which caused war to flare up in Europe once more. In the spring of 1940, Germany brought the war to North-Western Europe by invading several countries. Norway was among them. King Haakon and members of the Storting and the Cabinet fled to Great Britain. They established a government-in-exile in London and joined the wartime alliance against Nazi-Germany.

This established a second and most important dimension in Norway's foreign policy: a security policy based on membership in a wartime alliance of North-Atlantic sea powers. As Britain was exhausted by the war, the alliance was led by the United States. US President Franklin D. Roosevelt called the alliance "The United Nations". As the war approached its end, Roosevelt insisted that its cooperative spirit must continue beyond the war effort and be preserved in an international organization designed to establish and preserve a peaceful world according the principle of collective security. "The United Nations Organization" (UN) was established in 1944 and began its work in 1945. Norway was a staunch supporter of the UN from the very beginning.

The Cold War dashed all hopes of an efficient UN. The superpower rivalry between the USA and the USSR undermined the efficiency of the new organization and destroyed its hopes for a peace based on the principle of collective security. The first Norwegian reaction to the onset of the Cold War was to try to mediate between the rival superpowers. Norway's policy of "bridge-building"

10 Olav Riste, (2001) *Norway's Foreign Relations*. Oslo: Universitetsforlaget:75ff)

did not last long. In 1949 Norway cast its lot in with Great Britain and other north Atlantic powers, signed a common defence treaty, and joined in setting up The North Atlantic Treaty Organization (NATO), a military alliance dominated and led by a nuclear-armed United States.[11]

Since 1949, Norway's security-policy has been established on two legs: first a diplomatic leg, where Norway continues to rely on the principle of collective security, which is most conspicuously present in Norway's active support of the UN. This policy is designed to maintain a world order that is governed by liberal values and principles that are similar to Norway's own. It involves diplomatic efforts to establish norms and rules of international conduct and specify them in international law.

Second, Norway has based its security on a military leg, expressed in its NATO membership. The main purpose of NATO originally was to contain the Soviet threat – by a policy based on a fine balance and assurance and deterrence. In the years following the break-up of the Soviet Union, NATO altered its nature from being a military alliance to becoming an armed organization of collective security. Since the end of the Cold War, Norway has worked to reshape NATO into an important force of order in the world, and to actively participate in NATO operations in several corners of the world.[12]

Welfare – Production and Trade

Norway has a long tradition of seafaring and trade. It is often noted that Norway has a long history as a poor country. Yet, the Norwegian economy developed rapidly while the country was part of the union with Sweden. And this rapid development was an important reason why the union burst asunder in 1905. Economic growth began in earnest during the 1840s, after the British Parliament replaced its old protectionist Navigation Acts with a doctrine of free trade. This change opened up vast, new possibilities of maritime trade for Norwegian shipping, and within the next few decades Norway emerged as one of the major seafaring nations of the world. Economically, this boosted Norway's wealth and welfare. Politically, it pulled Norway into an orbit around Great Britain – at a time when Sweden was industrializing and tying faster contacts with the European Continent to the south, Norway was pulled westwards. Culturally, Norway's integration into a British-dominated world-economy stimulated the import of impulses from Britain and the British Empire. It also triggered some nationalist reactions at home.

11 (*ibid.*:202ff)

12 See Gjert Lage Dyndal and Torbjørn L. Knutsen, eds., (2012) *Exit Afghanistan*. Oslo: Universitetsforlaget

The second half of the 18th century, then, set Norway on a path as an emerging trading state with an open economy. Its growing merchant marine sustained an expanding economy, based in exports of goods and services. The greatest stimulus was initially provided by services; in particular by shipping. Norway's growing merchant fleet brought home an expanding income which allowed the Norwegians to make important investments at home. Over time, the nation developed industries which could exploit the natural resources of the land for the purposes of domestic consumption and foreign trade. The resources were first and foremost taken from the forests and from the ocean – ore, timber, wood and wood products on the one hand; fish and fish products on the other.

In addition, Norway's unique combination of mountains, fresh-water lakes, and rivers allowed the country to build hydroelectric plants and extract the energy of streams and water falls. This gave Norway a comparative advantage in the international division of labour: it enabled Norway to produce hydroelectric power at competitive prices, thus enabling the country to establish a service to industrialized countries of the West: smelting. Gigantic electrical ovens were built by several of Norway's deep-water harbours, to which foreign ships would come with ore and leave with metal ingots.

Long before its discovery of oil, then, Norway had evolved an industrial economy based on specialized services, international shipping, advanced technologies and pragmatic techniques of governance. When Norway began to extract and refine oil and gas during the 1970s, the nation's industry could draw on a skilled labour force, on technological know-how and a long tradition of centrally-planned industrial management.

Norway has in recent years become one of the world's largest exporters of fossil fuels – over 40% of its exports being crude petroleum and about 15% being gas. Thanks to these exports, Norway has enjoyed steadily growing surpluses on its trade balance with the outside world. As a result, Norway has become a very wealthy country – with a GDP per capita of about $65,000 (in 2013), according to the World Bank.

This wealth, it is important to add, is not the outcome of oil alone; it is the result of a political economy that has long emphasized the importance of robust social institutions and rational long-term planning. It is important to recall, that although the Norwegian petroleum sector yields an enormous income, very little of this income is spent at home. More than 95% of the petroleum profits are put into savings – or rather invested in global stocks and bonds. These investments – managed by the Government Pension Fund – represent values to the tune of over 700 billion USD and is the largest pension fund in the world. Petroleum profits, then, do not explain Norway's wealth. It does. However, explain why Norway is the largest stock holder in Europe, and why Norway, by virtue of its Pension Fund, wields more influence on Europe's financial sector than its modest number of inhabitants would otherwise suggest.

If petroleum does not explain the generous Norwegian welfare state, what does? High taxes do. The Norwegian welfare state is financed by citizens' taxes and tolls – which is to say that Norway finances its welfare state in the same way that other Scandinavian states finance their respective welfare states.[13] As a result Norway has some of the highest tax rates (and some of the highest prices) in the world. This is a price Norwegians pay for a radical policy of domestic redistribution of wealth.

Prestige

Norway's prestige is, like that of other countries, tied in with efforts to demonstrate to the world the good sides of Norwegian society and culture. The most immediately visible elements of a policy of prestige are associated with arts and sports. A cultural foreign policy involves a conscious broadcasting of the literature, the music and the images of the nation's most famous artists, e.g., though international festivals or world tours, displaying the works of Henrik Ibsen, Edvard Grieg and Edvard Munch. Less conspicuously, it involves the funding of sports – in the Norwegian case, winter sports are particularly important. The Olympic Winter Games in Lillehammer in 1994 may be seen as an element in a conscious policy of prestige.

But policies of prestige are also expressed in less obvious ways – through education, science and economic growth; through foreign aid and humanitarian activism. Norway is a highly developed and wealthy country. Norwegians are proud of the country's high rate of economic growth and level of welfare. They are also proud of the welfare state which redistributes wealth in ways that guarantee the citizens' material safety and security. And they are eager to display these achievements and the policy they represent. There is in Norwegian foreign policy a pronounced effort to display that policy and export social institutions which reflect it and which may recreate those achievements in other countries. Norway, in other words, has a policy of prestige that is intimately connected to the country's economic growth, technological progress, popular participation, the development and maintenance of a generous welfare state and with national pride.

This is apparent in a strong emphasis on humanitarian activism in Norwegian foreign policy. This emphasis has, since the mid-1990s, been more system-

13 Sweden and Denmark, Norway's social-democratic neighbours which have followed a similar policy of robust institutions and long-term planning but which do not export oil, have equally generous welfare states and are also among the world's most wealthy countries.

atically coordinated in the so-called "policy of engagement". Many Norwegians will perceive this activism as a moral obligation to assist victims of poverty, war and misfortune in the world. Norway has a long tradition of such activism, going back to nineteenth-century missionary work in countries in Africa and Asia. Relief- and refugee work was early established as an element of Norway's foreign policy, not the least through the relief work organized by Fridtjof Nansen in the wake of World War One on behalf of the League of Nations. After World War Two, such work of assistance, aid and relief was organized once more. Under the impact of the Cold War, such activities were pursued more systematically and evolved as elements in a broader policy of prestige – on behalf of the Norwegian nation as well as of the West in organizing their societies in liberal and democratic ways. Norway's long-standing activism in fronting liberal theories of peaceful interaction suited this development hand in glove.

Since the country gained independence in 1905, Norway's major prestige project has been to maintain an image as a nation of peace. The country has supported peace-projects run by the UN. It has also been engaged in unilateral initiatives towards conflict resolution and peace. The longest-lasting and the most visible of these prestige projects has been the annual award of the Nobel Peace Prize.

Autonomy

The question of autonomy is of concern for all nations. In Norway it has been a question of particular importance. Concerns for independence and autonomy have been deeply engrained in the Norwegian nation – perhaps because Norway obtained sovereign status comparatively late; perhaps because sovereignty was lost for five years of German occupation, perhaps because of pride in national achievement and confidence in Norway's corporate model, perhaps because of the nation's open economy which has made that model vulnerable to foreign influence… Regardless of the reason, Norwegian concerns for autonomy have been strong – so strong, at times, that it has been at loggerheads with other aspects of Norway's foreign policy and, at times, served to constrain the country's room for foreign-policy manoeuvre.

These constraints may be observed in an incongruity between Norway's internationalist rhetoric and the country's foreign-policy practice. On the one hand, Norway has traditionally fronted a rhetoric of internationalism – sometimes phrased as a liberal rhetoric of peace and free trade; sometimes as a radical rhetoric of international solidarity with those who are poor and disadvantaged. On the other, Norway has been reluctant to act upon this rhetoric and to engage in binding international relationships. This was evident when the

Norwegian Storting debated membership in the League of Nations in 1920 and objections were raised from radical parties on the left. Similar objections were raised on several occasions – in the mid- and late 1960s, in 1972 and in 1994 – when the prospect of Norway joining the European Community raised deep protests in many parts of Norwegian society.

On the one hand, then, Norway has conducted a foreign policy which has placed a heavy emphasis on peace and conflict resolution. On the other, Norway has refused to join one of the most significant peace projects in recent history: viz., the European project of cooperation and integration. The main reason for this refusal is not a distrust of the integration project as such – quite on the contrary, many Norwegians tend to praise the EU as a valuable force for stability and peace on the Continent (as the 2012 Nobel Peace-Prize award to EU suggests). However, the Norwegians fear for their autonomy – farmers fear that adjustments to EU rules will erode established arrangements of support and subsidies; fishermen fear that membership will open up for greater competition over dwindling stocks. Many Norwegians fear, in short, that EU membership will make it harder to maintain that complex web of regulatory arrangements that have buoyed the welfare, the social security and the egalitarianism of the nation. Besides, there may also be more than just a little national arrogance involved in Norway's attitude – a notion that whereas EU may alter European politics to the better, it may also change that of Norway to the worse.

Such debates about joining international partnerships have regularly provoked groups who argue that it is important to protect Norway's ability to shape its own destiny – to freely formulate its own political goals and define its own political priorities.[14]

Slovenia's Foreign Policy Tradition

Historical background

Slovenia proclaimed itself independent in the spring of 1991. Like Norway's, Slovenia's independence was the result of international changes brought about by upheavals in Russia. In the late 1980s, the weakening of the Soviet Empire had encouraged movements of (re-establishing) national independence all over Central and Eastern Europe. While one could argue that the idea about indepen-

14 See Torbjørn L. Knutsen, Gunnar M. Sørbø and Svein Gjerdåker, eds., (1997) *Norges utenrikspolitikk*. Oslo/Bergen: Aschehoug/CMI

dence of Slovenia is much older,[15] the history of actual independence begins in April 1990 when Slovenia, then still a part of the SFRY, held its first free elections for its own, independent government.

The elections were held in the context of a resentment against the federal government, which, dominated by the Serbian leadership, had drastically limited the influence of the six republics and autonomous provinces on the federal decision-making. On 23 December 1990, Slovenia held a referendum in which almost 90% of the voters (with a voter turnout of 93.5%) supported independence, which was declared on 25 June 1991. The Federal government reacted immediately and ordered the SFRY National Army to attack Slovenia in the vain hope of restoring both military and political control in the breakaway republic. The federal government gave up after 10 days. The so-called Brioni agreement ended the war on 7 July 1991, and *de facto* opened up the road for Slovenia to establish itself as an independent state. This agreement may be considered the first foreign policy success of Slovenia, although this was still the time when the foreign policy infrastructure was being built.

During the lifetime of Yugoslavia, the role of Slovenia in foreign policy decision-making gradually improved. From virtually no influence in the Kingdom of Yugoslavia, Slovenian diplomats wrote several important chapters in the history of SFRY. Edvard Kardelj, chief ideologist and a close associate of Yugoslav President Josip Broz Tito, was also an influential foreign policy strategist. Several Slovenian diplomats played a key role in formulating and implementing the positioning of Slovenia in the Non-Aligned Movement. Besides Kardelj, diplomats such as Aleš Bebler, Joža Vilfan, and Jože Brilej also played important roles. The 1974 Constitution afforded Slovenia, as one of the six constituent republics, relative independence in implementing foreign policy; the decision-making, however, rested with central authorities in Belgrade.

In 1991, then, as a newly independent state, with no history of sovereign statehood and limited experience in implementing foreign policy, Slovenia first had to establish its own foreign policy structure and institutions. This process had started before the declaration of independence. By that time, the then Assembly of the Republic of Slovenia had already published a document called

---

15 In particular, the so-called *Program zedinjene Slovenije* (the Programme of the United Slovenia) from 1848 called the Slovenians to use the momentum of the 'spring of nations' and press for greater autonomy within the Habsburg empire that would include the use of Slovenian as an official language and a substantial degree of self-governance, with its own "assembly". See Peter Štih,, Vasko Simoniti, and Peter Vodopivec. 2008. *Slovenska zgodovina: družba, politika, kultura*. Ljubljana: Inštitut za novejšo zgodovino, 269; see also Janko Prunk, 1999. *Kratka zgodovina Slovenije*. Ljubljana: Grad.

"Key Elements for a Foreign Policy Strategy of the Republic of Slovenia". That document included guidelines which narrowed down Slovenia's goals to basically two: first, to win universal recognition and, second, to join Euro-Atlantic institutions, notably the EU, as soon as possible. The secession from Yugoslavia, the establishment of the Slovenian diplomatic-consular network, and the membership in all major global organisations had been completed by the mid- 1990s. The first Slovenian foreign minister was Dr. Dimitrij Rupel.[16]

Security

In terms of its foreign policy orientation, Slovenia – like most other former communist states – set its eyes on the more advanced Western Europe. Even when independence was still only on the horizon, there were some debates about how Slovenia should negotiate its position in Euro-Atlantic institutions. Early in this discussion there were some politicians flirting with the idea of neutrality, but the discussion in that direction was quickly abandoned. As soon as Slovenia declared independence in 1991, the government began to steer its foreign policy away from the Balkans and away from the Non-Aligned Movement (NAM). The NAM was seen by Slovenian policy-makers at the time as a relic from the Cold War period, but also as the cornerstone of the foreign policy of socialist Yugoslavia with which Slovenian politicians did not want to have anything in common. At the same time, an effort to get rid of the NAM was also a clear sign that Slovenia would be looking for new alliances rather than trying to keep itself safe by a policy of neutrality. As for the Balkans, Slovenia was afraid that the inflaming war would cross its borders with the «South».

Slovenia applied for the UN membership and was quickly admitted to the Organisation (22 May 1992). However, the UN did not address Slovenia's security concerns, especially given the at times tentative and eventually disastrous performance of the UN in trying to keep peace and security in the War of Yugoslav Succession, which culminated in the inability of the UN to avoid the Srebrenica massacre in 1995. In an attempt to provide a security shield, Slovenia presented itself rather as a part of Central Europe. That region attracted huge sympathies during the Cold War from the West because of the resistance it offered to the Soviet Union (the 1968 Prague Spring in the Czechoslovakia, the 1956 Soviet intervention in Hungary, Poland's Solidarity Movement in the 1980s). Slovenia hoped to board that train of change, given that its population was among the first in Europe to have rebelled against the

16 See Dimitrij Rupel, Dimitrij. 2011. *Slovenija na svetovnem prizorišču*. Ljubljana: Slovenska matica.

Communist regime and signalled that the Cold War was coming to an end.[17] But the expectations that its part in the struggle against Communism would be rewarded by a quick solution to Slovenia's security dilemmas did not materialise. Unlike Slovenia, the Czech Republic, Hungary, and Poland, joined NATO in 1997. Whether Slovenia was less fit to join NATO than the three Central European states can be a matter of discussion. However, it must be said that Slovenia was at a disadvantage. The country was under the arms embargo during the Yugoslav war; the embargo was lifted only in 1994. The core Central European states did not have such problems. They exercised a tremendous pressure on NATO to get rid of the fears of how Russia would react to NATO's expansion to the East. Slovenia had not been part of the Soviet bloc, and could only join the queue for the "Round Two" enlargement of NATO. Slovenia finally became member in 2002.

After Slovenia had joined EU and NATO, its attitude to the Balkans gradually changed. Slovenia's foreign-policy planners developed an elaborate policy of «coming back» to the Balkan area. In July 2010, the National Assembly of the Republic of Slovenia adopted a Declaration on the Western Balkans, which outlined the measures of Slovenia's support and assistance to the stabilisation of the region.[18] The Declaration articulated various dimensions of Slovenian involvement in the region, in particular that of economic co-operation.[19] Institutionally, Slovenia's Ministry of Foreign Affairs even created a special department focused on the Western Balkans and regional initiatives, as well as a special office for assistance to the region.[20] From the Slovenian foreign policy perspective, the (Western) Balkans has finally returned from being an essen-

---

17 Arguably, one of the most important milestones in Slovenia's struggle against the Communist regime were the June 1988 protests against the imprisonment of three civilians and a Slovenian member of the Yugoslav National Army. The process, staged by the Yugoslav National Army, ended up in an indictment of all the four accused. The protests culminated in a massive demonstration in Ljubljana on 21 June 1988, the largest ever in the Slovenian history (attended by over 30,000 people). One of the imprisoned at that time is the current Prime Minister, Janez Janša.

18 The Declaration is available at http://www.mzz.gov.si/fileadmin/pageuploads/Zunanja_politika/Zahodni_ Balkan/A_declaration_on_the_WB.pdf.

19 The Guidelines are available (in Slovenian) at http://www.mzz.gov.si/ fileadmin/pageuploads/Novinarsko_sredisce/Sporocila_za_javnost/1007/Smernice_ZB.pd

20 See the website of the Centre for European Perspective (CEP), founded by the Government of the Republic of Slovenia, http://www.cep.si/. A description of the Western Balkans and regional initiatives department is available at http://www.mzz.gov.si/en/about_the_ministry/organisation/directorate_for_european_affairs_and_bilateral_political_relations/western_balkans_and_regional_initiatives_department/

tially security issue to a “normal” political realm.[21] Nevertheless, the Slovenian government keeps an eye on the developments in the Western Balkans, in particular to ethnic tensions in Bosnia-Herzegovina, Macedonia, and Kosovo. If escalated into conflicts, these tensions could arguably have a broader impact not only on the region but also on Europe as a whole.[22]

As for the approach toward the UN, Slovenia's foreign policy debates in the second half of the 1990s continued to display some ambiguity. There has often been talk about Slovenia’s limited capacities to play an active part in the UN activities. Ernest Petrič, former Slovenian Ambassador to the UN, admitted that this was partly due to the lack of resources (human and others), a typical problem of small states, but also because "other foreign policy priorities have been more relevant and important for Slovenia (such as EU accession, membership of NATO... the crisis in the Balkans)". Even the Slovenian non-permanent membership in the Security Council in 1998-99 did not change that.[23] In a discussion on future challenges for Slovenia's international relations, organised by the late President of Slovenia, Janez Drnovšek,[24] one of the main issues discussed was precisely how much of its foreign policy attention should Slovenia devote to regional and how much to global issues. In other words, how much of the UN could Slovenia afford?

Judging by the developments in the past decade, however, Slovenia has now become an active part of the UN's efforts in the maintenance of international peace and security.[25] Slovenia also uses its work in the UN in an effort to build its own international prestige as will be shown later in this chapter.

21 Zlatko Šabič and Annette Freyberg-Inan. 2012. Central Europe and the Balkans: So Close Yet so Far. In *Regional and International Relations of Central Europe* edited by Z. Šabič and P. Drulák. Houndmills, Basingstoke, Hampshire: Palgrave Macmillan.

22 Slovenian concerns about the situation in the (Western) Balkans have been exemplified by the Slovenian EU Presidency in 2008. The Slovenian government was particularly active in enhancing the status of Bosnia-Herzegovina and Serbia on their way to the EU – an effort which met success; the recognition of Kosovo took place under Slovenia's watch; and it tried to facilitate, albeit without success, negotiations between Greece and Macedonia that would open up the way for the latter to begin negotiating the terms of its membership.

23 Ernst Petrič, 2002. Združeni narodi in Slovenija. In Jožef Kunič et al., *10 let Slovenije v Združenih narodih / Slovenia's 10 Years in the United Nations*. Ljubljana: Ministrstvo za zunanje zadeve, 32-60, at p. 51)

24 These discussions are available (in Slovenian) at the home page http://www.prihodnost-slovenije.si/up-rs/ps.nsf/kn/8B499585B2D5283DC1256E940046C56C?OpenDocument

25 For a brief presentation, see http://newyork.predstavnistvo.si/index.php?id=2350&L=1

Welfare – Production and Trade

As part of socialist Yugoslavia, Slovenia had always had a relatively advanced economy. It successfully used the large Yugoslav market to market its products and services. When Yugoslavia unravelled in the early 1990s, Slovenia's economy was badly hit. Because of the loss of the Yugoslav market, Slovenia's GDP per capita fell from USD 8,658 in 1990 to USD 6,052 in 1992. Inflation soared as high as 247% in 1991, with unemployment topping 8% - nearly three times the 1989 level – and continuing to grow.[26]

In spite of this, Slovenia's economy was in much better shape than that of other Central and Southeast European countries. The proximity of Western markets (especially the neighbouring states of Austria and Italy) had made it easy for Slovenia to establish contacts with the capitalist economies in the West. This cushioned the economic shock. Consequently, Slovenia did not need to make a clean break with its socialist style economy; it could afford a gradualist transition to a market system.[27] Initially, the gradualist approach seemed to pay off. Slovenia's economy quickly improved, and its economic successes ensured that Slovenia was part of the group of countries that were included in EU's enlargement in 2004. Slovenia was also the first country from among the former socialist economies to embrace the Euro (2007). In the meantime, the cracks in the «Slovenian model» began to appear. The main reason for that seems to have been a complicated and ambiguous privatisation system with many legal loopholes.[28] The Slovenian economy became less of a success story of dedicated managers eager to strengthen the competitiveness of «their» companies by opening to foreign investments and creating jobs, and more of a place for all too many speculative moves in which (bought-out) companies‘ interests fell victim to individual preferences of the so-called new

---

26 Zlatko Šabič, 2002. Slovenia and the European Union: A different kind of two-level game In *Norms and nannies: the impact of international organizations on the central and east European states*, edited by R. H. Linden. Lanham: Rowman & Littlefield.:97)

27 Boris Majcen and Vlado Lavrač. 2006. Economic issues of Slovenia's accession to the EU, edited by B. Majcen. Ljubljana: Institute for Economic Research.

28 For example, according to Lorenčič, the privatisation legislation did not explicitly forbid management buyouts based on securing (often very generous) loans from the (state-owned) banks against the targeted company assets arguably a preferred way for managers, with little money of their own and unwilling to borrow against their own property, to raise loans for buyouts. See Aleksander Lorenčič, 2011. Proces gospodarske preobrazbe v Sloveniji. *MQ*, December, No 19, 54-55, http://www.zdruzenje-manager.si/storage/8593/31_Drugace-Proces_gospodarske_preobrazbe_v_Sloveniji.pdf. Pezdir remarked succinctly that the 'Slovenian type' of privatisation "would only allow state-owned monopolistic structures to be transformed into privately owned monopolistic structures." See Rado Pezdir, 2006. Thirteen Years of Gradualism – Inhibiting Transition in Slovenia? *Post-Communist Economies*, 18, 1, 51-68, at p. 52.

elite. The problematic privatisation is an important reason why the recent global crisis has hit Slovenia so hard, to the extent that it is "on the radar of the European Central Bank" as another country that might need to tap in the EU rescue funds.[29]

As for natural resources, Slovenia is relatively well endowed with forests, which cover almost 60% of the territory, and fresh water. In terms of calculation per capita on both forests and water, only two countries in Europe are better off than Slovenia: Finland and Sweden.[30] As already mentioned, Slovenia is not a land-locked country, although it has only 47 km of coastline. Its port of Koper plays an important role in the Slovenian economy, since it is "one of the closest ports for Central European states".[31] Slovenia's economy is focused on services, which account for 65-70% of the Slovenian GDP. In the service sector, tourism (45 % of the total services export) and transport (30 %) are the most important.[32] The current crisis has hit the service sector very hard, but some of the problems Slovenia's economy has spread over a longer period of time. For example, its trade balance is generally negative. In the period of 2000-2010, the total value of imports was higher than the value of exports.[33] Slovenia has a relatively high individual income tax rate (up to 41 %). Still, according to the 2010 data, 12.7% of the population in Slovenia was rated as living below the poverty line. In 2011, the percentage stood at 13.6% – a remarkable return to the year(s) before Slovenia entered the EU in 2004, when the poverty threshold stood at 12.1%.[34]

---

29 The quote is from the article "Slovenia Encounters Debt Trouble and May Need Bailout" by the New York Times from 14 September 2012 (http://www.nytimes.com/2012/09/15/business/global/slovenia-runs-into-debt-trouble.html?_r=1&pagewanted=all). See also "Slovenia's economy: next in line", *The Economist*, 18 August 2012 (http://www.economist.com/node/21560567).

30 The figures are from Eurostat (http://epp.eurostat.ec.europa.eu/statistics_explained/index.php/Water_statistics), Slovenia Forest Service (http://www.zgs.gov.si/eng/slovenian-forests/forests-in-slovenia/slovenian-forest-in-figures/index.html), and the Slovenian government (http://www.vlada.si/en/about_slovenia/geography/forests_in_slovenia/).

31 Damjan Kavaš, Matija Rojec, Klemen Koman, and Sonja Uršič. 2009. Izvedba sektorske analize slovenskega gospodarstva za privabljanje tujih neposrednih investicij in definiranje bistvenih konkurenčnih prednosti Slovenije kot lokacije za tuje neposredne investicije. Ljubljana: Inštitut za ekonomska raziskovanja.:3)

32 "Doing Business in Slovenia", Centre for International Cooperation and Development (CMSR), http://www.poslovniportal.si/

33 Simon Perše, Snježana Štuhec-Lončarević, Alenka Kozar, Almira Urbiha, Jana Živec, and Amira Mušić. 2012. Slovenia's Trade in Goods. Ljubljana: Statistical Office of the Republic of Slovenia:12)

34 The available data from: Statistical Office of the Republic of Slovenia, "Income and poverty indicators, Slovenia, 2010 – provisional data", http://www.stat.si/eng/novica_prikazi.aspx?id=

Prestige

Slovenia began to build its image and prestige surprisingly early. In 1986, a video appeared on the national television in which Slovenian uniqueness was portrayed by using images of unspoiled nature, hard-working people, and tourist attraction and a newly-designed logo; the word "Slovenia" with the linden leaf. The video entitled *Slovenija – moja dežela* (Slovenia – My Country) did raise some eyebrows in other parts of socialist Yugoslavia.[35] Drawing from the experience with the struggle for independence from a political system that was rapidly becoming a dictatorship, a struggle in which war could not be avoided, Slovenia began to build on its earlier representation. It wanted to be seen as a democratic, responsible, peaceful state, supporting multilateralism and universally shared norms such as human rights and the indivisibility of peace. To uphold this image, Slovenian foreign policy planners saw candidacies for high positions in, or presidencies of, various prominent international organisations as a useful means. Thus, Slovenia was elected a non-permanent member of the Security Council for the period 1998-1999. It took over the Chairmanship of the OSCE in 2005, presided the Council of the European Union in the first half of 2008, and the Committee of Ministers of the Council of Europe from May to November of 2009.

Beyond this "project-based diplomacy", Slovenia presented itself as a promoter of human security. Slovenia participated in the establishment of the Human Security Network, a 1998 initiative by Canada and Norway, which aimed to address issues such as respecting the Ottawa convention, children in armed conflicts, education in human rights.[36] One of the major contributors to the image of Slovenia as promoter of human security is the creation of the International Trust Fund for Demining and Mine Victims Assistance (ITF) in 1998. Recently, Slovenia has become more involved in supporting sustainable water management and will consider this topic as one of the priorities in its future foreign policy orientation.[37] In the past few years, however, Slovenia has also shown some tendency to become more inwardly oriented; it has tended to focus primarily on European and transatlantic affairs. Furthermore, the financial crisis could have some impact on its image globally. The role Slovenia

---

4177; http://www.stat.si/eng/novica_prikazi.aspx?id=4818; and http://www.stat.si/eng/novica_prikazi.aspx?id=708

35 The video is accessible at http://www.youtube.com/watch?v=mluKmCj_XXw.

36 More at http://www.mzz.gov.si/en/foreign_policy/foreign_policy/human_security_network_hsn/

37 "Minister Erjavec at the discussion 'Water as an opportunity for sustainable development and international co-operation of Slovenia'", http://www.mzz.gov.si/nc/en/newsroom/news/article//31852/

plays in the UN can be given as an example. Slovenia has been among the most active discussants of the UN Security Council Reform,[38] yet it is lagging behind paying its dues for the UN Peacekeeping forces.[39]

Autonomy

As a newly independent state, Slovenia found itself in an unusual position. A republic, which was a part of a 20-million state, all of the sudden found itself encircled with three formidable neighbours, with a centuries' long history of statehood and political independence, neighbours to which Slovenia at one point of history belonged or was occupied by them. Vulnerable as it was as a newly created state, and without any significant comparative advantages that would make it «big» in any particular field of co-operation (such as Luxembourg in the financial sector), Slovenia was eager to find as soon as possible a substitute for the Yugoslav federation that would address its security concerns. Slovenia naturally set its eyes on the NATO and the EU as guarantors of politico-military security and of access to a larger market. That, in turn, was bound to have an effect on its room for manoeuvre in international affairs, as Slovenia needs to align its positions with NATO and the EU.

Still, examples of Slovenia's particular views and positions on prominent international issues can be found. Such was the case with the hotly debated Goldstone Report, which was eventually endorsed by the General Assembly of the United Nations in November 2009. Of all the members of the EU only Slovenia, alongside Cyprus and Malta, voted in favour of the resolution.[40] In order to protect its national interests with regard to access to open seas, Slovenia did not hesitate to use its EU membership against Croatia to negotiate a commonly acceptable solution before giving Croatia a nod to conclude its accession negotiations.[41] The issue is being dealt with by means of arbitration to which both countries agreed in November 2010.

---

38 Elisabetta Martini, 2010. Restarting Negotiations for the Reform of the Security Council. Rome: Istituto Affari Internazionali., 7)

39 For current and past activities and projects of the Slovenian Ministry of Foreign affairs see http://www.mzz.gov.si/en/foreign_policy/foreign_policy/

40 For the minutes of the debate at the plenary session of the General Assembly and the voting record see https://www.un.org/News/Press/docs/2009/ga10883.doc.htm

41 In doing so Slovenia had good teachers in Italy and Austria. In the process of accession to the EU Slovenia had experienced the display of institutional power from these two countries, which simply seized an opportunity to accomplish some of their political interests *vis-à-vis* Slovenia in return for their support to the Slovenian EU membership. During the negotiations on Slovenia's Association Agreement, Italy had enough leverage in the EU to turn the essentially bilateral problem of property restitution into a European issue. Austria, too, used its

The Two Traditions Compared

Norway and Slovenia are small states.[42] Such states navigate the international system as well as they can. They seek to adapt. And they do this in ways which serve their own long-term interests – ways which enhance their own security, welfare, autonomy and prestige.

Yet, different states adapt in different circumstances. And although Norway and Slovenia both are European states, they are endowed with different resources, they are situated at opposite ends of the Continent, and they live in different neighbourhoods. Norway is surrounded by water. It has few neighbours. These are fairly similar to Norway in size and political orientation, Russia being the major exception. Norway lives in an orderly neighbourhood in the north-western corner of Europe. Slovenia is situated in a region which has evolved in the shadow of big, landed entities; it is a region where large composite actors, empires and federations, have regularly contested for power over the centuries.

Such differences in location have yielded different political economies and foreign-policy experiences. Norway has been an autonomous entity since the Napoleonic Wars and a sovereign state since 1905. She has experienced several foreign-policy shifts. Her record of security-policy includes an early phase of neutrality, followed by a phase of collective security and, since World War Two, a long-lasting phase of alliance policy. This record describes a slow evolution from fierce independence in 1905 towards greater foreign-policy commitments after 1945 – a record which suggests a reluctance to engage in binding commitments. This reluctance is nowhere more evident than in Norway's relations with EU.

Slovenia has been a sovereign state for over 20 years. Before that she was a part, first, of the Kingdom of Yugoslavia and then of Communist-ruled Yugoslavia. No sooner had she gained independence in 1991, than she worked to become a member of both NATO and the EU – and she was the first post-communist state to adopt the Euro on 1 January 2007. She has, over this short period, tied close links with the Great Powers of the West.

---

leverage over Slovenia to promote the idea of closing down the nuclear power plant Krško, of property restitution, and the so-called Cultural Agreement, clarifying the status of the German-speaking population living in Slovenia Petra Roter and Ana Bojinović, 2005. Croatia and the European union: a troubled relationship. *Mediterranean politics,* 10, 3, 447-454.; and Šabič, "Slovenia and the European Union", passim.

42 Bojko Bučar and Stein Kuhnle, eds. 1994. *Small States Compared: Politics of Norway and Slovenia.* Bergen Alma Mater.

On Security, Welfare, Autonomy and Prestige

The most significant historical difference between Norway and Slovenia may be that they have been situated at opposite ends of Europe and have belonged to different regional systems. They have had different great-power neighbours and have been affected by different regional dynamics.

Norway has been a North-Atlantic seafaring state with an open economy and friendly immediate neighbours. Her interests have been tied with those of Great Britain; her economy and political institutions have been deeply affected by the British liberal and democratic ideals. Whenever times have been uncertain, Norway has sought to tie her security to Great Britain and the sea power of the Royal Navy. Slovenia, by contrast, has been a near-landlocked state with agricultural traditions. Her interests have, on the whole, been connected up with the shifting great-power rivalries in the region; in the nineteenth century with the Habsburg Empire (after 1867, more commonly known as Austria-Hungary) and in recent centuries with Northern Italy. She has also been entangled in the rivalries of the smaller nations of the Balkans. After World War Two, Slovenia was pulled in as part of the Socialist Federated Republic of Yugoslavia (SFRY), an entity which occupied a unique place in the socialist world, but which was nevertheless perceived as part of the Eastern Bloc. Norway, by contrast, was solidly tied to the Western Bloc – to Great Britain in particular and, through Britain, to the USA.

Norway and Slovenia have different geopolitical vantage points, different political histories and different foreign policy orientations. These differences are still reflected in the political economies of the two countries.[43] Over the last 15-20 years, however, Norway and Slovenia have become more similar in outlook and political orientation. This is largely due to the collapse of the Soviet Union, the end of the Cold War and to changes in the political structures of Europe, which brought radical changes in Slovenia.

Norway and Slovenia both share the experience of becoming independent in the wake not merely of international changes but after changes brought about

---

43 It was noted above that Slovenia has about two million citizens, where Norway has two. Also, that whereas Slovenia's territorial area is about 20.000 km^2, Norway's is well over 15 times larger (about 325.000 km^2). In addition, Norway commands a maritime area which is 7 times larger than the size of its mainland. It may be added that Slovenia is an industrialized country – the degree of industrialization is reflected in its three largest sources of export earnings: machinery and transport equipment (38%), chemicals (14%) and furniture (5%). Norway's export earnings come from the sale of petroleum (43%), gas (15%), metals and machinery (16%) and fish (5%).

by upheavals in Russia.[44] Another similarity is that both countries had a relatively smooth transition from being a part of larger social formations to becoming independent states. Slovenia's road to independence was a bit bumpier than that of Norway – Slovenia's road involved (a ten-days) war, whereas that of Norway was peaceful. Once independent, the two countries had to focus their diplomatic attention towards gaining recognition, formulating foreign policy priorities, and establishing foreign policy services.

Another similarity is that Norway and Slovenia have both ended up as members of NATO – the longest-lasting of the anti-Soviet institutions. Again, Slovenia's membership is due to major changes in Slovenia's foreign-policy orientation after the end of the Cold War. During the early 1990s Slovenia tried hard to adjust its institutions of governance in order to satisfy these criteria of membership. Thus, it could be argued that for Slovenia NATO and EU were instrumental in introducing liberal values and liberal-democratic institutions to the country and guaranteeing the autonomy of the state. For Norway, which had a mature parliamentary system in place by the time of its independence in 1905, EU has rather been perceived as a threat to national autonomy and a challenge to a smoothly-working democracy.

In the beginning, neither Norway nor Slovenia had any particular comparative advantages that would make them influential actors in international affairs. The international importance of Norway, however, increased substantially in the late 1940s with the onset of the Cold War. The shortest distance between the two rival superpowers was a straight line drawn across the Arctic. In the age which introduced long-distance bombers and intercontinental ballistic missiles, Norway's strategic value rose steeply. Geography made Norway important in another, related aspect: Norway was the only NATO member to have a common border with the USSR – and that border was situated only a few miles away from the Kola Peninsula where the Soviets built one of their biggest ports. Northern Norway thus provided a unique vantage point for US surveillance and intelligence operations.[45]

Over time, however, Norway's geographical assets were offset by technological advances. Norway's strategic significance in the NATO-alliance diminished as the USA introduced new, steadily more sophisticated methods of surveillance – from submerged monitoring devices to high-flying, even space-based, vehicles.

---

44 Norway seized an opportunity afforded by the Russo-Japanese War (1905); Slovenia seized an opportunity afforded by the unravelling of the Soviet Union, which began in the late 1980s.

45 Rolf Tamnes, (1997) *Oljealder*. Oslo: Universitetsforlaget; and Torbjørn L. Knutsen, (2010) "Amerika i 50 års utenrikspolitikk", *Internasjonal politikk*, 68(1):139-49

Slovenia tried to play its geopolitical card in the 1990s. During the negotiations for NATO membership in the wake of the Soviet collapse, the Slovenian government argued that its geographic position was an asset for the alliance – it linked two NATO members now separated (Italy and Hungary).[46] The argument was that "Slovenia's admission would make NATO enlargement more geopolitically balanced, moving the area of security and stability in the direction of the volatile Balkans and [serve] as a positive incentive for good behaviour for the other Balkan aspirants to NATO and EU".[47] NATO, however, did not buy the argument. NATO strategists considered Slovenia to be far less important than say Poland, so Slovenian politicians had to wait until 2002 to finally become members of NATO.

Today, therefore, Norway and Slovenia are both members of the Atlantic alliance. Both countries have had their security policies deeply affected by this membership; efforts to reorganize their defence postures have been shaped by NATO priorities. Both countries have sought to adapt to American expectations and to convert their territorial defence forces into internationally deployable forces primarily aimed at peacekeeping. Both have participated in NATO operations in the Balkans and in Afghanistan. Norway and Slovenia both share a common concern with Russia.

Both Norway and Slovenia observe Russian behaviour carefully. However, they have very different views of Russia. Much of this difference is accounted for by geography. Norway and Slovenia also have different experiences with Russian relations and very different security histories. Neither country has been part of the Soviet-dominated Socialist bloc. In the Slovenian case this was very clear during the NATO membership negotiations. Moscow had incomparably lesser problems watching Slovenia to become a member of NATO than its former satellites, especially those with which it shares the border.

Geography also accounts for some of the economic differences between the two countries – differences in topography, for example, accounts for differences in available land; differences in climate accounts for differences in length of agricultural seasons. However, one of the most striking differences is the maritime environment. Norway is a wealthy country whose political economy is intimately tied in with the sea. Slovenia, too, has extracted wealth from the sea – the country has a large and regionally important seaport. However,

46 Zlatko Šabič and Ljubica Jelušič. 2003. Slovenia and NATO enlargement: twists, turns, and endless frustrations. In *Almost NATO: partners and players in Central and Eastern European security*, edited by C. Krupnick. Lanham: Rowman & Littlefield, passim

47 Anton Bebler,. 1999. Slovenia and the "Gray Zone" in Europe. In *The Challenge of NATO Enlargement*, edited by A. Bebler. Westport, CT: Greenwood Publishing Group, p. 157)

Slovenia has, in spite of this, not been affected by maritime activities to the degree that Norway has.

Norway has been a seafaring nation for centuries and has been moulded and shaped by maritime activities – by fishing and shipping and, more recently, by offshore extraction of oil and gas. Offshore drilling has provided an enormous income to the nation's coffers since the late 1970s. Before that, international shipping was a source of wealth for many towns in southern parts of Norway – especially during the several decades that covered the second half of the 19th century and the first half of the 20th. Fishing has been the oldest and most basic source of Norwegian wealth, sustaining entire towns along the Norwegian west coast and in northern Norway since the high Middle Ages, when new ships' technologies permitted Norwegians to transport salted herring and dried cod to the insatiable fish markets in the Catholic countries on the Continent.

The export of fish products is still a significant part in Norway's foreign trade. This is reflected in a foreign policy which is deeply preoccupied with the vast migrations of fish stocks in the North Atlantic. These stocks have been a traditional source of Norwegian wealth, and managing them through fishing quotas and regimes of tight control is an important part of Norway's foreign policy. Monitoring the activities of foreign vessels is a task of the coast guard. The effort to control the great, northern banks is a main reason why Norway has enjoyed good relations with the USSR/Russia; the two countries have recognized their common interests in protecting the fisheries of the North and evolved routines and institutions of cooperation. Also, the fear of losing control over the great, northern banks and of depleting traditional stocks through overfishing is a major reason why Norway has not joined the European Union. A good segment of the Norwegian population distrusts the fisheries policy of EU, and argues that Continental fishermen, driven by economic interests and market-based concerns, have exploited their own stocks beyond carrying capacity and destroyed them. Thus, the Norwegians want to protect the stocks which they have preserved through fisheries management and regulatory regimes. They are not eager to share the carefully husbanded stocks in the North Sea with industrial trawlers from the Continent.

Norway is part of the European market system through the EEA, but is not a full member of the European Union. Slovenia, by contrast, is tightly integrated into the EU. She joined the union in 2004, together with a group of other south-east European countries. Slovenia became, as of early 2007, the first new EU member to introduce the Euro as its currency – replacing the Tolar. Slovenia had very few if any alternatives. Its natural resources are limited, whereas its economy is decidedly service-oriented. Open markets represented the only window of opportunity for Slovenia to sustain its relative wealth among the post-communist countries.

Slovenia's integration into the EU has affected the foreign-policy course of the country. Norway's foreign policy orientation has been affected by a different factor: by climate change. For one of the most direct consequences of the global warming of recent decades has been to increase the average temperature of the Arctic, causing the ice cap to melt and the Arctic glaciers to retreat. This melting has uncovered new land and vast expanses of open sea. The new land offers new opportunities for mining and drilling. The uncovering of new expanses of open sea has opened up new opportunities for fishing, for drilling and for new routes of maritime transportation. Norway, as an "Arctic power",[48] has an important role to play as more of the Arctic is open for commercial activities – whether this is exploration of natural resources or development of new trade routes. Norway's wealth, national identity and prestige are tied to the Arctic.

Great Powers associate prestige with reputation for power; small states think differently.[49] Small states find other ways of gaining some level of high regard. For Norway and Slovenia, policies of prestige are associated with work to further justice and peace. Thus, Norway's national day, the 17th of May, is not celebrated by displaying the country's means of war, but with children's parades. Norway's foreign policy is tightly associated with a long tradition of peace activism – in efforts to create processes of arbitration and conflict resolution, in refugee and relief work, in development projects for the poorest regions of the world and in the promotion of human rights. Such projects are all connected to the Nobel Peace prize – an annual prize which is awarded by a Storting-appointed committee to that individual or organization which has made an important contribution to the cause of peace. Slovenia's cosmopolitanism is perhaps best displayed by its national anthem, which does not hail the «greatness of the Slovenian nation», but rather freedom and peaceful relations among all the nations of the world.[50]

---

48 Jody Ray Bennett, (2012) Vying for Power in the High North. Zurich: International Relations and Security Network (ISN).

49 Robert L. Rothstein, (1968) *Alliances and Small Powers*. New York: Columbia University Press

50 The anthem is an excerpt from the poem written by France Prešeren, called 'Zdravljica' (The Toast). The centre-right government, however, consistently tries to replace these verses with others in the same poem, which emphasise the 'Slovenian greatness' and its (Christian) legacy. For the official text of the anthem, see http://www.vlada.si/en/about_slovenia/political_system/national_insignia/text_of_the_slovenian_national_anthem_in_different_languages/

Closely related to this multidimensional peace work are Norway's active efforts to consolidate extant international law and to expand that law to new regions. This work is most immediately visible in Norway's work in the UN and in the work to expand the international law of the sea. The reason for this is easy to understand. The Norwegian economy is deeply dependent on the sea and has a deep interest in making sure that all powers obey common norms and rules of maritime behaviour. Norway invests much diplomatic effort in the UN because this organization is created and sustained by the Atlantic powers in an effort to establish and secure an orderly and liberal world, where relations among states rest on the principle of popular sovereignty at home, and abroad on the voluntarily obedience of international norms and rules defined in international law. This is a vision that is entirely consistent with the national interests of states democratic states like Norway and, in more recent years, Slovenia.

The UN is, in a sense, the first line of defence for small, open trading states. Norway and Slovenia are, consequently, working towards maintaining a secure, peaceful international community, based on sovereign equality and respect for international law. Both conduct policies of prestige that are perfectly in tune with the interests of small, liberal trading states. Both act as status quo powers, seeking to preserve the international order which has ensured their progress and wealth.

At the regional level, Norway is a founding member of NATO. Slovenia, for its part, has become a member in recent years, tying its future to both NATO and the EU. The geographical position and the political environment surrounding the two countries are very different. Unlike Norway, which is part of a strongly integrated environment in the Scandinavian region, Slovenia is geographically close to the restless Western Balkans where deeper integration is yet to be seen. In this respect, the reliance of Slovenia to the Western economic and military organisations is understandable.

Trade is extremely important for small states – they depend on free markets to generate and sustain their wealth as well as security. Here, Norway is in a better position than Slovenia because its maritime activities have afforded the nation a greater variety of natural resources to exploit for consumption or sale (fish, oil, and gas). Norway has a solid annual surplus in its foreign trade, running between 25 and 30 % of total trade. However, the continued exploitation of these vital resources is deeply dependent on education, knowledge and abilities of technological innovation. The Slovenian economy is vulnerable. The nation has some important natural resources (forests and water), but little beyond that. It is highly dependent on services, of which demand rises and falls with the economic situation in its most important trading partners such as Germany, Austria, Italy, and France. For over a decade, Slovenia's foreign trade has been negative; the nation has in recent years run an annual deficit of 4 to

5% of its total trade. The result has been a mounting trade imbalance which becomes even more problematic in the present global crisis.

Conclusion

As has been pointed out at the outset, differences among states can be many and hard to analyse in a systematic manner. No two states are alike, as the example of Norway and Slovenia, ostensibly two "small" states, clearly shows. In terms of population, the two states are comparable; in terms of the territory, given the vast territory of Norway, there is little to compare. Still, we argue that states can be compared, regardless of their size, if some common core concerns of the states are identified and analysed accordingly. We have identified four such concerns: security, welfare, autonomy, and prestige.

Using this approach, we see that there are many similarities between Norway and Slovenia and their foreign policy behaviour. A good number of them can be traced back to the fact that both countries are "small", democratic states that benefit from the present international system and which support the status quo and the work of the UN and international law. But there are also profound differences between the two countries. A good many of them can ultimately be traced back to different historical experience and geographical location. Norway continues to live in an orderly environment. As for Slovenia, its largest border has only recently been redefined, since Croatia has become the 28th member of the EU. Whether this will bring some more peace and less tension in the neighbourhood to the South remains to be seen.[51]

51 For additional readings, see also Odd-Bjørn Fure, (1996) *Mellomkrigstid, 1920-1940*. Oslo: Universitetsforlaget; and Polona Bunič and Zlatko Šabič. 2012. The Europeanization of Slovenian foreign policy: a one-way process? In *The New Member States and the European Union Foreign Policy and Europeanization*, edited by M. Baun and D. Marek. London: Routledge (forthcoming).

About the Editors

Kristen Ringdal is Professor of Sociology and Head of the Department of Sociology and Political Science at the Norwegian University of Science and Technology (NTNU) in Trondheim, Norway. He is the Norwegian National Coordinator for the European Social Survey, and is an elected member of the Royal Norwegian Society of Sciences and Letters. He has published articles in a broad range of journals including: *European Sociological Review, Administrative Science Quarterly, Human Relations, Journal of Applied Economics, Politics & Religion*, and *Quality of Life Research*. He has contributed to several books on comparative studies and is co-editor of *Nordic Social Attitudes in a European Perspective* (Edvard Elgar, 2008), *The Future of the Welfare State* (Edward Elgar, 2012), *The Aftermath of War: Experiences and social attitudes in the Western Balkans*, (Ashgate, 2012).

Sabrina P. Ramet is a Professor of Political Science at the Norwegian University of Science and Technology (NTNU), in Trondheim, Norway. Born in London, England, she was educated at Stanford University, the University of Arkansas, and UCLA, receiving her Ph.D. in Political Science from UCLA in 1981. She is the author of 12 scholarly books (three of which have been published in Croatian translations) and editor or co-editor of 32 books (31 published and one in production). Her books have also been published in French, German, Italian, and Serbian translations. Her latest book is *Gender (In)equality and Gender Politics in Southeastern Europe: A question of justice*, co-edited with Christine M. Hassenstab (Palgrave Macmillan, 2015),

Danica Fink-Hafner is Professor of Political Parties, Interest Groups and Policy Analysis and the Head of the Centre for Political Science Research at the Faculty of Social Sciences, University of Ljubljana (www.politoloske-raziskave.si). She was Vice Dean for Research, President of Slovenian Politological Association and member of the European Consortium for Political Research Executive Committee. Her recent publications include the edited book on *The Development of Civil Society in the Countries on the Territory of the Former Yugoslavia since the 1980s* (2015); article co-authored with Matej Knep, "Factors Affecting Green Party Development: Explaining the Decline of Green Parties in Slovenia", *Romanian Journal of Political Science* (2015) and an article on "A Typology of Populisms and Changing Forms of Society: Conceptualization and Slovenian Examples ", *Europe-Asia Studies* (in print).

About the Contributors

Mitja Hafner-Fink is Associate Professor of Social Science Methodology at the Faculty of Social Sciences, University of Ljubljana. He leads a continuous research program Slovenian Public Opinion at the Public Opinion and Mass Communication Research Centre at the same Faculty. He is Slovenian coordinator for the International Social Survey Programme (ISSP). In the period 1998-2001 he was president of Slovenian Sociological Association. His research interest includes (political) participation, citizenship, (national) identity, social values, and social science methodology. He has published in various journals including: *Quality and Quantity*, *Europe-Asia Studies*, *East European Politics and Societies*, and *Czech Sociological Review*. He has also contributed chapters to edited books on comparative studies or case studies published at publishers, such as Dartmouth, Texas A&M University Press, and Manchester University Press.

Christine M. Hassenstab worked as an attorney in Seattle for many years before moving to Trondheim, Norway, in 2001. She earned her J.D. in 1984 at Golden Gate University School of Law in San Francisco and her Ph.D. from the Norwegian University of Science and Technology in 2010 with a dissertation subsequently published by De Gruyter in 2015 under the title *Body Law and the Body of Law: A Comparative Study of Norm Inclusion in Norwegian and American Laws*. She is also co-editor, with Sabrina P. Ramet, of *Gender (In)equality and Gender Politics in Southeastern Europe: A Question of Justice* (Palgrave Macmillan, 2015). Her interests include the eugenics movement, the exclusion of women from the priesthood in the Catholic Church, and feminist theology.

Anders Todal Jenssen is a Professor of Political Science at the Norwegian University of Science and technology (NTNU). His field of research is political behaviour and he has published articles and contributed to books on a wide variety of topics in this field, including ethnic relations, politic values and value conflicts, referendums and electoral behaviour. He has taken a special interest in gender differences in political participation and representation and was a member of the Government appointed Gender Equality Committee that presented two white papers on gender equality in Norway (2012) and public policy on gender equality (2011).

Ola Listhaug is Professor of Political Science at the Norwegian University of Science and Technology (NTNU). He has published widely on topics like political trust and electoral behaviour. His books include, with Christopher J. Anderson et al. *Losers' Consent* (Oxford University Press, 2005) and co-edited with Sabrina P. Ramet, *Bosnia-Herzegovina Since Dayton: Civic and Uncivic Values* (Longo Editore, 2013).

Matej Knep worked on this publication as a research assistant at the Centre for Political Science Research at the Faculty of Social Sciences, University of Ljubljana in frame of P5-0136 Political science research programme and 10-ECPR-008 ARRS-N5-0014 European Collaborative Research Project in the Social Sciences (ECRP) Comparative Research on Interest Group Politics in Europe – INTEREURO (http://www.intereuro.eu/).

Torbjørn L. Knutsen is Professor of International Relations at the Norwegian University of Science and Technology (NTNU), in Trondheim. He has published journal articles on issues of foreign policy, peace and conflict. His books include *A History of International Relations Theory* (2016), *Exit Afghanistan* (2012, with Gjert Lage Dyndal), *Ways of Knowing* (2007), with Jonathon Moses, and *The Rise and Fall of World Orders* (1999). Knutsen is currently completing a book on Norwegian foreign policy.

Alenka Krašovec is Professor of Political Science at the Faculty of Social Sciences, University of Ljubljana, Slovenia. She has published articles in a broad range of journals including: *West European Politics, Journal of Southern Europe and the Balkans, The Journal of Communist Studies and Transition Politics, Communist and Post-Communist Studies, Electoral Studies*. She has contributed to several edited books on comparative studies, for example to *Social Pacts in Europe: Emergence, Evolution, and Institutionalization* (Oxford University Press, 2011), *Europeanising Party Politics? Comparative Perspectives on Central and Eastern Europe* (Manchester University Press, 2011), and co-authored a book *Governing New European Democracies* (Palgrave MacMillan, 2007).

Damjan Lajh is Associate Professor of Policy Analysis at the Faculty of Social Sciences, University of Ljubljana, and researcher in the Centre for Political Science Research at the same faculty. He is the Programme Coordinator of Master study programme *Political Science – Policy Analysis and Public Administration*. His research interests encompass public policies and policy-making processes in the national and EU context, Europeanization processes, and new forms of governance in the EU. As author or co-author he has published articles in a broad range of journals including: *West European*

Politics, Journal of Communist Studies and Transition Politics, Journal of Southeast Europe and the Balkans, Czech Sociological Review, Perspectives: The Central European Review of International Affairs, and *Studia Historica Slovenica*. He has contributed to several edited books, among others published at Routledge, Palgrave Macmillan and Manchester University Press.

Jože Mencinger is Professor emeritus of Economics at the Law School, University of Ljubljana. He received his Ph.D. in Economics from the University of Pennsylvania, Philadelphia, USA. He was active in politics and served as deputy prime minister and minister of the economy of the Republic of Slovenia (1990-1991), a member of the State Council (2002- 010), and a member of the Board, Bank of Slovenia (1991- 997). He was also rector of the University of Ljubljana (1998-2005). His interests have been empirical econometrics, comparative economics, economic policies, and EU economy. He is the author of the first Yugoslav econometric model and co-author of several econometric models, he published extensively on transition, economic policies, development of CEE countries, and EU economy. Since 1991, he has been editor of a monthly *Gospodarska Gibanja* (Economic Trends).

Marko Milosavljević is an Associate Professor with Ph.D. from the Department of Journalism, Faculty of Social Sciences at University of Ljubljana, Slovenia. He was Chair of Department of Journalism from 2007 to 2011. His research of media, new media and journalism in Slovenia and post-socialist countries, focusing on regulation and media economy, has been published in books and scientific journals in Germany, France, United Kingdom, United States, Bulgaria, Austria, Bulgaria, Croatia and Netherlands, in German, French, Croatian, Bulgarian and English language. Among the latest is a project "Media Pluralism Monitor - Monitoring Risks for Media Pluralism in EU Member States" with European University Institute – Robert Schuman Centre for Advanced Studies. He was a Chairman of the Expert commission for Pluralisation of Media at Slovenian Ministry of Culture from 2009-2010. He was a member of Experts' group for new Mass Media Act (2009) and Public Broadcasting Act (2009) at Slovenian Ministry of Culture. He is a member of National Committee for Information Society since 2010.

Espen Moe is Associate Professor in Political Science at the Norwegian University of Science and Technology (NTNU) in Trondheim. He received his PhD in Political Science from UCLA in 2004. He is the author of *Governance, Growth and Global Leadership* (Ashgate, 2007), the editor (with Paul Midford) of *The Political Economy of Renewable Energy and Energy Security* (Palgrave

Macmillan, 2014) and the author of *Renewable Energy Transformation or Fossil Fuel Backlash* (Palgrave Macmillan, 2015). He has published extensively on long-term processes of structural economic change, energy policy and transitions, and on renewable energy in journals such as *Review of International Political Economy*, *Energy and Energy Policy*.

Jonathon W. Moses is Professor of Political Science at the Norwegian University of Science and Technology (NTNU), Trondheim. He is also co-editor of *European Political Science (EPS)* and has also authored several articles and books on economic management and international migration, the most recent of which is *Emigration and Political Development* (Cambridge University Press, 2011).

Aleksandra Kanjuo Mrčela is Professor of Sociology of Work and Economic Sociology at the Faculty of Social Sciences, University of Ljubljana. Her research work and publications in Slovenia and abroad are in the fields of gender, industrial relations, organisation, post-socialist transition. She is among few academics in Slovenia who analyse gender and the economy. In 1996 published the book *Women in management,* the first work that has systematically discussed the topic in Slovenia. Since 2003 she is the coordinator of the national centre for the European Foundation for Living and Working conditions (Dublin) at the FSS, UL. Since 2004 she is a member of the Network of Experts in the Fields of Employment, Social Inclusion and Gender Equality Issues (European Commission, Employment and Social Affairs DG). From 2011 on she is an associate editor and from 2015 editor of *Social Politics* (Oxford: Oxford University Press, 1994). From 2015 she is Head of doctoral School of University of Ljubljana.

Zlatko Šabič is a Professor of International Relations at the University of Ljubljana, Faculty of Social Sciences. He is a Member of the Strategic Council for Foreign Affairs, the body of the Slovenian Ministry of Foreign Affairs. His presence in the International Relations professional networks is seen through his being the President of the Central and East European International Studies Association (CEEISA) from 2006 to 2010, and his being the founder and the first editor of the *Journal of International Relations and Development*, as well as being the founder and Member of the Governing Board of the European International Studies Association. He also co-edits, with Petr Drulák, the Book Series *Central and Eastern European Perspectives on International Relations* published with Palgrave. In the field of Higher Education, he has been a member of the Scientific Research Council for Social Sciences within the

Slovenian Research Agency (2010-2015). His most recent book project was on *International Relations in Central Europe* (Palgrave, 2012).

Marjan Smrke is an Associate Professor of Sociology at the Faculty of Social Sciences in Ljubljana, Slovenia. His main areas of scholarly interest entail church-state relations in post-communist societies, (de)secularization, modern atheism, modern superstitions, social dilemmas and social mimicry. His last book Družbena mimikrija (*Social mimicry*) was published in 2007. He has recently published in *East European Politics and Societies and Cultures* (2014) and in *Politicization of Religion, the Power of Symbolism* (Palgrave Macmillan, 2014). He is a member of ISORECEA (The International Study of Religion in Eastern and Central Europe Association).

Ola Svein Stugu is Professor of Public History/ the Didactics of History at the Norwegian University of Science and Technology (NTNU), Trondheim. He has published extensively on a broad range of historical topics, his latest books are *Historie i bruk* (Uses of History), 2008, and *Vegen til velstandslandet; norsk historie etter 1905* (The Road to the Affluent Society; Norwegian History since 1905), 2012. A select bibliography may be found at http://www.ntnu.edu/employees/ola.stugu. He is an elected member of the Royal Norwegian Society of Sciences and Letters.

Peter Vodopivec was from 1980 until 1999 First Lecturer and then Professor of Modern European History at the History Department of the University of Ljubljana. After 1999 until 2012, when he became retired, he served as a senior scientific adviser at the Institute of Modern History in Ljubljana. He has focused in his research and publications on 18th and 19th social, economic and political history. During the 1990s he was co-author of the first post-communist history curricula and participated in the reform of history teaching in Slovenia. His recent books include: *From Pohlin's Grammar to the Independent State, Slovene history from the end of the* 18th *until the end of the* 20th *century* (2006, 2007, 2010) and *Slowenische Geschichte, Politik-Gesellschaft-Kultur* (2008 – together with Peter Štih and Vasko Simoniti).

Toril Aalberg is Professor of Sociology and Head of Research at the Department of Sociology and Political Science, the Norwegian University of Science and Technology (NTNU), Trondheim. She is the Chair of a COST Action on Populist Political Communication in Europe, and is an elected member of the Royal Norwegian Society of Sciences and Letters. She has published extensively in a broad range of international journals including: *The British Journal* *of Political Science, Electoral Studies, European Journal of Political Research, European Sociological Review,* *International Journal of Comparative Sociology, International Journal of Press/Politics, the International Political Science Review, International Journal of Public Opinion Research* and *Public Opinion Quarterly.* She is the author or editor of 8 books, some in conjunction with others. These include *Challenges to Representative Democracy* (Fagbokforlaget, 1999), *Achieving Justice* (Brill, 2003), *Communicating Politics* (Nordicom, 2007), *How Media Inform Democracy* (Routledge, 2012) and *Populist Political Communication in Europe* (Routledge, 2016).